*Ian Stewart and David K. Stewart*

Conventional Choices:
Maritime Leadership Politics

**UBC**Press · Vancouver · Toronto

15 14 13 12 11 10 09 08 07    5 4 3 2 1

Printed in Canada on ancient-forest-free paper (100 percent post-consumer recycled) that is processed chlorine- and acid-free, with vegetable-based inks.

**Library and Archives Canada Cataloguing in Publication**

Stewart, Ian, 1953-
    Conventional choices: Maritime leadership politics / Ian Stewart and David K. Stewart.

Includes bibliographical references and index.
ISBN 978-0-7748-1341-9 (bound); ISBN 978-0-7748-1342-6 (pbk.)

    1. Leadership. 2. Political leadership – Maritime Provinces. 3. Political parties – Maritime provinces. 4. Maritime Provinces – Politics and government. I. Title.

JF1525.L4S74 2007              303.3'4              C2007-902085-2

Canadä

UBC Press gratefully acknowledges the financial support for our publishing program of the Government of Canada through the Book Publishing Industry Development Program (BPIDP), and of the Canada Council for the Arts, and the British Columbia Arts Council.

This book has been published with the help of a grant from the Canadian Federation for the Humanities and Social Sciences, through the Aid to Scholarly Publications Programme, using funds provided by the Social Sciences and Humanities Research Council of Canada.

UBC Press
The University of British Columbia
2029 West Mall
Vancouver, BC V6T 1Z2
604-822-5959 / Fax: 604-822-6083
www.ubcpress.ca

# Contents

# Tables and Figures

**Figures**

# Acknowledgments

This project had its genesis at a conference on New Brunswick politics organized by Bill Cross at Mount Allison University in October 2000. A joint paper given there, which grew out of David's doctoral work, engaged our shared interest in Maritime politics, highlighted the extraordinarily rich data that existed on party leadership elections in the region, and suggested a long-term project that might pull this data together. We extend our appreciation to Bill for organizing the conference, to those who attended for their insights, and to Ken Carty who provided encouragement and continued to challenge us with his valuable feedback along the way.

We owe a real debt of thanks to Agar Adamson and March Conley, who, during their years at Acadia, began this project and kept it going for a number of years. Ian Stewart continued this work after they had moved on to other projects. We also thank Bill Cross, who co-administered and co-financed two of the later surveys. Funding a project over such a long period is challenging, but Acadia University was most supportive with regard to providing financial assistance, and, towards the end, assistance was also provided by the University of Manitoba. We thank those institutions for their support. In particular, we wish to thank Suzanne Stewart and Danielle Fraser at Acadia for their administrative support and Richard Sigurdson at the University of Manitoba for providing David with time to work on this project. Thanks also to the students who provided research assistance (particularly Kiley Thompson and Steven Hobbs at the University of Calgary).

Versions of Chapters 4, 7, and 9 were presented at annual meetings of the Atlantic Provinces Political Studies Association, and we thank that organization for its support of research on the region and, more directly, the discussants who provided us with valuable feedback.

We are delighted with our experience with UBC Press and thank Emily Andrew and Holly Keller for their sterling work in shepherding us through this project. We also appreciate the valuable comments provided by the anonymous reviewers as these have improved the manuscript immensely.

Our depiction of the region's leadership contests is much enriched by the political cartoons contained in the appendix of this book. Political cartoonists make a distinct contribution to political debate and analysis, and we appreciate the willingness of so many of the top cartoonists in the Maritimes to allow their work to be reproduced in *Conventional Choices*.

Our families provided us with constant support throughout the project and cheerfully accepted the distractions and time away that accompanied it. Accordingly, we wish to express our deep gratitude to Audrey, Duncan, Gavin, Fraser, and Robyn Stewart as well as to Brenda O'Neill, and Rachel and Aidan Stewart.

There is much discussion in contemporary politics about disengagement and falling rates of participation. Our project is based on the willingness of many thousands of Maritimers to participate in the leadership selection processes of their parties and to provide the region's voters with the candidates from whom premiers would be drawn. The dedication and commitment of these activists to the political process should be celebrated. We are especially grateful to the thousands of delegates and voters who took the time to complete and return the surveys on which this book is based. Without their voluntary participation, the ability to analyze one of the most important parts of the political process would be impossible. We dedicate *Conventional Choices* to them.

# Conventional Choices

# 1
# Choosing Leaders

In representative democracies, leaders matter. They articulate, they persuade, they organize, they represent, and, most significantly, they choose. In some measure, we are all products of the activities of political leaders. Of course, the reverse is also true. Democratic leaders are not imposed from without; rather, they are imbued with the social structure and political culture of their particular body politic, and once elected to office, these pressures are more likely to be magnified than to be diminished. Even so, democratic leaders are not mere epiphenomenal froth driven by structural currents and breaking on institutional shoals; like all human agents, they combine idiosyncratic psychological and attitudinal profiles with a capacity for self-reflection. As a result, leaders can think and act with some degree of personal autonomy, and different leaders will confront the same set of political circumstances in different ways. In representative democracies, it bears repeating, leaders matter.

The selection of leaders is typically a two-stage process. The leadership of a political party is usually secured before the stewardship of the body politic can be won, although occasionally the former is a sufficient, as well as a necessary, condition of the latter. This is a book about the first of these stages, about the intraparty, rather than the interparty, struggle for power. In order to understand better their choices, we explore the backgrounds, the attitudes, and the motivations of those who select party leaders. We also consider what distinguishes winners from losers, what separates the few who succeed from the many who fail in their quest for party leadership. Parties and their leadership elections are an important part of political life in Canada, and relevant divisions in the wider polity are likely to animate leadership elections as well.[1] Analysis of leadership elections thus provide us with insight into political life more generally.

Leadership selection has been extensively scrutinized by the Canadian scholarly community. As Anthony Sayers notes: "Given that voters indirectly elect first ministers from among the leaders selected by their parties, this selection process has been a key concern of the study of leadership in Canada."[2] Beginning in 1968 with Donald Smiley's path-breaking article,[3] a number of this country's top political scientists have concentrated their analytical attention on the matter of leadership selection. We now know a great deal about the representativeness of convention attendees, about candidate motivations and career patterns, and about the influence on voting behaviour of money, ideology, the media, social structure, institutional rules, and a host of other variables. Indeed, the literature on leadership selection in our national parties grew so rapidly that, as early as 1976, Stephen Clarkson was openly questioning whether additional research would be "of any interest."[4]

Studies of provincial leadership conventions, however, were slower to emerge. In 1973, Courtney had reminded scholars that "the selection of provincial party leaders deserves nothing less than separate and complete studies."[5] Thirteen years later, however, Gibbins and Hunziker were still lamenting that "provincial leadership conventions have been ignored despite their greater frequency, their growing size and complexity and their growing importance to provincial political life."[6] Only in recent times has this disciplinary lacuna begun to be filled, most notably with two volumes from Carty, Erickson, and Blake and the Stewart and Archer treatise.[7] Even so, there remain vast gaps in our understanding of leadership selection in the provinces. Here, our focus will be on leadership selection in the three Maritime provinces of Nova Scotia, New Brunswick, and Prince Edward Island.

Since 1971, members of the Department of Political Science at Acadia University have been surveying participants at Maritime leadership contests.[8] As a result of this effort, a rich data set spanning twenty-five conventions over thirty-two years has been gathered (Table 1.1 provides an overview). As can be seen, the data set, while extensive, is not complete; data collection has been most comprehensive in Nova Scotia. In fact, from John Buchanan's second ballot victory in 1971 through to 2003, only one of that province's leadership contests (the 1997 Liberal gathering)[9] is absent from the data set. In the other two provinces, however, surveys have been conducted more sporadically. There have, for example, been no surveys of the New Democratic Party (NDP) in New Brunswick and only one in Prince Edward Island, omissions that speak volumes about the importance of the NDP in the political life of those provinces. However, a number of leadership elections held by major parties were not surveyed. For instance, the 1971 and 1978 gatherings of the New Brunswick Liberals (which elected Robert Higgins and Joe Daigle, respectively) and the 1989 (Barbara Baird-Filliter), 1991 (Dennis Cochrane), and 1995 (Bernard Valcourt) conventions of the New Brunswick Tories were not studied. And in Prince Edward Island, where the tenure of party leaders has typically been far briefer than that enjoyed by their counterparts in the other two Maritime provinces, the list of omissions includes the 1990 (Pat Mella) and 1996 (Pat Binns) Tory conventions. Nevertheless, one must not overreact to these lacunae; the data may not be completely comprehensive, but they afford unparalleled opportunities to examine thirty-two years of Maritime leadership conventions.

In *Conventional Choices*, we intend to utilize this incredibly rich data set to illuminate the nature and dynamics of Maritime leadership politics. Some generalizations across the data sets certainly emerge. But much of the story focuses on sources of variation. Table 1.1 reveals, for example, that, while many of the conventions were single-ballot coronations, others were close and protracted struggles. We anticipate that the voting calculus of delegates[10] will differ under different competitive circumstances. As well, six of the twenty-five conventions in Table 1.1 represent leadership changes in the governing party. Again, the task of choosing a premier, as opposed to an opposition leader, is likely to alter the convention dynamics. Moreover, it is apparent that the surrounding electoral contexts for these conventions varied widely. Those Nova Scotian New Democrats who gathered in the spring of 1996 to elect Robert Chisholm should have had no realistic ambitions that their party would soon escape decades of electoral oblivion. Two years later, by contrast, the New Brunswick Liberals who elected Camille Theriault as leader (and premier) were supremely confident that their stranglehold on provincial power would not soon be broken. One might reasonably anticipate, therefore, that patronage considerations, for example, would be more prominent among members at the Liberal rather than the NDP convention. Ironically, both sets of delegates were labouring under erroneous assumptions. The landscape soon shifted dramatically in both Nova Scotia and New Brunswick, and successive elections left Robert Chisholm far closer than Camille Theriault to the premiership of his province. We use the opportunities afforded by our analysis of these elections to address the region's political life more broadly.

Clearly, there are many potential sources of variation among the twenty-five leadership conventions under scrutiny. We pay particular heed to four key variables: (1) province, (2) time, (3) party, and (4) method of election. With regard to the first key variable, grouping Nova Scotia, New Brunswick, and Prince Edward Island (PEI) into a single analytical unit (the Maritimes) is a common practice. In reality, a variety of interprovincial differences exist in the region, and some of these are bound to affect leadership politics. In the three Maritime provinces, for example, only New Brunswickers must struggle to build bridges across a persistent and, at times, acrimonious ethno-linguistic divide. Prince Edward Islanders, by contrast, have the particular need to balance a xenophobic and pastoral self-identity with the economic and social consequences of tourist and development dollars "from away."

*Table 1.1*

## Maritime leadership elections in data set

| Year | Province | Party | Winner | Losers | No. of ballots | Surveys sent | Surveys returned | Response rate (%) |
|---|---|---|---|---|---|---|---|---|
| 1971 | NS | PC | Buchanan | Doucet, Thornhill | 2 | 736 | 405 | 55 |
| 1976 | PEI | PC | MacLean | Lee | 1 | 500 | 142 | 28 |
| 1978 | PEI | Liberal | Campbell | Mitchell | 1 | 480 | 163 | 34 |
| 1980 | NS | Liberal | Cameron | MacInnis, MacLean, Mooney | 3 | 914 | 437 | 47 |
| 1980 | NS | NDP | McDonough | Arsenault, MacEachern | 1 | 320 | 212 | 64 |
| 1981 | PEI | Liberal | Ghiz | Clement | 1 | 375 | 168 | 45 |
| 1981 | PEI | PC | Lee | Driscoll, Clark, Binns | 2 | 600 | 203 | 34 |
| 1982 | NB | Liberal | Young | Day, Frenette, Maher | 1 | 867 | 366 | 42 |
| 1985 | NB | Liberal | McKenna | Frenette | 1 | 550 | 274 | 50 |
| 1986 | NS | Liberal | MacLean | Cowan | 1 | 1,803 | 941 | 52 |
| 1988 | PEI | PC | Gass | Walker | 1 | 500 | 211 | 42 |
| 1991 | NS | PC | Cameron | Thornhill, McInnis, Callaghan | 3 | 2,434 | 1230 | 51 |
| 1992 | NS | Liberal | Savage | Downe, MacInnis, Drish, Hawkins | 2 | 3,500 | 1802 | 52 |
| 1993 | PEI | Liberal | Callbeck | Creed, Campbell | 1 | 1,800 | 984 | 55 |
| 1995 | NS | PC | Hamm | White, MacDonald | 1 | 1,800 | 957 | 53 |
| 1996 | PEI | Liberal | Milligan | Cheverie, MacDonald, Mullen | 1 | 1,000 | 365 | 37 |
| 1996 | NS | NDP | Chisholm | Atwell | 1 | 300 | 159 | 53 |
| 1997 | NB | PC | Lord | Betts, Allaby, Blaney | 2 | 2,000 | 593 | 30 |
| 1998 | NB | Liberal | Theriault | Byrne, Richard | 1 | 2,000 | 730 | 39 |
| 2000 | NS | NDP | H. MacDonald | Deveaux, M. MacDonald, Peters, Bitter-Suermann | 3 | 602 | 306 | 51 |
| 2002 | PEI | NDP | Robichaud | Bingham, Hawkes | 1 | 82 | 47 | 57 |
| 2002 | NS | Liberal | D. Graham | MacKenzie, B. Graham | 1 | 900 | 151 | 17 |
| 2002 | NB | Liberal | S. Graham | MacDougall | 1 | 1,500 | 166 | 11 |
| 2002 | NS | NDP | Dexter | MacDonell | 1 | 1,200 | 497 | 41 |
| 2003 | PEI | Liberal | Gliz | Buchanan | 1 | 1,800 | 248 | 14 |

As for Nova Scotians, they have been far more receptive to social democracy than have their counterparts elsewhere in the Maritimes. We anticipate that these and other provincial idiosyncrasies will impinge significantly upon our analysis; to paint the picture of "Maritime leadership conventions" with a needlessly broad brush would obscure as much as it would reveal. In light of this, an important part of our task is the identification of political phenomena of special relevance in only one of the provinces. As we show, PEI's leadership elections and politics are heavily influenced by the province's overwhelmingly rural nature. Linguistic divisions in New Brunswick animate political contests and attitudes in that province in a way that is simply irrelevant in the rest of the region. Finally, the space carved out by the NDP in Nova Scotia, and the challenges it has overcome to become a contender for power, reveal much that is unique about Nova Scotia.

With regard to time, the second key variable, it is something of a cliché to speak of exponential rates of political change in the modern world. Nevertheless, much has altered in the over three decades since John Buchanan was elected as leader of the Nova Scotia Progressive Conservatives: separatist provincial governments, patriation, an entrenched charter of rights, free trade, stagflation, an end to the Cold War, energy crises, neoconservatism, constitutional failure, fiscal crises, populism, 9/11, and, of course, globalization. A leadership convention may be akin to a cocoon, a place of partial and temporary insulation for attendees. Even so, the outside world inevitably comes crashing in on these gatherings. Neither candidates nor electors can check their socially laden conceptions at the gate; even if it were possible, few would do so willingly since social reference points often permit the attachment of meaning to convention events and outcomes. If the external milieu of Maritime leadership conventions has changed significantly over the three decades of our data collecting, and there seems to be little doubt on that score, we would expect to find evidence of same in our analysis.

The search for temporal change in our data, however, is less straightforward than one might have hoped. Predictably (and lamentably), different principal investigators have altered the research instrument over the years, dropping a few questions, adding many more, and tinkering with the wording of some of those that have endured. Even if the most recent iteration of the questionnaires provides optimal purchase on the perceptions and motivations of party members, longitudinal consistency has been sacrificed. Cognizant of the dangers of methodological artefacts, we interpret with caution any changes over time in our data.

With regard to party, the third key variable, our data set includes five leadership conventions from provincial New Democrats (all but one, alas, from Nova Scotia), seven from provincial Conservatives, and thirteen from provincial Liberals. Would one anticipate the emergence of interparty differences in our analysis? With respect to the NDP, with its distinctive traditions of electoral oblivion and social democratic ideology, convention delegates would presumably think and behave in a manner unlike their counterparts in either the Liberals or the Progressive Conservatives. With respect to differences between the two mainstream parties, however, our expectations would be more uncertain. After all, the Maritime branches of the Liberals and Tories are conventionally regarded as similarly pragmatic, vote-maximizing, brokerage parties. In Nova Scotia, for example, Murray Beck has observed that "differences in principle between the old parties are practically, non-existent"[11] and that the Liberals and Conservatives may be "a case of Tweedle-Dum and Tweedle-Dee."[12] Nevertheless, there is at least some evidence to the contrary. Elsewhere, we have argued that, contra Beck, the views of Nova Scotia Liberals and Conservatives differ at every level of political involvement – from voters to activists to candidates.[13] In New Brunswick, the notorious northwest to southeast diagonal line that divided the province into French, Roman Catholic Liberal and English, Protestant Tory fiefdoms has faded somewhat in modern times.[14] Nevertheless, as we demonstrate, the demographic makeup of the two parties' membership rolls remains easily distinguishable.

Finally, method of election is a key source of potential variation at leadership conventions. For over six decades, the institutional framework of leadership conventions in Canada was relatively stable. First adopted by the national Liberals in 1919 to select a leader after the sudden death of Sir Wilfrid Laurier, most subsequent rule changes amounted to tinkering at the margins, decreasing the role played by ex officio attendees, increasing the proportion of women or youth delegates, or controlling the extent of campaign expenditures (to take just three examples). None of these alternations, however, prevented leadership candidates from becoming progressively more skilful at manipulating the election of constituency delegates. Brazen machine politics became commonplace, and by the mid-1980s, Canada had both a prime minister and a leader of the opposition whose leadership triumphs had been secured, in part, through the effective organization at the delegate selection stage of ethnic blocs, children, non-residents, and even the homeless.[15]

Despite these unedifying features, the traditional leadership convention might have persisted in the absence of changes in the surrounding social context. The Canadian political culture, however, has altered significantly since the years immediately after the First World War. As the architects of the Meech Lake Accord were soon to discover, by the mid-1980s Canadians were growing suspicious of the mechanisms of representative democracy. Political elites were no longer the objects of deference, and an increasing populist enthusiasm for the devices of direct democracy could be detected. The Parti Quebecois was the first party to adapt to this social change. In 1985, it essentially cut out intermediaries by giving all registered party members a vote in the election of the new leader. The universal ballot, as it came to be known, was soon adopted by other parties, and, by the end of the twentieth century, it had become the norm.

Our thirty-two-year data set provides ample evidence of this transformation. The universal ballot was first employed in the Maritimes by the PEI Progressive Conservatives in 1990; although we lack survey data from that gathering, we do have information from eight other similarly structured conventions. Fortunately, for our purposes, not all of the recent leadership contests in the region have used the universal ballot. The PEI Liberals (in 1993), the Nova Scotia New Democrats (in both 1996 and 2000), and the New Brunswick Liberals (in 1998) elected their leaders through traditional delegated conventions. These conventions, and particularly that of the New Brunswick Liberals, help us to distinguish the impact of institutional change from the impact of time.

That there will be some effect from widening the franchise seems almost certain. Other studies of single leadership conventions have suggested that giving the vote to all party members changes the electorate's demographic composition, partisan commitment, and pace of decision making.[16] Our more comprehensive data set should permit us, with some degree of confidence, to establish the validity of these and other hypotheses.

Disentangling the impact of our four key variables (province, time, party, and method of election) is rarely straightforward. In a perfect world, one would have enough cases to hold the other three variables constant while scrutinizing the impact of change in the fourth. Even our data set of twenty-five different conventions falls far short of that ideal. In a perfect world, as well, the list of secondary variables that might impinge on the convention outcome would not be so extensive. Mention has already been made of governmental status, likelihood of electoral success, and number of ballots, but to that list could be added candidate personality types, nature and extent of media coverage, proximity of the next election, circumstances of the federal party wing, and many more. We allude to these factors on occasion but do not attempt a comprehensive overview of their impact.

There is, however, no need to be apologetic about the scope of this study. Twenty-five surveys over more than three decades may not be ideal, but they afford an unprecedented opportunity to examine the phenomenon of Maritime leadership conventions. Almost as important, this data set also enables us to speak more widely about the politics of Nova Scotia, of New Brunswick, and of Prince Edward Island. In contrast, for example, to the academic attention historically accorded the Prairie provinces of Alberta, Saskatchewan, and Manitoba,[17] the literature on the three Maritime provinces (both separately and as a grouping) remains lamentably sketchy. In part, this scholarly neglect may be rooted in a defensible commitment to methodological rigour: national public opinion soundings (including the influential Canadian Election Studies) typically contain too few respondents from any single Maritime province (and, especially, from PEI) to permit valid intraregional comparisons. In part, however, the academy's inattention can also be traced to a less defensible reliance on antiquated stereotypes about Maritime politics. Thus, the politics of Nova Scotia, New Brunswick, and Prince Edward Island have been perceived to be characterized by traditionalism, conservatism, stability, patronage, and dependence. This understanding, which regards Maritime politics of the early twenty-first century as different only in degree from the region's practices and mores of the late nineteenth century, is flawed in two important respects. First, it rests on an increasingly flimsy empirical base: exposing the shortcomings of these stereotypes has provided ample grist for some academic mills.[18] Second, it homogenizes that which is heterogeneous; that is, the traditional view of Maritime politics glosses over the fundamentally distinctive politics of Nova Scotia, New Brunswick, and Prince Edward Island. In *Conventional Choices,* we emphasize this latter shortcoming. Our twenty-five conventions over thirty-two years provide us with a series of windows through which we may regard the political cultures of the three Maritime provinces. There are, of course, alternative ways to gain some purchase on the political orientations of Maritimers, although it is worth noting that wide-ranging public opinion questionnaires have been quite uncommon in these three provinces. The validity of our particular measure, however, is easy to defend. Leadership conventions in the Maritimes, as we demonstrate, have brought together a diverse (albeit well-educated) cross-section of the provincial populace. These politically active and aware citizens should be particularly attuned to provincial orientations and mores. And in some instances, at least, the numbers involved have been quite impressive. Thus, approximately one out of every twenty adult Prince Edward Islanders attended the 1996 Liberal leadership convention. Ultimately, our twin purposes for this book work closely together. We are able to use data gathered from our leadership surveys to understand better the individuated political natures of Nova Scotia, New Brunswick, and Prince Edward Island. At the same time, this heightened awareness of provincial distinctiveness provides an illuminating backdrop for our close scrutiny of particular leadership contests.[19]

The twenty-five data sets also provide us with an opportunity to look at features of the leadership selection process in Canada that, previously, have not been examined in detail. We use this opportunity to look at the voters who backed fringe candidates and at attempts made by eliminated candidates to deliver their support to other candidates.

Our plan for *Conventional Choices* is straightforward. Combined with the appendix, the next two chapters provide overviews of the leadership elections, of the seventy-five candidates who sought their party's leadership, and of the tens of thousands of ordinary Maritimers who cast ballots in these contests. In Chapter 4, we systematically compare the political back-grounds and process involvement of those who participated in conventions with those who voted in universal ballots. We explore whether the change from delegated conventions to universal ballot has revolutionized the na-ture of leadership decision making. We note, in particular, that the substan-tial increase in the number of participants has not been accompanied by corresponding declines in political interest and activity.

The next three chapters demonstrate the impact of socio-economic vari-ables on voting behaviour. Chapter 5 emphasizes the continuing impor-tance of region, religion, and language, while Chapters 6 and 7 focus on community size and sex, respectively. We then consider, in Chapter 8, the role of party ideology. Using a range of measures, we demonstrate that ac-tivists in the Liberal, Progressive Conservative, and New Democratic parties have clearly different ideological perspectives.

Chapters 9 and 10 look at two aspects of convention dynamics that our extensive data set render susceptible to in-depth analysis. In the former, we analyze the process by which many voters (at the eleventh hour and with little conviction) come to support fringe candidates; in the latter, we high-light the limited extent to which eliminated candidates can "deliver" their supporters to another contestant.

The next section builds on our analysis of the twenty-five elections and scrutinizes phenomena that have emerged as peculiar to individual Mari-time provinces. In Chapter 11, we discuss the garden myth on Prince Edward Island and conclude that Islanders are continuing to define themselves as an independent farming people in an unspoiled cocoon. In Chapter 12, we highlight the continuing power of language to animate New Brunswickers, while in Chapter 13 we trace the evolution of the Co-operative Common-wealth Federation-New Democratic Party (CCF-NDP) in Nova Scotia from a minor Cape Breton-centred party to a major political force based princi-pally in metropolitan Halifax. In these three chapters, we use our leadership data to speak to broader political phenomena in each of the provinces.

In Chapter 14, we reflect on the enthusiasm academics retain for the lead-ership convention. While party activists have whole-heartedly embraced the all-member leadership vote, academics have, for the most part, been decidedly less enthusiastic about the change. Finally, in Chapter 15 we con-clude with a summary of our major findings.

As one might expect in a study of this magnitude, there are a number of methodological issues to keep in mind. For instance, there were minor meth-odological variations over this period. Typically, samples of convention attendees received mail questionnaires, and between one-third and one-half of these were generally returned. Until June 2002, the smaller scale of New Democratic Party gatherings obviated the need to draw a sample; prior to that time, all NDP delegates received a questionnaire. As well, the 2002

*Table 1.2*

**Maritime leadership elections in data set: actual vs. reported vote totals**

| Year | Province | Party | Candidate | First ballot Actual | First ballot Reported | Difference |
|------|----------|-------|-----------|--------|----------|------------|
| 1971 | NS | PC | Buchanan | 33 | 33 | 0 |
| | | | Doucet | 38 | 39 | +1 |
| | | | Thornhill | 29 | 27 | −2 |
| 1976 | PEI | PC | MacLean | 47 | 47 | 0 |
| | | | Lee | 43 | 43 | 0 |
| 1978 | PEI | Liberal | Campbell | 72 | 71 | −1 |
| | | | Mitchell | 28 | 29 | +1 |
| 1980 | NS | Liberal | Cameron | 37 | 40 | +3 |
| | | | MacLean | 27 | 29 | +2 |
| | | | Mooney | 21 | 17 | −4 |
| | | | MacInnis | 15 | 15 | 0 |
| 1980 | NS | NDP | McDonough | 74 | 80 | +6 |
| | | | Arsenault | 13 | 14 | +1 |
| | | | MacEachern | 13 | 6 | −7 |
| 1981 | PEI | Liberal | Ghiz | 65 | 68 | +3 |
| | | | Clement | 35 | 32 | −3 |
| 1981 | PEI | PC | Lee | 40 | 44 | +4 |
| | | | Clark | 24 | 25 | +1 |
| | | | Driscoll | 20 | 17 | −3 |
| | | | Binns | 16 | 14 | −2 |
| 1982 | NB | Liberal | Young | 51 | 56 | +5 |
| | | | Day | 31 | 27 | −4 |
| | | | Frenette | 12 | 11 | −1 |
| | | | Maher | 6 | 5 | −1 |
| 1985 | NB | Liberal | McKenna | 69 | 79 | +10 |
| | | | Frenette | 31 | 21 | −10 |
| 1986 | NS | Liberal | MacLean | 60 | 62 | +2 |
| | | | Cowan | 40 | 38 | −2 |
| 1988 | PEI | PC | Gass | 51 | 53 | +2 |
| | | | Walker | 49 | 47 | −2 |
| 1991 | NS | PC | Cameron | 32 | 35 | +3 |
| | | | Thornhill | 31 | 27 | −4 |
| | | | McInnis | 29 | 29 | 0 |
| | | | Callaghan | 8 | 8 | 0 |
| 1992 | NS | Liberal | Savage | 47 | 51 | +4 |
| | | | Downe | 41 | 38 | −3 |
| | | | MacInnis | 11 | 8 | −3 |
| | | | Drish | 1 | 1 | 0 |
| | | | Hawkins | 1 | 1 | 0 |
| 1993 | PEI | Liberal | Callbeck | 79 | 88 | +9 |
| | | | Creed | 16 | 10 | −6 |
| | | | Campbell | 5 | 2 | −3 |

▶

◄ *Table 1.2*

| Year | Province | Party | Candidate | First ballot | | |
|------|----------|-------|-----------|--------|----------|------------|
| | | | | Actual | Reported | Difference |
| 1995 | NS | PC | Hamm | 54 | 56 | +2 |
| | | | White | 37 | 34 | –3 |
| | | | Macdonald | 10 | 9 | –1 |
| 1996 | PEI | Liberal | Milligan | 52 | 50 | –2 |
| | | | Cheverie | 42 | 46 | +4 |
| | | | Macdonald | 5 | 3 | –2 |
| | | | Mullen | 1 | 1 | 0 |
| 1996 | NS | NDP | Chisholm | 77 | 79 | +2 |
| | | | Atwell | 23 | 21 | –2 |
| 1997 | NB | PC | Lord | 37 | 37 | 0 |
| | | | Betts | 32 | 31 | –1 |
| | | | Allaby | 17 | 21 | +4 |
| | | | Blaney | 14 | 11 | –3 |
| 1998 | NB | Liberal | Theriault | 56 | 55 | –1 |
| | | | Byrne | 27 | 25 | –2 |
| | | | Richard | 18 | 20 | +2 |
| 2000 | NS | NDP | H. MacDonald | 32 | 32 | 0 |
| | | | Deveaux | 29 | 29 | 0 |
| | | | M. MacDonald | 26 | 26 | 0 |
| | | | Peters | 8 | 8 | 0 |
| | | | Bitter-Suermann | 5 | 5 | 0 |
| 2002 | PEI | NDP | Robichaud | 73 | 84 | +11 |
| | | | Bingham | 22 | 13 | –9 |
| | | | Hawkes | 5 | 2 | –3 |
| 2002 | NS | Liberal | D. Graham | 60 | 74 | +14 |
| | | | MacKenzie | 33 | 20 | –13 |
| | | | B. Graham | 7 | 6 | –1 |
| 2002 | NB | Liberal | S. Graham | 75 | 77 | +2 |
| | | | MacDougall | 25 | 23 | –2 |
| 2002 | NS | NDP | Dexter | 63 | 70 | +7 |
| | | | MacDonell | 37 | 30 | –7 |
| 2003 | PEI | Liberal | Ghiz | 52 | 55 | +3 |
| | | | Buchanan | 48 | 45 | –3 |

Nova Scotia Liberals were surveyed electronically, while questionnaires were distributed on site without return postage to both the 2002 New Brunswick Liberals and the 2003 PEI Liberals. That these three surveys had many of the lowest response rates in our data set reveals the danger inherent in these cost-cutting initiatives. Although relying on party activists to answer a mail survey introduces an element of self-selection to the process, we nonetheless have good reason to be confident about the "representative" nature of our respondents. As Table 1.2 illustrates, the variation between the actual election results and the reported votes of our respondents is generally very small; the average discrepancy is only 3 percent, and, in some instances (such as the 2000 Nova Scotia NDP), the match is eerily close.

Not surprisingly, there is a slight tendency for those who supported the winning candidate to return their questionnaires, a trend that is magnified when the winner coasts almost uncontested to victory. All six of the cases in Table 1.2 where the gap between real and reported first ballot total exceeds 5 percent represent instances of this phenomenon. The coronations of Alexa McDonough, Frank McKenna, Catherine Callbeck, Danny Graham, Gary Robichaud, and Darrell Dexter were so convincing that those activists who backed minor candidates were significantly less willing to revisit, even vicariously, their deviant behaviour. No such pattern of response rate reactivity is apparent from highly contested leadership struggles. Even Rollie Thornhill's well-publicized arrest on charges of influence-peddling a few days after the 1991 Nova Scotia Progressive Conservative leadership convention did not deter an almost proportionate number of his backers from returning our survey. In general, therefore, Table 1.2 provides reassurance as to the representativeness of our data sets. With this reassurance, we turn to our analysis.

# 2
# The Conventions

In this book, our principal purpose is to discover and explain aggregate patterns of political behaviour. Hence, even our principal sources of variation (province, time, party, and method of election) permit us to analyze clusters of conventions rather than any single convention. Nevertheless, there are many occasions in subsequent chapters where outliers emerge from the data, where the results from specific leadership contests do not conform to the general pattern. It is easier to understand these cases if we have some purchase on the idiosyncratic dynamics that were in play on those occasions.

Each of the twenty-five elections featured particular variations on a set of more general themes. In this chapter, we focus upon just three of our twenty-five conventions: the 1996 Prince Edward Island Liberals, the 1997 New Brunswick Progressive Conservatives, and the 2000 Nova Scotia New Democrats (thumbnail sketches of the remaining twenty-two leadership contests can be found in the appendix of this book). The three contests featured here highlight some of the key variations at play in our study. They include, for example, one from each of the three major political parties. As well, the three contests showcase different methods of leadership selection. The 1996 PEI Liberals employed a single site all-member vote, while one year later, the New Brunswick PCs opted for the multiple-site variant of the universal ballot. By contrast, the 2000 Nova Scotia NDP chose its new leader at a traditional delegated convention. Finally, each of these three contests illuminates a distinctive feature of politics in their respective provinces: the garden myth of Prince Edward Island, the politics of language in New Brunswick, and the rise and transformation of the NDP in Nova Scotia. These are significant phenomena in the political life of each of the provinces, and exploring them enhances our general understanding of regional politics. We return to a fuller discussion of these three themes in Chapters 11 through 13.

## Prince Edward Island Liberal Party: 5 October 1996

For Catherine Callbeck, the fall from grace was precipitous. Three years after routing her opponents in both the Liberal leadership contest and the general election that followed, the first elected female premier in Canadian history was gone. When, in the mid-1990s, the federal Liberals unexpectedly converted to the faith of fiscal rectitude, there was widespread collateral damage (as such diverse individuals as Preston Manning and Doug Young could attest). Long dependent on Ottawa's munificence, the Callbeck administration was forced to cut programs and roll back public-sector salaries by 7.5 percent. When angry civil servants demonstrated outside the legislature, Callbeck left via a side exit, a particularly unfortunate gambit in a province where citizens are accustomed to face-to-face contact with their politicians. Callbeck took the province to the brink of a June 1996 election call but backed away; two months later, she announced her resignation.

Four candidates entered the race to succeed Callbeck. From the outset, the prospects of twenty-eight-year-old Charlottetown businessman Daniel Mullen were dismissed. Mullen had never previously run for elected office, and his incessant attacks on governmental arrogance seemed principally fuelled by a belief that a botched contract by the provincial ministry of education had precipitated the bankruptcy of Mullen's fledgling computer store. With the matter working through the courts, Mullen was, in effect, suing the very administration he aspired to lead. Mullen lacked both the resources and the inclination to run an effective campaign; his budget was only a thousand dollars and he summarized his approach to wooing voters thusly: "I'm not sucking up to these people ... What they are getting is me."[1] Still, Mullen could at least be credited with injecting some idiosyncratic policy positions into the race. The four all-candidates debates prior to the convention were low-key affairs, with all of the aspirants pledging to enhance health care, to preserve small rural schools, to oppose the Harmonized Sales Tax, and so on. On a few issues, however, Mullen proved to be an unlikely champion of the traditional image of PEI as a bucolic idyll. Unlike the other candidates, for example, Mullen advocated a total ban on video lottery terminals (VLTs) and promised even stricter land use regulations on farmers.[2]

The prospects of Tex MacDonald, a forty-eight-year-old teacher, were more difficult to gauge. A sports icon on PEI, MacDonald had served on Charlottetown city council for ten years, the last four as mayor. MacDonald's most obvious liability was his underdeveloped roots in the Liberal party. Indeed, it had been less than a year since MacDonald had renounced his Tory connections, and Island Liberals could legitimately wonder whether he had paid sufficient dues to seek the party's leadership. MacDonald ran an enthusiastic but troubled campaign, with recurrent allegations that his team was using the incentive of free hats to recruit instant-Liberals from local high schools.[3] MacDonald repeatedly emphasized both his own humble origins and his obeisance to the wisdom of the common folk; yet, in the eyes of one observer, MacDonald's self-styled "fresh new ideas" amounted to little more than "a vague but fervent desire to consult the people."[4]

The resumés of the two front-running candidates, Keith Milligan and Wayne Cheverie, manifested some obvious similarities. Both were forty-six years old, both had at least a decade of experience in the provincial legislature, and both had held prominent cabinet posts in the Ghiz and Callbeck administrations. Milligan had served as the minister of health and social services, agriculture, education and human resources, and transportation and public works, while Cheverie's postings had been in labour, health and social services, justice, and the Office of the Attorney General. Cheverie also had served as provincial treasurer and government house leader. As a result, both were obliged to defend the (increasingly unpopular) Liberal record, while simultaneously indicating that new policy directions could, and should, be taken. Hence, with respect to the public-sector wage rollback, both candidates supported it as necessary at the time but both also assured Liberal members that it would not be repeated.[5]

What differentiated Cheverie from Milligan were matters of style. The latter portrayed himself as a party outsider who would replace the dominance of the "backroom boy[s]" with a more "open" government: "Over the last 10 years, our government has tended to become more and more centralized ... government has surrounded itself with a very small group of advisers. The party I'd lead would reach out to all Islanders."[6]

As a silver fox rancher from Prince County, Milligan could successfully pander to the anti-Charlottetown sentiments harboured by many rural Islanders. Indeed, the "fervent, agrarian, anti-bureaucrat, anti-intellectual" edge to the Milligan campaign caused some to liken it to a "low-key Island version of the Khmer Rouge."[7] Few party luminaries were attracted to Milligan; in fact, Cheverie had four times as many cabinet ministers and twice as many backbenchers in his camp, and many of these must have dismissed as déclassé Milligan's boast to have set the record for paving the most roads in Kings County (no mean feat in itself).[8]

Charlottetown lawyer Cheverie presented quite a different image. Unlike Milligan, he did not seem to be particularly attached to the image of the Island as a pastoral ideal; at one point, he made the politically dangerous observation that "there's a balance that has to be struck here between those who farm and everyone else."[9] In fact, Cheverie's urban persona was such that he felt compelled to reassure Liberals that he did not actually believe the province "stops at North River" (i.e., just outside Charlottetown).[10] While Milligan was rounding up the support of party mavericks (both Larry Creed and the irrepressible Ron McKinley were onside), Cheverie quickly became the standard-bearer for the Liberal brass. Cheverie did nothing to discourage media reports that he was "cleaning up on Liberal establishment support;"[11] on the contrary, Cheverie boasted that he "fully expect[ed] to get the bulk" of the votes from long-time party activists.[12] Unfortunately, for Cheverie, this was to be the first PEI Liberal leadership race to be decided by an all-member ballot. When Callbeck announced her resignation in August, there were 5,500 paid-up party members; two months later, 9,874 Liberals were eligible to vote for the new leader.[13] Prior to the convention, the Milligan camp displayed photocopies to the press of 2,231 new membership applications.[14] Notwithstanding Cheverie's protestations that he was not actually a "cold fish,"[15] his campaign had clearly generated less enthusiasm than had that of his chief rival.

At the convention, Milligan continued to pay homage to the traditional image of Prince Edward Island as a garden. His speech emphasized the "down-home values" he learned at a one-room rural schoolhouse, while his parents "toiled long hours picking cucumbers."[16] Nevertheless, few expected the contest to be decided on a single ballot. Only 4,804 Liberals registered for the convention (or about one-half of those eligible to participate), and almost five hundred of these did not bother to cast a vote on the first round. Since Milligan's army of Prince County supporters had been bused in en masse and had nowhere else to go, it seems likely that most of the no-shows were Cheverie's Charlottetown backers who busied themselves with other activities while awaiting the (presumably decisive) second ballot. If so, they miscalculated grievously as the self-styled "little guy from Tyne Valley" was able to secure a narrow victory on the initial vote. Tex MacDonald's aspirations to be king-maker vanished when he received only about one-fifth of his anticipated total of one thousand votes. As Hillsborough MP George Proud observed: "The Roman Catholic Church accepts converts every day of the week but they don't appoint them cardinal the next day."[17] When Milligan took the stage for his victory address, he was dutifully flanked by the Liberal members of the legislature, nearly all of whom were sporting bright red Cheverie buttons and funereal expressions.[18] Exulted Larry Creed: "The backroom is dead. This convention was a victory of the ordinary over the extraordinary, and there are a lot more ordinary people about."[19] PEI was not, however, to remain Milligan's Island for long; two months after the convention, the *ancien* Liberal *régime* was defeated by Pat Binns' Tories.

| | |
|---|---|
| Keith Milligan | 2,237 |
| Wayne Cheverie | 1,836 |
| Tex MacDonald | 205 |
| Daniel Mullen | 51 |

SANDY CARRUTHERS / *GUARDIAN*, 9 OCTOBER 1996, A6

## New Brunswick Progressive Conservatives: 18 October 1997

The spectre of Frank McKenna loomed large over the Tory faithful in the fall of 1997. Three times in the past decade, the McKenna-led Liberals had routed the Progressive Conservatives, and over this period, five separate Tory leaders (Richard Hatfield, Mac MacLeod, Barbara Baird-Filliter, Dennis Cochrane, and Bernard Valcourt) had been tried and found wanting. With the party standing at only 18 percent in the polls,[20] and with Reform poised to launch a provincial alternative,[21] most New Brunswick Conservatives were understandably anxious to find a worthy foe for McKenna. The four contenders were thirty-two-year-old Moncton lawyer Bernard Lord, thirty-five-year-old former broadcaster Margaret-Ann Blaney of Saint John, forty-three-year-old Doaktown professor Norman Betts, and forty-six-year-old Fredericton lawyer Cleveland Allaby. Ironically, McKenna chose to resign as premier and Liberal leader on the Monday preceding the Tory convention; thus, voting calculations based on a future match-up against McKenna were suddenly rendered irrelevant.

This was a remarkably inexperienced field of candidates; none had previously held public office. Blaney was a losing Tory candidate (in Newfoundland) in the 1993 federal election, Allaby had been defeated (by then solicitor general Andy Scott) in the 1997 federal campaign, Lord had been a losing candidate in the 1995 provincial vote, while Betts had tried (and failed) to secure a Tory nomination in the same election. Hearing Allaby lord it over Betts at a CBC television debate ("I got the nomination, Norm!")[22] must have struck many viewers as rather droll.

As might have been expected, considerations of ethnicity intruded on the contest. Political folklore had it that New Brunswick francophones "tend[ed] to vote in a block;"[23] Bernard Lord was expected to be the principal beneficiary of this putative phenomenon. As the offspring of a Trudeauesque union between an anglophone father and a francophone mother, Lord was not only fluently bilingual but he also claimed to be genuinely "bicultural," to be able to "really understand the concerns of both language groups."[24] None of the other three Anglophone candidates could make such claims, although Betts' French was clearly superior to the variety offered up by both Blaney and Allaby. With the latter two candidates reduced to reading French from cue cards, Betts was emboldened to suggest that New Brunswick's premier needed to be bilingual: "There's nobody in this room who would argue that you can be a good premier if you don't look after and communicate with all the people of this province."[25] Such suggestions were particularly troublesome for Allaby, given that his campaign had been smeared by MLA Jeannot Volpe for being "anti-French." Volpe had only the flimsiest of evidence to substantiate this charge: he alleged that Allaby had made a speech comparing the Loyalist with the Acadian heritage, that Allaby had not invited all francophone media representatives to his campaign launching, and that Allaby had attracted the backing of several former adherents of the Confederation of the Regions Party.[26] Former party leader Barbara Baird-Filliter rightly decried Volpe's intervention as "miserable politics" and "calculated political opportunism,"[27] while editorialists thundered against "irresponsible mudslingers,"[28] and columnists speculated that the comments were part of a back-room conspiracy ("cooked up months in advance") to deliver the leadership to Betts.[29] Justifiably or not, Volpe's calumny cast a pall over the Allaby campaign.

Few policy disagreements emerged in the weeks leading up to the convention. Although Allaby's insistence that VLTs be removed from corner stores was idiosyncratic,[30] and Betts' desire to review the provincial tax system was similarly distinctive,[31] the overwhelming impression was that the candidates "differ[ed] little in actual policy statements."[32] Hence, at one debate, it was observed that, on many issues, "the four echoed one another, using different words to say much the same thing."[33] As a result, the contest between the two acknowledged front-runners (Betts and Lord) soon crystallized around questions of image and organization. With respect to the former, each had drawbacks. Lord had the "political liability" of being saddled with "a cherubic face that [made] him look like a truant from a Grade 10 algebra lesson."[34] In response, Lord could only urge Tory members not to "judge this book by its cover."[35] As for Betts, he attempted to counteract his image as an ivory tower wonk with lame puns ("our premier may be Frank, but he's not above the Norm")[36] and self-deprecating monikers ("a pulp cutter with a PhD").[37]

Ultimately, however, the contest may have been decided by superior organization. With the Tories employing an all-member ballot, the Lord team was apparently the most successful at signing up new recruits.[38] Hence, despite delivering what was arguably the worst speech at the convention, Lord enjoyed a slight lead after the first ballot. Both Blaney and Allaby were dropped from the second ballot (the latter by choice), and both decided to throw their support behind Lord (although many of Allaby's backers were visibly distressed by this manoeuvre).[39] The key to Lord's success now lay in his organization's ability to keep those members who had supported him at one of the four satellite voting stations (St. Stephen, Moncton, Bathurst, and St. Leonard) from drifting away before the commencement of the second ballot. In Moncton, a large group of Lord's instant conservatives were kept "entertained" at a local bar, the Cool Camel, until it was time to vote a second time. While Betts stopped short of accusing the Lord camp of vote-buying, he did openly question the dedication of these "Cool Camel Tories."[40] Thus, despite a slight erosion in turnout, Lord prevailed on the second ballot.

| Candidate | 1st ballot | 2nd ballot |
|---|---|---|
| Bernard Lord | 1,390 | 1,830 |
| Norm Betts | 1,223 | 1,413 |
| Cleveland Allaby | 663 | |
| Margaret-Ann Blaney | 527 | |

GREG PERRY / MONCTON TIMES & TRANSCRIPT, 21 OCTOBER 1997, D7

## Nova Scotia New Democratic Party: 15 July 2000

For Nova Scotia's New Democrats, the leadership convention of July 2000 was without precedent. At previous such gatherings, only the delusional had believed they were electing a future premier. But much had altered for the party in the four years since Robert Chisholm had won the leadership. From 18 percent of the vote and three seats in the provincial legislature after the 1993 election, the NDP catapulted to 35 percent of the vote and an extraordinary total of nineteen seats in 1998, before slipping back to 30 percent of the popular vote and eleven seats in 1999. Even though the 1999 results were far above the party's historic norms, they were nevertheless disappointing to most Nova Scotia New Democrats. Believing that momentum was very much in their favour, the party ran an overly cautious campaign in 1999. Chisholm's share of the blame for these ill-advised tactics is unclear, although he subsequently took full responsibility for the setback. Admittedly, the 1999 campaign was partially derailed when, after publicly denying any prior criminal misconduct, details of a two-decade-old Chisholm conviction for driving under the influence of alcohol were leaked to the media. After four years at the helm, and still only forty-three years old, Chisholm shocked many observers by resigning as leader, ostensibly to spend more time with his young family.

Who would succeed Chisholm? Early speculation centred on John Holm as the only long-serving member of the provincial caucus and Peter Mancini, the popular Cape Breton MP, but both declined to run. Ultimately, five individuals came forward: two Halifax MLAs (Maureen MacDonald and Kevin Deveaux), two former MLAs (Helen MacDonald and Hinrich Bitter-Suermann), and a former president of the Nova Scotia Government Employees Union (Dave Peters). The prospects of Bitter-Suermann and Peters were perceived by most observers to be negligible. Neither spent more than $2,600 on their leadership bid, while the other three candidates spent between four and five times that amount.[41] Peters entered the campaign late and had no prior electoral experience, while Bitter-Suermann had crossed the floor to the NDP from the Progressive Conservatives and was intent on making the NDP more business-friendly. But promising that, as leader, he would spend as much time consulting with chambers of commerce as with trade unionists,[42] and vilifying a bemused Dan O'Connor for allegedly using his chief of staff position to run a "smear campaign" against Bitter-Suermann's candidacy,[43] was hardly likely to endear him to the stalwarts of his new party. As one observer had inelegantly predicted at the outset of the leadership campaign: "If every party needs a pooper, count on the outspoken Bitter-Suermann to play the role in the months-long contest."[44] No clear favourite, however, emerged among the three front-runners. Each, for example, had the declared support of at least one member of the eleven-person provincial caucus. Of the three, former party president Helen MacDonald was the only one without a seat in the legislature, although her supporters made much of the fact that party icon Alexa McDonough had been similarly situated when she took over as leader in 1980. Helen MacDonald had actually won Cape Breton-The Lakes in a by-election in 1997 and had held the constituency in 1998. In the election of 1999, however, she had been upended by Liberal candidate Brian "Crusher" Boudreau, "whose troubles with the law have made him one of the legislature's more, ahem, colourful characters."[45] Helen MacDonald's campaign revolved around an oft-repeated commitment to return the party to the grassroots. The final edition of her campaign newspaper (*Helen Today!*) was entirely devoted to praising her commitment to party renewal. "Time and time again during the [leadership] debate Helen clearly articulated her theme of consultation and cooperation," it tendentiously observed. "Each time she spoke to the importance of working cooperatively with the membership she brought the enthusiastic crowd to their feet."[46] On most policy matters, however, Helen MacDonald was either evasive (pledging that a distinctively social democratic platform would emerge from meeting with the membership) or backward-looking (emphasizing the need to support the traditional industries of coal and steel).[47]

By contrast, Kevin Deveaux (MLA for Cole Harbour-Eastern Passage) released a blizzard of innovative policy proposals during the campaign. Deveaux pledged, among other things, to institute tax cuts to discourage forest clear-cuts,[48] to hold weekly internet chats with the party grassroots,[49] to axe the Economic Development Department, to establish a program at University College of Cape Breton (UCCB) in environmental remediation,[50] and, most controversially, to eliminate all postsecondary tuition fees.[51] When asked how he could be differentiated from his four competitors, Deveaux emphasized, with some justification, his "fresh new ideas that can present a real alternative based on our principles."[52]

In contrast to the other two favourites, Maureen MacDonald had some difficulty in carving out a distinctive campaign profile. Her policy initiatives (raising the minimum wage, fighting cuts to essential services, freezing postsecondary tuition, restoring educational funding, and so on) were something less than innovative. Somewhat defensively, Maureen MacDonald was to complain that Deveaux's plan to increase the NDP's caucus staff was unrealistic,[53] while his commitment to end postsecondary tuition was "very idealistic."[54] In a party that had previously been receptive to a woman as party leader, Maureen MacDonald's status as an incumbent female MLA had her well situated at the campaign's outset. She failed, however, to provide party members with a compelling reason to back her candidacy.

At the convention, Helen MacDonald held a narrow lead after the first ballot. As expected, neither Bitter-Suermann nor Peters achieved the 10 percent support level necessary to advance to the next ballot. Nor did they

MICHAEL DEADDER / *DAILY NEWS*, 15 JULY 2000, C3

throw their backing behind any of the other candidates. "I think whoever I support, it would be the kiss of death," observed Bitter-Suermann. "This was my worst thrashing ever in adult life."[55] On the second ballot, Helen MacDonald's vote total improved only marginally, and Kevin Deveaux took a narrow lead. Maureen MacDonald was dropped after this ballot, and the Halifax Needham MLA huddled briefly with her advisers. When she emerged to ask, "Where's Helen?" her decision was clear. "Helen MacDonald is rock solid," noted Maureen MacDonald, "She has a tremendous amount of maturity and experience."[56] With "most prominent members" of the Maureen MacDonald campaign following their candidate's lead and with the apparent assistance of the Alexa McDonough machine,[57] Helen MacDonald's third ballot victory was essentially assured. Faced with a candidate who offered youth and innovation, the NDP delegates instead opted for one who promised "to return the party to its traditional roots."[58]

|  | 1st ballot | 2nd ballot | 3rd ballot |
|---|---|---|---|
| Helen MacDonald | 193 | 207 | 322 |
| Kevin Deveaux | 172 | 211 | 262 |
| Maureen MacDonald | 154 | 177 | |
| Dave Peters | 47 | | |
| Hinrich Bitter-Suermann | 31 | | |

Taken together, the three leadership elections highlighted above, and the twenty-two others included in the appendix, display a rich diversity of political experiences. The number of voting participants ranges from a low of 82 (PEI NDP 2002) to a high of 11,536 (NS Liberal 2002), and the mean number of voters is 2,510. The winning candidates did extremely well with a mean vote share of 56 percent on the first ballot. On average, there were three candidates in the races, but the plurality of contests (ten of twenty-five) contained only two, and none had more than five. Consistent with earlier research,[59] more than three-fifths of the elections were held by the major opposition party,[60] and only one-quarter took place when the party was in government. Three elections were held by the New Democrats when the NDP was very much a minor party. As we noted earlier, five of the elections in our data set were held by New Democrats, seven by Conservatives, and thirteen by Liberals.

Obviously, no two contests were identical and some were decidedly idiosyncratic. Certainly, the spectre of criminal charges looming over Rollie Thornhill at the 1991 Nova Scotia PC convention was unique, and the aborted first ballot of the Nova Scotia Liberals the following year was equally distinctive. Even so, it is possible to extract some patterns from a tour of Maritime conventions.

First, it was customary for at least one sitting MLA to seek his or her party's leadership. In fact, only six of the twenty-five contests were without an incumbent legislator (including, not surprisingly, the 2002 PEI New Democrats). One might have surmised that discredited and dispirited opposition parties would have constituted the other five instances of this phenomenon. This presumption would have been correct with respect to the Nova Scotia Liberals in 1992 and 2002, the New Brunswick PCs in 1997, and the 2003 PEI Liberals but not with respect to the 1993 PEI Liberals. Finally, it is worth noting that, of the fourteen contests with candidates from both inside and outside the legislature, on only five occasions (or just over one-third) did victory go to a candidate from outside the caucus. We return to this matter when we scrutinize candidate backgrounds in the next chapter.

Second, it is apparent that at least some of these conventions did not unfold entirely as anticipated. Of course, everyone associated with the event was rightly certain that Catherine Callbeck would destroy her opponents in the 1993 PEI Liberal race. But the relative strengths of victorious candidates Alexa McDonough (NS NDP 1980), Joe Ghiz (PEI Libs 1981), and Keith Milligan (PEI Libs 1996) were all significantly underestimated by most observers, while, on the other hand, the winning vote totals for both Mel Gass (PEI PCs 1988) and Shawn Graham (NB Libs 2002) were substantially less than had been predicted. Handicapping Maritime leadership conventions continues to be a perversely inexact exercise.

Third, it was relatively uncommon to uncover discernible policy differences between the principal contenders for leadership. Leaving aside a few of the fringe candidates, in only eight of the twenty-five contests (or just under one-third) could party members have meaningfully cast their ballot on the basis of issue positions. This finding should not be taken, however, as support for the old chestnut about the non-ideological nature of Maritime politics. After all, a shared adherence to a party philosophy will certainly decrease the likelihood of policy disagreements among leadership contenders. As well, there are often wider strategic issues at play. Certainly, neither candidate for the leadership of the Nova Scotia NDP in 2002 wanted to jeopardize their party's arrival as a major player with fractious bickering over dogma. And for both the 1981 PEI Tories and the 1997 New Brunswick Liberals, the combination of deference to the principle of cabinet solidarity and satisfaction with the party's standing in the polls served to muffle any potential for policy discord. We return to this topic in Chapter 8.

Fourth, most of the leadership results represented continuity for the parties. We examined newspaper coverage for each of the elections and attempted to classify the winners as to whether they represented continuity or change for their party. The tone of the newspaper coverage suggests that the winner could be classified as a "candidate of continuity" more than 70 percent of the time. This tendency was particularly easy to detect when the race was generally perceived as a tussle between the establishment and the grassroots of the party.[61] Entering their respective conventions, there was no mistaking the fact that Alexa McDonough (NS NDP 1980), Doug Young (NB Libs 1982), Catherine Callbeck (PEI Libs 1993), Wayne Cheverie (PEI Libs 1996), Darrell Dexter (NS NDP 2002), and Danny Graham (NS Libs 2002) were the overwhelming choice of party insiders. Of the six, only Cheverie failed to triumph. When the party brass is divided, however, there are clearer opportunities for candidates who represent change. On five such occasions, the race was explicitly primed between experience and newness. Three times the candidate of renewal triumphed (Joe Ghiz [PEI Libs 1981], Frank McKenna [NB Libs 1985], and Robert Ghiz [PEI Libs 2003]), while only twice did victory go to the candidate of experience (Bennett Campbell [PEI Libs 1978] and Vince MacLean [NS Libs 1986]).

Fifth, most of these elections (eighteen), ended on one ballot, and only two went all the way to a third ballot before a decision was made. On all but one occasion, the candidate who led on the first ballot ultimately secured victory. Elections employing the universal ballot were somewhat more likely to end after a single ballot (ten of twelve) than were those that used the traditional delegate system (eight of thirteen). Given that the former mechanism permits a well-organized and well-financed candidate to expand the electorate to the point where victory is all but secured, this pattern is not particularly surprising. We now turn to scrutinize the backgrounds of the seventy-five men and women who sought their party's leadership as well as the backgrounds of the thousands of Maritimers who voted in these elections.

# 3
# From J. Buchanan to A. Buchanan: Candidates and Voters

Leadership elections involve two separate sets of participants: the candidates who vie for the leadership and the voters who determine which of the candidates will be successful. In this chapter, we profile each of these groups in pursuit of our partisan, provincial, temporal, and selection method comparisons. Those who choose Canada's party leaders have attracted significant academic and media attention. A good deal of this scrutiny has focused on the personal characteristics of the voters who actually make the leadership choice. The leadership electorates have been profiled in terms of their social and economic characteristics, and much ink has been spilled regarding their representativeness. Such profiles, implicitly at least, carry with them a concern over whether the delegates in some way reflect the society for which they are trying to select a leader. In fact, the literature on leadership conventions is quite direct in its assessment of the representativeness of convention delegates in socio-economic terms. The delegates who perform the crucial job of leadership selection have not been, as Courtney demonstrated, "a true cross section of Canadian society."[1] Lele, Perlin, and Thorburn, in their study of the 1967 and 1968 national conventions, indicate the nature of this distortion. As they put it, "delegates to the two conventions were predominantly representative of the most privileged groups in Canadian society [and] were drawn from a strikingly narrow socio-economic base."[2]

The elite background of the delegates was not just a phenomenon of the 1960s. Frizzell and McPhail, with the benefit of the 1976 national PC convention, repeated the Lele, Perlin, and Thorburn charge that "all delegates come from a remarkably narrow socio-economic base."[3] Similarly, Courtney and Perlin, in an examination of the national conventions of 1983 and 1984, concluded: "In their socio-economic status delegates are manifestly unrepresentative."[4] Brodie pointed specifically to discrepancies in income, education, and gender,[5] while, with respect to age, Perlin, Sutherland, and

Desjardins observed that "people under 30 were somewhat underrepresented among Liberal delegates and somewhat overrepresented among Conservative delegates" and that "in both parties, the number of delegates over 60 was underrepresented."[6] These trends continued through the end of the century. Courtney reported that, at the 1993 PC leadership convention, only 34 percent of the delegates were women, and only 12 percent were over the age of sixty. The 1990 Liberal convention was generally similar.[7] In essence, then, delegates to national conventions have been mainly male, middle-aged, relatively affluent, and well educated. However, Courtney and Perlin also noted: "On other demographic divisions the delegates are more or less representative of distinctive regional characteristics."[8] Presumably, this would include such features as language, ethnicity, religion, and (possibly) community size.

Evidence of the background of provincial delegates is less overwhelming but points in the same direction. Blake, Carty, and Erickson, in a study of the 1986 BC Social Credit convention, found that the "average delegate was the sort of middle-aged, well-educated, relatively affluent individual usually seen at party conventions in Canada."[9] Adamson, in discussing the 1971 Nova Scotia PC convention, also noted that delegates "were middle aged and overwhelmingly male Protestants of Anglo Saxon origin with a moderately high level of education and at least by Nova Scotian standards well to do."[10]

The Protestant dominance of the 1971 Nova Scotia Conservative convention suggests a somewhat different kind of gathering than those found nationally. At national conventions, delegates represent the provinces and founding ethnic groups quite adequately; indeed, conventions were partially created for that purpose.[11] The failure of certain parts of the electorate to return MPs of a particular party was not regarded as sufficient reason for denying such groups the opportunity to participate in leadership selection. As Courtney explains:

> That the Liberal Parliamentary membership in 1919 was drawn overwhelmingly from the province of Quebec and that the Conservative caucus in 1927 was composed almost entirely of MPs from Ontario, British Columbia and Nova Scotia distressed the politicians of the day. Understandably they were attracted to an institution which overcame their representational concerns by ensuring an equal number of participants from every constituency in the country.[12]

Thus, by holding conventions, and organizing conventions around constituencies, parties did not have to fear that particular regions would be excluded from the leadership selection process. Indeed, regional exclusion was not the only concern in 1919. Laurier felt it important that he be succeeded by a

Protestant, and the general belief was that an English-speaking Protestant leader was essential for the electoral health of the Liberal party.[13] A caucus dominated not only by Quebec but also by French Catholics was not regarded as the appropriate body for selecting such a leader. Far better to have a national convention that would draw delegates from all over the country and that, with constituencies as the basic unit, would certainly bring a majority of English Protestants. The 1971 Nova Scotia convention was also organized around constituencies, as indeed were all Nova Scotia and New Brunswick conventions (although conventions on PEI used polls as the basic unit). Yet Catholics, in spite of their importance in Nova Scotia politics, were decidedly underrepresented. Catholics generally did not favour the Conservatives, and the Conservatives apparently made little effort to include them in their leadership convention. Thus, we cannot assume that the representational successes and failures at the national level will necessarily be replicated in the provincial arena. The twenty-five leadership elections for which we have data enable us to map representation and to indicate the differences that may cross party or provincial lines. Even more important, they allow us to track representation over three decades in order to identify continuity and change in Maritime politics.

In this chapter, we profile Maritime leadership election voters. Do they "represent" their societies? Are they drawn from the same relatively elite and male substratum of the population as are national delegates? Two contrary answers have some surface validity. On the one hand, given the cadre nature of Maritime parties and the fact that they are dominated by the leadership, voters are likely to be of relatively high status. On the other hand, given that the costs in time, distance, and money to attend a Maritime convention are not overly onerous, delegates are likely to be of lower status than are their counterparts elsewhere. The geographic compactness of the three provinces makes attendance at a convention relatively easy and inexpensive – particularly on PEI, where delegates anywhere in the province can commute daily to a convention. The general movement to universal ballots should exacerbate this tendency.

In developing these profiles, we look at a number of characteristics. We first look at gender and age since, as MacIvor points out, parties have used conventions "to manipulate the composition of the electorate to achieve particular representational goals: gender parity, inclusion of younger people."[14] Then, by focusing on education, we examine questions of status and the concerns identified in the literature regarding the elite nature of participants. Following this, we turn to a discussion of community size and then, finally, to the traditional Maritime cleavage of religion.

This chapter also scrutinizes the backgrounds of leadership candidates. In contrast to the extensive research on leadership voters, however, the Canadian scholarly community has had relatively little to say about leadership candidates. John Courtney's work is a notable exception: in both *The Selection of National Party Leaders* (1973) and *Do Conventions Matter* (1995), Courtney provides us with much background detail on the candidates for federal leadership. We are thus able to contrast national patterns with those we uncover from our Maritime data set. In this chapter, then, we profile both the leaders and the voters from our twenty-five Maritime leadership conventions.

## Gender

The most commonly shared characteristic of the seventy-five candidates is gender. As in federal leadership races, the vast majority of Maritime candidates were men, and only seven of the candidates who sought the leadership were women. On this dimension, however, we see a substantial amount of variation over time and among parties.

Before 1988, Alexa McDonough was the only woman to seek the leadership of a Maritime party. Since 1988, six women contested the leadership elections contained in our data set,[15] and it seems that the process has become somewhat more open. Nonetheless, the leadership contestants in the Maritimes remain overwhelmingly male.

Women were far more likely to seek the leadership of the NDP than they were to contest Liberal or Conservative elections. Five of the fifteen candidates who sought the NDP's leadership were women, while only one of the twenty-three PC candidates and just one of the thirty-seven Liberal candidates were female.[16] The literature on women in Canadian parties offers a clear explanation for this trend.[17] Women are more likely to lead parties that have little chance of forming a government, and the New Democrats have never won an election in the region. However, there are exceptions, most notably Catherine Callbeck, who won an easy victory in the 1993 PEI Liberal election (an election held when the party was in power) and went on to become the first woman to lead a provincial party to victory in a general election. As we discuss in Chapter 13, the New Democrats in Nova Scotia became realistic contenders for power over this time period,[18] but it was clearly a minor party when two of the women in our data set (Alexa McDonough and Yvonne Atwell) sought the leadership.

Intriguingly, the success rate of the women who sought the leadership was somewhat higher than was that of the men. Three of the seven women (43 percent) won their leadership elections compared to just 32 percent of the men.

As with candidates, the vast majority of the voters in Maritime leadership elections are male. However, we again see evidence of change as the proportion of leadership electorates made up by women has doubled during the three decades covered by our data. In 1971, women constituted only 24 percent of the Nova Scotia Tory leadership voters, while in 2003, women

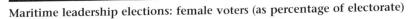

Figure 3.1

**Maritime leadership elections: female voters (as percentage of electorate)**

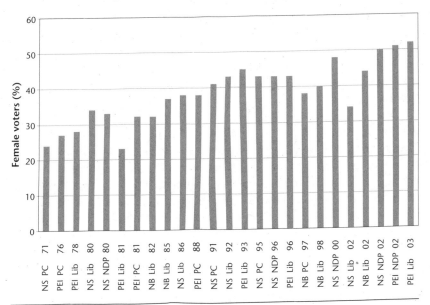

accounted for 52 percent of those who voted in the PEI Liberal leadership election. Indeed, there is a clear secular pattern in the representation of women (see Figure 3.1). Before 1990, the percentage of the electorate formed by women never surpassed 40 percent, while since, it has only twice fallen below 40 percent.

This trend cannot be attributed to the change from conventions to universal ballots as the 1997 New Brunswick Conservative universal ballot and the 2002 Nova Scotia Liberal universal ballots were the two elections that did not exceed the aforementioned 40 percent plateau. Moreover, the difference between the universal ballot utilized by Nova Scotia New Democrats in 2002 and the more traditional convention in 2000 was a minuscule two percentage points. There was a similarly tiny gap between the PC universal ballot in New Brunswick in 1997 and the Liberal delegated convention the following year.

In the three most recent elections for which we have data, women have accounted for more than half of the electorate. There does not appear to be much of a partisan division with respect to the representation of women. In 1980, the level of female representation was almost identical for the Nova Scotia Liberals and New Democrats, and, in 1995-96, women were present in identical proportions at the Nova Scotia Tory, Nova Scotia New Democrat, and Island Liberal leadership electorates. Finally, in 2002-3, women made up similar proportions of the Island New Democratic and Liberal electorates.

The increase in the representation of women is one of the most striking features of change in our data set. Women account for an increasing proportion of leadership electorates, and it is becoming more difficult to describe these processes as predominantly involving males. The general nature of this change over time is particularly remarkable when one considers that, as recently as 1981, the Nova Scotia Tories were reluctant even to have women candidates.[19]

### Age

The candidates who sought the leadership in the 25 elections were relatively young, with ages ranging from 28 to 67 and averaging 44. Youth appeared to be well served, as more than one-third of the candidates were under the age of 40 when they sought the leadership. In contrast, the population over 60 was very poorly represented in the ranks of leadership candidates, accounting for only 5 percent of the total.

No partisan differences seemed important with respect to age. The mean age ranged from a low of 43.7 for the Liberals to a high of 45.2 for the New Democrats. Comparing provincial data, we found that youthful candidacies were most common on PEI, where 11 of the 24 candidates were under 40. Three of the four candidates who were over sixty contested leadership elections in Nova Scotia. We ran a correlation between vote share and age and found that the relationship was negative (Pearson's R -.207), albeit relatively weak, indicating that older candidates generally received lower vote shares.

The age data provided one surprise. Courtney's research at the national level found that the "average age of candidates running in recent leadership conventions has been considerably lower than before"[20] However, our data on the Maritimes produced somewhat divergent results. The mean age of candidates who contested leadership elections between 1971 and 1987 (roughly the mid-point) was 41.4, while the mean age of those who contested later elections increased to 45.7. We initially felt that this might be due to the change to universal ballots, which have been associated with a higher participation rate by older voters. However, even when we limited the comparison solely to conventions, the mean age remained almost identical.

The representation of younger Canadians at leadership conventions has been controversial. Parties have generally regarded it as important to ensure adequate representation for youth and have put in place requirements that a certain proportion of constituency delegations be under a specified age. As Perlin, Sutherland, and Desjardins pointed out in the mid-1980s, "this form of guaranteed representation has progressively broadened so that delegates under 30 now constitute the largest age group attending conventions."[21]

Needless to say, no similar requirements have ever been put in place with respect to older Canadians.

The age profile of leadership voters in the Maritimes has changed dramatically over time. Specifically, the proportion of voters under the age of thirty has declined, while the proportion over the age of sixty has grown (see Figure 3.2). Before 1988, in only one leadership election did those under thirty account for less than 15 percent of the delegate total. Since 1988, the share of younger voters has surpassed 15 percent only twice, and it is more usually around 10 percent. Indeed, in five of the most recent eight elections, the representation of youth has not reached double digits (in percentage terms). In the conventions held before 1990, youth generally outnumbered those over sixty. In subsequent conventions and universal ballots, those over 60 have always outnumbered youth.

The representation of older Maritimers in leadership elections appears to be related to the emergence of all-member votes. Voters over the age of sixty accounted for about one-third of the voters in the 1997 New Brunswick universal ballot but made up only one-quarter of the delegates to the Liberal leadership election held the next year. As well, the percentage of older voters doubled in the four years separating the 1991 Nova Scotia PC convention from that party's 1995 tele-vote.

*Figure 3.2*

**Maritime leadership elections: voters over 60 and under 30 (as percentages of electorate)**

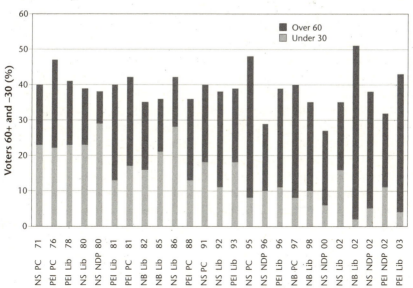

New Democratic conventions can be distinguished by the lower levels of representation for older voters. In 1980, such voters comprised less than 10 percent of the delegate total, and while this figure had more than doubled (to 21 percent) by 2000, the proportion was much lower than were those recorded by the party's provincial Liberal and Tory counterparts. The New Democrats, of course, had not, to that point, used a universal ballot. The proportion of voters over sixty increased to 33 percent in the 2002 Nova Scotia universal ballot.

It is possible to make too much of a generational change in representation. One should keep in mind that the majority of voters in 24 of the 25 leadership elections were between the ages of 30 and 60. In fact, this group generally accounted for at least 60 percent of total voters. Nonetheless, it seems clear that there has been a shift in the age of those who participate in leadership elections and that older voters now have a stronger voice.

### Status

Traditional portraits of politicians depict them as lawyers; indeed, law is often seen as the preferred background for politicians. But, as Courtney has shown, other paths are becoming more common for leadership candidates, particularly within the NDP.[22]

Law remained the most common occupation of Maritime leadership candidates, with 31 percent possessing such a background. Business was also a frequent preparatory path, with 19 percent of the candidates coming from this occupational group. Fifteen percent of the candidates were educators, 9 percent possessed an agricultural background, and 4 percent were union activists. The other 23 percent of the candidates were dispersed among a wide variety of backgrounds, including medicine, social work, and broadcasting. No other occupation was represented by more than one candidate.

Partisan differences were apparent on this measure. While lawyers accounted for more than one-third of the Liberal and Conservative candidacies, only 13 percent of the NDP candidates were lawyers. New Democratic candidates were more likely to be teachers than lawyers or businesspersons. Almost one-quarter of the Liberals and Conservative candidates had business occupations, but none of the New Democrats could be so characterized. The "other" category[23] accounted for almost half (47 percent) of the NDP candidates but for less than 20 percent of the older parties' candidates.

Provincial comparisons are complicated by the fact that 80 percent of the NDP candidates were from Nova Scotia. Nonetheless, business and law accounted for 81 percent of the New Brunswick Liberal candidates but for only about half of the party's total in either Nova Scotia or PEI. Overall, 73 percent of the New Brunswick candidates, 42 percent of the Nova Scotia candidates, and 54 percent of the Island candidates came from backgrounds in either business or law.

It appears that the background of candidates is becoming more diverse over time. Prior to 1988 (essentially the mid-point of our study) 88 percent of the candidates came from law, business, education, or farming, while after 1987 only 74 percent had such backgrounds.[24]

Finally, we found that candidates from law, business, education, or farming were more successful than were those from other backgrounds. Two-thirds of the candidates from the above backgrounds garnered more than 30 percent of the vote in their elections, while more than half of the candidates with other occupations came in with less than 20 percent of the vote.

The status of leadership candidates must also be assessed in terms of their previous political background. We look first (Table 3.1) at the political offices held by candidates as they entered their leadership race.

More than half of the candidates held a political office at the time they entered the leadership race. Three of the seventy-five candidates were sitting MPs, while twenty-three were backbench MLAs. Only thirteen candidates were members of the provincial cabinet at the time they sought their party's leadership. This latter figure is not surprising since, as mentioned above, most leadership elections in the Maritimes, like most provincial leadership elections generally, take place when the party is out of office. On those occasions when the party was in office, almost two-thirds of the candidates (thirteen of twenty) occupied seats in the cabinet. Only five did not hold any political office, while one was a sitting mayor (Tex Macdonald, PEI Liberals 1996) and the other was an MP (Catherine Callbeck, PEI Liberals 1993). Callbeck was the only person not in a provincial cabinet to win a leadership election held when a party was in power (although she had previously served in Alex Campbell's cabinet).

Our analysis shows relatively few partisan differences in the political backgrounds of candidates (see Table 3.2). Some of the differences we do see are obvious as no NDP candidate in the region could have occupied a position in the cabinet.

*Table 3.1*

**Maritime candidates: pre-entry political status**

|                      | N   | %   |
|----------------------|-----|-----|
| Provincial cabinet   | 13  | 17  |
| Mayor                | 3   | 4   |
| Backbench MLA        | 23  | 31  |
| MP                   | 3   | 4   |
| Private              | 33  | 44  |
| Total                | 75  | 100 |

*Table 3.2*

**Maritime candidates: pre-entry political status by party**

|  | Liberal (%) | PC (%) | NDP (%) | Total (N) |
|---|---|---|---|---|
| Cabinet | 16 | 30 | 0 | 13 |
| Mayor | 5 | 4 | 0 | 3 |
| MLA | 30 | 22 | 47 | 23 |
| MP | 3 | 9 | 0 | 3 |
| Private | 46 | 35 | 53 | 33 |
| $N =$ | 37 | 23 | 15 | 75 |

A somewhat higher proportion of Conservative candidates were cabinet ministers, which is surprising since, while 35 percent of the Conservative candidates sought the leadership when their party was in power, the corresponding figure for the Liberals was a comparable 32 percent. The proportion of candidates sitting in the provincial legislature (cabinet plus MLA) was quite similar for all three parties (46 percent of the Liberals, 52 percent of the Conservatives, and 47 percent of the New Democrats).

Notable differences were, however, apparent over time. Only 21 percent of the candidates in the elections held before 1988 were not serving politicians. In contrast, twenty-seven of the forty-seven candidates (57 percent) in later leadership elections did not hold a political office at the time they contested the leadership. As Courtney found nationally, holding political office has become less important for potential leaders.

We also examined whether those who sought the leadership had ever previously held political office. Only a slight majority of candidates (forty of seventy-five) had held (or were currently holding) some form of provincial or federal office; obviously, having held such a position was not a prerequisite for seeking the leadership. There were minor partisan differences in this area. Fifty-one percent of the Liberal candidates had held provincial office, as had 52 percent of the Conservatives and 60 percent of the New Democrats. The New Democratic proportion of office holders would be even higher if the three PEI candidates were excluded. Only one New Democrat has ever been elected to that province's legislature, and he did not attempt to succeed himself in the 2002 leadership race. Excluding the three Island New Democrats from the examination would increase the proportion of office holders within that party to 75 percent, well above that of the Liberals or Conservatives. In terms of provincial comparisons, the candidates with federal experience were all from PEI, but there were no other glaring patterns.

In contrast, change over time was discernible. For the New Democrats, the proportion of those who had held provincial office did not change much over the time under study. After 1988, seven of the ten candidates in Nova Scotia had some experience in the provincial legislature, but, in 1980, two of the three candidates also had such a background. For the Liberals and Conservatives, however, we see a notable decline in the proportion of candidates who had held provincial office. The proportion of Liberals with experience as MLAs dropped from 73 percent to 36 percent. And the drop within the Conservative party was also dramatic, falling from 70 percent to 39 percent. Again, provincial electoral success was not seen as a requirement for seeking the leadership. Liberal and Conservative candidates in universal ballots were even less likely to have provincial experience – with figures of just 31 percent and 14 percent, respectively – than were NDP candidates.

Those without previous electoral success, however, posted poorer results in the leadership contests. The mean vote share of those who had held a political office was always higher than was that of those who had not held a particular office. Indeed, federal office proved most advantageous as the three MPs who entered provincial leadership contests (Prince Edward Island's Angus MacLean, Catherine Callbeck, and Mel Gass) were all victorious. Moreover, while 38 percent of those who had served in a provincial legislature were able to win a leadership contest, the success rate of those without such a background was only 29 percent. Similarly, only 15 percent of those with experience as MLAs received less than 15 percent of the votes, while almost one in three of the candidates without such experience suffered that fate. Although political experience is not a prerequisite for entering a race, it certainly seems to give candidates a leg up.

Leadership candidates in the Maritimes were very well educated: four-fifths had at least one university degree. More strikingly, seven of the eleven candidates without degrees received less than 15 percent of the vote and accounted for almost 47 percent of this group. In partisan terms, a somewhat higher proportion of New Democrats did not hold university degrees. Huge majorities of the candidates in each province held degrees, with the percentage ranging from a low of 71 percent on PEI to a high of 86 percent in Nova Scotia. There were some differences between the two time periods as well: 71 percent of those who sought the leadership before 1988 were university graduates, and this proportion increased to over 85 percent of the candidates thereafter.

Given the nature of our data, it proved difficult to discuss voters in terms of occupation, and, indeed, the literature has rarely done so. As well, in the next chapter we focus in detail on the political experience of voters and so do not develop this point here. Thus, at this time our descriptions of leadership voters focuses on education. As discussed earlier, traditionally, leadership electorates were better educated and more affluent than were members of society in general – a factor that has been shown to have some ramifications for leadership choice.[25] Overall, our data offer further evidence that leadership elections are largely the purview of higher-status individuals. The 1991 Census reports that about 10 percent of Maritimers over the age of fifteen held university degrees. By this standard, the educational attainments of those who vote in leadership elections are truly impressive (see Figure 3.3). The New Democratic delegates stand out from those from other parties as, in most cases, more than half of them held university degrees. This did not diminish much with the universal ballot in Nova Scotia in 2002 as 51 percent of the voters reported holding a university degree. A provincial difference was also clear: delegates to Island conventions appear considerably less educated than do those in the other provinces. The lowest percentage of delegates with university degrees was recorded by the PEI Liberals in 1993 and 1996 (18 percent and 22 percent, respectively). And in none of the Island Liberal or Conservative leadership elections did the percentage of university educated voters surpass 33 percent. Even those who participated in the Island NDP leadership election were less likely to have degrees than were their counterparts in Nova Scotia. However, fully 45 percent of those who voted in the Island NDP leadership election had degrees.

In Nova Scotia and New Brunswick, those with university degrees never fell below the 30 percent mark, and the lowest score recorded – the New

*Figure 3.3*

**Maritime leadership elections: voters with a university degree (as percentage of electorate)**

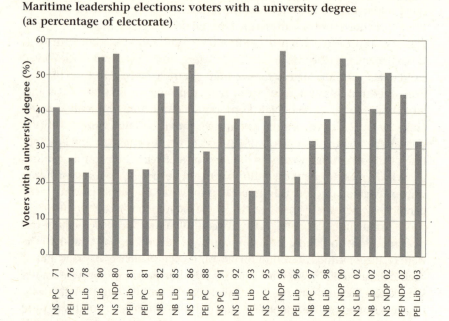

Brunswick Conservative's universal ballot in 1997 – was 32 percent. There appeared to have been somewhat of a decline in educational status among New Brunswick Liberals, with the lowest proportion of those with degrees occurring in 1998. The party, of course, had made a conscious decision to increase the number of delegates that year, which probably accounts for this change. The proportion with degrees recovered to 41 percent in 2002. However, this election (see appendix) was essentially decided at the delegate selection stage, and many eligible voters did not bother to attend the ratifying convention.

The Nova Scotia Conservatives, like both Island parties, displayed a stable pattern with 39 percent to 41 percent of its voters possessing degrees. On the other hand, sharper fluctuations could be seen among the Nova Scotian Liberals. While more than half of those who attended the leadership conventions of the 1980s held university degrees, only 38 percent of those who participated in the 1992 tele-vote were that well educated. The percentage of university educated voters rebounded to 50 percent in the 2002 ballot. Essentially, in partisan and provincial terms, New Democratic delegates were clearly the best educated, while delegates from PEI were least likely to hold degrees.

## Geography

There are interesting patterns with respect to the regional origins of the seventy-five candidates, although on this measure the possibility of provincial comparisons is limited. In Nova Scotia, 53 percent of the candidates came from the Halifax-Dartmouth area, while 17 percent were from Cape Breton and 30 percent from the rural mainland. On PEI, 63 percent were from Queens County, 21 percent from Kings, and 17 percent from Prince. In New Brunswick, 53 percent came from the three largest cities (20 percent from Fredericton, 20 percent from Moncton, and 13 percent from Saint John). In general, a substantial proportion of candidates (45 percent) came from the major urban centres, but there were also a large number of rural candidates (although not as many as one might expect given the rural nature of the Maritimes).[26]

The intraprovincial partisan differences are noteworthy. Seventy-five percent of Island Conservative candidates came from Queens County compared to 62 percent of the Liberals. Liberal candidates were more likely to come from Kings County. Prince Edward Island is the most rural of the Maritime provinces, but a large portion of the Island's leadership candidates were residents of the Charlottetown area. Fifteen of the twenty-four Island candidates resided in Queens County – which comprises 53 percent of the Island population – and most of these were from the Charlottetown area. However, an urban base appears to be a rather mixed blessing on PEI as only two of the winners in our elections came from the City of Charlottetown:

Joe and Robert Ghiz. Three leaders came from other parts of Queens County; one winner, Bennett Campbell, came from Kings County. Three of the four candidates from Prince County (Catherine Callbeck, Keith Milligan, and Gary Robichaud), which contains Summerside, the Island's second city, were able to win their contests.

In New Brunswick, three of the four PC candidates came from the major cities, but only five of the eleven Liberal candidates resided in those centres. However, the rural candidates were quite successful as Graham (2002), Theriault (1998), McKenna (1985), and Young (1982) all went on to win their party's leadership. The only victorious candidate to come from an urban centre was Bernard Lord, who had previously contested a riding in the City of Moncton. Thus, while most leadership candidates were from urban areas, most winners were not.[27] Regionally, more than half of the Liberal candidates came from the areas above "the diagonal from Grand Falls in the Northwest to Sackville in the southeast."[28] None of the Conservatives came from this area,[29] which remains predominantly Catholic and contains most of the province's Acadian population.

Candidates from the Halifax/Dartmouth area were quite common in Nova Scotia leadership elections. Indeed, nineteen of the thirty-six candidates who sought the leadership were from this area. In contrast, only eleven candidates represented the rural mainland (where the bulk of the population resides), and just six candidates were from Cape Breton. The success rates of the candidates were strongest for Cape Breton, with 50 percent of them winning their elections. Three of the candidates from the rural mainland were victorious, as were five of the Halifax-based candidates. Three of the latter were from the NDP, which has not yet had a leader representing the rural mainland. A Halifax base appears to be a firmer foundation for an aspirant for the NDP leadership than it does for those in other parties. Although urban candidates represented 45 percent of our sample, only 32 percent of the leadership contests went to one of these candidates. Thirty-nine percent of the candidates from outside the major urban areas went on to victory, while only 27 percent of the city-based candidates were successful.

Not only were rural candidates less common than the rural proportion of the provincial electorates might suggest, but, as Table 3.3 shows, voters from the most rural areas (population under one thousand) are also underrepresented. This is especially true of the Nova Scotia New Democrats. In none of the four elections for which we have data did the rural voters constitute a plurality of the electorate; indeed, the largest proportion they ever comprised was 27 percent. In all four elections, the rural voters were outnumbered by both Halifax voters and those based in small towns and cities. The lack of representation for rural voters in New Democratic elections may be both a cause and an effect of the relative weakness of the party on the rural mainland. The absence of rural voters was particularly

*Table 3.3*

**Maritime provinces: urban-rural distribution**

|  | Rural (under 1,000) | Betwixt | Major urban centres |
|---|---|---|---|
| PEI | 55% | 17% | 28% (Charlottetown, over 20,000) |
| NS | 44% | 26% | 30% (Halifax, over 100,000) |
| NB | 50% | 18% | 32% (Fredericton, St. John, and Moncton, over 50,000) |

*Source:* 2001 Census.

acute at the 1996 convention, where both candidates were from the Halifax area. At that gathering, Haligonians accounted for almost half of those voting, while voters from rural areas made up only about 10 percent. Surprisingly, the underrepresentation of rural areas does not seem to be a regional problem for the New Democrats since, in PEI, rural members accounted for more than half of the 2002 electorate.

The Nova Scotia Liberals and Tories provided a better reflection of the provincial population distribution, but even in 1971 rural voters made up only 38 percent of the PC voters. This share had fallen to 20 percent by 1995. Rural Liberals consistently comprised around one-quarter of their party's leadership electorate. The 2002 Liberal universal ballot stands out, with a disproportionate share of the voters being from Halifax. This was, of course, where both the major candidates resided.

Although the underrepresentation of rural areas was especially noteworthy among Nova Scotia New Democrats, it occurred in other parties and provinces as well. Table 3.4 makes clear that Liberals in New Brunswick were also substantially less likely to be from rural areas than were New Brunswick residents in general. The proportion of Liberal leadership voters from these areas did not reach the 25 percent mark in any of the four elections for which we have data, and in three cases it was under 20 percent. Our data on New Brunswick Tories are limited, but we do note that residents from the major urban areas were slightly underrepresented.

The PEI parties provided the best representation for rural areas. Voters from villages of less than one thousand people made up a plurality or majority of the vote in all seven elections for which we have data. The representation of voters from the Charlottetown area was also close to that found in the general population.

In neither New Brunswick nor Nova Scotia is the relative absence of rural voters an indication that voters from the major urban centres dominate the process. With the exception, again, of the Nova Scotia New Democrats, where Halifax voters were always more numerous than one would expect given

*Table 3.4*

**Maritime leadership elections: urban-rural distribution**

|  | Rural (%) | Betwixt (%) | Urban (%) |
|---|---|---|---|
| **Nova Scotia** | under 1,000 | 1,000-100,000 | over 100,000 |
| PC 1971 | 38 | 46 | 16 |
| PC 1991 | Not collected | | |
| PC 1995 | 20 | 65 | 15 |
| Liberal 1980 | 28 | 50 | 22 |
| Liberal 1986 | 26 | 60 | 14 |
| Liberal 1992 | 25 | 58 | 17 |
| Liberal 2002 | 15 | 50 | 35 |
| NDP 1980 | 27 | 34 | 39 |
| NDP 1996 | 10 | 42 | 48 |
| NDP 2000 | 16 | 49 | 35 |
| NDP 2002 | 17 | 49 | 34 |
|  | | | |
| **New Brunswick** | under 1,000 | 1,000-50,000 | over 50,000 |
| Liberal 1982 | 17 | 59 | 24 |
| Liberal 1985 | 18 | 64 | 18 |
| Liberal 1998 | 17 | 65 | 18 |
| Liberal 2002 | 21 | 53 | 26 |
| PC 1997 | | | 26 |
|  | | | |
| **Prince Edward Island** | under 1,000 | 1,000-10,000 | over 10,000 |
| PC 1976 | 64 | 18 | 18 |
| PC 1981 | 63 | 23 | 14 |
| PC 1988 | Not collected | | |
| Liberal 1978 | 60 | 25 | 15 |
| Liberal 1981 | 57 | 24 | 19 |
| Liberal 1993 | Not collected | | |
| Liberal 1996 | 44 | 29 | 27 |
| Liberal 2003 | 43 | 36 | 21 |
| NDP 2002 | 51 | 29 | 19 |

the area's share of the province's population,[30] the major urban areas in the provinces also consistently received less representation than their populations warranted. This has not changed over time, despite movements to universal ballots and to closer approximations of representation by population. This suggests that the concerns of voters outside major urban centres must be taken seriously by leadership candidates, and, with the possible exception of the Nova Scotia NDP, the road to victory requires a substantial degree of rural support.

Provincial differences can be seen with respect to the urban nature of the leadership electorate. Island electorates are clearly more rural than are those in the other provinces. However, in Nova Scotia Liberal and Conservative elections, the proportion of voters from communities of fewer than one thousand voters was generally higher than was that from the major urban centre. Party is relevant on this dimension as well, with the Nova Scotia (but not the PEI) New Democrats appearing as the most urban party in the region. The movement to universal ballots had no discernible impact on the representation of rural Maritimers.

## Religion

Religion has long been associated with Maritime politics. For decades, the Liberal party in Nova Scotia had an unwritten rule requiring that its leadership alternate between Protestants and Catholics. Candidates violated this norm at their peril, and the defeat of Harold Connolly in 1954 is seen as a classic illustration of the rule at work. A plurality of the candidates who sought to lead a party was Catholic. Forty-five percent of the candidates came from the Roman Catholic faith, 32 percent from Protestant denominations, and 23 percent could not be identified according to faith. The religious backgrounds of the candidates demonstrate both partisan and provincial differences. Table 3.5 presents the partisan differences.

Catholic candidates were much more common in the Liberal party, where they accounted for 60 percent of the total. Protestants were much more numerous in Conservative ranks, where they provided 52 percent of the candidacies. In contrast, we could not identify the religious background of 80 percent of the NDP candidates. We were not able to determine whether four of the Liberal candidates had a religious affiliation (in any event, three of these individuals received almost no support).

Provincial differences were also notable as most of the candidates in New Brunswick, regardless of party, were Catholic. On PEI, there was essentially an even split between Catholics and Protestants, at least within the Liberal and Conservative parties (eleven Protestants, nine Catholics). This distribution reflects the general population share in the province. Nova Scotia displayed the greatest dispersion. More than 60 percent of the Liberal candidates in the province were Catholic, more than 60 percent of the Conservative

*Table 3.5*

**Maritime candidates: religion by party**

|  | Catholic (%) | Protestant (%) | Not identified (%) |
|---|---|---|---|
| Liberal (37) | 60 | 30 | 11 |
| PC (23) | 48 | 52 | 0 |
| NDP (15) | 13 | 7 | 80 |

candidates were Protestant, and we were not able to identify the religious affiliation of 75 percent of the New Democrats.

Not surprisingly, we again find partisan dispersion among the election winners. For instance, we were only able to identify the religious affiliation of one of the NDP winners, while eight of the thirteen Liberal winners were Catholic, and five of the seven PC victors were Protestant. Despite their greater number, Catholic candidates possessed the lowest success rates. While 47 percent of the candidates were Catholic, they were successful only 40 percent of the time. In contrast, 32 percent of the contestants were Protestant, but Protestants won 44 percent of the elections. None of the Protestant candidates won less than 15 percent of the vote, but one in four of those for whom we could not identify a religious preference fell into this category, as did 17 percent of the Catholics.

Maritime leadership voters can also be distinguished on the basis of religion. This is not perhaps surprising as religion has been an important part of Maritime politics since before Confederation, with various efforts made in all of the provinces to pay attention to the Protestant-Catholic division. However, overrepresentation of one religious group, as Adamson found with Protestants at the NS PC 1971 convention, is actually the norm in Maritime leadership elections (see Figure 3.4). According to the 1991 census, Catholics

*Figure 3.4*

**Maritime leadership elections: Catholic voters (as percentage of electorate)**

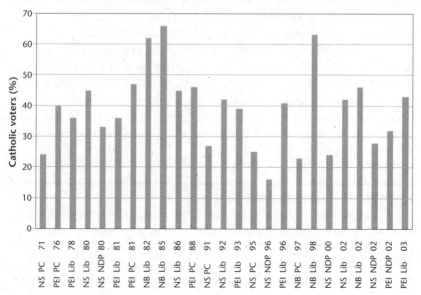

comprised 54 percent of the NB population, 47 percent of the Island population, and 37 percent of Nova Scotia's. A look at Figure 3.4 shows that Catholics are rarely represented in percentages resembling the provincial populations. Only once, at the Island Conservative convention of 1981, were Protestants and Catholics present in their actual population shares (47 percent Catholic). It should also be noted that, contrary to British Columbia, where Blake, Carty, and Erickson found the plurality of delegates would not avow any religious affiliation,[31] most Maritime Liberals and Conservatives made such a designation. The New Democrats again proved exceptional on this dimension. At each of their contests, between 24 percent and 33 percent declared no religious affiliation. Only small percentages of Liberals or Conservatives made similar claims.[32]

In terms of descriptive representation, Island gatherings proved most accurate. However, Catholics were somewhat underrepresented in all of the Liberal elections. The historic preference of Island Catholics for the Conservatives[33] was apparent in both 1981 and 1988, with Catholics comprising just under half of the electorate (although curiously, this tendency was not apparent in 1976).

Catholics were consistently underrepresented in Conservative elections in Nova Scotia. The percentage of Catholics at these gatherings never exceeded 27 percent, well below their population share. Given the traditional preference of Catholics for Liberals, this relative absence is not difficult to understand, but it is worth noting that it has not changed over time. Conversely, Catholics were somewhat overrepresented at the two Liberal conventions as well as in the two universal ballots in 1992 and 2003. The Catholic proportion of the Liberal electorate was consistently in a tight range, from 41 percent to 46 percent.

In New Brunswick, where Catholics constitute a provincial majority (54 percent) and historically have preferred the Liberals, one might expect that the Liberal electorate would be more heavily Catholic. This was certainly the case in the first three Liberal elections. In each of those gatherings, the Catholic percentage was at least 60 percent. Protestants were obviously not present at Liberal conventions in the same proportions as they were in the general population. The New Brunswick Conservative party reversed this trend. Although more than half of New Brunswickers were Catholic, this was true of less than one in four of the 1997 Conservative voters. The 2002 New Brunswick Liberal convention represents something of an outlier on this dimension as only 46 percent of the voters were Catholic. While this is substantially higher than the Conservative figure, it is well below the earlier Liberal figures. It may well be the case that the peculiarities of that election, in which one of the two major candidates dropped out after the delegates were selected (effectively leaving no doubt about the outcome), created a somewhat uncharacteristic body of voters.

It appears that, when Maritime parties choose their leaders, rather than brokering the supposedly strong religious divisions, the parties disproportionately attract delegates or voters from the religious group that supports them most strongly in elections. This lends support to Winn and McMenemy's contention that "the cultural backgrounds of party activists reflect the particular electoral support of the parties ... Each party tends to possess activists among those groups from which it draws voting strength."[34] In Maritime leadership selection, this also describes delegates and voters. Movements away from conventions to universal ballots have had no discernible impact on this tendency.

## Discussion

Our examination of the seventy-five candidates who sought their party's leadership revealed a number of partisan differences. Candidates for the New Democratic Party were less likely than were candidates for other parties to have an identifiable religious affiliation and to have never have participated in government. They tended to be somewhat older than candidates for the old line parties, and their leadership was more likely to be contested by a woman. Conservative and Liberal candidates also differed in some areas, most notably in their religious affiliation, with the traditional association of Liberals with Catholics being manifest.

The differences in religious composition could also be seen in provincial comparisons, with the prevalence of Catholic candidates much higher in New Brunswick. PEI saw the only candidates who were MPs and was home to the largest group of candidates without university degrees. The highest proportion of youthful candidates was also found on the Island.

Changes over time were also evident. In the latter half of the thirty-two-year period, women became more likely to seek party leadership and the mean age of candidates increased, as did the proportion of candidates with university degrees.

Our profile of the characteristics of leadership voters over three decades reveals both continuity and change. The representation of women has grown over time, and this trend crosses both provincial and partisan lines. Similarly, there has been a general increase in the proportion of older voters in leadership electorates and a concomitant decline in youthful voters. Nonetheless, the majority of voters in leadership elections in the region continues to be between thirty and sixty years of age.

Provincial differences are noteworthy. In particular, delegates and voters on PEI were distinctive. They were less educated, relatively older, and far more likely to come from rural communities than were delegates from other provinces. Island voters and delegates could also be distinguished by the reversal of the Protestant-Catholic representation found elsewhere in the region, with Catholics being more numerous at Conservative gatherings.

In Nova Scotia and New Brunswick, the Liberal and Conservative party electorates could be easily distinguished on the basis of religion. Catholics were far more likely to be found among Liberal electorates, and this trend has not diminished in the thirty-two years covered in our data set. On the other hand, it is also worth noting that the ethnic background of both the New Brunswick Liberal and Conservative leadership voters broadly reflected the duality of New Brunswick, with francophones constituting between 21 percent and 38 percent of the electorate. The New Democratic delegates in Nova Scotia differed from Liberal and Conservative voters on two quite important dimensions. First, they were much more likely to claim no religious affiliation. Second, they were far more likely to reside in the metro Halifax area, with only a small proportion coming from the province's most rural communities. Island New Democrats shared the religious dimension with their counterparts in Nova Scotia, but they were even more likely to be from rural areas than were Island Liberals or Conservatives.[35]

Our data also suggest that the change from conventions to universal ballots has had some effect. In New Brunswick, where we have data on a universal ballot and a convention held only one year apart, we find that the convention enfranchised a higher proportion of voters with university degrees, while the universal ballot increased the share of the electorate that was over the age of sixty. This latter tendency was also apparent in the 1995 Nova Scotia Conservative all-member vote. Universal ballots were not, however, associated with an increase in voters from more rural areas.

Finally, it is clear that Maritime leadership electorates, like Maritime leadership candidates, are not fully representative of their societies. Admittedly, the distortions (especially with respect to gender and education) are less evident among voters than among candidates. Even so, voters did not generally provide an accurate descriptive representation of provincial societies. Those who vote in Maritime leadership elections provide a portrait of party activists, not of the province. Indeed, each party's leadership electorate seems to overrepresent societal groups from which the party draws its support. Even at conventions, the constituency basis did not ensure that all politically salient groups received a proportionate voice in leadership selection. Leadership elections, and even conventions, are gatherings of the faithful, not an opportunity to broaden the face of the party.

It is also obvious that the leadership electorates, to some degree, present something of a varied face. They are not exclusively the preserve of educated, male, middle-aged party regulars nor do they represent only one religious or ethnic group. Various groups are represented in these elections, but it remains to be seen which of the potential cleavages has been associated with voting.

# 4
# Tourists or Partisans? Political Background and Leadership Election Engagement

In the previous chapter, we examined the socio-demographic and geographic patterns of participants in Maritime leadership elections. We saw that the shift to universal ballots had some impact on participation. In general, there was greater representation of women, and older people were better represented. These are obviously positive changes, but many concerns have been raised about the negative effect of an all-member vote. With the movement to such universal ballots in recent years, much attention has been paid to issues of political background and engagement with the leadership election process. Courtney notes: "Much of the evidence to date suggests that those who participate in a universal vote on a party's leadership have far less commitment to the party than the regulars who have served as convention delegates."[1] Whitaker makes a similar point and warns of the emergence of "virtual" parties in the Canadian context.[2] Empirical evidence of this can be found in studies of the Alberta Conservative party, which identified clear differences in the political background and involvement with the leadership election between Conservative convention delegates in 1985 and universal ballot voters in 1992.[3] Cross found a similar gap between participants in the New Brunswick PC universal ballot in 1997 and the province's Liberal convention a year later.[4] In essence, the universal ballot participants possessed less extensive backgrounds in their party and did not participate in election activities in the same manner as did delegates. Previous national studies have documented the deep roots convention delegates had in their parties. As Courtney summarizes, those who participated in national conventions, regardless of party, "were usually experienced activists with many years of party membership under their belts."[5]

Despite the extensive literature on national leadership selection, there have been relatively few opportunities to assess partisan and provincial differences in the political backgrounds of leadership voters or to chart changes over more than a couple of elections. In this chapter, we do this. We look at how long voters had been members of their political party, focusing specifically on those who have been members for less than a year or more than ten years. We also determine whether voters had previously supported another party or worked for the party in whose election they voted. We then turn to a discussion of how voters participated; we look at when the voting decision was made, whether voters were influenced by speeches, and whether voters attempted to persuade others to vote as they did. We look for differences among parties, provinces, and over time. Our analysis of Maritime leadership elections provides little evidence of "virtual" parties tied to a particular leader. Even the more recent universal ballots were dominated by voters with extensive roots in their parties. The choice of leaders in the Maritimes is essentially made by voters with extensive party backgrounds, suggesting another way in which Maritime politics may be distinct.

One of the major concerns expressed by critics of universal ballots is the role played by so-called instant members – those recent members who may have joined just to participate in the process. Nationally, Joe Clark described such individuals as "tourists," exposing their lack of ongoing commitment to the party.[6] We find that these newcomers formed only a small proportion of the voters in leadership elections. Their numbers never reached the one-third point, peaking at 32 percent in the first NDP convention in our data, the 1980 Nova Scotia convention. This convention represented a historic shift for the party (as we show in Chapter 13), from its traditional Cape Breton stronghold to a base in metro Halifax. Certainly, the party has never subsequently attracted newcomers in such large numbers. The only other election in which the proportion of newcomers was greater than one-fifth was the 1997 PC universal ballot in New Brunswick. This race was also somewhat idiosyncratic. "After a decade in the electoral wilderness, and with no signs of imminent success, the party was eager to appear more open, democratic, and contemporary than its opponents," notes one observer. "The party also hoped to attract new members by offering them a direct vote."[7] Obviously, the party's hopes were realized on this occasion.

Overall, the mean percentage of newcomers was only 9 percent, and in eleven of the sixteen elections for which we have data, the percentage was below 10 percent (see Figure 4.1). This includes recent universal ballots in PEI and Nova Scotia, indicating that, in contrast to the Alberta situations, universal ballots in the Maritimes have not generally opened the floodgates to tourists, despite the previously noted difference between New Brunswick Liberals and Conservatives in 1998 and 1997.[8] We find no further evidence of partisan differences in this area. Somewhat ironically, it does appear that tourists are less common in PEI than in the other provinces. On average, only 5 percent of Island voters had been members for less than a year, while the corresponding figures were 9 percent in New Brunswick and 12 percent in Nova Scotia.

*Figure 4.1*

**Maritime leadership elections: voters who were party members for less than a year (as percentage of electorate)**

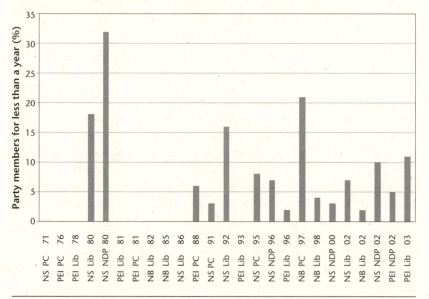

Expanding our examination to look at the proportion of voters who had first joined their party more than ten years previously provides us with more evidence that Maritime elections are largely peopled by party veterans. On average, 63 percent of the voters had been members of the party for over ten years. The proportion ranged from a low of 28 percent, at the previously discussed Nova Scotia NDP convention in 1980, to a high of 89 percent at the coronation of Catherine Callbeck on PEI in 1993. As Figure 4.2 shows, in eighteen of the twenty-three elections for which we have data, more than half of the voters were relatively long-standing members. Figure 4.2 also highlights a partisan difference on this dimension. Reflecting its relatively shallow political roots in the region, the NDP was less likely to have a majority of long-term members than were the other parties. This contrasts sharply with the national picture. "More than the other parties," notes Courtenay, the NDP "seems to view conventions as the business of the party's long time established activists."[9] It seems that, in the Maritimes, there are far fewer of these party veterans; certainly, in none of the five NDP elections had a majority of voters been members for more than ten years. In contrast, a majority of the voters in the old-line parties always reported such a background.

*Figure 4.2*

**Maritime leadership elections: voters who joined a party more than ten years previously (as percentage of electorate)**

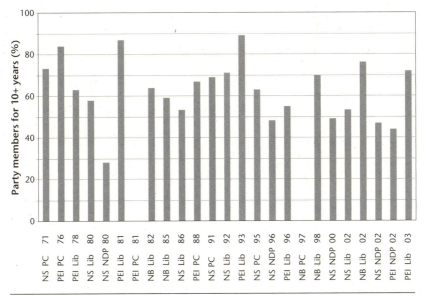

Given that four of our five NDP elections were in Nova Scotia, it is not surprising that the mean proportion of voters in that province with initial memberships dating more than ten years was only 54 percent, 13 percentage points below the comparable figure for New Brunswick and 15 points below that for PEI. We do see a slight difference between universal ballots and conventions on this dimension. For universal ballots, 58 percent of the voters reported first joining the party more than ten years earlier; the corresponding figure for conventions was 64 percent. Still, the universal ballots were scarcely populated by party neophytes.

The strong commitment of leadership voters to their party can also be seen when we examine data on support for another party. As Figure 4.3 indicates, in the twenty-three elections for which we have data, only an average of 25 percent of the voters report *ever* having belonged to or supported another party. There is quite a wide deviation among the various elections on this dimension, ranging from a low of 11 percent at the PEI Liberal convention in 1978 to a high of 47 percent at the 2000 NDP convention in Nova Scotia.

Once again, this is an area where we can see strong partisan differences. Only in NDP elections did we find more than 35 percent of the voters reporting previous support for another party. Thus, not only were New Democratic

*Figure 4.3*

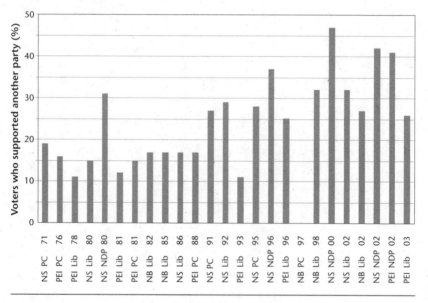

**Maritime leadership elections: voters who supported another party (as percentage of electorate)**

voters less likely to be long-term party members, they were also more likely to have previously supported another party. Again, this contrasts with the national picture of New Democrats as "long-time" partisans.

With most NDP elections held in Nova Scotia, it comes as no surprise to find that the Nova Scotian elections have the highest proportion of voters who had previously backed another party (an average of 31 percent). This proportion declined to 23 percent in New Brunswick and to just 21 percent on PEI.

It appears that the relative openness of universal ballots made them more attractive to voters who had the audacity to support some other party in the past. While just over one in five of the convention delegates acknowledged supporting another party, almost one-third of the universal ballot voters made such an admission. Still, even in these open elections, two-thirds of the voters claimed never to have backed another party. Maritime leadership elections remain the purview of the committed.

This perspective is further buttressed by an examination of previous party work. Here we sought simply to determine whether a voter had worked for the party in whose leadership election she or he was participating. The evidence points to strong partisan backgrounds. On average, four-fifths of the voters claimed to have worked for their party in a previous election. As

Figure 4.4

**Maritime leadership elections: experienced party workers (as percentage of electorate)**

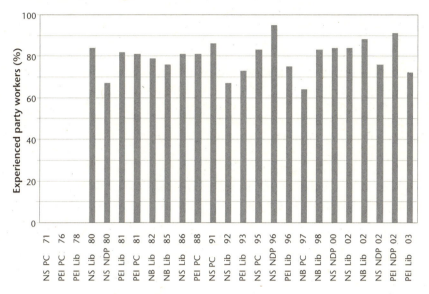

Figure 4.4 shows, the vast majority of voters were invariably experienced party workers. The proportion ranged from a low of 64 percent for the New Brunswick PCs in 1997 to a high of 95 percent among the Nova Scotia New Democrats in 1996.

This is one area where the New Democratic voters resembled their counterparts in both the Liberal and Conservative parties. Indeed, a slightly higher percentage of New Democrats, 83 percent, reported previous party work. This is not to suggest that Liberal and Conservative voters were non-workers (since the figure for both parties was 79 percent); rather, this is an area where the New Democrats in the region had comparable partisan records. While the NDP elections were less likely to be populated with those possessing long memberships or an unbroken record of support for the party, once they had joined, New Democrats were as likely as were Liberals or Conservatives to work for their party.

We see no clear provincial differences in this area and only a limited change between conventions and universal ballots. Essentially, in all of the leadership elections held in the region, the vast majority of voters were party workers. This may ease to some degree the concern that parties using this method are going to be overrun with temporary members "who are not really committed partisans."[10]

Our analysis of the party backgrounds possessed by Maritime leadership voters indicates that these voters were experienced and long-time party members. Indeed, most of them have never even supported another political party. The vast majority worked for their chosen party in the past, and most joined their party initially more than ten years before the leadership elections. Tourists are in very short supply at these gatherings.

We do see partisan differences that reflect the differential status of the NDP in the region. NDP participants were far more likely than were other participants to have previously supported another party and were much less likely to have joined the party more than ten years previously. Participants in Island elections were more likely than their mainland counterparts to report joining more than ten years earlier and less likely to have ever supported another party.

Differences over time can be seen, with the proportion having previously backed another party on the increase. Universal ballot participants were somewhat less likely to have joined their party ten years previously and more likely to report support for another party at some point in their lives. However, these differences were only of degree, and not only had a majority of universal ballot voters never supported another party but they also reported memberships of more than ten years.

Having ascertained that the vast majority of those who participate in Maritime leadership elections are possessed of an extensive party pedigree, we now turn to an examination of leadership election participation. Specifically, we look at whether voters made their choices before the convention or the day of the vote, whether they were influenced by the candidate speeches, and whether they tried to persuade others to support the candidate they backed.

It is clear that most of those who participated in Maritime leadership elections made up their minds relatively early. A majority of voters had always made their choice before showing up at the convention or, in the case of universal ballots, before the day of the vote. On average, only 20 percent of the voters indicated that they made up their minds at the convention or on the day of the universal ballot. However, as Figure 4.5 illustrates, we see a wide variation in this area, with the proportion making up their minds late ranging from a low of 5 percent (Nova Scotia Liberals and New Democrats in 2002) to a high of 38 percent (PEI PC 1988). In the appendix of this book, it is noted that, at the latter convention, Andrew Walker's final total was unexpectedly close to that of winner Mel Gass. Our data indicate that, among those delegates who came to a voting decision at the convention, a statistically significant proportion opted for Walker.

There do not appear to be major differences among the three parties in this area, but we do see a rather striking provincial difference, with Island voters more likely to make up their minds on the day of the vote. An average

*Figure 4.5*

**Maritime leadership elections: voters who made their choice at convention or on day of vote (as percentage of electorate)**

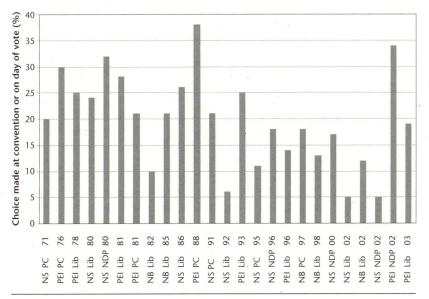

of 26 percent of Island voters report making up their minds on the day of the vote or at the convention, while in Nova Scotia only 17 percent make such a claim and in New Brunswick only 15 percent.

The switch to a universal ballot also appears to have slightly changed the nature of the election, with a much higher proportion of the voters making up their minds before the event. While an average of 23 percent of the convention delegates indicated that they made up their minds at the convention, only 14 percent of universal ballot voters made their decisions on voting day. This is hardly surprising since, in some cases, those who vote in universal ballots may not have an opportunity to observe the candidates on voting day. Presumably, then, there would be less reason to wait for election day to make a decision.

Of course, even for those who participate in universal ballots, election day events could prove important to the outcome. Indeed, a surprisingly high proportion of voters indicated that they were influenced by the candidate speeches. Figure 4.6 illustrates that more than two-fifths of the voters made such an assertion, with a high of 65 percent (New Brunswick Liberals 1985) and a low of 27 percent (New Brunswick Liberals 1998). With the high and low recorded by the same party, we see little evidence of partisan or provincial differences.

*Figure 4.6*

**Maritime leadership elections: voters who were influenced by candidate speeches (as percentage of electorate)**

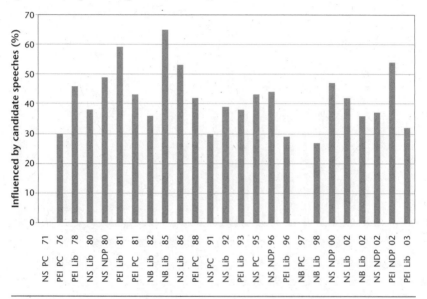

The high proportion reporting that the speeches influenced them in 1985 is consistent with the discussion of the conventions presented in the appendix. At that convention, the losing candidate made a direct attack on his opponent, and this was widely seen as a tactical blunder. In 1998, the successful invasion of the delegate selection process by candidate organizations likely rendered that convention particularly immune to speeches.

We see little difference between universal ballots and conventions on this variable. Despite the fact that most universal ballot voters might be seeing or hearing the speeches over television or radio, almost as many of them claimed to be influenced by the speeches – political phenomena that are relatively unmediated.

Candidate speeches continue to be important, and their relative significance does not seem to be declining over time. Thirty percent of the Island PC voters in 1976 said they were influenced by these speeches, as did 32 percent of the Island Liberal voters in 2003. Given the earlier data we presented, which indicate that most voters made up their minds before the convention or voting day, it seems that, for many voters, the speeches must confirm the choices they made earlier. Nonetheless, the possibility of candidates gaining or losing support as a result of their speeches continues to

*Figure 4.7*

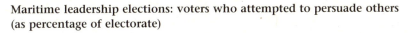

**Maritime leadership elections: voters who attempted to persuade others (as percentage of electorate)**

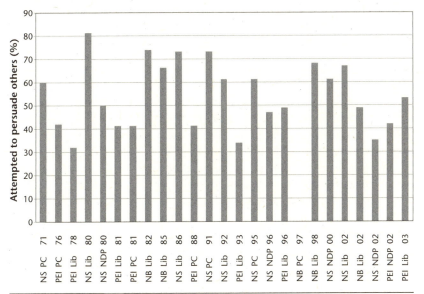

exist. It is obviously important for television and/or radio to provide coverage of the speeches associated with universal ballots.

Although many voters were, to some degree, open to persuasion by candidate speeches, most were actively engaged in campaigning for their own candidates of choice, as Figure 4.7 indicates. An average of 54 percent of voters indicated that they tried to persuade others to support a particular candidate. Two PEI Liberal conventions were relatively impervious to voter persuasion. The 1978 Liberal convention (in which almost half the delegates claimed to be influenced by the speeches) and the Callbeck coronation in 1993 both saw less than 35 percent of the delegates attempt persuasion. In contrast, over four-fifths of the delegates to the Nova Scotia Liberal convention in 1980 tried to persuade others to vote for a particular candidate.

Island voters seemed more willing to allow their fellow partisans to make up their own minds than did voters in the other provinces. While only 43 percent of Island voters attempted to persuade their fellow voters to behave in a particular manner, the corresponding figures for Nova Scotia and New Brunswick were 61 percent and 64 percent, respectively. New Democrats were marginally less likely to try to persuade others than were Liberals or Conservatives.

This is another area where we see that the movement from conventions to universal ballots has had little impact on voter behaviour. While 55 percent of the convention delegates attempted to persuade others, 53 percent of the universal ballot voters did so. Clearly, those who participated in the universal ballots seized the opportunity to convince others to follow the same path. This bodes well for parties seeking to re-energize themselves with a change in leadership. Most of those who participate in Maritime leadership elections made their voting decisions before a convention or the day of a universal ballot. Most were also engaged in the election to the extent that they attempted to persuade others to support a particular candidate. Despite these factors, a relatively high proportion of voters indicated that they had been influenced by the candidate speeches. The voting day events of leadership elections continue to be important, even though most people have made up their minds before the fact.

Island elections appear to be somewhat different from those in Nova Scotia and New Brunswick. Island voters were more likely to make up their minds at the convention or on the day of the vote and were less likely to try to persuade others. Of course, universal ballots on PEI were held at a single site, making the experience much more of a shared one than was the case on the mainland.

The shift from conventions to universal ballots had virtually no impact on the willingness of voters to persuade others or, somewhat surprisingly, on the likelihood of voters saying that they had been influenced by the speeches. Universal ballot voters were, however, more likely to make up their minds before voting day. Of course, conventions were changing too, as candidate organizations increasingly engaged in "trench warfare." As Cross explains in reference to the 1998 New Brunswick Liberal convention: "Campaign workers organized supporters at the riding level to run slates of committed delegates in an attempt to guarantee the selection of supporters as delegates and thus not have to rely on being able to win the support of large numbers of uncommitted delegates later on."[11] We discuss the implications of this kind of competition in more detail in Chapter 14. It does seem that, given the absence of deliberation involved in more recent conventions, many of the academic laurels applied to delegated conventions are undeserved.

Our examination of political background and participation suggests a good deal of continuity. This continuity is particularly impressive, given the changes in Maritime leadership elections since 1971. In order to assess changes over time, we arranged the twenty-five elections into three time periods: 1971-81, 1982-91, and 1992-2003.[12] As Table 4.1 indicates, over thirty-two years there was a steady increase in the number of voters and candidates but a corresponding decrease in the number of ballots.

We sought to determine the degree to which these changes reflected the growing use of universal ballots in leadership selection. If we look at the

*Table 4.1*

**Maritime leadership elections: changes over time**

| Time period | | Candidates | Voters | Ballots | FST vote |
|---|---|---|---|---|---|
| 1971-81 | Mean | 2.86 | 1,027 | 1.71 | 54 |
| | N | 7 | 7 | 7 | 7 |
| | Minimum | 2 | 320 | 1 | 33 |
| | Maximum | 4 | 1,462 | 3 | 74 |
| 1982-91 | Mean | 2.80 | 2,135 | 1.40 | 54 |
| | N | 5 | 5 | 5 | 5 |
| | Minimum | 2 | 1,171 | 1 | 32 |
| | Maximum | 4 | 2,748 | 3 | 69 |
| 1992-2003 | Mean | 3.15 | 3,452 | 1.31 | 58 |
| | N | 13 | 13 | 13 | 13 |
| | Minimum | 2 | 82 | 1 | 32 |
| | Maximum | 5 | 11,536 | 3 | 79 |
| Total | Mean | 3.00 | 2,510 | 1.44 | 56 |
| | N | 25 | 25 | 25 | 25 |
| | Minimum | 2 | 82 | 1 | 32 |
| | Maximum | 5 | 11,536 | 3 | 79 |

thirteen elections held since the first universal ballot in 1992, we observe that universal ballots are generally shorter than conventions. The four traditional conventions lasted an average of 1.5 ballots, while the eight universal votes took only 1.25 ballots. The mixed system used by the New Brunswick Liberals in 2002 was over on the first ballot. Both conventions and universal ballots recorded identical mean scores with respect to the number of candidates.

The average vote share of the leader on the first ballot was somewhat higher in the time period in which universal ballots were utilized. However, distinguishing between universal ballots and conventions indicates that the former were not responsible for this increase. The average vote share of the first ballot leader in the universal ballot was 54.5 percent, while in the four conventions the first ballot leader averaged a 61 percent vote share. Universal ballots, then, were scarcely less competitive than were conventions.

Unquestionably, the shift to universal ballots has increased the number of people directly participating in the selection of the party leader. Indeed, Table 4.1 somewhat masks this dramatic change. Looking simply at the recent conventions, we see that the number of voters actually declined from the second period to under two thousand. In contrast, the mean number of voters in universal ballots is almost three times larger than the convention average – this despite the fact that the smallest election in our data set is a universal ballot (the PEI NDP in 2002).[13] Contrary to the warnings of many political scientists, these changes in the number of people participating and in the kind of election used have not had dire implications with respect to the political background and involvement of participants. This may, to some degree, assuage the concerns of critics of universal ballots. In the Maritimes at least, continuity coexists with change, and tourists are vastly outnumbered by partisans.

# 5
# Leadership Election Support Patterns: Friends and Neighbours?

The selection of a leader is one of the most important decisions a political party makes. The choice of a leader sets the direction of the party for the future, influences the views citizens have of the party, and has a direct impact on government formation. What divides parties when they make these decisions is thus of great interest. "A leadership convention," notes Carty, "opens a window into a party to reveal its inner structures and dynamics."[1] Studies of party leadership elections have revealed that the cleavages that divide citizens in elections are also of significance in leadership elections. As Krause and Leduc put it, "clearly the division of a party by factors such as East and West, French and English, left and right, old and young, is an important part of the fabric of Canadian party politics, and cannot be neglected in any analysis of convention behaviour."[2]

Empirical investigations of leadership selection at both the federal and provincial levels have highlighted the importance of region as well as a variety of demographic characteristics. Our data enable us to look at the impact of demographic and geographic factors in twenty-five leadership elections taking place over a thirty-two-year period. It permits us to identify the factors that have an enduring impact and it also allows us to explore differences based on party or province. In his earlier examination of nine Maritime leadership conventions held between 1971 and 1985, David Stewart identified distinctive patterns of delegate support based on region (described as the neighbourhood effect) and religion or ethnicity (described as support from a friend).[3] Extending that analysis over all twenty-five leadership elections clearly indicates that divisions of this nature remain important in Maritime politics. Regionally based voting cleavages could be identified at twenty of the twenty-five conventions, including elections held by all three parties and in all three provinces. These divisions persisted across time. Such gaps were evident at the first convention in 1971 and could still be identified in 2003. Moreover, regional cleavages were as evident in universal ballots as they were at conventions.

Differences in patterns of delegate support on the basis of religion were also quite common, and twelve of the elections exhibited divisions of this sort. As well, all five of the elections in New Brunswick exhibited division based on language or ethnicity, including three elections where there were no discernible religious divisions. As Table 5.1 shows, it was possible to identify distinctive patterns of voting in other areas as well, but regional and religious and ethno-linguistic divisions require significant individual attention. Subsequent chapters address cleavages on the basis of gender and community size, but for now we focus on issues relating to region and religion (and, in New Brunswick, ethnicity and language).

### The "Neighbourhood" Effect

We begin our analysis by examining the regional divisions. Given the general relationship we see between region and candidate choice, it is easier to begin by noting the small number of cases in which we could not identify significant voting differences on this basis. With regard to the 2002 PEI NDP leadership election, it may well be the case that the small number of voters who participated in that election precluded statistically significant relationships: only eighty-two New Democrats actually voted in this election, and the absence of significant statistical differences (for region, as, in fact, for all other demographic variables) is therefore scarcely surprising. In two other conventions, the Nova Scotia New Democrats in 1996 and the PEI Conservatives in 1976, there were only two contestants, and both were from the same area of the province. In the Liberal universal ballot in Nova Scotia in 2002, the two major candidates (who shared more than 90 percent of the vote) grew up and resided in the same regions, again undercutting neighbourhood claims. The only other convention at which we could not identify regional differences was the New Brunswick Liberal convention of 1985; but, even here, as we discuss later, deeper probing allowed us to identify local support for one of the candidates.

The degree to which region is a container for divisions based on other factors is not the prime focus of this chapter. Evidence from national politics suggests that the container argument does not capture the reality of regionally based voting. As Blais et al. note, "regional differences are not simply a matter of differences in the socio-demographic make-up of the regions."[4] Our review of newspaper coverage of the twenty-five elections indicates that evidence of regionally based leadership campaigns is generally absent. That said, regional differences have historically been significant in Maritime politics. Fitzpatrick's vivid description of the north-south divide in New Brunswick illustrates this tradition.[5] Similarly, divisions in Nova Scotia between Cape Breton and the Mainland, and, more recently, between Halifax and the rural Mainland, have had an impact on provincial politics.[6] In PEI, movement away from the relatively equal representation of the three

*Table 5.1*

**Maritime leadership elections: selected demographic attributes by vote**

| Election | Region | Religion | Language | Rural | Education | Income | Age | Gender |
|---|---|---|---|---|---|---|---|---|
| PEI LB 03 | 0.27 | | | 0.20 | | | | |
| NS LB 02 | | | | | 0.27 | | | 0.22 |
| NB LB 02 | 0.49 | | 0.21 | | | | | |
| PEI NDP 02 | | | | | | | | |
| NS NDP 02 | 0.44 | 0.14 | | 0.23 | | | | |
| NS NDP 00 | 0.42 | | | 0.21 | | | 0.18 | 0.22 |
| NB LB 98 | 0.61 | 0.23 | 0.43 | 0.13 | 0.2 | 0.11 | 0.14 | |
| NB PC 97 | 0.21 | 0.4 | 0.33 | | 0.14 | | | |
| NS NDP 96 | | | | | 0.14 | | | 0.31 |
| PEI LB 96 | 0.26 | 0.22 | | 0.16 | | 0.18 | | |
| NS PC 95 | 0.35 | | | 0.13 | | 0.08 | | |
| PEI LB 93 | 0.16 | 0.14 | | | 0.08 | 0.09 | 0.09 | |
| NS LB 92 | 0.23 | 0.08 | | 0.13 | 0.08 | 0.09 | 0.07 | |
| NS PC 91 | 0.27 | | | | 0.08 | | 0.11 | |
| PEI PC 88 | 0.21 | 0.18 | | | 0.21 | 0.21 | | |
| NS LB 86 | 0.37 | 0.19 | | 0.14 | | | 0.12 | |
| NB LB 85 | | | 0.18 | 0.23 | | | | 0.18 |
| NB LIB 82 | 0.34 | | 0.18* | 0.24 | 0.16 | | | |
| PEI PC 81 | 0.32 | 0.25 | | 0.25 | | | | |
| PEI LB 81 | 0.26 | | | | | | | |
| NS NDP 80 | 0.31 | | | 0.15 | | | | |
| NS LB 80 | 0.4 | 0.27 | | 0.16 | | 0.13 | | |
| PEI LB 78 | 0.32 | | | 0.23 | | | 0.2 | |
| PEI PC 76 | | 0.23 | | | | 0.23 | | |
| NS PC 71 | 0.23 | 0.22 | | | | | 0.13 | |
| | 20 of 25 | 12 of 25 | 5 of 8 | 14 of 21 | 9 of 24 | 8 of 25 | 8 of 25 | 4 of 25 |

* Indicates that the variable was ethnicity rather than language.

*Note:* Cramer's V is only reported when the association with voting is statistically significant. (Cramer's V is a measure of association based on chi square. Values range from 0-1, with the higher values indicating a stronger association.)

unequal counties was resisted for years, and changes responding to representation by population required court action. Nonetheless, our analysis suggests that, in these Maritime leadership elections, as is often the case elsewhere in the country, regional differences relate principally to the residency of the candidates.

Recall that the 1976 PEI PC convention and the 1985 New Brunswick Liberal convention were two of the five instances in Table 5.1 where regional voting was not apparent. Yet a closer scrutiny reveals patterns of support not captured by our simple regional variable. In 1976, PC candidates Jim Lee and Angus MacLean came from different parts of Queens County, and when we divided that region on the basis of community size we saw strong levels of support for each candidate in her/his own area. Similarly, in 1985, Ray Frenette was able to win significantly higher levels of support among delegates from his hometown of Moncton, when the remainder of the region was joining the rest of the province in providing huge levels of support to Frank McKenna. An examination of the data illustrates the ubiquity of such patterns, and we look at these patterns in each of the provinces in turn.

As Table 5.2 shows, of the seventy-five leadership candidates, only ten failed to improve on their average vote share among their neighbours. This pattern repeated itself in both conventions and universal ballots and crossed both partisan and provincial lines. In fact, as is made clear in the appendix of this book, some candidates openly bragged about the almost monolithic support of their neighbours.[7] With regard to the few candidates who did not receive a boost from their neighbours, this can generally be explained quite simply. In the 2003 Liberal election on PEI, Robert Ghiz and Alan Buchanan were both from Queens County, although Ghiz had not actually lived there for some time (he was working for the Chretien government in Ottawa). A neighbourhood boost for Buchanan left no room for Ghiz. In New Brunswick in 1985, Frank McKenna was somewhat difficult to place in regional terms as he represented one area in the legislature but was originally from another part of the province. His mobility might diminish his ability to benefit from the general neighbourhood effect since, as Putnam notes in *Bowling Alone*, "frequent movers have weaker community ties."[8] Regardless, McKenna won huge majorities among all delegates other than those from his opponent's hometown, so his failure to receive a neighbourhood boost should not be seen as terribly important. Similarly, in 1971, John Buchanan faced candidates from both his region of birth (Cape Breton) and his place of residence (Halifax), factors that undoubtedly cut into his ability to attract support on this basis. In the case of Atwell at the 1996 Nova Scotia NDP convention, there was only one other candidate and he represented the same area. Barry Clark, at the 1981 PC PEI convention, was challenged by two other candidates from Queens County, making it difficult

*Table 5.2*

## Maritime candidates: neighbourhood boost

| Party | Province | Year | Candidate | Boost |
|---|---|---|---|---|
| Liberal | PEI | 1978 | Campbell | 22 |
| Liberal | PEI | 1978 | Mitchell | 29 |
| Liberal | NS | 1980 | Cameron | 38 |
| Liberal | NS | 1980 | Maclean | 55 |
| Liberal | NS | 1980 | Mooney | 41 |
| Liberal | NS | 1980 | MacInnis | 14 |
| Liberal | PEI | 1981 | Ghiz | 1 |
| Liberal | PEI | 1981 | Clements | 29 |
| Liberal | NB | 1982 | Young | 30 |
| Liberal | NB | 1982 | Day | 36 |
| Liberal | NB | 1982 | Frenette | 23 |
| Liberal | NB | 1982 | Maher | 11 |
| Liberal | NB | 1985 | McKenna | -3 |
| Liberal | NB | 1985 | Frenette | 23 |
| Liberal | NS | 1986 | Maclean | 43 |
| Liberal | NS | 1986 | Cowan | 7 |
| Liberal | NS | 1992 | Savage | 16 |
| Liberal | NS | 1992 | Downe | 42 |
| Liberal | NS | 1992 | MacInnis | -2 |
| Liberal | NS | 1992 | Drish | 3 |
| Liberal | NS | 1992 | Hawkins | 2 |
| Liberal | PEI | 1993 | Callbeck | 10 |
| Liberal | PEI | 1993 | Creed | 15 |
| Liberal | PEI | 1993 | Campbell | 1 |
| Liberal | PEI | 1996 | Milligan | 40 |
| Liberal | PEI | 1996 | Chevrie | 27 |
| Liberal | PEI | 1996 | MacDonald | 1 |
| Liberal | PEI | 1996 | Mullen | 2 |
| Liberal | NB | 1998 | Theriault | 41 |
| Liberal | NB | 1998 | Byrne | 71 |
| Liberal | NB | 1998 | Richard | 79 |
| Liberal | NB | 2002 | S. Graham | 24 |
| Liberal | NB | 2002 | MacDougall | -7 |
| Liberal | NS | 2002 | D. Graham | 5 |
| Liberal | NS | 2002 | MacKenzie | -1 |
| Liberal | NS | 2002 | B. Graham | 44 |
| Liberal | PEI | 2003 | R. Ghiz | -24 |
| Liberal | PEI | 2003 | Buchanan | 24 |

▶

| Party | Province | Year | Candidate | Boost |
|-------|----------|------|-----------|-------|
| PC | NS | 1971 | Doucet | 24 |
| PC | NS | 1971 | Buchanan | 0 |
| PC | NS | 1971 | Thornhill | 10 |
| PC | PEI | 1976 | Maclean | 10 |
| PC | PEI | 1976 | Lee | 14 |
| PC | PEI | 1981 | Lee | −1 |
| PC | PEI | 1981 | Clark | −2 |
| PC | PEI | 1981 | Driscoll | 19 |
| PC | PEI | 1981 | Binns | 33 |
| PC | PEI | 1988 | Gass | 10 |
| PC | PEI | 1988 | Walker | 23 |
| PC | NS | 1991 | Cameron | 26 |
| PC | NS | 1991 | Thornhill | 7 |
| PC | NS | 1991 | McInnis | 3 |
| PC | NS | 1991 | Callaghan | 4 |
| PC | NS | 1995 | Hamm | 46 |
| PC | NS | 1995 | White | 43 |
| PC | NS | 1995 | MacDonald | 5 |
| PC | NB | 1997 | Lord | 14 |
| PC | NB | 1997 | Betts | 3 |
| PC | NB | 1997 | Allaby | 11 |
| PC | NB | 1997 | Blaney | 19 |
| | | | | |
| NDP | NS | 1980 | McDonough | 13 |
| NDP | NS | 1980 | Arsenault | 20 |
| NDP | NS | 1980 | MacEachern | 19 |
| NDP | NS | 1996 | Chisholm | 11 |
| NDP | NS | 1996 | Atwell | −12 |
| NDP | NS | 2000 | H. Macdonald | 68 |
| NDP | NS | 2000 | Deveaux | 17 |
| NDP | NS | 2000 | M. Macdonald | 9 |
| NDP | NS | 2000 | Peters | 29 |
| NDP | NS | 2000 | Bitter-Suerman | 29 |
| NDP | NS | 2002 | Dexter | 9 |
| NDP | NS | 2002 | MacDonell | 66 |
| NDP | PEI | 2002 | Robichaud | 19 |
| NDP | PEI | 2002 | Bingham | 13 |
| NDP | PEI | 2002 | Hawkes | −3 |

for each of them to receive disproportionate support. Ken MacInnis, in the 1992 Nova Scotia Liberal tele-vote, was faced with a much more popular candidate from the Halifax area in John Savage, a factor that undoubtedly reduced any possibility of a neighbourhood effect for MacInnis. In his earlier try for the leadership in 1980, his fellow Haligonians were more supportive. In 2002, Nova Scotia Liberal candidates Francis MacKenzie and Danny Graham shared the same home area, making it difficult for both to receive a boost. The remaining candidate, who was without any extra support from his neighbours, was New Brunswick Liberal Jack MacDougall, who participated in the anomalous election of 2002, for which many eligible delegates did not bother to show up.

It is striking that so many of the weak candidates in these elections nonetheless received disproportionate support from their neighbours. In a later chapter, we distinguish between fringe and serious candidates and note that both candidate types benefit from the neighbourhood effect. In general, neither the hopelessness of a candidate's chances nor the inevitability of his or her victory can be seen as eliminating the neighbourhood effect. In most cases, but for the support of their neighbours, a title less envious than "fringe" would be required for many minor candidates. At any rate, support of this type demonstrates that voters are likely not attempting to jump on a bandwagon. The neighbourhood effect is visible in all areas of the region and, on average, candidates received support levels from their neighbours 19 percentage points higher than their vote elsewhere.

### The "Friendship" Effect

Religion has historically been important in Maritime politics. The north-south division in New Brunswick is magnified by a Protestant/Catholic split, PEI parties often utilized balanced tickets to try to keep religion out of politics, and the Protestant/Catholic division in Nova Scotia was recognized by a Liberal party tradition of alternating their leaders – a tradition that persisted until the first universal ballot in 1992. Thus, it is not surprising that significant divisions on the basis of religion could be identified in twelve of the twenty-five conventions for which we have data. Such divisions were found in five of the nine conventions on which David Stewart's initial analysis was based, and its presence in seven of the remaining sixteen elections suggests that it remains important, albeit without the ubiquity of the neighbourhood effect.

It is important to keep in mind that religion does not seem to be as important for the NDP. As we saw in the previous chapter, New Democratic voters and candidates can be distinguished from Liberal and Conservative voters by the presence of substantial numbers who claim no religious affiliation. Recall that such individuals make up only a tiny proportion of Liberal and Conservative voters. Not surprisingly, religion was not a significant source of division in four of the five NDP elections in our data base. Only the 2002 Nova Scotia NDP universal ballot was an exception to this tendency, with John MacDonell performing significantly better than Darrell Dexter among those with no religion. Otherwise, and in marked contrast to the other two parties, the relative unimportance of religion in NDP leadership elections is further buttressed by the difficulty in obtaining information about the religious background of most NDP candidates. Given the absence of statistical significance for this variable at NDP gatherings, we do not view this as problematic.

Religious divisions were absent from a number of other conventions as well. On Prince Edward Island, for example, there were no significant religious differences in the support bases of the candidates at the Liberal conventions of 1978, 1981, and 2003. In 1978, the leadership was contested by two Catholics; and in 1981 and 2003, two Protestants were the only candidates. In all cases, the candidates drew similar levels of support from both religious groups.

The 1982 and 1985 New Brunswick Liberal conventions did not demonstrate religious divisions either. In 1985, both Frenette and McKenna were Catholic. In 1982, one of the candidates, Joe Day, was a Protestant; however, unlike Protestant candidates in Nova Scotia and PEI, his co-religionists were not significantly more likely to vote for him. He did, however, draw disproportionate support from voters of British origin. The fluently bilingual Young, who has been described as an Acadian,[9] won 72 percent of the votes cast by those who described their ethnicity as French, but only 47 percent from those who claimed a British origin. Divisions on the basis of ethnic origin were much more firmly associated with voting, suggesting that religious politics were being suppressed by linguistic politics in New Brunswick. In fact, when we consider ethnic or linguistic divisions as part of the "friendship" effect in New Brunswick, we find this dimension to be omnipresent.

The 1985 leadership convention was contested by only two candidates: Frank McKenna and Ray Frenette. McKenna cruised to an easy victory; however, notwithstanding the massive nature of his defeat, Frenette, an Acadian, was able to attract disproportionate support from his fellow Acadians. Indeed, Frenette's support from rank-and-file Acadians was somewhat masked by the strong support given to McKenna from Acadian delegates who attended the convention in an ex officio capacity. Thus in the two early New Brunswick cases, the absence of ties based on religion are not inconsistent with support following a friendship pattern: the pattern is simply ethnic rather than religious. The 2002 New Brunswick Liberal convention was also unmarked by religious divisions but, again, saw linguistically based divisions. That leadership election, as we have shown, was rather idiosyncratic, and the division was not consistent with linguistic support for a "friend."

Religious divisions were absent from other conventions as well. The 1993 Liberal convention on PEI won by Catherine Callbeck displayed no significant religious cleavage; however, her competitors had very little public profile and their ability to mobilize any co-religionists was limited. Similarly, the 2002 Nova Scotia Liberal election, in which religious differences among the candidates could not be identified,was not marked by religiously based voting decisions. Neither the 1991 nor the 1995 PC conventions in Nova Scotia revealed much in the way of religiously based support. When the provincial PCs met to choose a successor to long-serving premier John Buchanan in 1991, two of the four candidates (Clair Callaghan and Tom McInnis) were Roman Catholic and two (Donald Cameron and Rollie Thornhill) were Protestant. Nonetheless, voting by "friends" at this convention was negligible, with the three major candidates all receiving essentially the same support from Protestants and Roman Catholics. In 1995, the only Catholic candidate, Michael MacDonald, actually performed marginally better among Protestant delegates, and the pattern for the two Protestant candidates (John Hamm and Jim White) was relatively consistent across the religious cleavage.

In the remainder of the elections, a significant religious division was present. In every case save one, this took the form of disproportionate support for a candidate from his or her co-religionists. The exception was the 1988 PEI PC convention, where a significant division was apparent despite the fact that both candidates were Protestant. What seems to be driving the observed pattern, in fact, is a spill-over from federal-provincial relations. Prior to the convention, the Supreme Court of Canada had struck down the country's abortion legislation as contrary to the Charter of Rights and Freedoms. With the federal Conservative government of Brian Mulroney vacillating on whether to fill this regulatory vacuum, PEI's legislators, in their spring 1988 session, sent a "strongly" worded message to Ottawa rejecting the principle of abortion on demand and endorsing the procedure only in cases where the life of the mother was at risk.[10] Provincial MLA Andy Walker's hard line on abortion would thus have been flagged to Catholic Tories on the Island; conversely, federal MP Mel Gass would have been tarred by his association with the presumably more permissive national elites. Thus the obvious link between religion and vote at the 1988 convention was likely driven by a (perhaps erroneous) perception of a shared value rather than a shared demographic tie.

As discussed above, although the 1982 and 1985 New Brunswick Liberal conventions were not marked by significant divisions on the basis of religion, the same could not be said for language and ethnicity. The leadership elections held by the Progressive Conservatives in 1997 and the Liberals in 1998 allow us to look for the continued existence of linguistic support in

New Brunswick while also exploring the significance of religion. The friendship effect, as it relates to mother tongue, remained noteworthy. Three of the candidates were francophone, and each of these candidates received disproportionate support from francophone voters. In general, the anglophone candidates, most of whom had a limited facility in French, were unsuccessful in attracting support from francophone voters. Inevitably, their backing was substantially stronger among anglophone voters. The two winning candidates, Theriault and Lord, were both ultimately successful in winning majority support from each of the linguistic communities; but for both, the support from their francophone friends was substantially higher.

Language was rarely far from the surface during the 1998 Liberal campaign. Twenty-five years previously, Bernard Richard had been a vocal supporter of Acadian nationalism; for some New Brunswickers, these youthful activities still resonated. "It has been difficult for me in certain areas, related to my Parti Acadien involvement in the early seventies and that's fair," acknowledged Richard. "It has been more difficult for me in certain anglophone areas."[11] As a unilingual anglophone, Greg Byrne had the opposite problem. Byrne might insist that "whether they are anglophones or francophones, New Brunswick Liberals want the best leader for this party and for this province," but his "somewhat laboured French" ensured that his support would be largely confined to the anglophone community.[12] The high degree of anglophone support for Greg Byrne in the Liberal race is particularly striking since Byrne was not often mentioned in the early lists of potential candidates, and some observers pointed to the fact that, according to the traditions of the Liberal party, it was a francophone's turn to lead the party. As Condé Grondin asserted in handicapping the major contenders for the leadership, "You'll notice the names are all French ... That's because the New Brunswick Liberal party has developed what they call an alternation mode – they alternate between French and English leaders."[13] Obviously, as in 1985, many anglophone voters did not accept this alternation thesis.

Such friendship considerations effectively trumped any A-B-C (Anybody-But-Camille) alliance against obvious front-runner Camille Theriault. Many doubted that Greg Byrne would be able either "to convince Mr. Richard's many francophone supporters to join him despite his unilingual anglophone background or persuade his mostly anglophone block of delegates to back Mr. Richard, a former Parti Acadien candidate."[14] As for Bernard Richard, irrespective of any personal desire to block a Theriault victory, most observers believed it would "be hard for his Acadian supporters to miss the chance to make an Acadian the next premier of New Brunswick."[15] Ultimately, only Camille Theriault was seen as having support that transcended his immediate friends and neighbours; yet even Theriault's support base proved to be consistent with this phenomenon.

Unlike the earlier New Brunswick conventions, both the 1997 and 1998 gatherings were also marked by a statistically significant difference in the votes cast by Protestants and Catholics. At the 1998 Liberal convention, Byrne's support among Protestants was substantially higher than it was among Catholics, and the association between religion and voting was stronger than was that of any of the other socio-economic variables, save language. Further investigation, however, reveals this to be essentially an artefact of language. There were no self-described francophone Protestant voters at the Liberal convention, and when we limit examination of voting to anglophones, we see that Byrne did better among Catholics than he did among Protestants – 45 percent versus 38 percent – and actually led both Theriault and Richard among English-speaking Catholic voters.

In the 1997 Conservative election, religion was more strongly associated with voting than was language. Lord did particularly poorly among Protestants on the first ballot, finishing third; and on the final ballot, despite being endorsed by the two eliminated candidates, he still won just 55 percent of the Protestant vote, while his support from Catholic voters surpassed 80 percent.

This essentially replicates the results with regard to language and leaves one pondering the respective influence of these traditional variables. Given the earlier results in New Brunswick, it seemed possible that what we were seeing was an overlapping of the religious and linguistic divisions. In other words, most of the anglophone voters were Protestant, so we were simply seeing the linguistic division in another form. Certainly, virtually none of the francophone voters (less than 3 percent) was Protestant. However, 15 percent of the anglophone voters were Catholic, so the religious dimension was not completely a redisplay of language differences.

In an attempt to sort out these differences, we placed religion and ethnicity in a set of regression equations, along with other socio-economic variables as well as the variables used to identify the "neighbourhood" effect. The results were somewhat unexpected. When we examined Lord's support on the first ballot, we found that the religious variable was significant: all things being equal, Protestants were 20 percent less likely to vote for Lord than were Catholics. In contrast, the coefficient for language was not significant. Thus, even when we controlled for age, education, income, and the neighbourhood effect, the religious division remained significant. This cleavage appeared even stronger when Lord voters were individually examined against Betts and Allaby voters.

Regressions examining paired choices for each of the candidates provided further confirmation of a neighbourhood effect. Controlling for religion and language does not eliminate the significance of the neighbourhood effect for Betts and Blaney in their competition with Lord, and the neighbourhood effects are the only variables distinguishing supporters of Betts from both Blaney and Allaby.

The support of friends and neighbours remains an important factor in New Brunswick leadership elections. All things being equal, candidates do substantially better among voters from their home regions and among voters with the same mother tongue. However, in the Conservative election, divisions based on the Protestant-Catholic divide were actually stronger than were those based on language, raising questions about claims that language has superseded religion in Canada's only officially bilingual province. It is important, however, not to overestimate the religious element since, ultimately, Lord won majorities from both communities.

It seems clear that ethno-linguistic cleavages are extremely important in New Brunswick and that religion remains an issue that often divides voters in Maritime leadership elections. While such divisions are not as strong as are those based on region, they often remain significant, at least when major candidates of different faiths confront each other. The rumours of the demise of religious divisions in the region may have been exaggerated.

## Friends and Neighbours

Our analysis of twenty-five leadership elections in the Maritimes suggests that the friends and neighbours thesis remains of relevance. In particular, the neighbourhood effect was almost ubiquitous, with virtually all of the candidates receiving disproportionate support from voters who were from their home area.

The evidence with respect to friends and neighbours support was somewhat mixed. It was not present in New Democratic elections, but it was usually present in some form in New Brunswick, and, when there were serious Catholic and Protestant candidates in the other provinces, religious divisions were almost always evident. In short, we see clear evidence of a continuing pattern of linguistically based friendship in New Brunswick and, most of the time, of religiously based friendship in Nova Scotia and PEI.

On the other hand, there were eight Liberal or Conservative leadership elections in Nova Scotia and PEI where the friendship factor was not readily identifiable; some might infer from this evidence that religion is of declining importance in the region. One should be cautious, however, about drawing such conclusions. When we look at the eight leadership elections in which religion played no role, we see that, on four occasions, the candidates shared the same friends (PEI 1978, 1981, 1988, 2003). Moreover, in three other contests (PEI 1993 and Nova Scotia 1995, 2002),[16] the candidates with distinctive sets of friends were very weak and attracted less than 10 percent of the votes cast. Thus only one of the recent leadership elections (Nova Scotia 1991) directly contradicts the "friends" thesis. It may well be that Rollie Thornhill's unique position in promising not to privatize the Sydney Steel Corporation enabled him to make substantial inroads among voters in Cape Breton, Nova Scotia's most heavily Catholic region. Correspondingly, the unwillingness of the Catholic candidates to make such a commitment may have diminished their ability to attract support from their co-religionists provincewide. One might anticipate that friends and neighbours politics would be more likely where there was little policy differentiation. The presence of such a clear policy differentiation in 1991 may well have weakened the friendship effect. On the one occasion when a religious cleavage appeared despite all candidates being of the same faith (PEI 1988), abortion views provided the explanation. The influence of religion on Maritime politics then, is not always policy-free, but policy can certainly affect the way it manifests itself. Leadership elections based more on policy might well diminish the friendship factor; however, there is little evidence that such elections are becoming policy contests, and it is possible that even this might not eliminate religious divisions in candidate choice. At present, the politics of friends and neighbours remains part of the story of leadership choice in the Maritimes.

The preceding analysis of voting behaviour paints a picture of friends and neighbours support. The continuing significance of geographic influences, let alone religious ones, deals a blow to those eager for evidence of "modernization" in Maritime politics. It does not indicate a polity being "subtly eroded by the processes of change."[17] The importance of localism and religion/ethnicity in Maritime leadership elections leads us to doubt that such primordial ties can be important in these events and irrelevant elsewhere.

The presence of friends and neighbours support is not something some observers of Maritime politics will point to admiringly. Wilson called the geographic and religious influences on Maritime politics "pre-industrial,"[18] and the notion that, as polities develop, ties of this type will decline is widely held:

> In modernization theories, place is viewed as significant only in traditional or parochial societies and not in modern ones ... as societies "modernize" they undergo certain determinate mutations that create new conditions for political life. In particular, national functional cleavages (such as class) displace older territorial and communal cleavages (such as region and religion).[19]

V.O. Key, the creator of the term "friends and neighbours," was quite negative in his assessment of the phenomenon. As he put it: "The chances are that the friends and neighbours appeal can assume overriding importance only in an immature politics in which issues are either nonexistent or blurred."[20] He further describes this kind of voting as based on a "more or less totally irrelevant appeal."[21] It is possible, however, to view such support more positively. Assessing friends and neighbours support negatively assumes that it is an unreflective and automatic occurrence. Yet there is no reason to assume that support from friends and neighbours is something that every candidate could take for granted. Even Key grudgingly admitted this when he wrote: "the harshest criticism that can be made of a politician is that he cannot win in his own beat or precinct. If his friends and neighbours do not support him, why should those without this advantage trust such a candidate?"[22]

As discussed in Chapter 3, the Maritime provinces are predominantly rural, and this provides fertile soil for "friends and neighbours" support. Friends and neighbours support in the Maritimes must be understood within the context of "a sense of place," and that sense of place is predominantly rural. As Wilson observes, "there is in the Maritime culture a deep sense of place, of belonging, of beginnings: cities and towns are small and many of their inhabitants are not many steps removed from the country ... there is nothing superficial about the Maritimer's common and deep sense of place, his sensitivity to family and local traditions."[23] Individuals can be quickly identified in terms of their "place" or whether they "belong." Maritimers have elevated the phrase "come from aways" to a level of deep significance, an indication that someone does not belong and that newcomers do not fully fit in. As Bruce points out: "Beneath the celebrated friendliness of Maritimers, there lurks a bowel-deep suspicion of outsiders."[24] Others have contended that, in small towns and villages, "a noticeable fissure in the social structure ... runs along the line of old versus new residents ... It is difficult for newcomers to penetrate such networks, they remain isolated."[25] This may partially explain the lack of much in the way of a neighbourhood effect for either McKenna or Buchanan.[26]

There is one other feature that contributes to the strength of localism in the Maritimes: the competition among various communities. Again, as Bruce points out,

> from province to province, island to island, county to county, town to town and from bay to cove and river to beach, Maritimers have been fighting and plotting to get the upper hand over one another for a couple of centuries. Down Home communities are often about as co-operative as the Hatfields and McCoys, as harmonious together as a convention of fishwives. Each town has its own way of doing things, its own self interest, history and traditions to protect, and perhaps its own grudges to nurse and grievances to cherish.[27]

The evidence that religious affiliation remains associated with candidate choice in Maritime leadership elections should not be overly surprising, given the importance of religious affiliation in national voting data. If religion remains associated with political choices nationally, surely a similar tendency should be found in the country's "Bible Belt."[28] Admittedly, in the period covered by our analysis, the percentage of Maritimers claiming no religious affiliation has increased, while the percentage of those attending church regularly has decreased. However, the Atlantic region continues to stand out in terms of Christian affiliation and participation in religious services. As the 2001 census revealed, the vast majority of Maritimers describe themselves as Christian. Eighty-seven percent of Nova Scotians claimed affiliation with a Christian denomination, as did more than 90 percent of the residents of New Brunswick and PEI. Moreover, as the 2003 General Social Survey on Social Engagement reveals: "Frequency of attendance at religious services was greatest among individuals in the Atlantic region."[29] More than 75 percent of Islanders, 69 percent of New Brunswickers, and 63 percent of Nova Scotians reported attending church at least a few times a year. These figures surpass those of all provinces but Newfoundland.

Indeed, Frank Jones, in his 2003 study of religious commitment in Canada, found that the percentage of "potential attendees" (those who are religious but do not attend church regularly) was highest in the Atlantic region.[30] He also found that what he called the "religious" population (those claiming religion is at least somewhat important in their lives) was more prevalent in Atlantic Canada than elsewhere. As he put it: "The religious rate varies from 46 percent to 47 percent in British Columbia and Quebec, to 62 percent in Ontario and the prairie region, to 67 percent in the Atlantic region."[31]

Similarly, historian George Rawlyk, in his major 1996 study of religious belief and practice in Canada, reports that residents of Atlantic Canada were most likely to agree that religion was important in their lives, to pray regularly, and to believe that the Bible was the inspired word of God. They were least likely to agree that "Jesus Christ was not the divine son of God." [32] Overall, Rawlyk suggests that we must be cautious in interpreting declining rates of church attendance and that this decline "should not necessarily be equated with a collective loss of faith."[33] Religion, particularly of the Christian variety, remains vibrant in the Maritimes and is far from absent in Maritime leadership elections. The higher rates of religious participation in the Maritimes likely feed back into the neighbourhood effect since, as Clark reveals, "people who attended religious services on a regular basis were more likely to feel a very strong connection to their community."[34]

In a largely rural society, with a culture that places such importance on the sense of place, the presence of friends and neighbours voting is not something that should come as a shock. The decline of this phenomenon in the region would likely require changes in the nature of both Maritime society and culture.

One cannot push this argument too far. Friends and neighbours are by no means restricted to the Maritimes. Carty, Erickson, and Blake examined leadership contests across Canada, concluding, "One variable does emerge as significant in all of our cases: region."[35] Similarly, in their analysis of the 2000 federal election, Blais et al. hint that reports of the disappearance of such influences are exaggerated. In their words:

> The impact of social cleavages on vote choice may well have declined in most advanced industrial states between the 1960s and 1980s. Whether this trend has continued along this same trajectory is not clear. What is clear is that there is no such pattern in Canada. Region and religion remain as crucial now as they once were.[36]

Religious affiliation was not always associated with voting, but it seems that knowledge of a candidate's religious background may provide some sort of common identification and, thus, enable leadership voters to be aware of whether or not they share a particular tie with a candidate. Given the strength of religion in Maritime society, it would be surprising if this did not occasionally affect voting. Religious voting patterns were more difficult to detect in New Brunswick, but in that province another form of kinship existed: language and ethnicity, which provides a kind of shared identification that is even more obvious than is that provided by religion. It is also an identification whose political salience is unquestionable. All things being equal, Maritime voters have generally provided disproportionate support to their "kin."

# 6
# Town versus Country: Urban-Rural Divisions

Recently, there has been discussion in Canada about the emergence of a new cleavage, one that distinguishes rural and urban Canada. In recent federal elections, for example, rural Canadians have been significantly less likely than their urban counterparts to vote Liberal.[1] Thomas also highlights the growing relevance of this division. As he puts it, "Canada appears to be developing two distinct electoral groupings: (1) progressive-heterogeneous large urban; and (2) conservative-homogeneous-smaller cities (edge) and rural areas."[2]

The distinctions between urban and rural areas in the Maritimes are not as extreme as they are in many parts of the country. The largest city in the region, Halifax, contains fewer than 300,000 people[3] and has only about 30 percent of the provincial population. In New Brunswick, there are only three cities greater than 50,000 in population (Saint John, Fredericton, and Moncton). In total, only 32 percent of the New Brunswick population lives in these cities. Prince Edward Island has the smallest urban centre, Charlottetown, and its population, which is less than 40,000, comprises just over a quarter of the provincial population.

The Maritime provinces are decidedly more rural than is the Canadian norm. The standard approach in Canada is to classify all areas with a population of more than one thousand people as urban.[4] Even using this intuitively implausible definition of urban, we see from Table 6.1 that it applies to only 56 percent of Nova Scotians, 50 percent of New Brunswickers, and 45 percent of Islanders. Indeed, the proportion of urban voters has changed only slightly over the last thirty years. The 1971 census revealed the proportion of urban Maritimers to be 58 percent in Nova Scotia, 51 percent in New Brunswick, and 38 percent in PEI.[5] These large and consistent numbers suggest that rural voters are likely to be influential in the region's politics; and, indeed, this has been a recurring theme in the thirty-two-year-period covered by our study. As Table 5.1 revealed, significant voting divisions were found in fourteen of our data sets. It is possible that this figure might have

*Table 6.1*

**Maritime provinces: rural distribution over time**

| Year | PEI | New Brunswick | Nova Scotia |
|---|---|---|---|
| 2001 | 55% | 50% | 44% |
| | 74,619 of 135,294 | 361,596 of 729,498 | 400,998 of 908,007 |
| 1991 | 60% | 53% | 47% |
| | 77,952 of 129,765 | 376,610 of 716,495 | 416,230 of 890,950 |
| 1981 | 64% | 49% | 45% |
| | 77,991 of 122,506 | 343,183 of 696,403 | 380,600 of 847,442 |
| 1971 | 62% | 49% | 42% |
| | 68,860 of 111,640 | 304,563 of 616,788 | 317,132 of 756,039 |

*Source:* 1971, 1981, 1991, and 2001 Census of Canada.

been greater, but some of our data sets do not include measures of community size, rendering analysis of this measure impossible. The measures of association for this variable equal those for any other demographic variable, save region.

As the previous chapter demonstrates, it is quite clear that geography is a major part of the story of Maritime leadership selection and that this dimension of political competition crosses partisan and provincial lines. The rural nature of the Maritimes and its implications for regional politics is not given the attention it deserves. The absence of data on this measure in a number of our surveys is indicative of this oversight.

**Urban-Rural Voting Divisions**

Table 5.1 revealed that urban-rural differences were significant at fourteen of the twenty-one conventions for which we have data on community size. In many of these cases, however, the possibility existed that these results were to some degree replicating the neighbourhood effect discussed in Chapter 5. To take but one obvious example, John Savage's strength among urban voters in the 1992 Liberal leadership race might simply have been a function of the strength of his support among his metropolitan Halifax neighbours. To disentangle the impact of these two variables, we removed a candidate's neighbours from the sample and examined the impact of the urban-rural dichotomy on the voting behaviour of the remaining respondents.[6] The results are displayed in Table 6.2 and reveal an average gap of almost nine percentage points between urban and rural support.[7] As can be seen, in four cases (PEI Liberals 1978 and 2003, New Brunswick Liberals 1982, and Nova Scotia NDP 1980), there were no statistically significant findings.

*Table 6.2*

---

**Maritime candidates: urban-rural support outside neighbourhood**

| Leadership election | Candidate | Rural (%) | Urban (%) | Gap in support |
|---|---|---|---|---|
| PEI Liberal 2003 | Buchanan | 38 | 31 | 7 |
| | R. Ghiz | 63 | 69 | 6 |
| NS NDP 2002* | MacDonell* | 38 | 23 | 15 |
| | Dexter | 60 | 68 | 8 |
| NS NDP 2000* | Bitter-Suermann* | 14 | 1 | 13 |
| | Peters | 2 | 7 | 5 |
| | MacDonald, H. | 22 | 23 | 1 |
| | MacDonald, M.* | 33 | 17 | 16 |
| | Deveaux | 18 | 22 | 4 |
| NB Liberal 1998* | Theriault | 61 | 53 | 8 |
| | Richard* | 9 | 18 | 9 |
| | Byrne | 26 | 23 | 3 |
| PEI Liberal 1996* | Milligan* | 52 | 32 | 20 |
| | Chevrie | 30 | 32 | 2 |
| NS PC 1995* | Hamm* | 39 | 61 | 22 |
| | Macdonald | 11 | 7 | 4 |
| | White* | 39 | 29 | 10 |
| NS Liberal 1992 * | Downe* | 44 | 31 | 13 |
| | Savage* | 40 | 50 | 10 |
| | MacInnis | 11 | 8 | 3 |
| NS Liberal 1986* | MacLean | 49 | 55 | 6 |
| | Cowan* | 33 | 41 | 8 |
| NB Liberal 1985* | Frenette* | 5 | 24 | 19 |
| | McKenna* | 97 | 77 | 20 |
| NB Liberal 1982 | Young | 55 | 49 | 6 |
| | Frenette | 4 | 7 | 3 |
| | Day | 28 | 19 | 9 |
| | Maher | 4 | 4 | 0 |
| PEI PC 1981* | Clark* | 30 | 12 | 18 |
| | Driscoll | 8 | 12 | 4 |
| | Lee | 43 | 50 | 7 |
| | Binns | 6 | 8 | 2 |
| NS NDP 1980 | Arsenault | 13 | 9 | 4 |
| | McDonough | 83 | 72 | 11 |
| | MacEachern | 2 | 3 | 1 |
| NS Liberal 1980* | Cameron* | 74 | 59 | 15 |
| | MacLean* | 14 | 28 | 14 |
| | Mooney | 10 | 12 | 2 |
| | MacInnis | 11 | 8 | 3 |
| PEI Liberal 1978 | Campbell | 73 | 61 | 12 |
| | Mitchell | 18 | 8 | 10 |

\* $\chi^2 < .05$

What appeared to be an urban-rural division in 1978 was simply dispro-portionate support for Gerard Mitchell from his Charlottetown neighbours. Distinctions in the urban and rural support for Mitchell on the rest of the Island were not statistically significant. A comparable result was found in 2003. Although Alan Buchanan drew disproportionate support from rural Islanders, this came largely from his fellow residents in Queens County. In Prince and Kings counties, the difference between his rural and urban sup-port was not statistically significant. Similarly, what initially appeared to be greater urban support for Joe Day and Ray Frenette in New Brunswick in 1982 should also be understood as a neighbourhood boost. When we ac-count for their respective homes in Saint John and Moncton, we no longer find the urban-rural cleavage to be significant. Finally, the 1980 Nova Scotia NDP convention follows a similar trend. Alexa McDonough does especially well in her Halifax base, and her two competitors do well with the support of their Cape Breton neighbours. When we control for these factors, the urban-rural cleavage loses significance. For the ten other races, however, at least one of the candidate's support patterns was directly linked to commu-nity size.

We begin by looking at the Nova Scotia New Democrats. In 2000, Hinrich Bitter-Suermann had substantially more support from rural than from ur-ban voters once his Lunenburg neighbours were removed from the sample. Somewhat surprisingly, a parallel pattern is apparent in the support of third place finisher Maureen Macdonald. Despite representing a Halifax constitu-ency, her support in the remainder of the province was concentrated dis-proportionately among rural Nova Scotians. The 2002 NDP election provides an even more dramatic urban-rural split, with John MacDonell winning 38 percent the rural vote outside of his Hants county home but securing less than a quarter of the votes from more urban voters. This split was perhaps not surprising given that, as is made clear in the appendix of this book, MacDonell was intent on expanding the NDP's presence in rural Nova Scotia. In both these elections, the eventual NDP winners did not demonstrate as much strength in rural areas as they did in urban areas; however, this did not prove problematic, and each won comfortable victories.

In 1992, John Savage was also able to overcome a relatively weak showing in rural Nova Scotia. His main competitor, Don Downe, outpolled him among the most rural Nova Scotians, but Dr. Savage's ability to carry the urban vote was enough to propel him to victory. Downe's support declined as community size rose. High levels of support in the more urban areas of both Cape Breton and the rural mainland allowed Savage to overcome Downe's dominance of the rural vote. If the universal ballot had turned Nova Scotian Liberals out in a proportion similar to that found in the gen-eral population, Downe's base among rural voters might have been suffi-cient for victory.

Urban-rural differences in candidate choice could also be seen at other Nova Scotia Liberal conventions. In 1986, Jim Cowan not only drew disproportionate support from his Halifax neighbours but also from urban areas outside of Halifax. Sandy Cameron's victory in the Nova Scotia Liberal convention in 1980 also displayed an urban-rural split, with Cameron's popularity with rural Nova Scotians running 15 percentage points above that of urban voters on the final ballot. Support for candidates at the 1995 PC convention in Nova Scotia could also be distinguished on the basis of community size. Outside of his home in Pictou County, John Hamm was far more popular with Nova Scotians who were not from rural areas. In contrast, Jim White's candidacy was much stronger in the more rural areas.

This brief look at urban-rural splits in Nova Scotia illustrates the importance of being competitive in rural areas. Cameron and MacLean were able to secure comfortable wins based upon large rural vote totals. Savage and Hamm won by combining strong urban support with an almost even division of the rural vote. It was their ability to be at least competitive in rural Nova Scotia that helped them secure victory. Strikingly, Savage was the *only* Liberal or Conservative winner who, in the final analysis, could not carry a majority of rural voters. For the New Democrats, rural support was less necessary.

Rural-urban splits were also found on PEI. The 1981 PC convention saw Barry Clark make it a three-ballot race largely on the basis of his support from rural Islanders. Eventually, Jim Lee won all areas, but Clark achieved his best results in the rural areas. An urban-rural division was more prominent in the Liberal leadership race in 1996. Keith Milligan's success with rural voters easily overwhelmed Wayne Cheverie's urban Charlottetown base and put Milligan in the premier's office. Milligan's support from voters outside his Prince County home was 20 percentage points higher among rural voters.

When we consider these results in the light of our discussion on candidate success in Chapter 3, a pattern emerges. Successful candidates tended to be more competitive in rural areas, and an urban base could not compensate for weakness in rural areas. Every Island winner, except Robert Ghiz, was able to win at least a plurality of the rural vote, but a number of candidates who had greater urban appeal went down to defeat. The efforts of Joe Ghiz in 1981 to demonstrate his familiarity with the rural Island (by stressing his potato-picking and lobster-eating experiences) demonstrates the importance of the rural vote. Even Robert Ghiz won a majority of the votes cast by rural voters outside of Alan Buchanan's base in Queens County.

In New Brunswick, the rural vote went overwhelmingly to Frank McKenna when he won his easy 1985 victory over Ray Frenette. McKenna carried all areas of the province, but Frenette's support was greater with the more urban voters and he had virtually no support from rural residents. The landslide nature of McKenna's victory was a function of his stranglehold on rural voters, more than 90 percent of whom supported him.

The last place finisher at the 1998 New Brunswick Liberal convention was also extremely weak with rural voters. Outside his home county, Bernard Richard's support was almost twice as strong in urban areas. As we discussed in Chapter 3, an urban base was not much of an asset in New Brunswick leadership elections. Most of the winners were from rural areas, and on three occasions the victor was not the choice of urban New Brunswick. In contrast, on every occasion the successful leadership candidate was also the choice of a majority of rural New Brunswickers.

### Discussion and Conclusions

The earlier suggestion that there is a polarization between Canada's major urban centres and the rest of the country does not completely depict the Maritime reality. Nonetheless, our look at twenty-five leadership elections reveals that urban-rural distinctions are central to Maritime politics and that divisions of this sort can be found among electorates in all parties and provinces.[8] As we saw in Chapter 3, the candidates popular in the major urban centres are not necessarily those most likely to win a party's leadership. The concentration of media, particularly the electronic media, in urban centres may well provide a somewhat unrealistic view of the strength of urban candidates both to the province at large and to the candidates themselves. The exception to the general pattern was the Nova Scotia NDP, which once again emerged as distinctive. Just as that party differed from its provincial counterparts with respect to religiously based "friendship" patterns, so it differed in its more urban nature. Chapter 3 demonstrates that the Nova Scotian NDP leadership electorates were predominantly urban and, thus, that it was possible for an urban base to provide the foundation for victory for NDP elections in a way that it did not for Liberal or Conservative elections.[9]

Some of the urban-rural differences we found in Table 6.2 increased our appreciation of the neighbourhood effect. For some candidates, like Gerard Mitchell, Joe Day, and Alan Buchanan, their disproportionate support from either urban or rural voters was largely driven by their neighbours. Once we controlled for this feature, the split was not so strong. On the other hand, for candidates such as Barry Clark, Don Downe, Keith Milligan, John Hamm, Ray Frenette, John MacDonell, and Bernard Richard, the impact of community size existed independently of the neighbourhood effect. The pull of geography on those who vote in Maritime leadership elections, be they conventions or universal ballots, goes beyond the ubiquitous neighbourhood effect.

The salience of urban-rural cleavages in some leadership elections, and the greater success of candidates based in rural areas, must be understood within the unique Maritime context. In Canada, the 2001 census showed that only 20 percent of the population was rural. By contrast, 47 percent of

Maritimers live in a rural setting. Applying the rural definition of Statistics Canada, we see that the three Maritime provinces are the most rural in the country; however, even that does not fully capture the rural nature of the region. Hodge and Quadeer, in their study of towns and villages in Canada, found that 40 percent of the 9,500 small communities in Canada were in the Atlantic region, even though it has only 11 percent of the total population.[10]

The first post-Confederation premier of Nova Scotia, William Annand, once commented that the City of Halifax was not the Province of Nova Scotia, and in studying the Maritimes today, a similar viewpoint must be adopted. One must not assume that the urban areas are as dominant as they seem to be elsewhere in the country, and one must be very wary of any attempt to extrapolate from their environs to the region as a whole. Contrary to general perception, the urban areas in the Maritimes are, electorally, secondary actors.[11] In the Maritimes, it is quite possible to win elections without carrying the major urban areas. The 2004 Nova Scotia election highlights this point, as John Hamm and the Conservatives were re-elected with a solid minority government, despite gathering only 30 percent of the votes in metro Halifax and winning just three of the seventeen seats there. Indeed, the fact that Halifax, by far the largest city in the Maritimes, contains just 33 percent of the seats in the Nova Scotia legislature illustrates the electoral dominance of rural areas.

Politics in such a rural setting has a number of rather specific features. Hodge and Quadeer indicate that "in the public mind, towns and villages and the countryside have come to be associated with intimate social relations and with a more healthful way of life."[12] While the more healthful way of life is likely mythical, the more intimate social relations are politically important. Hodge and Quadeer go on to note three important parts of this social intimacy, the first of which is visibility: in small "towns and villages almost everybody can be seen, on the main street or in the supermarket: similarly in a somnolent village street the few comings and goings cannot help being observed. Mutual acquaintances, familiar faces and the visibility of daily routines are staples of living in small communities."[13] In such small settings, political elites are highly visible, their strengths and weaknesses relatively common knowledge. Residents of small towns and villages are well placed to evaluate such individuals.

The second feature of life in small towns is what Hodge and Quadeer call "an ethos of mutual help."[14] In a similar vein, Bollman and Biggs point out that "smaller centres possess a greater sense of community then the less socially cohesive 'big city.'"[15] In essence, not only are individuals well known, but the pervading sense of community might well include helping your neighbour at the ballot box. Hodge and Quadeer define the final feature as personalized decision making: "Important functionaries are personally well known to residents and they are approached on that basis even for routine matters."[16] Add to this Clark's claim, based on the General Social Survey of 2003, that "people living in smaller communities also are more likely to have a feeling of belonging."[17]

Such features have obvious links to the neighbourhood effect we discussed earlier. Given these factors, one would expect the neighbourhood effect to be substantially stronger for candidates from more rural areas. This is indeed the case. When we dissect the neighbourhood boost by distinguishing between candidates from the major urban centres (Halifax, Saint John, Moncton, Fredericton, and Charlottetown) and the candidates from more rural areas, we see clear and statistically significant differences (see Table 6.3). "Metropolitan" voters were certainly supportive of local candidates. On average, the support for these thirty-four candidates was almost ten percentage points higher among their neighbours. However, this figure pales in comparison to the boost received by more rural candidates.[18] Their support from their neighbours was fully 26 percentage points higher than it was elsewhere. Moreover, while only 45 percent of the candidates came from the major urban centres, 70 percent of the candidates who did not receive a neighbourhood boost had such origins. The ethos of mutual help was certainly working well for candidates from rural areas.

In smaller communities, then, candidates likely benefit from enhanced visibility, an ethos of mutual help, and a strong sense of community. Moreover, the personalized decision-making style helps assure ordinary citizens, or delegates, that they will be able to approach their neighbour on this basis in the future. Not only can supporting one of your own be based on a shared sense of community or a desire for some sort of reflected glory, but the expectation of being able to deal more personally with that individual on relevant matters, of having a friend at court, is also important. If "your" candidate is victorious, the scope of issues on which this kind of special access can be used is broadened.

*Table 6.3*

**Maritime candidates (major only): urban-rural background by neighbourhood boost**

|  | Boost | | |
| --- | --- | --- | --- |
|  | Mean | Minimum | Maximum |
| Major urban candidates | 10.1 | −24 | 71 |
| Rural candidates | 26.7 | −3 | 79 |
| All candidates | 19.2 | −24 | 79 |

*Note:* Difference of means significant at < .001.

The geographic patterns of support at Maritime conventions point to the continued existence of a "distinct" Maritime political society, one marked by the arrangements and divisions typical of a region of small towns and villages. The perceptions of change suggest that the small-town nature of the Maritimes has not been given the attention it deserves.[19] The majority of Maritimers continue to reside in small towns and villages, and this fact is consequential in the region's politics. The rural nature of the region likely affects the role religion plays in politics since, as Clark points out, "rural and small town Canadians have traditionally attended religious services more frequently than people living in big cities ... In smaller communities, religious organizations are a significant contributor to local social and cultural life."[20]

Metropolitan academics and journalists may focus on changes in urban areas (perhaps because they are the main destination of the relatively few outsiders who come to the region),[21] but these are far from the Maritime norm. It is thus quite dangerous to extrapolate from such areas (in, for example, support for the NDP) to the region in general. Understanding political competition in the Maritimes requires a focus on small towns and villages. As Dasgupta explains in reference to national data, "significant differences continue to persist in almost every sphere of social and cultural life. The different environments of rural and urban Canada continue to produce different behaviours and attitudes."[22] As in 1867, the City of Halifax is not the Province of Nova Scotia. Nor, for that matter, is Saint John equivalent to New Brunswick, or Charlottetown to PEI. Rural communities remain home to large proportions of Maritimes, and woe betide the Maritime leadership candidate who fails to travel the secondary highways and the back roads in search of votes.

# 7
# Brothers and Sisters? Gender-Based Voting at Party Conventions

Our discussion of convention behaviour has thus far focused on the seemingly primordial cleavages of religion, ethnicity, and territory. Yet even those votes cast for friends and/or neighbours needed, in some sense, to be primed. Recall that, when several candidates were from the same part of the province (as in the 1991 Nova Scotia Progressive Conservative race), the neighbourhood influence was considerably diminished. Recall, as well, that when all candidates were of the same religious faith (as in the 1978 Prince Edward Island Liberal contest), the friendship effect could be entirely eliminated. Thus, the fact that sex has only been weakly associated with voting behaviour at Maritime leadership conventions (as revealed in Table 5.1) must be approached with some interpretive caution. Perhaps considerations of gender have genuinely been inconsequential for the vast majority of Maritime party activists. But perhaps a potentially significant sex cleavage has effectively been suppressed by the nature of Maritime leadership contests. To be made manifest, any social cleavage requires a contextual cue.[1] As Brodie suggests in her analysis of the gender factor in national conventions: "Political constituencies rarely exist as independent factions in electoral contests. They are created and structured by the appeals of the candidates and the range of choices on the ballot."[2] Thus, where leadership candidates not only are of the same gender but also speak as one (when they speak at all) on gender-related issues, it would be very surprising for male and female voters to diverge sharply. In fact, for nineteen of the twenty-five conventions in our data set, all the leadership aspirants were men. Nevertheless, this chapter demonstrates that, where appropriately primed not only by the presence of a credible female candidate but also by a competitive contest, an otherwise latent gender cleavage can easily rise to the surface.

Research on the impact of gender in Maritime politics is limited. However, national research has demonstrated that Canadian men and women differ politically. For example, men have been shown, on a number of measures, to be more politically active than are women.[3] Similarly, a gender gap

Table 7.1

**Canadian candidates (female only): first ballot vote by sex**

| Year | Jurisdiction | Party | Candidate | Vote (%) | | |
|------|--------------|-------|-----------|----------|---|---|
| | | | | Female | Male | Gap |
| 1976 | Canada | PC | Flora Macdonald | 14 | 10 | 4 |
| 1986 | BC | Social Credit | Kim Campbell | 3 | 2 | 1 |
| 1986 | BC | Social Credit | Grace McCarthy | 21 | 16 | 5 |
| 1989 | Canada | NDP | Audrey McLaughlin | 45 | 21 | 24 |
| 1990 | Canada | Liberal | Sheila Copps | 13 | 11 | 2 |
| 1992 | Alberta | PC | Nancy Betkowski | 46 | 30 | 16 |
| 1993 | Canada | PC | Kim Campbell | 57 | 46 | 11 |
| 1994 | Alberta | NDP | Clancy Teslenko | 14 | 7 | 7 |

has also been readily apparent in Canada on a range of political issues, with men typically evincing more hawkish, more individualistic, and more market-oriented attitudes than do women. One observer nicely summarized these differences as "Economic Man – Social Woman."[4] Men and women have also been shown to diverge in their voting behaviour. In the elections immediately prior to 1993, women typically favoured the Liberal party by a small amount; men, to a corresponding extent, were marginally more likely to back the New Democratic Party and Progressive Conservative party. The breakdown of the third party system[5] somewhat sharpened Canada's gender contradictions. While the 2000 Canadian Election Study found no voting differences between men and women in the Province of Quebec (where the Alliance party was not a significant player), a different story emerged elsewhere. In English Canada, 32.7 percent of men, but only 21.5 percent of women, voted Alliance.[6]

When one shifts the level of analysis from the party to the individual candidate, however, the available evidence becomes much sketchier. Admittedly, some analysts have professed to have uncovered no differences in the relative vote-winning capacities of male and female candidates (at least none after the introduction of controls for party label, incumbency, previous voting patterns, and so on). Hence, Heather MacIvor claims that "there is no evidence to support the belief that voters will not vote for women. In fact, some observers now believe that women have a slight electoral advantage because they represent a change from the old boys who have always run Western political systems."[7]

Yet even if male and female candidates are equally popular with the Canadian electorate (and studies in the United Kingdom and Australia have replicated this finding),[8] it does not follow that male and female voters within that electorate are behaving in an identical fashion. On the contrary, there may be countervailing trends, with men and women being attracted to the same extent by candidates of their own gender and likewise being repelled to the same extent by candidates of the other gender. Identity politics of the sort hypothesized here typically have both a cognitive and an affective component. With respect to the former, Johnson et al. note that "it is entirely reasonable to ask how much like oneself the political agent is. The more an agent resembles oneself the more he or she might be expected reflexively to understand and act on one's own interests."[9] Or, as Sheila Copps succinctly puts it: "You expect farmers to speak for farmers. Women should speak for women."[10]

Identity politics are not merely the product of rational calculations of self-interest; they are also rooted in the emotional bonds forged from a shared sense of community. Do these cognitive and affective forces exist within each gender? And can they underlie voting behaviour? A number of American scholars have attempted to answer this question experimentally. Surveys taken throughout the 1960s probed American willingness to vote for a hypothetical female presidential candidate. Somewhat surprisingly, men were 6 percent more likely than were women to do so, although this gap had essentially vanished by the early 1970s.[11] More controlled experiments, in which large numbers of university students were asked to choose between different pairs of hypothetical candidates, produced some startling results. Sigelman and Sigelman, for example, discovered that 61.5 percent of the white females in their study (but only 39.6 percent of the white males) were prepared to vote for a white, middle-aged female over a white, middle-aged male. Gender affinities could only be pushed so far, however, as white females tended to prefer hypothetical white male candidates to their equally fictional black female counterparts.[12] Other studies also emphasized the importance of candidate sex as a basis of voting choice. Hence, Ekstrand and Eckert concluded that female voters "exhibited a bias in favour of the liberal leaning candidate when the contestant was a woman,"[13] while Hedlund et al. discovered that women were statistically more likely than were men to vote for hypothetical female office-seekers (although not, intriguingly, when the candidate was depicted as the mother of small children).[14]

Initial attempts to replicate these experimental findings in the real world of American electoral politics proved to be difficult. One analysis of the 1982 mid-term elections discovered that a link existed between female voters and female candidates only when the former were self-identified Independents and the latter were perceived to be supporting issues that were "important" to women; otherwise, the votes of men and women were "not a major reflection of the sex of the candidate."[15] In the 1990s, however, this connection became much stronger. With a larger pool of female candidates and with the Republican Party campaigning on a coded commitment to "family values,"

American voters were increasingly sensitized to the politics of gender identity. After uncovering a statistically significant tendency for women voters to back women candidates, Plutzer and Zipp ominously suggested that "the existence of identity politics represents a threat to the current party system and may play a pivotal role in deciding electoral outcomes."[16]

Canadian analysts of this phenomenon have generally come to less apocalyptic conclusions. Most researchers have focused on the gender of party leaders. In the 1993 federal election, two of the five major parties had female leaders (Kim Campbell of the PCs and Audrey McLaughlin of the NDP); although both parties suffered electoral reverses in 1993, they did manage, according to Brenda O'Neill, to enjoy "substantially higher rates of recruitment among women voters than among men."[17] Nor does grouping the 1993 and 1997 elections together alter the conclusion. According to Fred Cutler, Canadian voters during this period "were less likely to support a party whose leader was of the opposite sex."[18] Given that impressions of local candidates are part of the voting calculus of some Canadians,[19] it would be surprising if only the gender of party leaders had left any imprint on the data.

Clearly, gender-based voting exists. But would we anticipate this phenomenon to be more or less pronounced when attention shifts from the interparty struggle for election to the intraparty contest for leadership? On the one hand, those who participate in leadership conventions are manifestly more interested and engaged in the political process than are their counterparts in general elections. As a result, one might surmise that leadership voters would be less likely to rely on what Fred Cutler has dubbed "the simplest shortcut of all"; that is, the electoral cue provided by a shared demographic attribute. On the other hand, many observers have noted that, in regular elections, the tugs of party and of gender can pull the voter in different directions, with the former often trumping the latter. In leadership races, however, no such cross-pressures exist; since all participants belong to the same party, any inclinations towards gender-based voting would remain unalloyed. Thus, our expectations about the prevalence of this phenomenon in leadership contests remain rather murky.

Fortunately, this question can be tested empirically. Table 7.1 focuses upon Canadian leadership conventions outside the Maritime provinces in which there was at least one woman candidate and about which survey data are readily available. In 1976, Flora Macdonald became the first woman seriously to seek the leadership of a national party (the Progressive Conservatives), and her campaign bore the indelible imprint of that fact. Thus, Macdonald confidante "Fast Eddie" Goodman importuned male convention delegates to make their wives "happy" and vote for Flora.[20] As can be seen from Table 7.1, female leadership aspirants after Macdonald invariably received a greater share of the votes from the female, as opposed to the male, portion of the electorate. Admittedly, the differences are relatively small in some cases. Both men and women, for example, regarded Kim Campbell's 1986 candidacy for the leadership of the British Columbia Social Credit Party as a hopeless cause. Similarly, the small gender gap for Sheila Copps in 1990 may have been rooted in a campaign that "was not explicitly feminist in message."[21] In contrast, the sizable sex cleavages apparent in Table 7.1 in the support patterns of Nancy Betkowski in 1992 and Kim Campbell in 1993 can be attributed to the fact that, in both instances, sex became a centrepiece of the leadership campaigns. In the former case, this occurred after backers of rival Ralph Klein bluntly raised doubts about whether, as a woman, Betkowski could be an effective premier of Alberta.[22] As for Campbell, her explicit self-identification as a "feminist," in conjunction with the frisson associated with selecting the country's first female prime minister, ensured that the sex of the candidate would not go unheeded by the Conservative delegates.

Nor is there any reason to suspect that the pattern of gender-based voting apparent in Table 7.1 would not have been reproduced at those Canadian leadership conventions contested by women but for which no survey data exist. Certainly, there is impressionistic evidence that, at least with respect to some of these contests, the issue of gender was much on the minds of party members. Thus, when Rosemary Brown exceeded most observers' expectations at the 1975 national New Democratic Party convention, former leader Tommy Douglas attributed her showing to "a sort of prejudice in reverse," a determination on the part of rank-and-file members to display that they were not biased against blacks or women.[23] Similarly, when Sheila Copps (described at the time as "some jumped-up combination of Jayne Mansfield and Joan of Arc") sought the leadership of the Ontario Liberals in 1982, one observer claimed that delegates were confronted with a "simple" question: "Will the voters of Ontario in 1985 choose a government led by a 32-year-old woman, albeit an attractive, intelligent one?"[24] Finally, Alexa McDonough's candidacy for the 1995 national New Democratic Party leadership was haunted by the fact that the departing leader, Audrey McLaughlin, had been both a woman and an electoral liability. Confronting the issue head-on, McDonough chose as her slogan: "Two is not too many."[25] In all of these instances, delegates were obliged to view the leadership contest at least partially through the prism of gender; some degree of gender-based voting likely ensued.

What, then, has been the pattern in Maritime leadership contests? At nineteen of our twenty-five conventions, only male candidates sought the leadership; as a result, matters of gender were sublimated. Certainly, the media coverage of these contests did not bring this latent cleavage to the fore. Women's voices were typically only heard in human interest stories about candidates' wives. Some of these women were presented as openly non-political: Julie McKenna, for example, asserted, "I'd rather be married to a plumber,"[26] while Wilma Clements confided, "I leave the politics to Gilbert."[27] Other candidates' wives clearly played a more active role in their husbands' campaigns. Thus, the attentive reader was informed that Diane Lord was a "petite blonde" who was "an incredible political asset" due to her skill at working a crowd,[28] while Lois Gass was said to be ready to be the wife of PEI's opposition leader but was actually "aspiring to be the wife of the next premier."[29] Substantive women's issues were almost entirely absent from the campaign discourse of the nineteen Maritime contests in which there were only male contenders. Rollie Thornhill's commitment, made during the 1991 Nova Scotia Progressive Conservative contest, that he would bring more women into cabinet and the senior civil service and that he would make it a "priority" to ensure that women's issues would be "dealt with by a sensitive and compassionate government"[30] represents a partial exception to this generalization. On the other hand, Thornhill may simply have been responding to the fact that, at the campaign's outset, Donald Cameron and Tom McInnis were attracting the most attention from Progressive Conservative women.[31]

Under such circumstances, it is not surprising that the gender cleavage in voting behaviour was not statistically significant in seventeen of the nineteen conventions that had only male candidates.[32] Indeed, it is the two exceptions to the rule (the 1982 and the 2002 leadership contests of the New Brunswick Liberals) that require closer scrutiny. Why anti-establishment candidate Jack MacDougall in 2002 would receive the backing of 18 percent more female than male delegates remains mysterious, but at least the 1982 data are more explicable. During that race, the New Brunswick Advisory Council on the Status of Women took the unusual step of distributing a voting guide to delegates. While not mentioning any candidates by name, the pamphlet did contrast some "common attitudes" that men purportedly assume towards women, ranging from "cavalier" to "sensitive and aware."[33] Irrespective of front-runner Doug Young's other virtues, most observers would have placed him closer to the former than to the latter end of such a continuum. This, after all, was a candidate who urged Premier Hatfield's Acadian lieutenant Jean-Maurice Simard to "think seriously about the fact he is seated in the Legislature next to a man who collects dolls,"[34] who had openly acknowledged his ambition and aggression, and who had been characterized as "a go-for-the-jugular Tough Guy."[35] Perhaps cued by the Advisory Council's guide, 15 percent fewer women than men cast their votes for Doug Young.

For our purposes, those Maritime leadership conventions that had both male and female contenders are of greater interest than are those that had only male contenders. As Table 7.2 reveals, those six contests tell what is, by now, a familiar story. In every instance, female candidates received a disproportionate share of their vote from the female section of the electorate. Yet at only half of these conventions was the sex cleavage statistically significant – a finding that seems to be rooted in the different competitive positions of the women candidates. In those instances where the prospects of the female aspirants were widely regarded either as hopeless (Deborah Kelly-Hawkes, Margaret Ann Blaney) or as unassailable (Catherine Callbeck), the gender gap did not approach statistical significance. At the other three conventions (intriguingly, all featuring the Nova Scotia New Democratic Party), the presence of women candidates in relatively more competitive circumstances served to prime the sex cleavage. A second look at Table 7.1 suggests that a similar phenomenon may have been at work in conventions outside the Maritimes. Of course, factors other than the competitive context sensitized Nova Scotia New Democrats to the importance of gender at these three conventions. In 1980, for example, Alexa McDonough was bidding to become the first female party leader in Canada, and media coverage of the event unconsciously reflected this fact. In one account of the three candidates, Len Arsenault was characterized as a "teacher," Buddy MacEachern as "outspoken," and Alexa McDonough as "attractive."[36] Indeed, one columnist enthused that McDonough was "pretty enough to catch the eye of any man at 100 yards."[37] Sixteen years later, as the appendix details, New Democratic delegates were jolted by Yvonne Atwell's allegation that she had been victimized during the campaign by "sexism."[38] And, at the 2000 convention, the gender conflicts were rendered explicit after the second ballot, when departing candidate Maureen MacDonald chose to crown a queen rather than a king, despite the fact that fellow MLA Kevin Deveaux had overtaken Helen MacDonald on the second ballot. Helen MacDonald secured the party leadership on the third ballot.

Even leaving aside voting behaviour, support for politicians of the same gender is apparent in our data. Since 1995, our surveys have typically asked respondents to identify the national leader of their party (past or present) with whom they feel the greatest affinity. As Table 7.3 makes clear, male and female New Democrats have differed sharply on this measure. For women, a strong affinity to Alexa McDonough is apparent; men, by contrast, tend to prefer Tommy Douglas (although Ed Broadbent's star has been rising in the most recent surveys). Respondents were also asked about past and present provincial leaders, and Table 7.4 reproduces these data. Again, a clear pattern emerges. Female New Democrats felt the greatest affinity with Alexa McDonough (in her previous incarnation as provincial party leader), while the men were relatively more inclined to identify with Robert Chisholm. What is particularly interesting in Tables 7.3 and 7.4 is that Alexa McDonough's appeal to women existed independently of whether there

*Table 7.2*

**Maritime candidates (female only): vote by sex**

| | Year | Jurisdiction | Party | Candidate | Vote (%) | | | Ratio of male to female vote | d/sigma d* |
|---|---|---|---|---|---|---|---|---|---|
| | | | | | Female | Male | Gap | | |
| First ballot | 1980 | NS | NDP | Alexa McDonough | 87.1 | 76.3 | 10.8 | 1.14 | 2.06 |
| | 1993 | PEI | Liberal | Catherine Callbeck | 89.0 | 87.9 | 1.1 | 1.01 | 0.53 |
| | 1996 | NS | NDP | Yvonne Atwell | 34.8 | 10.3 | 24.5 | 3.37 | 4.01 |
| | 1997 | NB | PC | Margaret Ann Blaney | 11.9 | 9.1 | 2.8 | 1.30 | 0.98 |
| | 2000 | NS | NDP | Helen MacDonald | 34.9 | 29.7 | 5.2 | 1.17 | 3.63 |
| | | | | Maureen MacDonald | 33.6 | 18.7 | 14.9 | | |
| | 2002 | PEI | NDP | Deborah Kelly-Hawkes | 4.3 | 0 | 4.3 | 1.80 | 0.79 |
| Second ballot | 2000 | NS | NDP | Helen MacDonald | 34.2 | 29.5 | 4.7 | NA | 2.46 |
| | | | | Maureen MacDonald | 35.6 | 26.9 | 8.7 | | |
| Third ballot | 2000 | NS | NDP | Helen MacDonald | 66.0 | 46.5 | 19.5 | 1.16 | 3.49 |

* Any d/sigma d over 1.96 is statistically significant.

were credible female contenders (Nova Scotia 1996 and 2000), whether there was only a fringe aspirant (PEI 2002), or whether women candidates were entirely absent (Nova Scotia 2002). Only in the latter two contests, however, did the inclination to gender-based voting remain latent.

This phenomenon merits closer scrutiny. Recall that candidates' gender had a statistically significant influence on voting choice at the 1980, 1996, and 2000 conventions of the Nova Scotia NDP. What distinguished the female delegates who backed a female candidate from those who did not? Unfortunately, the 1980 convention must be excluded from the analysis since the number of respondents in the latter category is in the single digits. Nevertheless, the findings from 1996 and 2000, as revealed in Table 7.5, are illuminating. In contrast to those who vote for men, New Democratic women who vote for female candidates tend to be long-standing party members, tend to perceive themselves as left wing, and are less inclined to see the NDP, in Walter Young's well-known dichotomy,[39] as more of a political party

Table 7.3

**Maritime NDP leadership elections: national leader affinity by sex**

|  | 1996 NS NDP | | 2000 NS NDP | | 2002 NS NDP | | 2002 PEI NDP | |
|---|---|---|---|---|---|---|---|---|
|  | Female | Male | Female | Male | Female | Male | Female | Male |
| McDonough | 60.3% | 26.8% | 47.3% | 22.0% | 47.2% | 26.8% | 42.9% | 13.0% |
| Douglas | 24.1% | 48.8% | 31.0% | 48.0% | 28.4% | 37.9% | 28.6% | 30.4% |
| Other | 15.5% | 24.6% | 21.7% | 30.0% | 24.4% | 35.3% | 28.5% | 56.6% |
| $N =$ | 58 | 82 | 129 | 150 | 218 | 224 | 21 | 23 |
| $\chi^2$ | < .01 | | < .01 | | < .01 | | < .05 | |

Table 7.4

**Nova Scotia NDP leadership elections: provincial leader affinity by sex**

|  | 2000 NS NDP | | 2002 NS NDP | |
|---|---|---|---|---|
|  | Female | Male | Female | Male |
| Chisholm | 36.8% | 49.7% | 21.9% | 40.9% |
| McDonough | 56.6% | 41.2% | 70.5% | 51.1% |
| Other | 6.6% | 9.1% | 7.6% | 8.0% |
| $N =$ | 136 | 153 | 224 | 225 |
| $\chi^2$ | < .05 | | < .01 | |

than a social movement. For such a woman voter, backing a female candidate was seemingly perceived to be part of a wider political project of equality and social justice. Nevertheless, Table 7.5 also indicates the importance placed on the "appealing" personal characteristics of the female candidate. Taken together, this evidence is perfectly consistent with the melange of cognitive and affective considerations that typically underlie identity politics.

One final manifestation of gender-based voting is apparent in our data set. Recall that when Maureen MacDonald was eliminated after the second ballot of the 2000 Nova Scotia New Democratic Party convention, she opted to throw her support behind Helen MacDonald rather than Kevin Deveaux. Generally speaking, Maureen MacDonald's delegates followed her lead on the third ballot. But Table 7.6 reveals an interesting division: many more of her male backers "defected" to Kevin Deveaux on the convention's final ballot. Even among Maureen MacDonald's female second ballot supporters, an intriguing cleavage is apparent. Despite the tiny sample size, Table 7.7 reveals a statistically significant relationship between personal affinity to female national party leaders and third ballot voting behaviour. In other words, the small coterie of female backers of Maureen MacDonald who did not follow their champion's lead on the convention's final ballot were notably atypical in their relative lack of affinity for Alexa McDonough and Audrey McLaughlin.

What, then, can be concluded from this analysis? First, gender-based voting has undeniably been a political reality at Maritime leadership contests. When properly cued by the presence of a viable female candidate within a genuinely competitive context, male and female party members have made

*Table 7.5*

**Nova Scotia NDP leadership elections (women only): vote by selected attributes**

| Variable | Value | Voted for female | Voted for male | $\chi^2$ |
|---|---|---|---|---|
| Length of party membership | 5 years or less | 27.5% | 47.7% | < .01 |
| Self-ascribed political views | Left | 30.8% | 19.3% | < .10 |
| Perception of NDP | More party than movement | 20.2% | 31.5% | < .10 |
| First reason for first ballot vote | Personal characteristics appealing | 16.8% | 2.2% | < .01 |
| *N* | | 120 | 89 | |

*Table 7.6*

---

**Nova Scotia NDP leadership election, 2000 (Maureen MacDonald voters only): third ballot vote by sex**

|  | Female | Male |
|---|---|---|
| Kevin Deveaux | 17.3% | 36.6% |
| Helen MacDonald | 82.6% | 63.4% |
| N | 52 | 41 |

$\chi^2 < .05$

*Table 7.7*

---

**Nova Scotia NDP leadership election, 2000 (Maureen MacDonald female voters only): third ballot vote by national leader affinity**

|  | Greatest affinity for Alexa McDonough or Audrey McLaughlin | Greatest affinity for male national leader | N |
|---|---|---|---|
| Voted for Kevin Deveaux on third ballot | 11.1% | 88.9% | 9 |
| Voted for Helen MacDonald on third ballot | 51.2% | 48.8% | 43 |

$\chi^2 < .05$

sharply divergent electoral choices. There is no reason to doubt that similar studies elsewhere in Canada would uncover the same phenomenon. It is noteworthy, however, that all three of the cases where gender identity was appropriately primed (and, thus, where men and women differed significantly in their voting behaviour) involved the Nova Scotia New Democratic Party. At first glance, this pattern might seem surprising. After all, the New Democratic Party has long been in the forefront in the struggle for sexual equality, and both male and female adherents likely share in this commitment. On the other hand, that very commitment is likely to induce women to seek the leadership of the New Democratic Party and, accordingly, to jump-start the emergence of gender-based voting. Moreover, it seems likely that there are a higher proportion of feminists among NDP women than there are among their counterparts in other parties. If so, New Democratic women are particularly apt to attach a wider meaning (both symbolic and substantive) to the election of a female party leader and to vote accordingly. Therefore, it is not coincidental that much of this chapter is devoted to leadership politics in the New Democratic Party. The party that has arguably the greatest allegiance to sexual equality is the party that is most likely to be riven by sexual differences in voting behaviour.

Second, while the pattern of gender-based voting is clear, the underlying process is not. Without a single exception, female leadership candidates (both inside and outside the Maritimes) have received a disproportionate share of their votes from women voters. But is this a function of attraction (to a candidate of one's own sex), repellence (away from a candidate of the opposite sex), or both? Are men and women equally attracted to aspirants with whom they happen to have a common chromosomal composition (and equally repelled by those with whom they do not)? One might reasonably surmise that the frequency of all-male fields in the past has served, over time, to moderate the reactions of both men and women voters to male candidates. By this logic, neither men's attraction to, nor women's repellence from, male candidates should be especially strong. By contrast, the relatively more uncommon entry of a woman contender might serve to heighten the responses of both genders, with female voters being especially enthused and their male counterparts being decidedly put off by a female candidate. But this is mere conjecture; without firmer empirical footing, attempts to adduce any electoral advantage from the presence of a sex cleavage in the electorate should be avoided.[40]

Finally, it is worth considering the likely role of the gender cleavage at future Maritime conventions. That women will seek leadership positions with more frequency in the future than they have in the past seems self-evident. What is less clear, however, is whether or not this will ultimately encourage voters to disregard, or at least to downplay, considerations of candidate gender as a basis for electoral choice. Much depends, presumably, on whether gender identity politics remain commonplace in other social settings. If so – and this seems to be a reasonable surmise – the heretofore largely sublimated tugs of "brothers" and "sisters" may come to rival the more established claims of "friends" and "neighbours" at Maritime leadership conventions.

# 8
# Inter- and Intraparty Attitudinal Differences

Traditionally, little controversy has attended the role of ideology in Maritime politics. If there was one thing upon which the academy was united, it was the irrelevance of ideology to politics in the region. According to Dyck, "one would look in vain for any consistent ideological differences between the Liberals and Conservatives,"[1] while Wearing maintains that "neither ideology nor major policy questions have much to do with party lines – the last big issue to divide Liberals and Conservatives was that of entering Confederation over a hundred years ago."[2] Similarly, the three major historic accounts of Maritime politics – Beck's *The Government of Nova Scotia*, MacKinnon's *The Government of Prince Edward Island*, and Thorburn's *Politics in New Brunswick* – all conclude that parties do not differ ideologically and that differences in voting choice cannot be established on that basis.

Some of our previous work questioned these assumptions. We noted that the supporting evidence was far from overwhelming and we used data from candidate studies, leadership conventions, and public opinion soundings in Nova Scotia to test the conventional wisdom. Our analysis suggested that "ideological differences between the Liberals and Progressive Conservative parties are in fact apparent at several levels of analysis."[3]

Controversy also exists regarding the role of ideology in leadership elections. Of the media's role in conventions, Fletcher concludes: "Meaningful policy debate has been largely abandoned."[4] However, works by Krause and Leduc as well as Johnston suggest that opinions on issues influence voting behaviour and are highly salient in understanding the outcome of leadership elections.[5] Work on the Maritimes, within this context, has been limited, but earlier work by Stewart indicates that such "divisions were seldom associated with voting in any structured fashion."[6]

In this chapter, we look for attitudinal differences among the parties in the three provinces as well as for provincial differences and change over time. We follow this with a discussion of how party delegates and leadership voters relate to key political concepts. In the final portion of the chapter we discuss intraparty attitudinal differences as they relate to voting choice. We expect to find evidence of difference between the parties in terms of ideology but not so much in the way of ideologically structured voting divisions. These expectations are largely borne out as our analysis provides evidence of partisan differences in the collections of attitudes held by participants in leadership elections. We also found that intraparty differences of opinion on political issues were only occasionally associated with candidate choice in a significant or coherent manner.

Unlike the socio-demographic data we present in earlier chapters, the attitudinal questions asked of voters in our twenty-five surveys vary considerably. Some questions were asked with great regularity in early surveys and then essentially disappeared. Others emerged later and continued to be asked, while still others were only asked in a handful of elections. As well, the questions asked of delegates and voters usually include some specific references to the province and the time in which the election was held. In this chapter, we do not examine questions of this sort; rather, we look mainly at issues addressed either throughout the three-decade time period or for some substantial portion of that period.

We begin by looking at the self-placement of voters on a five-point ideological scale – a question asked regularly since 1992. We follow this up with questions relating to the role of government and the scope of its activities. These include questions on the regulation of foreign capital, whether social programs should be universal, and whether governments should always balance their budgets. We then look at answers to questions that probe the importance of unions for democracy and views on the free trade agreement. Questions relating to the expansion of provincial powers and the recognition of Quebec as a distinct society are also examined. We conclude by looking at views on patronage. As our analysis shows, it is possible to differentiate among the region's three parties in a number of areas.

Our first look at how one might ideologically distinguish Maritime parties is based on a question first asked of voters in the Nova Scotia Liberal tele-vote of 1992 and repeated in eleven of the twelve surveys subsequently conducted. This question asked voters to place themselves on a five-point scale, ranging from left, to left-centre, to centre, to centre-right, and, finally, to right. As Figure 8.1 indicates, this scale proved quite useful in distinguishing members of the three parties.

An examination of Figure 8.1 (with 0 representing "left" and 4 representing "right") shows modest polarization among the region's parties. The scores range from 0.54 for the Nova Scotia New Democrats in 1996 to a high of 2.55 for the Nova Scotia Conservatives in 1995. Calculating the mean scores for the three parties (see Table 8.1) produces an average of 0.90 for the New Democrats, 1.94 for the Liberals, and 2.38 for the Progressive Conservatives. Statistical tests for differences of mean proved significant, providing

*Figure 8.1*

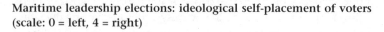

**Maritime leadership elections: ideological self-placement of voters (scale: 0 = left, 4 = right)**

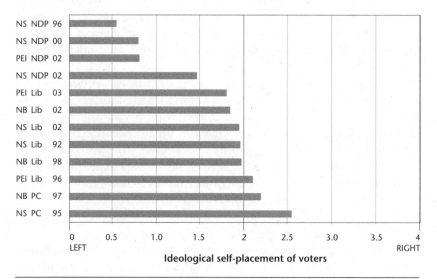

Ideological self-placement of voters

*Table 8.1*

**Maritime leadership elections: attitudes by party**

|  | NDP | Liberal | PC |
|---|---|---|---|
| Self-placement*+ | 0.90 | 1.94 | 2.38 |
| Right to regulate foreign capital* | 94% | 82% | 76% |
| Social programs should be universal* | 98% | 87% | 76% |
| Governments should always balance budgets* | 34% | 76% | 74% |
| Unions are essential to democracy*+ | 91% | 62% | 43% |
| Free trade has been beneficial*+ | 13% | 40% | 75% |
| Provincial power should be expanded*+ | 38% | 45% | 65% |
| Quebec should be recognized as a distinct society* | 64% | 35% | 33% |
| Patronage is a fact of life* | 54% | 71% | 76% |

\* Indicates that differences among the three parties are statistically significant.
+ Indicates that differences between the Liberals and Conservatives are statistically significant.

further evidence regarding the existence of ideological differences among Maritime parties.

The range among parties is also instructive. The two scores for Conservative parties are each higher than are any of the Liberal scores, and all of the Liberal scores are higher than are all those for the NDP. The trend for the Nova Scotia NDP is an interesting one as the self-placement of participants in their elections increases from 0.54 in 1996 to 0.79 in 2000 to 1.47 in 2002. We return to this subject in Chapter 13.

Both moderate polarization and partisan differences can also be seen when we look at opinions on the regulation of foreign capital (see Table 8.1).[7] Majorities from all parties believed that foreign capital in Canada needs regulation, but the divisions within the parties differ. Ninety-four percent of New Democrats believed in regulating foreign capital, but the percentage with that view fell to 82 percent among Liberals and 76 percent among Conservatives. There are no obvious patterns over time, and differences among the three provinces were not readily apparent on this measure. The opinions expressed by delegates and voters on this question suggest a general acceptance of government involvement in the economy that crosses partisan and provincial lines. The Conservatives, however, have the largest proportion of voters wary of such regulation.

This impression was again borne out when we asked delegates and voters (after 1986) whether social programs should remain universal. Virtually all New Democrats took this position (98 percent), as did 87 percent of Liberals and 76 percent of the Progressive Conservatives. All parties were in general agreement on the subject, and again there was little in the way of variation by province or over time. Nonetheless, the difference in the mean scores for the three parties was statistically significant, with Conservatives the least cohesive on the issue and the New Democrats the most united.

The New Democrats possessed less cohesion on whether governments should always balance their budgets. This question distinguished regional New Democrats from their counterparts in the Liberal and Conservative parties. While three-quarters of respondents from the traditional parties took this stance, only one-third of the New Democrats saw this as a requirement. This is one of the issues that showed some provincial variation as well, with the Liberals in New Brunswick and PEI being much more likely than their fellow partisans in Nova Scotia to see balanced budgets as essential.

Over time, we also see changes in perspective regarding whether governments should always balance their budgets, and these differences seem related to the political context. These differences are broken down by leadership election in Table 8.2. Following the actions of the Liberal government in PEI from 1993 to 1996, the percentage of Island Liberals believing the budget should always be balanced increased by seventeen points. In 2003, with the Liberals again in opposition, the percentage holding this view declined. Similarly, the New Brunswick Liberals in 2002, after four years in opposition, were no longer quite as convinced of the merits of balanced budgets as they had been in 1998. Support for balanced budgets increased within the Nova Scotia New Democrats from 26 percent in 1996 to 38 percent in 2002.

Questions relating to the role of trade unions in Canadian democracy returned New Democrats to near unanimity. Questions relating to unions or strikes were asked in seventeen of our surveys, and, on average, 91 percent of New Democrats agreed that unions were an important part of Canadian democracy (after 1986) and that there should not be limits on the right to strike (1986 and earlier). A tiny majority of Liberals (53 percent) held the same position, but only 43 percent of Conservatives did so. On the question of the right to strike, we note much wider differences between the Liberals and Conservatives on PEI (1976 and 1978) than we do in Nova Scotia (1971 and 1980). The differences between the Liberals and Conservatives on the essential role of unions in a democracy again produced statistically significant differences. On this issue, we detect little in the way of provincial variation or change over time.

With respect to free trade, however, we saw obvious differences among the three parties. While very few New Democrats saw free trade as having benefited their province, 40 percent of Liberals expressed the view that it had been beneficial and three-quarters of the Progressive Conservatives took that position.

Given the bitterly divisive federal election in 1988 on the subject of free trade with the United States, it is not surprising to see these sorts of divisions. It is noteworthy that the perspective of Liberals has changed on this issue over time. In 1986, 35 percent of Nova Scotia Liberals supported, in principle, the "idea" of free trade with the United States, but in 1992, after the federal Liberals campaigned against the agreement in 1988, only 8 percent of them felt the deal had been beneficial. And, in 1993, only 12 percent of Island Liberals took this position. However, the Liberal impressions of the benefits of free trade have improved over time, as most Liberals in recent elections now think the deal has been beneficial.

It may well be that, with federal Liberal governments effectively complicit in free trade since 1993, provincial Liberals no longer associate the agreement so closely with former Prime Minister Mulroney and are more likely to assess the agreement without the lens of partisanship. This is also an issue that is characterized by intraregional variation, at least within Liberal ranks. Positive evaluations of free trade by New Brunswick Liberals were consistently high. This may be because the provincial party disagreed with the stance taken by the federal party in 1988 or because we do not have data available on this issue prior to 1998.

The most commonly asked attitudinal question in our data set addresses provincial powers and whether or not provinces should have more power. This was an issue that placed the Liberals and New Democrats on one side and the Conservatives on the other. On average, 65 percent of Progressive Conservatives felt that provinces should have more power. This perspective was shared by only 45 percent of Liberals and 38 percent of New Democrats. The issue of provincial powers was also one that enabled us to observe differences based on province. Island Liberals, for instance, were more

*Table 8.2*

**Maritime leadership elections: agreement with selected attitudes (%)**

| Leadership election | Right to regulate foreign capital* | Social programs should be universal | Unions essential for democracy* | Government must balance budget | Free trade good for province | More power for province | Recognize Quebec as Distinct Society | Patronage is a fact of life |
|---|---|---|---|---|---|---|---|---|
| NS PC 1971 | 74 | | 35 | | | 64 | 23 | |
| PEI PC 1976 | 86 | | 40 | | | 65 | 15 | |
| PEI Lib 1978 | 89 | | 20 | | | 50 | 31 | |
| NS Lib 1980 | 84 | | 37 | | | 29 | 43 | |
| NS NDP 1980 | 88 | | 83 | | | 34 | | |
| PEI Lib 1981 | 64 | | | | | 33 | 24 | |
| PEI PC 1981 | 65 | | | | | 83 | 35 | |
| NB Lib 1982 | 86 | | | | | 26 | 26 | |
| NB Lib 1985 | 87 | | | | | 39 | 39 | |
| NS Lib 1986 | | | | | 35 | 43 | 26 | |
| PEI PC 1988 | | 79 | 52 | | 83 | | | 85 |
| NS PC 1991 | 75 | 64 | 43 | | 58 | 55 | | 72 |
| NS Lib 1992 | 89 | 83 | 66 | | 8 | 47 | | 66 |
| PEI Lib 1993 | 87 | 81 | 61 | 66 | 12 | 57 | | 86 |
| NS PC 1995 | 79 | 77 | | 66 | 68 | 59 | 45 | 71 |
| NS NDP 1996 | 97 | 96 | 96 | 26 | 4 | 24 | 75 | 47 |
| PEI Lib 1996 | 85 | 85 | 58 | 83 | 43 | 53 | 45 | 73 |
| NB PC 1997 | | 85 | | 81 | | 64 | 45 | |
| NB Lib 1998 | 81 | 89 | 59 | 88 | 56 | 62 | 50 | 84 |
| NS NDP 2000 | 95 | 97 | 92 | 33 | 19 | 40 | 67 | 53 |
| NS Lib 2002 | 72 | 86 | 56 | 62 | 60 | 36 | 28 | 82 |
| NB Lib 2002 | 80 | 94 | 64 | 77 | 58 | 51 | 41 | 73 |
| PEI NDP 2002 | 93 | 100 | 95 | 40 | 14 | 42 | 57 | 53 |
| NS NDP 2002 | 95 | 98 | 88 | 38 | 15 | 52 | 55 | 62 |
| PEI Lib 2003 | 83 | 94 | 67 | 78 | 54 | 60 | 36 | 87 |

* Indicates that wording for the question changed over time.

supportive of increased provincial powers than were their counterparts in Nova Scotia. Only in 1981 were a majority of Island Liberals opposed to expanding provincial powers, while a majority of Nova Scotia Liberals always opposed such an expansion. The New Brunswick Liberals offered majority support for more provincial power in 1998 but were significantly less enthusiastic in both 1982 and 1985. In 2002, the percentage expressing support for more provincial power was eleven percentage points below the 1998 figure. The position of the New Democrats in Nova Scotia on this issue also appears to change over time, and we see a dramatic increase in support for provincial power in 2002 when, for the first time, a majority expressed support for this option. This is, of course, also the first time the party allowed all members to vote for the leader, so we are unable to separate issues of timing from type of election.

Another thorny issue in Canadian federalism has been whether to recognize Quebec as a distinct society. This question was raised in twenty of our surveys, and the partisan differences are significant and striking. On average, 64 percent of New Democrats favoured such recognition. The corresponding figures for the Liberals and the Conservatives were 35 percent and 33 percent, respectively. Variations on this measure over time and within parties were noteworthy. Although those in favour of such recognition always remained a minority within the Conservative party, the minority grew much stronger over time. In the 1970s, less than one-quarter of the Conservatives supported this recognition, but in the 1990s almost 45 percent were willing to see Quebec recognized in this manner. Liberal opinion on this issue also moved over time, albeit not to the same degree and with less consistency. Forty-three percent of the Nova Scotia Liberal delegates in 1980 were willing to recognize Quebec in this fashion, but in 2002 only 28 percent held this position. That same year, 41 percent of the New Brunswick Liberal delegates were willing to recognize Quebec as a distinct society, as were 36 percent of the PEI Liberal voters in 2003. The latter two scores reflect increases since 1978 and 1982. Support for such recognition was generally somewhat higher among New Brunswick Liberals, and the increase in the proportion of voters holding such views there was more dramatic than it was elsewhere.

The last issue for which we can identify partisan differences relates to patronage. This issue was raised in surveys after 1986, and it dramatically demonstrates differences between New Democrats, on the one hand, and Liberals and Conservatives, on the other. Interestingly, majorities from all parties accepted patronage as a fact of life, but the New Democrats were the most internally divided, with an average of only 54 percent taking this position. Agreement was highest among Conservatives at 76 percent, while 71 percent of Liberals took this position.

It appears that the New Democrats, at least in Nova Scotia, became more resigned to patronage over time. In 1996, only 47 percent of their delegates held this position, but by 2002, this figure had grown to 62 percent. However, even this level of support was below that expressed by any Liberal or Conservative group at any time. The traditional parties seem quite united in the view that patronage cannot be avoided. New Democrats in Nova Scotia seem increasingly resigned to this as well.[8]

Our analysis of party positions on various issues suggests that differences among the parties in the region appear strong when the New Democrats are compared to the Liberals and the Conservatives. However, limiting the comparison to Liberals and Conservatives also revealed some significant differences, most notably in self-placement. That Conservatives designated themselves as significantly to the right of the Liberals indicates that activists in the two parties see themselves differently in political terms. Moreover, we could identify clear differences between the two traditional parties with respect to free trade and enhanced provincial power. As well, the issue of whether unions were an essential part of Canadian democracy placed a majority of Liberals on one side and a majority of Conservatives on the other. Thus, the old line parties could be distinguished on a number of issues.

The issue questions we asked were obviously contextually bound and certainly did not cover the full spectrum of political issues. There are many ways to obtain analytical purchase on party ideology. Heretofore in this chapter we have relied on the ideological self-placements of respondents and drawn upon inferences from their opinions on a range of policy questions. Now we propose to take a slightly more unconventional tack. For ten of the surveys undertaken since 1994, respondents were asked to rank in order the importance of the following concepts to their party's philosophy: the church, the community, the Constitution, the family, the individual, the market, the monarchy, the state, and the trade union movement. These nine concepts are admittedly abstract, but they are all encumbered with understandings about what is central to a just and well-ordered society. If the Maritime region's Liberal, Progressive Conservative, and New Democratic parties represent different ideologies, the concepts should be ranked differently by activists.

Table 8.3 provides an initial look at this question. Unfortunately, there is only a single Conservative sampling, so the bulk of our attention is centred on the differences between Liberals and New Democrats. Table 8.3 displays the percentage in each survey who gave top ranking to a particular concept. On some dimensions, there is little evidence of partisan division. Virtually no one in any party ranks either the church or the monarchy as most central to their party philosophy. Nor, somewhat surprisingly, is there much difference with respect to the state. New Democrats may have a reputation for being statophiles, for wanting a strong state to correct for the inequities of the market, but there is no evidence of this in Table 8.3. On each of the other six concepts, however, New Democrats differ sharply from their Liberal and Conservative counterparts. Put briefly, NDP activists are significantly less likely than are the others to claim the centrality of the Constitution, the family, the individual, and the market, and they are dramatically more likely than are Liberals and Tories to emphasize the importance of the trade union movement and, especially, the community. This difference in emphasis is perfectly consistent with the NDP's avowal of social democracy. Between the other two parties, there is little of note, although the Conservatives' outlier status with respect to the market, combined with their disinclination to aver the importance of either the church or the monarchy, speaks volumes about the party's ideological displacement of high toryism with business liberalism.

Table 8.3 only displays data on the most important concepts; Table 8.4, by contrast, reveals the order and mean figures for all the concepts. Generally speaking, partisan differences are less obvious in this table. Thus, like their NDP counterparts, Liberal and Conservative activists tend to rank the community first (although generally, the median figure is almost a full point higher for the latter group) and the monarchy last. The intervening order is also broadly similar across parties, with two notable exceptions. While Liberal and Conservative activists place the market somewhere between third and fifth in the rankings, the corresponding figure for New Democrats is consistently seventh. With respect to the trade union movement, on the other hand, the pattern is almost exactly reversed. Otherwise, the differences are largely ones of nuances. It is important to realize that respondents are evaluating the importance of these nine concepts to the philosophy of their party rather than to that of their person. It would be surprising, however, if there was no leakage from the latter to the former, if no respondents externalized their own ideals onto those of their beloved party. True, there is little evidence of this phenomenon among Liberal and Conservative activists; perhaps ideology matters less to these individuals. For New Democrats, however, the story is quite different. As Table 8.5 makes clear, those who ascribe left-wing views to themselves perceive the trade union movement and the state to be more important, and the individual, the family, and the market to be less important, than do their more centrist cohorts. In most cases, the gap between the two groups exceeds the combined standard error of the means. Thus, the data reviewed in this section confirm that Maritime New Democrats can be ideologically distinguished from their Grit and Tory counterparts not only in terms of the concepts they regard as central to their party philosophy but also in their inclination to read their own views on to those of their compatriots.

Table 8.3

**Maritime leadership elections: concept most important to party philosophy (%)**

| Leadership election | Church | Community | Constitution | Family | Individual | Market | Monarchy | State | Trade union movement |
|---|---|---|---|---|---|---|---|---|---|
| NS PC 1995 | 3 | 24 | 12 | 19 | 17 | 17 | 1 | 10 | 2 |
| PEI Lib 1996 | 4 | 24 | 13 | 27 | 15 | 8 | 0 | 7 | 1 |
| NB Lib 1998 | 5 | 21 | 10 | 21 | 22 | 8 | 0 | 7 | 1 |
| NB Lib 2002 | 1 | 23 | 12 | 17 | 37 | 11 | 0 | 10 | 1 |
| PEI Lib 2003 | 9 | 31 | 19 | 25 | 21 | 7 | 3 | 7 | 5 |
| NS Lib 2003 | 2 | 27 | 16 | 18 | 32 | 5 | 2 | 10 | 2 |
| NS NDP 1996 | 1 | 60 | 0 | 11 | 14 | 0 | 0 | 5 | 10 |
| NS NDP 2000 | 0 | 51 | 2 | 17 | 10 | 1 | 0 | 7 | 12 |
| NS NDP 2002 | 1 | 51 | 5 | 10 | 14 | 0 | 0 | 6 | 12 |
| PEI NDP 2002 | 0 | 47 | 5 | 8 | 8 | 3 | 0 | 6 | 13 |

*Note:* Totals may exceed 100 percent if respondents designated more than one concept as most important to party philosophy.

Table 8.4

Maritime leadership elections: concept's relative importance to party philosophy (order/mean)

| Leadership election | Church | Community | Constitution | Family | Individual | Market | Monarchy | State | Trade union movement |
|---|---|---|---|---|---|---|---|---|---|
| NS PC 1995 | 7/6.73 | 1/2.90 | 5/4.50 | 2/3.16 | 4/3.94 | 3/3.89 | 9/7.47 | 6/5.02 | 8/7.09 |
| PEI Lib 1996 | 7/6.02 | 2/2.82 | 4/4.14 | 1/2.61 | 3/3.79 | 5/4.65 | 9/8.08 | 6/5.79 | 8/6.92 |
| NB Lib 1998 | 7/6.73 | 1/2.94 | 5/4.50 | 2/3.02 | 3/3.45 | 4/4.30 | 9/8.04 | 6/5.04 | 8/6.95 |
| NB Lib 2002 | 8/7.21 | 1/2.75 | 4/4.15 | 2/2.87 | 3/2.95 | 5/4.51 | 9/7.93 | 6/5.69 | 7/6.97 |
| PEI Lib 2003 | 7/5.62 | 1/2.62 | 4/3.69 | 2/2.67 | 3/3.46 | 5/4.55 | 9/7.22 | 6/5.58 | 8/6.22 |
| NS Lib 2003 | 8/7.20 | 1/2.99 | 4/3.65 | 3/3.19 | 2/3.02 | 5/4.79 | 9/7.69 | 5/4.79 | 7/7.16 |
| NS NDP 1996 | 8/7.44 | 1/1.92 | 6/5.64 | 2/3.35 | 4/3.84 | 7/5.79 | 9/8.61 | 5/4.81 | 3/3.43 |
| NS NDP 2000 | 8/7.29 | 1/2.01 | 6/5.19 | 2/2.95 | 3/3.87 | 7/6.16 | 9/8.58 | 5/5.04 | 3/3.87 |
| NS NDP 2002 | 8/7.47 | 1/2.17 | 5/4.66 | 2/3.19 | 3/3.71 | 7/6.06 | 9/8.36 | 6/5.20 | 4/4.19 |
| PEI NDP 2002 | 8/7.37 | 1/1.74 | 5/4.42 | 2/3.34 | 3/4.08 | 7/6.03 | 9/8.76 | 6/5.16 | 4/4.11 |

Table 8.5

**Nova Scotia NDP leadership elections: concept's relative importance to party philosophy**

|  | Family | Individual | Market | State | Trade union movement | N |
|---|---|---|---|---|---|---|
| **NS NDP 2000** |  |  |  |  |  |  |
| Left | 3.28/.20 | 4.38/.21 | 6.39/.15 | 4.47/.23 | 3.44/.18 | 87 |
| Other | 2.85/.12 | 3.58/.15 | 6.10/.12 | 5.18/.17 | 4.08/.16 | 154 |
| **NS NDP 2002** |  |  |  |  |  |  |
| Left | 3.48/.16 | 3.96/.19 | 6.13/.15 | 4.79/.22 | 3.71/.17 | 112 |
| Other | 3.13/.11 | 3.68/.14 | 6.03/.12 | 5.27/.15 | 4.34/.15 | 203 |

## Intraparty Attitudinal Divisions

The possible influence of attitudinal differences on voting has long been a source of interest for those studying leadership selections. Analysts of these events often seemed positively eager to map the impact of attitudes or ideology on voting. Historically, however, competition for the leadership has not been viewed as an "engagement of principles." Early on, Smiley argued that convention rules, and the consequent necessity of creating a coalition of support, would prevent candidates from issuing ideological appeals.[9] It was, therefore, not surprising when Perlin found little evidence of an ideological cleavage at the 1967 and 1976 Conservative national conventions.[10] Gibbins and Hunziker, in their study of delegate voting in Alberta, also argued that policy preferences had no significant impact on delegate voting behaviour.[11] Yet contrary evidence has also emerged. In their study of the 1976 PC convention, Krause and Leduc found that 40 percent of the delegates claimed ideological labelling as important in their voting choices.[12] Clark was able to win a fourth ballot victory partly because he won "impressive majorities among those delegates classifying themselves to the left-centre of the party."[13] However, he also fought the more right-wing Wagner to a virtual stand-off among delegates who placed themselves on the right of the party.

Johnston, in his examination of the final choices at the 1983 and 1984 conventions, also found important attitudinal divisions. In his assessment of the relative weight of social group, geographic, and attitudinal variables, he provides strong evidence that voting was ideologically based. As he concludes: "At their respective leadership conventions, each party was divided between left and right."[14] In terms of ideological self-placement, delegates who put themselves on the right of their party were more supportive of Mulroney in 1983 and of Turner in 1984. Moreover, voting divisions could be seen when delegate opinions on continentalism, bilingualism, and provincialism were taken into account.[15] Evidence from provincial leadership elections also identified attitudinally based divisions. Work by Carty, Blake, and Erickson[16] on British Columbia, and by Stewart and Archer[17] on Alberta, has pointed out significant attitudinal divisions in candidate support bases. In this part of the chapter, we examine each of the twenty-five Maritime leadership elections and assess the degree of attitudinal difference in the support bases of the candidates.

Analysis of newspaper coverage of the twenty-five elections clearly indicates that most of these races were not seen as battles among candidates with differing policy perspectives, let alone ideological differences. Indeed, we could identify only eight elections in which substantive policy differences were evident. One of the conventions we identified as a potential conflict of ideology was the first in our data set – the 1971 Progressive Conservative convention in Nova Scotia.[18] On the first ballot, eight of the thirty attitudinal variables were significantly associated with voting, while, on the second ballot, nine variables were so associated. The disagreement appeared particularly salient on issues that could be considered French/English. Certain other areas of disagreement could be considered in a liberal versus conservative context. Examination of John Buchanan's victory in 1971 thus indicates that it was, at least partially, a victory for the "conservative" wing of the party.

The Nova Scotia Conservative convention in 1991 also appeared to be affected by the positions delegates took on various issues. Our analysis of the media coverage in 1991 indicated that attitudinal differences had an impact on the outcome; and, indeed, our analysis of voting showed significant differences between Thornhill and Cameron supporters on a number of dimensions. However, these differences were matters of degree only, and Cameron won comfortably across the attitudinal spectrum. Media coverage of the 1992 Liberal tele-vote suggested the possibility of attitudinal divisions affecting candidate choice. Indeed, the ideological self-placement of voters differed significantly, with Downe drawing more support from voters placing themselves on the right of the political spectrum and Savage drawing more from those placing themselves more to the left. With respect to specific policy matters, Downe drew more of his support from those who did not believe that social programs should be universal or that unions were essential for democracy. He was also more popular with those who believed that the Nova Scotia Power Corporation should be privatized. Unfortunately for Downe, most voters did not hold those views, providing Savage with a much wider base. Reversing the tendency at the 1971 PC convention in 1992, the victory was one for the Liberal party's left wing.

Media coverage of the four Nova Scotian NDP leadership elections indicated that two of them might be marked by attitudinal differences in candidate choice. The first of these was held in 1980 and was won handily by Alexa

McDonough. Surveys of these early conventions did not provide us with a short-hand ideological self-placement question to look at, and, indeed, relatively few attitudinal questions were asked. The only questions that were significant, as we see in Chapter 13, related to internal party matters.

The 1996 convention was another one-sided victory, and there appeared to be clear differences between the two candidates. However, there was no significant difference on ideological self-placement, and the victory secured by Chisholm was so all-encompassing that the only question that produced a significant difference concerned the inevitability of patronage.

Interestingly, although the 2000 convention did not appear as divisive in the media as did the 1996 gathering, delegates choosing different candidates could be distinguished on the basis of their answer to the self-placement question. For instance, while only 21 percent of Deveaux's supporters placed themselves on the left, more than 50 percent of those who supported the MacDonalds (Helen and Maureen) did so.[19] Backers of Deveaux were more supportive of a Triple-E Senate, much more likely to believe that free trade was beneficial, that budgets should always be balanced, and that the Nova Scotia NDP should emulate Tony Blair's "Third Way." They were less convinced that unions were essential for democracy and that the NDP had a bright future in the province. Not surprisingly, they were also more in favour of allowing all members to vote for the party's leader. With the exception of this last issue, the majority of delegates took different positions and preferred the MacDonalds to Deveaux. Helen MacDonald's third ballot victory certainly appears to be one of the left over the centre-left.

None of the surveys of the three Island Conservative leadership elections asked questions about self-placement, and the media coverage did not suggest much in the way of policy division among the candidates. Our analysis of voting confirms that these elections were not generally marked by attitudinal differences in candidate support bases.

Similarly, media coverage of the five Liberal elections on PEI provided few hints of policy division, and analysis of the five data sets revealed little in the way of systematic attitudinally based voting. The ideological self-placement question was first asked in 1996, and it was not significant, even though media coverage provided hints of divisions. Certainly, as Chapter 6 shows, there was evidence of a rural-urban split that might have attitudinal divisions at its heart, but we were unable to find much in the way of attitudinal divisions in voting.[20]

Somewhat surprisingly, the 2003 election saw significant differences in the self-placements of Buchanan and Ghiz voters. Buchanan voters placed themselves further to the left then did those who backed Ghiz. Such divisions were not identified by media commentators, and our examination of the individual attitudinal questions revealed few differences.

Virtually no evidence of attitudinally based voting could be found at the 1982, 1985, and 2002 Liberal conventions in New Brunswick.[21] The two other New Brunswick leadership elections revealed more significant divisions, but in none of them was the ideological self-placement variable significant. As we discuss in more detail in Chapter 12, questions relating to the place of French and English in the province, and New Brunswick's bilingual and bicultural nature, were highly divisive and significant. In general, anglophone candidates did better with voters who were not as committed to bilingualism and recognition of Acadian culture. The only Conservative election in our collection (1997) was clearly home to divisions based on French-English relations, but differences on other matters were extremely limited.

Our review of the association of positions on attitudinal questions with candidate choice suggests that this influence is not common in Maritime leadership elections. Our analysis of the media coverage of the leadership elections resulted in our identifying seven of the twenty-five elections as potential battles over policy.[22] Examining these in conjunction with our attitudinal questions indicated that three were not riven by substantive divisions in these areas.[23] In contrast, we found three additional elections where the responses suggested a division among voters not hinted at in the media coverage.[24] Even assuming that all of these elections were marked by attitudinal divisions of some sort, we would still be dealing with only a minority of elections. In short, relatively few leadership elections appear to have been affected to a substantial degree by attitudinal differences. In only five of the twelve elections in which the ideological self-placement question was asked was it significant, and in three of these, the ability of voters to pick up on candidate cues seems problematic.

We do see some provincial variation in this area. Although we found clear examples of intraparty cleavages in elections in all three provinces, attitudinal divisions appear more common in Nova Scotia than they do in the two other provinces. Such divisions were least common in PEI, where we did not find a single convention or election in which it appeared that issue positions were associated with voting in a significant and coherent fashion. New Brunswick occupies the mid-point, with one major exception. As we discuss in Chapter 12, there are huge differences of opinion on issues relating to language and culture in this province, and these positions are clearly associated with voting choice.

There appears to have been little change over time in this area, and there is certainly little evidence that attitudinally based support coalitions are becoming more common. One of the most obvious divisions was found at the first convention in 1971, but some of the more recent elections, despite an expanded set of attitudinal questions, reveal few such cleavages in candidate choice. Finally, when it came to ideological battles, we were not able to identify much in the way of differences between conventions and universal ballots.

## Conclusion

It is not our contention that differences of opinion do not exist within political parties. Indeed, the ideological self-placement question alone reveals a fair degree of dispersion within parties. However, these and other divisions are only infrequently associated with voting choice. There are wide differences of opinion within parties, but it appears that these rarely intrude in the voting process. It likely takes a particular sort of campaign to prime this kind of behaviour, and these sorts of campaigns do not abound within Maritime parties.

It is, however, quite possible to identify differences among the various parties in terms of attitude. New Democrats stand out from Liberals and Conservatives on many issues, and they consistently place themselves farther to the left. As well, they are more likely to place a higher priority on trade unions and community in terms of their importance to party philosophy.

We were also able to identify differences between Liberals and Conservative participants. Conservative voters placed themselves farther to the right and were more supportive of free trade and the expansion of provincial powers. They were also less convinced that unions were essential to democracy. On occasion, we were able to identify provincial differences, for example on patronage and free trade. In general, however, these differences were less dramatic than were those among the three parties.

There were relatively few differences over time. Admittedly, attitudes towards free trade and balanced budgets jumped around among Liberals, but these seemed to flow from proximity to power or positions taken by federal parties rather than temporal shifts. As we elaborate later, the New Democrats in Nova Scotia appear to have grown more moderate over time, but in general neither time nor method of selection had a clear impact on attitude.

# 9
# Rebels without a Cause?
# Supporters of Fringe Candidates

Many Canadians are likely bemused by the intense contests over leadership that characterize the country's major political parties. Why, they must ask themselves, would anyone struggle so vigorously to gain a position that is so relentlessly unpleasant? Nevertheless, the actions of most leadership aspirants do admit of a certain rationality. One of the "serious" contenders for the job will obviously be able to enjoy the fruits of power, while his or her major rival(s) will, at the very least, have re-established their claims to influence in the party. Even the actions of "second-tier" candidates are generally explicable. Their chances of victory may well be remote; even so, the undertaking may be considered worthwhile if they are able to barter successfully the backing of their supporters, if they are able to shift the party's ideological profile, or if they are able to establish themselves as putative heirs apparent.[1] But what about the "fringe" candidates, the no-hopers? Neil Fraser received five votes from a total of 2,991 at the 1983 leadership convention of the Progressive Conservative party. Three years later, Kim Campbell had only fourteen supporters from the 1,294 British Columbia Social Credit delegates gathered to select a new party leader. Nuisance candidates such as these are not usually entirely irrelevant to the proceedings. They usually irritate television executives (e.g., by occupying valuable air time).[2] And, by ensuring that none of their more formidable opponents will be eliminated after the first ballot, they also provide both voters and candidates with a precise support breakdown to assist them in the hard choices still to come.[3]

Yet few fringe candidates can be driven by such other-directed considerations. In their stead are likely to be an unhealthy attachment to self and an equally unhealthy detachment from political reality. Fringe candidates are determined to have their instant of notoriety, and the likelihood of public humiliation is either denied, ignored, or enjoyed. Such conduct may not be to everyone's taste, but it is at least comprehensible. What, however, is one to make of those who vote for fringe candidates? Their preferred choice for leader at least experiences a Warholian moment of fame; by contrast, these people anonymously expend a variety of resources (including their first ballot vote) in an endeavour inevitably doomed to failure. Ultimately, we show that, for a disproportionate number of such individuals, voting for a fringe candidate is a last minute decision taken with little conviction.

It is essential to clarify the central concept of this analysis. What precisely is meant by a "fringe candidate?" Two problems with the use of this term are immediately apparent. The first is perceptual: whether a particular leadership aspirant is a "fringe candidate" is very much in the eyes of the beholder. Lacking an accepted objective standard, reasonable people might well disagree about whether, for example, Tom Wappel's 1990 bid to secure the leadership of the national Liberal party fell into that category. The second problem is that any operationalization of "fringe candidate" must be sensitive to the size of the leadership field. To take an extreme example, Joe Clark managed to emerge victorious from the 1976 convention of the national Progressive Conservative party despite securing only 277 votes from a first ballot total of 2,360. Clark's improbable victory owed much to the fact that there was a large field of eleven candidates. Had there been only one or two other contenders, Clark's 12 percent share on the first ballot would likely have been insufficient to avoid the tag of "fringe candidate." The second problem is easier to overcome than the first. In this analysis, we employ a sliding scale of $< \frac{1}{2x}$, where x represents the number of candidates. Thus, fringe candidates for party leadership are those who received less than one-quarter of the first ballot vote in a two-person contest, less than one-sixth in a three-person contest, less than one-eighth in a four-person contest, less than one-tenth in a five-person contest, and so on. While this operationalization is defensible, it remains inherently subjective. We address the reasonableness of this subjective standard shortly.

Table 9.1 makes clear that a number of fringe candidates can be identified in our data set; these were concentrated in eleven of the twenty-five leadership contests. The table reveals some apparent anomalies. In 1993, Larry Creed received 16 percent of the first ballot vote in a three-person contest; accordingly, he was classified as a fringe candidate. Twelve years earlier, Patrick Binns had garnered an identical share of the vote. Because there had been an additional candidate in the 1981 race, however, Binns narrowly escaped being tagged with the same label. Yet, since similar circumstances will confront any dichotomy between fringe candidates and otherwise, there is no reason to abandon the method outlined above. Aggregating the data from ten of the surveys from the bottom panel of Table 9.1 produces a pool of 507 respondents who voted for a fringe candidate on the first ballot (30 for Arsenault, 13 for MacEachern, 34 for Frenette, 19 for Maher, 102 for Callaghan, 18 for Drish, 7 for Hawkins, 90 for Creed, 15 for Campbell, 88 for Michael MacDonald, 32 for Atwell, 8 for Tex MacDonald, 3 for Mullen,

*Table 9.1*

## Maritime leadership elections: serious and fringe candidates by first ballot support

| Leadership election | Candidates (% support) | | | | |
|---|---|---|---|---|---|
| | 1 | 2 | 3 | 4 | 5 |
| **Conventions without a fringe candidate** | | | | | |
| NS Lib 1971 | Doucet 38 | Buchanan 33 | Thornhill 29 | | |
| PEI PC 1976 | MacLean 57 | Lee 43 | | | |
| PEI Lib 1978 | Campbell 71 | Mitchell 28 | | | |
| NS Lib 1980 | Cameron 37 | MacLean 27 | Mooney 21 | MacInnis 15 | |
| PEI PC 1981 | Lee 40 | Clark 25 | Driscoll 19 | Binns 16 | |
| PEI Lib 1981 | Ghiz 65 | Clements 35 | | | |
| NB Lib 1985 | McKenna 69 | Frenette 31 | | | |
| NS Lib 1986 | MacLean 60 | Cowan 40 | | | |
| PEI PC 1988 | Gass 51 | Walker 49 | | | |
| NB PC 1997 | Lord 37 | Betts 32 | Allaby 17 | Blaney 14 | |
| NB Lib 1998 | Theriault 56 | Byrne 27 | Richard 18 | | |
| NB Lib 2002 | S. Graham 75 | MacDougall 25 | | | |
| NS NDP 2002 | Dexter 63 | MacDonell 37 | | | |
| PEI Lib 2003 | Ghiz 52 | Buchanan 48 | | | |
| **Conventions with at least one fringe candidate** | | | | | |
| NS NDP 1980 | McDonough 74 | Arsenault* 13 | MacEachern* 13 | | |
| NB Lib 1982 | Young 69 | Day 31 | Frenette* 11 | Maher* 6 | |
| NS PC 1991 | Cameron 32 | Thornhill 31 | McInnis 29 | Callaghan* 8 | |
| NS Lib 1992 | Savage 47 | Downe 41 | MacInnis 11 | Drish* 1 | Hawkins* 1 |
| PEI Lib 1993 | Callbeck 79 | Creed* 16 | Campbell* 5 | | |
| NS PC 1995 | Hamm 54 | White 37 | MacDonald* 10 | | |
| PEI Lib 1996 | Milligan 52 | Cheverie 42 | MacDonald* 5 | Mullen* 1 | |
| NS NDP 1996 | Chisholm 77 | Atwell* 23 | | | |
| NS NDP 2000 | H. MacDonald 32 | Deveaux 29 | M. MacDonald 26 | Peters* 8 | |
| PEI NDP 2002 | Robichaud 73 | Bingham 22 | Kelly-Hawkes* 5 | | |
| NS Lib 2002 | D. Graham 60 | MacKenzie 33 | B. Graham* 7 | | Bitter-Suermann* 5 |

* Denotes fringe candidate.

15 for Bitter-Suermann, 24 for Peters, and 9 for Bruce Graham).[4] This data set is the focus of the subsequent analysis.[5]

Has our particular understanding of fringe candidacies gathered an appropriate harvest? Would other observers cavil at tarring any or all of the sixteen leadership hopefuls with such a label? One check on the method involves scrutinizing the media treatment afforded each of these candidates in the weeks immediately prior to the convention. As Fred Fletcher and Robert Drummond observe,

> To be taken seriously, and to attract capable organizers and financial supporters, a candidate must be seen as viable, that is having a reasonable chance to win the leadership race. To a large extent, viability depends on media attention. When network news producers and major newspaper editors write off a candidate, he or she is unlikely to get very far in the race.[6]

Did the media suggest that the particular candidacies of Len Arsenault, Buddy MacEachern, Ray Frenette, Allan Maher, Clair Callaghan, George Hawkins, John Drish, Larry Creed, Bill Campbell, Michael MacDonald, Tex MacDonald, Daniel Mullen, Yvonne Atwell, David Peters, Hinrich Bitter-Suermann, and Bruce Graham were not viable? In general, yes. In fact, only the 1980 Nova Scotian NDP race provided an exception to this pattern. In the days preceding the vote, press reports trumpeted "a three-way race, too close to call,"[7] while one commentator suggested that Len Arsenault might "enter the convention as a slight favorite in a close race."[8] In actuality, Alexa McDonough obliterated her opponents; one abashed analyst acknowledged that "her margin in the first-ballot victory stunned most observers."[9]

For the remaining conventions in our sample, the media were far more prescient in distinguishing between serious and fringe candidates. To take but a few examples: Clair Callaghan was derided as someone facing "a formidable task if he's to pull off what would be the upset of the century."[10] George Hawkins was "destined to drop out of the race on the first ballot."[11] John Drish was mocked as "Candidate Moonbeam."[12] Larry Creed and Bill Campbell were dismissed as "fellow fringe candidate[s]"[13] who had "a tough road to climb."[14] Michael MacDonald was labelled as an "outsider."[15] Daniel Mullen was characterized as a "dark horse candidate"[16] whose campaign would "realistically" prove "to be no more than a soapbox."[17] Finally, the "challenges" to Hinrich Bitter-Suermann winning the leadership were adjudged to be "far more numerous than [just] lacking a constituency to call home."[18]

Such media coverage provides some support for our method of identifying fringe candidates. Significant doubts about the viability of almost all of our sixteen candidacies were repeatedly raised by the media in the weeks immediately prior to the vote. Hence, while it might be suggested that the criteria employed herein is too exclusive (i.e., there may have been other fringe candidates in the wider data set), it is difficult to argue that the method is too inclusive (i.e., the net designed to catch fringe candidates has also scooped up some serious ones). Admittedly, one must be cautious about pushing this argument too far. After all, the media's treatment of the various leadership aspirants and the subsequent distribution of votes on the first ballot are not entirely discrete phenomena. There is an element of self-fulfilling prophecy in the media's decision to label someone as a fringe candidate as potential donors, workers, and voters may well decide to expend their resources on an apparently less hopeless cause. Nevertheless, the media are neither omnipotent nor arbitrary in this matter. With respect to the latter, Fletcher and Drummond assert:

> The news organizations do not, of course, divide the candidates between the serious and non-serious on whim. They respond to a variety of indicators, the most important of which are public profile (name familiarity in the jargon of voting experts), degree of support from other notables, including the key backroom experts in fundraising and campaign organization, the appearance of broad ... appeal, capacity to raise funds, and certain personal characteristics such as speaking ability and television performance.[19]

As to the media's power essentially to "create" fringe candidates through selective labelling, the findings in Table 9.2 (derived from the ten specific conventions under scrutiny) are illuminating. One might have anticipated that those who voted for a fringe candidate would have been insulated, to some extent, from the media's indictment of their hopeful's prospects. Since an absence of media exposure and support for fringe candidates are not, in fact, strongly correlated, it would be prudent not to exaggerate the media's capacity to torpedo legitimate contenders. Accordingly, the media's treatment of the sixteen leadership aspirants under scrutiny has provided some credence to our operationalization of fringe candidates.

Given that Arsenault, MacEachern, Frenette, Maher, Callaghan, Hawkins, Drish, Campbell, Creed, M. MacDonald, T. MacDonald, Mullen, Atwell, Peters, Bitter-Suermann, and B. Graham were not, in fact, serious candidates,

*Table 9.2*

**Maritime leadership elections: media exposure by fringe candidate vote**

|  | Read newspapers every day | Watch television news every day | N |
|---|---|---|---|
| Voted for a serious candidate | 82% | 73% | 5,206 |
| Voted for a fringe candidate | 80% | 67% | 408 |

what motivated people to vote for them? Most analyses of party activists suggest that they are driven by a mixture of policy, patronage, and social motivations,[20] yet neither of the latter two are likely to underlie support for a fringe candidate. For those who regard party activity as an enjoyable form of social interaction (the party-goers), the prospect of backing a fringe candidate must have negligible appeal; on the contrary, they would shun the pervasive sense of isolation, the largely empty or non-existent hospitality suites, and the funereal post-convention gatherings that are inextricably tied to fringe candidacies. Nor would one expect to find evidence of those for whom party activity is a method of material advancement (the gold-diggers). Patronage is essentially the preserve of winners; coming from fringe candidates, any promises of future booty are scarcely credible.

Our expectations would be quite different, however, with respect to those activists who are principally motivated by policy concerns (the zealots). Such individuals might well prefer to vote for a hopeless cause than to sacrifice or compromise an intensely held set of principles. After all, the closest political analogue to voting for a fringe candidate in a Canadian leadership convention is to vote for such a candidate in a general election contested under the single-member plurality electoral system.[21] In countries employing some variant of this method, as Maurice Duverger postulates, voters are disinclined to "waste" their ballots on minor-party candidates.[22] Leaving aside parties of political satire,[23] only those with a strong doctrinal base will continue to struggle against the conversion bias inherent in the electoral system. These ideological parties survive "more from their activists' faithful commitment to party doctrine or creed than from any genuine hope of electoral victory."[24] There is, unfortunately, little empirical evidence pertaining to this question: most national voting surveys unearth only a handful of respondents who admit to voting for one of these parties.[25] The conclusion of doctrinaire voting, therefore, is generally inferred from the nature of the act itself. In other words, voting for a party with an idiosyncratic ideological profile and no prospects of electoral success can best be understood if the voter strongly identifies with the party's creed. That there are alternative psychological explanations cannot be denied. Nevertheless, a strong commitment to party dogma remains the most credible explanation for having cast a ballot for such parties as the Christian Heritage Party in Canada, the Libertarian Party in the United States, the National Front in Great Britain, and the Natural Law Party in all three countries.

Are such zealots to be disproportionately found in the camps of the sixteen fringe candidates under scrutiny? Surprisingly, only a negative answer to this query is possible. On a range of issues, those who backed serious candidates and those who supported fringe aspirants had, in aggregate, remarkably similar views. Admittedly, this might be deceptive: ideological cleavages between the backers of fringe and serious contenders might exist

*Table 9.3*

**Maritime leadership elections: policy rationale by fringe candidate vote**

|  | Yes | No | N |
|---|---|---|---|
| Supporters of serious candidates | 43% | 57% | 5,713 |
| Supporters of fringe candidates | 42% | 58% | 500 |

in any or all of the individual conventions under scrutiny without necessarily appearing in the aggregate data. In other words, the ideological distinctiveness of a right-wing fringe candidate for the leadership of the Progressive Conservatives could easily be negated in the larger data set by the presence of a similarly distinctive fringe aspirant (either in the same or in a different contest) on the left of the PCs (or, for that matter, on the left of the Liberals). As it turns out, these concerns are largely without foundation. In none of the eleven particular conventions under scrutiny are there significant differences between the policy views of those who backed serious contenders and those who supported fringe aspirants for party leadership. Moreover, as Table 9.3 indicates, the two groups of party activists did not differ significantly in the extent to which they provided a policy rationale for their first ballot vote. This does not, of course, mean that some activists have not supported a fringe candidate for ideological reasons. It does mean, however, that, contrary to expectations, zealots have not been disproportionately concentrated in the camps of fringe candidates.

Our scrutiny of the primary motivations that ostensibly underlie party activity has not greatly enriched our understanding of those who support fringe candidates in Maritime leadership conventions. Given the irregular and idiosyncratic character of these contests, however, it is not implausible that activists behave at such gatherings in a manner largely unrelated to their primary motivations for party work. One possibility is that they use leadership conventions as an opportunity to express solidarity with their neighbours. Given our discussion in Chapter 5, it is not surprising that the data in Table 9.4 clearly support this speculation. Of the thirty-six leadership aspirants under scrutiny, only three – Ken MacInnis, Yvonne Atwell, and Francis MacKenzie – did not benefit from "the neighbourhood effect," and in all three cases, other candidates with the same home county were in the contest. Have fringe candidates benefited disproportionately from the activists' urge to support a local candidate? Much depends on how one measures the phenomenon. If one simply subtracts the votes share in the rest of the province from that obtained in the home area (as in the middle numeric column of Table 9.4), then the answer is clearly negative. In fact, the four largest instances of neighbourhood effect, according to this method, were all enjoyed by serious candidates. This approach, however, is inherently

*Table 9.4*

**Maritime candidates (fringe only): neighbourhood boost**

| Candidate | | Home county | % in home area | % in rest of province | % increase $(a - b)$ | % increase $\dfrac{(a-b)}{b} \times 100$ | Haberman's adjusted residuals* |
|---|---|---|---|---|---|---|---|
| McDonough | Serious | Halifax | 87 | 76 | 11 | 14 | 2.0 |
| Arsenault | Fringe | Cape Breton | 30 | 10 | 20 | 200 | 3.4 |
| MacEachern | Fringe | Cape Breton | 21 | 2 | 19 | 950 | 4.5 |
| Day | Serious | St. John–Charlotte–Kings | 55 | 11 | 44 | 400 | 5.8 |
| Young | Serious | Gloucester–Northumberland Kings | 79 | 50 | 29 | 58 | 4.4 |
| Frenette | Fringe | Moncton–Westmorland | 29 | 6 | 23 | 383 | 5.7 |
| Maher | Fringe | Restigouche–Madawaska-Victoria | 15 | 4 | 11 | 275 | 3.4 |
| Cameron | Serious | Pictou | 60 | 34 | 26 | 77 | 4.4 |
| McInnis | Serious | Halifax | 31 | 28 | 3 | 11 | 1.3 |
| Thornhill | Serious | Halifax | 32 | 24 | 8 | 33 | 3.0 |
| Callaghan | Fringe | Halifax | 10 | 8 | 2 | 25 | 1.7 |
| Downe | Serious | Lunenburg | 73 | 34 | 39 | 115 | 9.8 |
| MacInnis | Serious | Halifax | 8 | 9 | –1 | –11 | –0.9 |
| Savage | Serious | Halifax | 64 | 47 | 17 | 36 | 6.4 |
| Drish | Fringe | Digby | 4 | 1 | 3 | 300 | 2.2 |
| Hawkins | Fringe | Halifax | 1 | 0.1 | 0.9 | 800 | 3.0 |
| Callbeck | Serious | Prince | 95 | 85 | 10 | 12 | 4.4 |
| Campbell | Fringe | Queens | 2 | 1 | 1 | 100 | 1.3 |
| Creed | Fringe | Kings | 22 | 7 | 15 | 214 | 5.8 |

▼ *Table 9.4*

| Candidate | | Home county | % in home area | % in rest of province | % increase $(a-b)$ | % increase $\dfrac{(a-b)}{b} \times 100$ | Haberman's adjusted residuals* |
|---|---|---|---|---|---|---|---|
| Hamm | Serious | Pictou | 95 | 49 | 46 | 94 | 10.0 |
| White | Serious | Hants | 74 | 31 | 43 | 139 | 7.1 |
| MacDonald | Fringe | Halifax | 13 | 8 | 5 | 63 | 2.3 |
| Chisholm | Serious | Halifax | 83 | 71 | 12 | 17 | 1.6 |
| Atwell | Fringe | Halifax | 17 | 29 | -12 | -41 | -1.6 |
| Cheverie | Serious | Queens | 57 | 31 | 26 | 84 | 4.5 |
| Milligan | Serious | Prince | 81 | 41 | 40 | 98 | 6.0 |
| MacDonald | Fringe | Queens | 3 | 2 | 1 | 50 | 0.9 |
| Mullen | Fringe | Queens | 2 | 0 | 2 | 8 | 1.6 |
| H. MacDonald | Serious | Cape Breton | 92 | 24 | 68 | 284 | 8.3 |
| Deveaux | Serious | Halifax | 37 | 20 | 17 | 85 | 3.3 |
| M. MacDonald | Serious | Halifax | 30 | 21 | 9 | 43 | 1.8 |
| Peters | Fringe | Pictou | 35 | 6 | 29 | 483 | 4.3 |
| Bitter-Suermann | Fringe | Lunenburg | 32 | 3 | 29 | 967 | 6.0 |
| D. Graham | Serious | Halifax | 78 | 71 | 7 | 10 | 1.1 |
| MacKenzie | Serious | Halifax | 18 | 20 | -2 | -10 | -0.2 |
| B. Graham | Fringe | Hants | 50 | 6 | 44 | 733 | 2.5 |

* Haberman's adjusted residuals control for any differences in the size of the categories' marginals. Any absolute values larger than 1.96 are statistically significant.

biased against fringe candidates: they simply do not receive enough votes anywhere to make possible gaps of the magnitude apparent in the record of some serious candidates. The candidacies of Ray Frenette and Larry Creed illustrate this point nicely since, under this method, both are clearly pushing the upper limits of the neighbourhood effect. Had they received many more votes in their home area, they would no longer have been considered fringe candidates, and it is difficult to conceive their negligible total in the rest of the province being reduced any further.

Yet using a measure of proportionate increase to assess the neighbourhood effect (as in the second column from the right of Table 9.4) is not necessarily an improvement. Using this method, most of the largest gains in home area voting are experienced by the fringe candidates: Buddy MacEachern, George Hawkins, and Hinrich Bitter-Suermann all register improvements of at least 800 percent in their home counties. Unfortunately, this method is also flawed as it, too, is manifestly biased – this time, against serious candidates. The lower the vote total a candidate receives in the remainder of the province, the easier it is for that candidate to enjoy a large proportionate increase in his or her home area. John Drish, for example, received the support of only two of the forty-six surveyed activists from his home county of Digby. His even more abysmal record elsewhere in Nova Scotia ensured, however, that, under this method, he would be credited with a 300 percent increase. Accordingly, the final column of Table 9.4, which displays Haberman's adjusted residuals, probably offers the fairest assessment of the neighbourhood effect since it controls for the size of the marginals in each category. Using this method, it appears that serious candidates profited from being regarded as "favourite sons or daughters" slightly more than did their fringe counterparts. For the former, the average Haberman's adjusted residual figure was a highly significant 4.2; for the latter, the corresponding number was a still significant, but smaller, 2.9.

Given that other aspects of social structure were also not correlated with support for a fringe candidate, it would appear that the problem needs to be approached from a different direction. It has been assumed heretofore that only those activists who are fundamentally attached to some aspect of a fringe candidate's campaign will remain steadfastly supportive in the face of growing evidence that the cause is a hopeless one. Our attempts to uncover the source of this attachment have, however, been largely fruitless. Only when we look for evidence of ambivalence, rather than commitment, does the picture suddenly become clearer. Table 9.5 provides five different measures of delay, confusion, and uncertainty, and all of them are strongly correlated with support for fringe candidates. Activists who only came to a voting decision at the convention, who were in some manner influenced by the speeches, who did not try to persuade others to vote in a like fashion, who could not or would not provide a conventional explanation for their

*Table 9.5*

**Maritime leadership elections: measures of ambivalence by fringe candidate vote**

| | | Supported serious candidate | Supported fringe candidate | N* |
|---|---|---|---|---|
| Decided on vote | No | 88% | 66% | |
| at the leadership | Yes | 12% | 34%** | |
| convention | N = | 5,661 | 501 | 125 |
| | | | | |
| Voting decision | No | 64% | 53% | |
| affected by | Yes | 36% | 47%** | |
| speeches | N = | 5,575 | 496 | 1,078 |
| | | | | |
| Attempted to | No | 38% | 55% | |
| persuade other | Yes | 62% | 45%** | |
| delegates to vote | N = | 5,597 | 493 | 435 |
| same way | | | | |
| | | | | |
| Most important | • policy agreement | 94% | 82% | |
| reason for vote | • best vote-getter | | | |
| | • appealing personal characteristics | | | |
| | • approached by workers | | | |
| | • promised support | | | |
| | • help my area | | | |
| | • help me politically | | | |
| | • appeal to women | | | |
| | • appeal to youth | | | |
| | • best decision maker | | | |
| | • asked by prominent people | | | |
| | | | | |
| | Other | 6% | 18%** | |
| | N = | 4,618 | 399 | 229 |
| | | | | |
| Voted for first | No | 7% | 37% | |
| preference | Yes | 93% | 63%** | |
| | N = | 3,767 | 219 | 68 |

* Sample size necessary to produce statistical significance at the .05 level.
** $\chi^2 < .01$.

action, and who did not support their first preference on the initial ballot were all disproportionately to be found in the camps of fringe candidates. Some of the relationships are quite striking. Of those activists who had decided on their vote before the convention, only 6.2 percent backed a fringe candidate; for those who only made up their mind at the convention, however, the corresponding figure is 20.3 percent. The inability or unwillingness of a disproportionate number of backers of fringe candidates to indicate a specific rationale for their action is also notable. On a range of other matters, such individuals were not similarly reticent.

The phenomenon of delegates voting for a fringe candidate rather than for their actual first preference merits particularly close scrutiny. Although their sample of delegates supporting fringe candidates was very small (only nine by the criteria employed here, Krause and Leduc uncovered a similar pattern in their analysis of the 1968 national Liberal convention and the 1976 national Progressive Conservative meeting. Hence, while 77 percent of the delegates at the latter and 75 percent of those at the former voted their "true preference" on the first ballot, the figure for fringe candidate Howard Grafftey was actually 0 percent.[26] What is one to make of such behaviour? Certainly, political party folklore is replete with instances of people "parking" their first ballot votes with aspirants who have no chance of success so that they might subsequently move to the winning candidate without the risks attendant upon having supported another serious contender at the outset. At the 1968 Liberal convention, for example, the *Globe and Mail* interviewed one party notable who planned to vote for Joe Greene on the first ballot:

> He knows perfectly well that Mr. Greene will not win, but he also knows that a first ballot vote for Mr. Greene will leave him clear to support the winner from the time of Mr. Greene's elimination. To the experienced politician, this is vital. If you are not with the winner, you are nowhere.[27]

Were delegates at the eleven Maritime leadership conventions under scrutiny simply "parking" their first ballot support with fringe candidates? It seems unlikely. In the first instance, only three of the eleven contests even went to a second ballot. For delegates to the 1993 PEI Liberal leadership convention, in particular, the strategy of waiting until after the first ballot in order to jump on the winning bandwagon would have been nonsensical: there was, after all, only one serious candidate in the race. Nor is there much evidence of parking in the three conventions that took more than a single ballot to declare a winner. Only 33 percent of those activists who supported John Drish and George Hawkins on the first round opted for the victorious John Savage on the decisive second ballot. One year previously, only 36 percent of Clair Callaghan's first round delegates switched to eventual winner Don Cameron on the second ballot; instead, a clear plurality lurched, like medieval body-collectors, into the camp of the doomed Tom McInnis. And at the 2000 Nova Scotia NDP convention, thirty-nine respondents supported Hinrich Bitter-Suermann and Dave Peters on the first ballot.

Amazingly, only one of these found her/his way into the camp of the eventual winner, Helen MacDonald, on the second ballot; the other thirty-eight opted instead for either Kevin Deveaux or Maureen MacDonald. Of course, it might be argued that some of these activists were attempting to engage in strategic voting and simply "backed the wrong horse." Such colossal miscalculation, however, jibes poorly with the political sophistication inherent in the parking gambit.

In fact, Table 9.6 suggests that there are two quite different explanations required to understand the support patterns of fringe candidates. Those activists who not only voted for, but genuinely preferred, a fringe candidate were difficult to distinguish from their cohorts who backed serious candidates. They reached their decision well in advance of the convention, they were not particularly influenced by the official speeches, and they did try to persuade other delegates to vote in a like fashion. Moreover, their motivations were not especially difficult to comprehend. Fully 80 percent of these individuals were either from the candidate's home area or indicated that agreement with the candidate's views on policy was the principal reason for their vote – a relationship that had been obscured earlier when the entire sample of fringe candidate supporters had been considered. For those activists who supported a fringe candidate but whose true preference lay elsewhere, the picture is completely different. Table 9.6 confirms that it is this group that is driving a good portion of the differences observed earlier, and the strength of the associations is apparent from the relatively low sample size throughout the table. What is particularly interesting is the interaction effect between support for fringe candidates, first preference, and time of decision. Table 9.7 reveals that, in the weeks before the convention, the fringe candidacies were hemorrhaging. Of the activists who came to a decision at this time, only 52 percent of those who genuinely preferred a fringe candidate remained loyal. The remainder, somewhat sadly, defected for potentially greener pastures. There was, admittedly, a smaller, countervailing flow from those who decided to support fringe candidates over their own first preferences, but the cruel side of politics was still clearly exposed.

For those who only came to a voting decision during the convention, however, the trend was reversed. Those who had not already fled from the fringe candidate's standard tended to stay the course, and their numbers were somewhat surprisingly swelled by defectors from other camps. Given that information about the relative prospects of the various candidates grows throughout the campaign until peaking at the convention, there would seem to be only one possible way to interpret this phenomenon. Fringe candidates apparently profited from a combination of ambivalence towards the favourites and sympathy for the underdog. Even if their true preference was for a serious candidate, the failure of some activists to make a definitive commitment before the convention indicates that they were harbouring

*Table 9.6*

**Maritime leadership elections (fringe voters only): measures of ambivalence by first preference**

| | | Supported fringe candidate who was first preference | Supported fringe candidate who was not first preference | N* |
|---|---|---|---|---|
| Decided on vote at the leadership convention | No | 78% | 51% | |
| | Yes | 22% | 49%** | 49 |
| Voting decision affected by speeches | No | 61% | 52% | |
| | Yes | 39% | 48% | 492 |
| Attempted to persuade other delegates to vote the same way | No | 43% | 57% | |
| | Yes | 57% | 43% | 219 |
| Most important reason for vote | • policy agreement<br>• best vote-getter<br>• appealing personal characteristics<br>• approached by workers<br>• promised support<br>• help my area<br>• help me politically<br>• appeal to women<br>• appeal to youth<br>• best decision maker<br>• asked by prominent people | 86% | 61% | |
| | Other | 14%<br>N = 136 | 39%**<br>N = 77 | 47 |

\* Sample size necessary to produce statistical significance at the .05 level.
\*\* $\chi^2 < .01$.

some misgivings. They came to the convention looking for a reason to confirm the true preference; inevitably, some did not find that reason, and the fringe candidate stole into this vacuum of commitment. A solid performance in the policy bear-pits or an inspired speech to the convention was sufficient to seduce the support of these ambivalent activists; even if the effect was merely temporary, it needed only to last until the first round of balloting. Magnifying this doubt towards their true preference were apparent feelings of sympathy towards the underdog. Fully 15 percent of those PC delegates who voted for Clair Callaghan in 1991 revealed such sentiments in unsolicited marginal notes appended to their returned questionnaires. Typical comments were that they "wanted [the] candidate to recover [his] deposit," that they "wanted to give the underdog a chance," that they "didn't want him to lose pride," and that they "wanted him to have a good showing [respectable] on first ballot." It would seem that the pattern in Table 9.7 betrays a curious paradox. Many activists defected from fringe candidates before the convention because they perceived the cause to be futile. Come the convention, however, and the same perception of futility suddenly worked to the fringe candidates' advantage. In short, that fringe candidates had no prospects of success was both initially repellent and subsequently attractive.

What, then, can be concluded from this analysis? Two observations stand out. First, and most obviously, there are two distinct types of party activists who support fringe candidates. One group is distinguishable from the rest of the party stalwarts largely by virtue of their preferred candidate. In virtually all other aspects, they think and behave like those who back serious candidates; that is, they come to a decision early, attempt to persuade other delegates to vote in a like fashion, are not particularly influenced by the speeches, and are motivated principally by regional and/or ideological concerns. By contrast, the second group of fringe candidate supporters tends to share none of these attributes. In their stead are a combination of ambivalence towards the favourites and sympathy for the underdogs. This ambivalence does not reflect a strategic concern to jump on a winning bandwagon

*Table 9.7*

**Maritime leadership elections: first preference by time of decision by fringe candidate vote**

|  | Fled* | Held** | Lured*** | Ratio of fled to lured |
|---|---|---|---|---|
| Decided on first ballot vote before convention | 91 | 105 | 40 | 2.3:1 |
| Decided on first ballot vote during convention | 14 | 30 | 39 | 0.3:1 |

\* "Fled" refers to those delegates whose first preference was a fringe candidate but who cast their first ballot for a different candidate.
\*\* "Held" refers to those delegates whose first preference was a fringe candidate and who cast their first ballot for that candidate.
\*\*\* "Lured" refers to those delegates who voted for a fringe candidate on the first ballot even though that candidate was not their first preference.

after the initial ballot; rather, from one perspective, they can be seen as rebels without a cause.[28]

Second, the analysis suggests that opinion polls on the relative standing of the candidates taken prior to the convention will ignore two countervailing tendencies. On the one hand, they will reinforce the climate of opinion that suggests that fringe candidates have no legitimate prospects for success.[29] As such, they will contribute to the pre-convention flight from these candidates. It might, therefore, be assumed that the polls will slightly overestimate the support base of fringe candidates. On the other hand, many public opinion soundings either ignore the undecided or factor them into the analysis in the same proportions as they do decided voters. Recall, however, that only 6.2 percent of those activists who made up their mind prior to the convention supported fringe candidates, while the corresponding figure for those who reached a last minute judgement was a healthy 20.3 percent. By ignoring this phenomenon, therefore, it might be thought that the polls will slightly underestimate the size of fringe candidate support. Yet, since these two factors work in opposite directions, they may effectively cancel each other out. One can surmise, however, that the closer to the convention a poll is taken (that is, after the viability of a fringe candidate's chances have been repeatedly called into question by the media and most of those who might be so inclined have already jumped ship), the more likely the poll is to underestimate a fringe candidate's eventual first round total.

Leadership candidates and their supporters generally exist in a symbiotic relationship. In return for the latter's efforts on their behalf, the former provide (or pledge to provide) a range of material, ideological, social, and symbolic benefits. With respect to fringe candidates, however, the symbiosis is incomplete. The peculiarity of fringe candidate behaviour and the willingness to embrace certain humiliation is noted at the outset of this chapter. Their public abasement is less than complete, however, only because the fringe candidate's apparent masochism is not matched by a commensurate level of sadism among the party activists.

# 10

# Going My Way? "Delivering" Votes after the First Ballot

Voters at Canadian leadership conventions enjoy significant autonomy in choosing their favourite candidate. In obvious contrast to their American counterparts, delegates to Canadian leadership conventions have not been shepherded under the watchful eyes of regional notables, have not been compelled to cast public ballots, and have not had their options profoundly constrained by the choices of local caucuses and primaries. True, Canadian leadership delegates may have owed their status to participation in candidate slates at the constituency level, but once so elected, their freedom has been inhibited only by the self-imposed dictates of conscience and duty.[1] However, the extent of that autonomy has been questioned for those voters whose standard-bearers are, at some point, eliminated from the contest. Although there has been much media discussion of the impact of candidate endorsements, there has been relatively little in the way of systematic academic analysis of these vote transfers. Our data permits us to explore and analyze such transfers over a number of elections. We begin this chapter with a brief review of the predominantly national literature dealing with this phenomenon.

The folklore of Canadian leadership conventions is rich in tales of "intense back-room dealing,"[2] and of pledges to "deliver" blocks of delegates in return for a variety of benefits. Thus, Alvin Hamilton, a leadership candidate at the 1967 national Progressive Conservative convention, could refer to supporters, in revealingly paternalistic terms, as his "boys,"[3] at the same time as fellow contender George Hees was being urged to make a deal while he still had "some marbles left to roll."[4] Finally, it is worth recalling the events of the 1961 Ontario Progressive Conservative leadership convention. After five ballots, Robert Macaulay was eliminated and only Kelso Roberts and John Robarts remained in the contest. According to one account, Macaulay's supporters were numerous enough to give the victory to whichever of the two remaining candidates he guided them towards. The crucial decision was his ... [Macaulay] stood silent for a few moments, his forehead creased ... Macaulay turned to those around him and said: "Go tell our people to vote for Robarts. We don't want Roberts." With that, he left his seat and strode smilingly over to Robarts.[5]

Admittedly, most leadership candidates will exaggerate their influence and most media commentators are overeager to personalize power relations. Nevertheless, these accounts stand in sharp contrast to the understanding of voter autonomy sketched at the outset.

Can these two perspectives (delegate as subject versus delegate as object) be reconciled? All voters, even those who are interested and informed, respond to political cues from their immediate environment. It might be naive to dismiss its import when such a cue comes from someone to whom a delegate has made a genuine emotional commitment (and the frequent scenes of weeping in the camps of defeated candidates would suggest that this is not an uncommon phenomenon). Thus, some formally autonomous delegates may choose to be loyal to, and guided by, their fallen hero (even if the language of "choice" likely misrepresents the process involved). Put differently, such voters are free to be unfree.

At the national level, most eliminated leadership candidates have opted to provide a cue to their supporters. In the period between 1967 and 1993, as Table 10.1 reveals, a total of fifty-three candidates sought the leadership of the Liberals (1968, 1984), NDP (1989), or Progressive Conservatives (1967, 1976, 1983, 1993).[6] Of the thirty-eight who failed to reach their convention's final ballot, only ten made no signal. In convention vernacular, such candidates are said to have "released" their followers; such language, it is worth noting, implies that the delegates had previously been enjoying something less than total autonomy. The other twenty-eight candidates all indicated a preference among the remaining contenders. Was this group effectively able to "deliver" its support? The amount of attention paid to such endorsements by delegates, candidates, and media observers alike is certainly suggestive, but only that. Unfortunately, reaching a definitive conclusion on this matter is difficult. A first glance at Table 10.1 suggests that endorsements do matter. Twenty-eight eliminated candidates indicated a preference among the remaining contenders; in only five such instances did a plurality of their supporters vote otherwise on the next ballot. Even some of these deviant cases come with rather substantial caveats. Joe Greene's apparent inability in 1968 to direct his delegates to Pierre Trudeau, for example, is based on an N of only 14; just the movement of a single Greene supporter from the Winters to the Trudeau column would erase the former's plurality. Likewise, the Grafftey and Nowlan exceptions are based on Ns of 7 and 6, respectively. As for Jim Edwards' failure to deliver en masse to Kim Campbell on the second ballot of the 1993 Tory leadership convention, it is worth noting that only 6 percent of delegates who genuinely preferred Edwards and voted for him on the first ballot had Kim Campbell as their second choice. By contrast, 63 percent of such individuals regarded Jean Charest as their second preference, with a further 27 percent being unsure. Given that initial distribution of opinion, the ability of Edwards to "deliver" 42 percent of his support to Campbell on the second ballot might be adjudged a "success."

The Edwards example highlights some of the problems that bedevil this sort of analysis. Isolating the precise impact of a candidate endorsement would require close tracking of delegate opinions during the convention. To date, however, even the most sophisticated leadership survey instrument has only entailed pre- and post-convention sampling, and this is insufficient to disentangle the effect of an endorsement from, for example, that of candidate speeches or media coverage of the convention or discussions with other delegates or even self-reflection. The Edwards case also suggests that one cannot apply fixed benchmarks to assess the ability of departing candidates to deliver their votes. John Courtney, for example, has suggested that a successful endorsement requires that at least 70 percent of the directed delegates vote in the prescribed manner.[7] However, this standard is not sensitive to the size of the field; it is presumably more impressive if 65 percent follow a candidate's lead when there are still six contenders left in the race than it is if 70 percent do so when only two remain on the ballot. As well, it takes no account of delegate preferences independent of any candidate endorsement. Of course, Courtney is also aware of this problem, for he quotes the nineteenth-century French politician Ledru-Rollin: "There go my people and I must follow them for I am their leader."[8] If followers and leaders frequently switch roles in this fashion, all of the high correlations apparent in Table 10.1 become immediately suspect.

Are there no paths around these exceedingly murky waters? Do we lack the means to infer whether defeated candidates' endorsements are primarily causal of, or consequential upon, their supporters' voting patterns? With definitive answers to such questions in short supply, analysts will continue to disagree about the significance of endorsements. Hence, Blake, Carty, and Erickson concluded that, at least with respect to the 1986 BC Social Credit race, "once the balloting began these endorsements had little impact."[9] In contrast, Krause and LeDuc decided that the evidence makes it "impossible" to reject the hypothesis that "candidate endorsements are a significant factor in convention political behaviour."[10]

*Table 10.1*

**Canadian leadership elections: candidate endorsements**

| Convention | Supporters of | Directed to | Vote % on next ballot | | | N |
|---|---|---|---|---|---|---|
| 1967 PC | | | **Roblin** | **Stanfield** | **Other** | |
| | McCutcheon | Stanfield | 18 | 41 | 41 | 39 |
| | Hees | Stanfield | 34 | 42 | 24 | 81 |
| | Fulton | Stanfield | 29 | 64 | 7 | 154 |
| | Diefenbaker | None | 34 | 26 | 40 | 54 |
| | Hamilton | None | 51 | 37 | 12 | 59 |
| | Flemming | None | 22 | 32 | 46 | 50 |
| | Starr | None | 21 | 11 | 68 | 19 |
| 1968 Liberals | | | **Trudeau** | **Winters** | **Other** | |
| | Greene | Trudeau | 36 | 50 | 14 | 14 |
| | MacEachen | Trudeau | 47 | 28 | 25 | 70 |
| | Hellyer | Winters | 23 | 69 | 7 | 156 |
| | Martin | None | 21 | 35 | 44 | 111 |
| | Kierans | None | 52 | 13 | 35 | 48 |
| 1976 PC | | | **Clark** | **Wagner** | **Other** | |
| | MacDonald | Clark | 92 | 3 | 5 | 39 |
| | Stevens | Clark | 46 | 18 | 36 | 28 |
| | Fraser | Clark | 44 | 13 | 43 | 16 |
| | Gillies | Clark | 38 | 8 | 54 | 13 |
| | Grafftey | Clark | 14 | 0 | 86 | 7 |
| | Horner | Wagner | 29 | 66 | 5 | 35 |
| | Hellyer | Wagner | 35 | 56 | 9 | 34 |
| | Nowlan | Wagner | 50 | 0 | 50 | 6 |
| | Mulroney | None | 67 | 33 | 0 | 42 |

▼ *Table 10.1*

| Convention | Supporters of | Directed to | Vote % on next ballot | | | | N |
|---|---|---|---|---|---|---|---|
| **1983 PC** | | | **Clark** | **Crosbie** | **Mulroney** | **Other** | |
| | Crombie | Crosbie | 30 | 55 | 15 | 0 | 20 |
| | Gamble | Crosbie | 0 | 100 | 0 | 0 | 3 |
| | Pocklington | Mulroney | 0 | 50 | 50 | 0 | 20 |
| | Wilson | Mulroney | 12 | 35 | 49 | 4 | 43 |
| | Crosbie | None | 21 | 0 | 75 | 4 | 192 |
| **1984 Liberals** | | | **Chretien** | **Turner** | **Other** | | |
| | Roberts | Chretien | 56 | 40 | 4 | | 50 |
| | Munro | Chretien | 59 | 35 | 6 | | 17 |
| | Whelan | Chretien | 32 | 68 | 0 | | 25 |
| | MacGuigan | Turner | 24 | 73 | 3 | | 29 |
| **1989 NDP** | | | **McLaughlin** | **Barrett** | **Langdon** | **Other** | |
| | Langdon | McLaughlin | 59 | 33 | 0 | 8 | 177 |
| | De Jong | McLaughlin | 55 | 23 | 21 | 1 | 138 |
| | McCurdy | Langdon | 23 | 15 | 45 | 17 | 90 |
| | Waddell | Barrett | 29 | 37 | 20 | 14 | 122 |
| | LaGassé | None | 19 | 23 | 31 | 27 | 26 |
| **1993 PC** | | | **Campbell** | **Charest** | **Other** | | |
| | Edwards | Campbell | 42 | 57 | 1 | | 84 |
| | Boyer | Charest | 15 | 85 | 0 | | 13 |
| | Turner | None | 41 | 59 | 0 | | 17 |

When we turn to examining voting practices at Maritime leadership conventions, similar problems emerge. Admittedly, departing candidates in this region have been less prone than have those in other regions to signal their preference among the remaining contenders: Table 10.2 illustrates that only six of the fifteen individuals in our data set chose to do so. Of those six, all but one was able to deliver at least a plurality of their supporters to their chosen ally. The single exception concerned Pat Binns' idiosyncratic declaration for the third place candidate in the 1981 Prince Edward Island Progressive Conservative's contest: Fred Driscoll. With Driscoll's own support hemorrhaging on the second ballot (he retained only 67 percent of his first ballot backers, while the corresponding figures for the two front-runners, Jim Lee and Barry Clark, were 95 and 90, respectively), Binns was able to deliver only a modest number of his delegation to Driscoll. The other five candidates who chose to direct their supporters were far more successful than was Binns, although only three (Allaby, Blaney, and Maureen MacDonald) achieved John Courtney's 70 percent benchmark for success. On the other hand, Table 10.3 reveals that the supporters of three of the other fallen candidates (Mooney, Hawkins, and Bitter-Suermann) moved

*Table 10.2*

**Maritime leadership elections: candidate endorsements**

| Convention | Eliminated candidate | Endorsement | Next ballot | N |
|---|---|---|---|---|
| NS PC 1971 | Thornhill | Buchanan | 66% Buchanan, 34% Doucet | 108 |
| NS Lib 1980 | MacInnis | MacLean | 48% MacLean, 32% Cameron, 20% Mooney | 56 |
|  | Mooney | None |  |  |
| PEI PC 1981 | Binns | Driscoll | 41% Lee, 30% Driscoll, 30% Clark | 27 |
|  | Driscoll | None |  |  |
| NS PC 1991 | Callaghan | None |  |  |
|  | McInnis | None |  |  |
| NS Lib 1992 | Hawkins | None |  |  |
|  | Driscoll | None |  |  |
|  | MacInnis | None |  |  |
| NB PC 1997 | Blaney | Lord | 96% Lord, 4% Betts | 49 |
|  | Allaby | Lord | 73% Lord, 27% Betts | 89 |
| NS NDP 2000 | Bitter-Suermann | None |  |  |
|  | Peters | None |  |  |
|  | M. MacDonald | H. MacDonald | 74% H. MacDonald, 26% Deveaux | 93 |

*Table 10.3*

**Maritime leadership elections: absence of candidate endorsement by subsequent vote**

| Convention | Candidate supported | Plurality preference for | % vote on next ballot for preferred candidate | $\chi^2$ | Adjusted residual |
|---|---|---|---|---|---|
| NS Lib 1980 | Mooney | Cameron | 80 | *** | +3.2 |
| | Others | – | 59 | | |
| PEI PC 1981 | Driscoll | Lee | 59 | – | +0.5 |
| | Others | – | 64 | | |
| NS PC 1991 | Callaghan | McInnis | 44 | * | +1.8 |
| | Others | – | 35 | | |
| NS PC 1991 | McInnis | Cameron | 68 | ** | +2.6 |
| | Others | – | 60 | | |
| NS Lib 1992 | Drish | Downe | 56 | – | +1.0 |
| | Others | – | 44 | | |
| NS Lib 1992 | Hawkins | Downe | 86 | ** | +2.2 |
| | Others | – | 44 | | |
| NS Lib 1992 | MacInnis | Downe | 66 | *** | +5.6 |
| | Others | – | 42 | | |
| NS NDP 2000 | Bitter-Suermann | Deveaux | 80 | *** | +3.5 |
| | Others | – | 35 | | |
| NS NDP 2000 | Peters | M. MacDonald | 50 | ** | +2.1 |
| | Others | – | 29 | | |

\* $\chi^2 < .10$
\*\* $\chi^2 < .05$
\*\*\* $\chi^2 < .01$

almost as one into another camp, even in the absence of any overt signal from their fallen champion.

How are we to make sense of this data? One way to test for the impact of candidate endorsements is to make the (admittedly artificial) assumption that, in the absence of any given candidate, supporters of that individual would be distributed among the other contenders in approximately the same proportions as are found in the remainder of the electorate. One could then contrast the anticipated and actual results for those delegates whose standard-bearer had been eliminated on the previous ballot. If candidate endorsements are significant, two phenomena should be apparent in the data. First, support for the endorsed by followers of the endorser should be consistently higher than one would anticipate, other things being equal. Second, the deviations from the expected outcome should be consistently higher than they are in the absence of such directions from departing candidates. The final two columns of Tables 10.3 and 10.4 undertake this exercise. As is apparent, the actual vote totals for the endorsee in Table 10.4 do, in every

*Table 10.4*

---

**Maritime leadership elections: candidate endorsement by subsequent vote**

| Convention | Candidate supported | Directed to | % vote on next ballot for endorsed candidate | $\chi^2$ | Adjusted residual |
|---|---|---|---|---|---|
| NS PC 1971 | Thornhill | Buchanan | 66 | *** | +3.6 |
| | Others | – | 46 | | |
| NS Lib 1980 | MacInnis | MacLean | 48 | ** | +2.3 |
| | Others | – | 32 | | |
| PEI PC 1981 | Binns | Driscoll | 30 | * | +1.7 |
| | Others | – | 16 | | |
| NB PC 1997 | Allaby | Lord | 73 | * | +1.9 |
| | Others | – | 62 | | |
| NB PC 1997 | Blaney | Lord | 96 | *** | +4.9 |
| | Others | – | 61 | | |
| NS NDP 2000 | M. MacDonald | H. MacDonald | 74 | *** | +4.3 |
| | Others | – | 48 | | |

* $\chi^2 < .10$
** $\chi^2 < .05$
*** $\chi^2 < .01$

instance, exceed expectations. Even more important, the significance tests are generally stronger and the adjusted residuals are generally higher in Table 10.4 than they are in Table 10.3. Thus, one can tentatively conclude that the presence of a candidate endorsement is associated with a more constrained distribution of votes. The nature of the linkage between the two, however, remains problematic.

One way to explore this connection is to consider the motivations of those involved. In George Perlin's well-known typology, party activity can be animated by considerations of affect, of patronage, and/or of policy;[11] the relative importance of these different concerns might well underlie the impact of candidate endorsements. Unfortunately, it is not just the motivations of the suddenly homeless voters that are relevant but also those of the departing candidates themselves. At the national level, candidate endorsements have ostensibly been animated by a wide range of considerations. Those motivated by policy concerns have probably been the most straightforward. Peter Pocklington and Michael Wilson are alleged to have moved to Brian Mulroney rather than to John Crosbie at the 1983 Progressive Conservative convention because "both men want[ed] the economy to be the issue in any future election," and a Crosbie victory might have precipitated a campaign hijacked by matters of language and national unity.[12] Other candidates have apparently been driven by concerns of patronage and power. Perhaps the most blatant instance of this phenomenon occurred at the 1979 convention of the Newfoundland Conservatives. After a disappointing result on the first ballot, tourism minister James Morgan was heard "frantically murmuring to himself that he had to 'pick a winner.'" After taking "a deep breath," Morgan took himself out of the contest and declared for (eventual victor) Brian Peckford.[13] Even though few candidates are as frank about their pursuit of political interests, one does not have to be a jaded cynic to detect the not infrequent presence of same.

Most inscrutable of all for the political outsider are those endorsements animated by affective attachments. Sometimes these emotional considerations involve the positive bonds of loyalty, respect, and friendship. Thus, John Roberts at the 1984 Liberal leadership tilt was being urged by his advisers to move to John Turner and save his career but "out of friendship and principle" opted to back the doomed candidacy of Jean Chrétien.[14] Similarly, after the penultimate ballot of the 1961 Ontario Progressive Conservative leadership convention, Robert Macaulay was mistakenly believed to be leaning towards fellow Torontonian Kelso Roberts over John Robarts. "Proponents of a Toronto-versus-the-hinterland strategy," notes one observer, "did not take into account other factors affecting political loyalties such as ties of youth and friendship." In the end, the latter proved decisive and Macaulay endorsed Robarts.[15] Finally, despite having earlier pledged to support Dave Barrett in return for an appointment as caucus whip,[16] Simon de Jong justified his surprising move to Audrey McLaughlin at the 1989 New Democratic Party national convention thusly: "My head told me to go to Dave Barrett, my heart told me to go to Audrey."[17]

On other occasions, however, candidates have seemingly been driven by feelings of visceral hostility. Thus, despite pledges to that effect from a campaign manager, Sinclair Stevens never considered moving to the camp of Jack Horner in 1976. Acknowledged Horner: "He knew I didn't hold him in very high esteem."[18] Similarly, Mitchell Sharp's dramatic declaration for Pierre Trudeau on the eve of the 1968 Liberal leadership convention was partially motivated by Sharp's "personal antipathy" for Trudeau's chief rival Robert Winters.[19] Finally, many had assumed that David Crombie would be a natural ally of Joe Clark at the 1983 Progressive Conservative convention. But Crombie "had never forgiven Clark for not putting him in the inner cabinet,"[20] and he moved instead to the camp of John Crosbie. Indeed, Crombie's animus towards Clark was so intense that he purportedly stayed in the race for a second ballot partly to forestall any growth in Clark's vote total.[21]

Clearly, the endorsements of defeated candidates are animated by a rich variety of impulses. Moreover, the same range of motivations is apparent among delegates; while some attach themselves to a candidate for policy reasons, others act on the basis of patronage or affective concerns. Can we make any sense of this motivational stew? It seems plausible that some combinations of candidate and delegate motivation will increase, while others will decrease, the likelihood that the two will act as one even after the former has been eliminated from the race. For example, when a defeated candidate endorses another contender for policy reasons, it is likely to resonate positively with those supporters whose initial attachment was likewise motivated by policy. In contrast, many who support a candidate for affective reasons will be completely unmoved when, in defeat, that candidate is also driven by affective considerations into the camp of another contender.

Unfortunately, teasing out these linkages is very difficult. Human motivation is much more complex than the basic trichotomy sketched here. Even if an action's primary motivation can be identified, it is likely to be shaped, altered, or reinforced by the presence of subsidiary influences. Thus, Peter Pocklington's aforementioned endorsement of Brian Mulroney in 1983 may well have been largely impelled by policy concerns. But power motivations were also part of Pocklington's calculations. Pocklington had promised to endorse John Crosbie if the ebullient Newfoundlander was within two hundred votes of Brian Mulroney: "Crosbie wasn't," summarizes one account, "and Pocklington didn't."[22] In fact, Pocklington had already negotiated the price of his endorsement in any future Mulroney administration: he was to have a prominent role (perhaps as a cabinet minister or as chair of a royal commission on taxation).[23] Finally, Pocklington's actions were also driven by affective motivations. Pocklington may have been a political neophyte with idiosyncratic views, but Mulroney was consistently solicitous towards him. This, according to one observer, helped to cement the deal between the two: "Here was a man [Pocklington] looking for respect and getting it, from one of the leading contenders."[24] Thus, disentangling the motivations behind Pocklington's actions in 1983 is not straightforward. Once one realizes that almost all participants at Canadian leadership conventions have personalities at least as complex as that of Peter Pocklington, the magnitude of this problem becomes apparent. Moreover, candidates cannot be relied upon to provide straightforward motivational accounts. Whether they are consciously dissembling or unconsciously deluded, their comments for public consumption will usually emphasize other-regarding concerns. Thus, Ken MacInnis justified his move to Vince MacLean after the first ballot of the 1980 Nova Scotia Liberal leadership convention on the grounds that the two men had "similar positions on the major issues."[25] Perhaps, but MacInnis had made provincial control over offshore development the centrepiece of his campaign, while MacLean had pointedly told delegates that he had yet to formulate a position on the matter. Moreover, MacInnis' campaign manager had, earlier that day, allegedly informed the Fraser Mooney team that, if eliminated, his man would move to their camp.[26] Under such cloudy circumstances, making complete sense of MacInnis' actions is next to impossible. Similar ambiguities are apparent with each of the five other relevant candidates in our data set.

Fortunately, these sorts of problems appear less daunting when we turn our attention to the followers of these candidates. While respondent reactivity is an endemic feature of survey research, these individuals are not only much less likely to have complicated motivational underpinnings to their convention behaviour but they are also much more prone to provide forthright responses about same. Finally, they exist in much larger numbers. Merging the supporters of the six defeated candidates who subsequently endorsed another contender produces a sample of 384 respondents, 254 of whom joined their former standard-bearer in another camp, 130 of whom did not. The results from Table 10.5, however, are somewhat disappointing. As anticipated, those who had an affective basis for their first ballot were less "reliable" in their voting behaviour once the object of their affections had been eliminated from the race. The difference, however, is relatively small and does not quite approach statistical significance. In fact, there are no notable structural, attitudinal, or motivational differences between those electors who voted on the next ballot with their fallen champion and those who did not. While not decisive, this finding permits us to draw some inferences about the leader-follower relationship. Recall our earlier uncertainty about how best to interpret the high correlation between candidate endorsements and the subsequent voting behaviour of their followers. Put bluntly: were candidates generally leading or following their supporters? If the former were true, one might anticipate finding some imprint of their actions in the data, some sign that, for example, younger voters, or members of the party brass, or place-seekers, or those without university education were more (or less) likely to follow the direction of their ousted standard-bearer. That no such imprint can be found suggests that candidate

*Table 10.5*

**Maritime leadership elections: principal motivation by vote for endorsed candidate**

| Principal motivation | Voted for endorsed candidate (%) | Did not vote for endorsed candidate (%) | N |
|---|---|---|---|
| Policy | 68 | 32 | 155 |
| Patronage | 62 | 38 | 78 |
| Affective | 55 | 45 | 56 |
| Other | 73 | 27 | 95 |
| | | | 384 |

endorsements are more likely to be dependent than independent factors in the chain of convention causality.

For the most part, the data contained in Table 10.6 strengthen this understanding. Respondents to our survey of the 1997 New Brunswick PC race were asked to provide their candidate preference ranking as well as their voting behaviour. Admittedly, the data must be approached cautiously as respondents might just be harmonizing their thoughts and their actions after the fact. Nevertheless, Table 10.6 indicates that the overwhelming proportion of former Allaby and Blaney supporters preferred Lord to Betts and voted in a fashion consistent with that rank ordering. Thus, for either Allaby or Blaney to have endorsed Betts rather than Lord would have been not only improbable (assuming that candidates and their supporters have generally similar views on many matters) but also, for the most part, ineffective. True, that minority of Allaby and Blaney supporters who preferred Betts to Lord were more likely than were the others to have voted for their less preferred candidate on the second ballot. Had those who preferred Betts defected to the same degree as did those who preferred Lord, then Lord would have received seven fewer votes (from a total of 124) from our second ballot sample. It is not unreasonable to attribute at least part of that relatively modest total to the endorsements of Lord by Allaby and Blaney (although the general tendency for leading candidates to hold their support more effectively than their trailing competitors must also carry part of the explanatory load). Even in the absence of candidate endorsements, in other words, the second ballot outcome would have been only slightly different.

Because we only have six instances of candidate endorsements in our data set, it is impossible to pick out specific provincial, temporal, or partisan patterns. It may be, however, that the move to the universal ballot will decrease still further the frequency with which this phenomenon will figure prominently in future conventions. First, as we have seen, all-member votes tend to be decided on a single ballot, thus removing the need for eliminated candidates to signal a preference to their supporters. Second, in most all-member votes (excluding, of course, those on Prince Edward Island), the bulk of the electorate is not physically present at the convention and might well, as a result, be oblivious to the sorts of visual cues often provided

*Table 10.6*

**New Brunswick PC leadership election, 1997 (Allaby and Blaney voters only): candidate preference by second ballot vote**

|  | Voted Lord | Voted Betts |
| --- | --- | --- |
| Preferred Lord | 95 | 3 |
| Preferred Betts | 8 | 18 |

by departing candidates. Finally, some parties (such as the Nova Scotia Liberals in 2002) have employed a preferential ballot in their all-member votes. Clearly, an exiting candidate cannot influence the direction of votes that have already been cast.

Two conclusions flow logically from this analysis. First, candidate endorsements are clearly a useful predictor of electoral behaviour. Wherever such endorsements occur, in other words, we can be confident that the candidate's former supporters will move disproportionately in the indicated direction. Second, the dynamics of this phenomenon have frequently been misinterpreted. Most followers of a departing candidate are not waiting for a signal to move from one corral to another. On the contrary, the evidence suggests that any candidate declaration is more likely to reflect than to induce such a stampede. The political folklore of Canadian leadership conventions, in other words, mistakenly downplays the importance of voter autonomy.

Accordingly, some of the language employed to characterize Canadian leadership conventions needs to be either modified or reinterpreted. To take but one example: departing candidates are frequently said to "deliver" the votes of supporters to another contender, as though they exercised some form of proprietary control over these ballots. Such terminology should only be retained if the candidate's delivery function is seen to be more akin to that of mail-carriers, who, after all, have little effective authority over that which they deliver and whose "deliverables" arrive at a destination determined by others.

# 11
# Prince Edward Island and the Garden Myth

At the heart of Prince Edward Island's provincial identity is the myth of the garden. As depicted in the early twentieth-century writings of Lucy Maud Montgomery, the Island has been understood to be a veritable Eden, a bucolic redoubt from the chaos of modern, urban life. At a number of points in our analysis, particularly in Chapters 3 and 6, we saw the significance of the Island's rural nature in leadership politics, and in this chapter we explore the implications of the province's rural nature in more depth.

Prince Edward Island is the most rural of the Maritime (and Canadian) provinces, and rural Islanders were well represented at all leadership conventions. The importance of the province's rural nature was highlighted in the judgment rendered in *MacKinnon v. Prince Edward Island et al.*, the 1993 case that ended the rough equality of county representation in the Island legislature. As Justice DesRoches wrote: "The importance of the rural economy cannot be overestimated and the rural nature of the Island should continue to be reflected in the composition of the legislature."[1]

In a perceptive essay first published in 1982, David Milne argues that the garden myth "organized for Islanders an ideal picture of themselves as an independent agricultural people protected from the world in an unspoiled pastoral setting."[2] Of course, not all aspects of life on PEI conformed to this sense of collective identity, but nor was the disconnect so profound as to render it risible. In Milne's formulation of the garden myth, three key elements could be distinguished. First, Islanders are understood to be farmers; other pursuits are legitimate only in so far as they advance agrarian interests. Second, the marriage of three centuries of small-scale human endeavours with the Island's natural topography has produced a landscape of incomparable beauty. Third, there is virtue in being a geographic, economic, and cultural hinterland; isolation from the Canadian, continental, and global mainstream has permitted the preservation of a distinctive and valuable Island way of life. A quarter-century of surveying Island activists at leadership conventions permits us to gain some purchase on each of these orientations. As will become apparent, only some aspects of the garden myth retain a prominent place in most Islanders' consciousness.

## The Pre-eminence of Agriculture

Whatever the cultural mythology, agriculture's social and economic domi-nance of Prince Edward Island dropped precipitously throughout the twen-tieth century. Admittedly, the data on land under cultivation do not do justice to the extent of this decline. Of the 1.4 million acres of land that constitute Prince Edward Island, an astonishing peak of 1.2 million acres was being farmed in 1931. By 1976, the year of our first leadership conven-tion on the Island, this figure had dropped somewhat to 730,000 acres;[3] in 2001, the corresponding number was 646,000 acres.[4] What these figures disguise, however, is the extraordinary reduction in the number of farms on PEI. In the sixty years between 1941 and 2001, fully 85 percent of Island farms disappeared, and the bottom has apparently not yet been hit. Al-though about half the Island is still under cultivation, farms have grown much larger and the community of farmers has grown much smaller. In short, agribusiness has largely supplanted the small family farm.[5] This is not, needless to say, how the garden myth was supposed to play out on Prince Edward Island. After over a century of exploitation by absentee Brit-ish landlords, the land question for Island farmers was ostensibly settled at Confederation. Thereafter, notes one observer, "the society of independent yeoman ought to grow, prosper, and become celebrated in song and story. Unfortunately, only the last occurs. Growth and progress soon come to a halt, and despite the folk culture the Island increasingly finds itself locked into agrarian backwardness."[6] In fact, Prince Edward Island farm income during the middle portion of the twentieth century was typically about 25 percent of the average Canadian personal income.[7] Perversely, the value of farm land on Prince Edward Island continued to rise during this period; thus, Island farmers were doomed to "live poor and die rich."[8] Not surpris-ingly, many Island farmers opted out of this scenario; those who remained (and their numbers fell from 21,000 in 1901 to 7,800 as of 1996) turned to mechanization, consolidation, and monoculture in order to secure a living.

Notwithstanding this social transformation, the vision of the Island as a society of independent farmers has not perished. Even as it no longer cap-tured the reality of conditions on Prince Edward Island, it remained as a powerful, albeit increasingly utopian, ideal. Successive Island governments (with the partial exception of Alex Campbell's administration of the 1960s and 1970s) have striven to prop up traditional rural society by blocking land sales to non-residents, limiting the number of acres that any single landowner can possess, and so on. Thus, Angus MacLean, who headed a government dedicated to a "Rural Renaissance" in the early 1980s, has mused that "all societies of the past collapsed when they became highly urbanized."[9] When the Island's electoral boundaries were challenged in the early 1990s, MacLean came to the defence of rural areas. In the former premier's view, "the protection of rural interest in Prince Edward Island requires that representation for rural areas not be reduced. The Island is almost dependent on farming and fishing, the basic industries on which the Island society exists."[10] Then agriculture minister and future premier Keith Milligan was similarly supportive and "stated that any redistribution which would tend to urbanize representation would not be necessarily healthy. He said that the voice of the farming community must be heard and any reduction in the power of that voice would exacerbate already existing problems."[11] Even current premier (and full-time bean farmer) Pat Binns employs rhetoric that is "pointedly nostalgic."[12]

Do these aspects of the garden myth continue to resonate among ordinary Prince Edward Islanders? Are the primacy of agriculture and the sanctity of land still central to their collective sense of identity? Over a twenty-seven-year period, we have surveyed Island activists at leadership conventions on eight separate occasions. The data relevant to this part of the garden myth are reproduced in Table 11.1.

A number of patterns are present in Table 11.1. First, there is apparent homogeneity on each of these four measures. Virtually no one thought Cavendish Farms should be able to buy up large tracts of farmland, and essentially everyone agreed that foreign investment in Prince Edward Island should be regulated and that government must protect agricultural land and institute provincewide land-use zoning regulations. Second, there are no partisan differences over these matters: even New Democrats, who are often perceived to be outside the Island's political mainstream, share completely in this consensus. Finally, the data have remained remarkably consistent over time: there is no indication that this particular cornerstone of the garden myth is beginning to erode.

### Pastoral Beauty

Many have commented on the bucolic charms of Prince Edward Island. "Fly over in autumn," rhapsodizes one enthusiast, "and you will see below the greatest panorama of quaintness and color you have ever witnessed."[13] The Island is widely regarded as an unspoiled refuge in an increasingly urbanized and industrialized world. Perversely, the virtual unanimity on this point threatens to undercut its validity as large numbers of tourists flock to Prince Edward Island every summer.

Islanders have long regarded the annual inundation of visitors "from away" with some ambivalence. On the one hand, tourism provides much-needed revenues for the province's beleaguered economy; indeed, like agriculture,

*Table 11.1*

## PEI leadership elections: agriculture attitudes (% agree)

| | 1976 PCs | 1978 Liberals | 1981 Liberals | 1981 PCs | 1993 Liberals | 1996 Liberals | 2002 NDP | 2003 Liberals |
|---|---|---|---|---|---|---|---|---|
| The PEI government should permit Cavendish Farms to buy more land. | | | 15 | 9 | | | | |
| Foreign investment should be regulated. | 86 | 89 | 91 | 87 | 87 | 85 | 93 | 83 |
| Government must protect and preserve agricultural land. | | | | | 95 | 97 | 98 | 97 |
| PEI requires a system of provincewide land-use zoning regulations. | | | | | 88 | 90 | 100 | 87 |

tourism now contributes about $300 million annually to the Island's GDP. The number of tourists per year has grown from half a million in the mid-1970s to 800,000 in the early 1990s to 1.2 million since the opening of the Confederation Bridge in 1997. Thus, the tourist-to-permanent resident ratio now stands at approximately 9:1, and even though this figure is somewhat deceptive (since all the visitors are not in situ simultaneously), shoe-horning so many people into a relatively confined area every summer must obliterate some of the Island's special appeal. Even so, some would like to see traffic volumes ramped up even further. A publication of the Canadian Institute for Research on Regional Development, for example, suggests that "the tourist industry is an area in which opportunities appear to outnumber obstacles,"[14] while the provincial Department of Tourism trumpets its mandate "to promote continued growth in the tourism sector, aggressively market Prince Edward Island as a premier destination, [and] proactively facilitate product and plant development."[15]

To those Islanders enamoured of the garden myth, however, the prospect of transforming Prince Edward Island into "the Bermuda of the North"[16] has been decidedly unappealing. For such folk, tourism has been, at best, a necessary evil, and that only when its baneful impact has been substantially mitigated. Thus, one speaker in the debate over the Automobile Act, 1908, observed:

> The proposition that the government widen the roads for the convenience of autoists is too ridiculous to be seriously dealt with. As far as tourists are concerned, we wish to encourage them in every way and for this reason automobiles should be prohibited.[17]

Since 1960 (when the provincial Department of Tourism was first established), such voices have become louder and better organized. Named for a xenophobic anti-Confederate, the Brothers and Sisters of Cornelius Howatt satirized the Campbell government for its "wholesale marketing of the soul of 'the Island' as a tourism gimmick."[18] Such concerns obviously resonated with most Islanders: a 1974 survey, taken at a time when yearly visitors were approximately 40 percent of the present level, revealed that 76 percent of Islanders did not want any increase in the number of tourists.[19] Inevitably, the imperatives of agriculture and of tourism have clashed; typically, the former has held the master trump. Thus, plans were quashed to prevent the use of manure near major thoroughfares during the tourist season, while, over protest, a piggery was constructed adjacent to the Mill River Resort. "The public reception and retelling of such events," notes one observer, "makes it clear that farming ... enjoys moral hegemony as a superior way of life."[20] Of course, modern agricultural practices are also despoiling the garden aesthetic; corporate farming has ostensibly "done much to uglify

*Table 11.2*

| PEI leadership elections: tourism attitudes (% agree) | | | | | | | |
|---|---|---|---|---|---|---|---|
| | 1978 Liberals | 1980 Liberals | 1981 PCs | 1993 Liberals | 1996 Liberals | 2002 NDP | 2003 Liberals |
| Tourism is more important than farming and fishing. | 22 | 7 | 5 | | | | |
| PEI is too dependent on tourism. | | | | 49 | 61 | 84 | 60 |

the district around Bedeque."[21] Nevertheless, it is tourism that is usually singled out for special criticism in this regard. The crowded beaches, the garish theme parks, and the cheap Anne memorabilia, all raise legitimate questions about whether the Island's unspoiled charms can survive the annual summer onslaught of visitors.

Do such concerns exist among Prince Edward Island party activists? Table 11.2 features two attitudinal measures that tap into this aspect of the garden myth. Appropriately enough, the data confirm the reservations that Islanders have about their burgeoning tourism industry. In fact, the trend line for both indicators suggests that Prince Edward Island party activists have become more, rather than less, uneasy about the annual onslaught of visitors from away. Once again, the presence of a key component of the garden myth has been illuminated.

## Isolation and Independence

As an island, PEI is both physically and psychologically removed from the Canadian mainstream. While some might lament this backwater status, celebrants of the garden myth treasure their apparent ability to resist the baneful effects of modernity. Yet there are two problems with this understanding of Prince Edward Island. First, it is demonstrably untrue: Prince Edward Island is not Rivendell. On the contrary, it is subject to a myriad of economic and political forces beyond its control – from federal government laws and regulations to internationally determined prices for agricultural commodities. Indeed, one analyst roots the twentieth-century exodus from Prince Edward Island farms in the Island's status as a "residual" agricultural supplier to outside forces with which it has essentially no bargaining power.[22] Second, even the (inevitably doomed) attempt to construct "Fortress PEI" has had unfortunate consequences; at times, Islanders have exhibited "a parochialism which bordered on the xenophobic."[23] Examples of this attribute have abounded. A 1951 act of the provincial legislature, for instance, dubbed all non-residents (including other Canadians) as "alien[s]."[24]

Yet even if Islanders' collective sense of autonomy is naive, it remains as a central component of the garden myth. In fact, it partly accounts for the antipathy with which Islanders customarily greet fresh tourist ventures. Yes, there is a concern that the Island's pastoral beauty will be blighted by yet another trailer park. But equally, there is a fear that a community of independent farmers will be transformed "into a pandering people – a province of flunkies and attendants."[25]

Welcome or not, the outside world has come crashing in on Prince Edward Island in recent decades. Particular heed must be paid both to the amorphous forces of globalization and neoliberalism as well as to such tangible events as the signing of the Canada-United States Free Trade Agreement (which inextricably tied Prince Edward Island's economic future to markets far beyond its borders) and the construction of the Confederation Bridge (which not only almost doubled the number of annual visitors but also had the singular effect of morphing Prince Edward Island from an island into a peninsula).[26]

How have Islanders responded to these manifest incursions on their collective sense of autonomy? Apparently, with open arms. Table 11.3 reveals that Islanders have embraced many facets of their integration with the outside world. Leaving aside the curious findings on maritime union, Islanders overwhelming accept that the maritime provinces should be more closely integrated, that Confederation has been good for Prince Edward Island, and that interprovincial trade barriers should be removed. The Confederation Bridge proposal may have intensely divided Islanders in the 1980s; in fact, the referendum on proceeding with the fixed link only passed by a margin of 59 percent to 41 percent. Nevertheless, Table 11.3 suggests that relatively few doubts remain about the benefits of this project, with support levels in the Prince Edward Island Liberal party climbing from 72 percent to 90 percent to 99 (!) percent over a ten-year period. A similar, albeit less dramatic, evolution is apparent with respect to the Free Trade Agreement (FTA) with the United States. The FTA being the centrepiece of the national Tories' successful 1988 re-election campaign, it is not surprising that Table 11.3 reveals, at least initially, sharp partisan differences on this matter (with 82 percent of the 1988 Conservatives, but only 12 percent of the 1993 Liberals, expressing approval of the deal). Over time, however, Liberal (but not New Democratic) support for the FTA has ramped upward – first, to 43 percent and, more recently, to 53 percent.

Table 11.3 may reveal a clear attitudinal pattern, but interpretive difficulties remain, especially when it is juxtaposed with Tables 11.1 and 11.2. One possibility is that Table 11.3 signals the beginning of the end to the garden myth and that support for the traditional pastoral aesthetic and for the

Table 11.3

**PEI leadership elections: integration attitudes (% agree)**

|  | 1976 PCs | 1978 Liberals | 1980 Liberals | 1981 PCs | 1988 PCs | 1993 Liberals | 1996 Liberals | 2002 NDP | 2003 Liberals |
|---|---|---|---|---|---|---|---|---|---|
| Maritime union is good idea. | 34 | 82 | 43 | 50 | | | | | |
| PEI government must support proposals to remove interprovincial trade barriers. | | | | | | 87 | 91 | 86 | 92 |
| The maritime provinces should be more closely integrated. | | | | | | 79 | 74 | 77 | 78 |
| The fixed link will benefit/has benefited PEI. | | | | | 78 | 72 | 90 | 79 | 99 |
| Confederation has been a good thing for this province. | | | 97 | 92 | 92 | 96 | 95 | 93 | 98 |
| The Canada/US free trade deal will be/has been good for PEI. | | | | | 82 | 12 | 43 | 14 | 53 |

social pre-eminence of agriculture will likewise soon fall away. Tables 11.1 and 11.2, however, provide no hints that erosion in support for these two aspects of the garden myth is imminent. Thus, it seems more likely that Islanders have effectively disaggregated the garden myth, that they believe integration with the outside world does not preclude preserving a bucolic idyll at home.

The apparent homogeneity with which Islanders regard most aspects of the garden myth makes it difficult to uncover any internal cleavage patterns. Indeed, in the most recent surveys of Island delegates, this group-think is apparent in all the indicators, save two: attitudes towards overdependence on tourism and evaluations of the US-Canada free trade pact. On these matters, where public opinion is much more sharply divided, one might have surmised that differences in age and in community size would have emerged from the data (especially given the evidence in Chapters 5 and 6 of urban-rural cleavages in convention behaviour on PEI), with young and urban Islanders being more supportive of the FTA and less alarmed by the growth of the tourist industry than their elderly and rural counterparts. Surprisingly, the findings from the two most recent Prince Edward Island Liberal conventions provide only modest support for this expectation. As Table 11.4 reveals, the data generally move in the anticipated direction; in only one of the four instances, however, is the difference of a magnitude to be statistically significant.

## Conclusion

For students of Canadian politics, this discussion of Prince Edward Island political culture may seem familiar. There are, after all, striking parallels

*Table 11.4*

**PEI Liberal leadership elections: tourism and FTA attitudes by age and community size (% agree)**

|  | PEI too dependent on tourism | | FTA good for PEI | |
|---|---|---|---|---|
|  | 1996 Liberals | 2003 Liberals | 1996 Liberals | 2003 Liberals |
| Old rural residents* | 69.6 | 59.6 | 40.4 | 45.0 |
| Young urban residents | 39.7 | 59.1 | 50.0 | 60.9 |
| N = | 173** | 80 | 164 | 73 |

* The dividing line between old and young is 50 years, and the dividing line between rural and urban is 5,000 people.
** $\chi^2 < .01$
*Note:* In an attempt to isolate Charlottetown and Summerside residents from other Islanders, we have used 5,000 inhabitants as the line between urban and rural, as opposed to the 1,000 division employed elsewhere in the book.

between the Prince Edward Island case and the much better known twentieth-century transformation of Quebec. Prior to the 1960s, both provinces celebrated a rural mythology, even as the domestic sociological underpinnings were being gradually eroded. In defence of a particular way of life, both have turned to the provincial state to provide legislative bulwarks against change from without. In spite of all efforts, the distinct societies of both Quebec and Prince Edward Island have begun to unravel; many inhabitants have responded by clinging tenaciously to the remains of identity. Finally, most Quebecers and Prince Edward Islanders now accept that their provinces must be more closely integrated into the national and international political economy.

Does this mean that the garden myth will soon disappear from Prince Edward Island, that Islanders will no longer define themselves as an independent farming people in an unspoiled cocoon? It seems doubtful. First, there are obvious commercial benefits to be derived from ensuring that the reality of Prince Edward Island does not stray too far from the garden ideal. Well over a million tourists flock to Prince Edward Island every summer; if their experiences are not at least proximate with the garden ideal, then no amount of ersatz Anne of Green Gables bric-a-brac will keep them coming back. Second, and more fundamentally, most Islanders remain attached to this sense of collective identity. The testimony of former premiers MacLean and Milligan in defence of rural overrepresentation in the legislature make that sense of identity clear. Transformations in social and economic structures need not, especially in the short run, engender corresponding changes in attitudes and orientations. Much depends, first, upon the degree of tension between myth and reality and, second, upon the words and deeds of both established and emerging socio-political elites. It is here that the parallel between Quebec and Prince Edward Island ceases. In the former province, the social transformations wrought by a half-century of urbanization and industrialization rendered the dominant image of a rural, conservative people under the aegis of a parish priest insensible to large numbers of Quebecers. Moreover, these sociological changes had stimulated the rise of new elites wedded to a bourgeois secular individualism and with an obvious interest in challenging the established orthodoxy. After less than a decade of serious contestation (although that period might have been extended but for Duplessis' timely demise), the Quiet Revolution ensued.

Even a half century later in Prince Edward Island, however, comparable phenomena are much less in evidence. There are no Island counterparts either to such industrial towns as Sherbrooke and Shawinigan or to the metropolitan sprawl of Montreal. Nor are there elites extant with an obvious interest in challenging the garden myth;[27] and, as is made clear in the appendix to this book, most Island leadership candidates have professed their allegiance to same. The present-day establishment seems content to use the Island's identity for political and economic gain, and the counter-cultural voices of artisans and environmentalists are, if anything, even more likely to be raised in defence of the garden myth. Of course, the Island way of life could be subtly subverted even by its ostensible defenders. According to Lorraine Begley, this process is already well under way:

> At the whim of the socially dominant, words such as "home" and "community" become in Prince Edward Island, the words of alienation. As the currency of the Department of Tourism, they have been drained of their meaning and then refilled, bloated, discoloured.[28]

On this understanding, the mythological aspects of the original garden identity may, at last, be fully realized. As David Milne has observed, there has been increasing tension between the garden as a description of Prince Edward Island and the garden as a prescription for Prince Edward Island.[29] Even as the Island's reality has progressively deviated from the bucolic idyll of yesteryear, enthusiasm for this vision has continued largely unabated. Of course, such dissonance has its limits (which is not to suggest that they have yet been approached on Prince Edward Island). Resolving such tension is, in this instance, more likely to involve altering the ideal to more closely conform to the reality than shaping the reality to more closely approximate the ideal. If Begley's pungent critique is to be believed, the Island's political and business elites are striving to resolve the contradiction by redefining the terms of the ideal (i.e., by retaining the central concepts while substituting fresh operationalizations of same). Whatever else can be said about such a stratagem, it would at least have the salutary effect of rendering equally mythical both the reality and the pre-transmogrified ideal of Prince Edward Island as a garden.

But that harmonization of the garden myth is clearly some way off. As we saw in Chapter 3, the dominance of rural areas in Island leadership elections shows no signs of abatement, and the majority of Islanders continue to reside in communities of less than one thousand people. This chapter has demonstrated that the Island's rural myths continue to resonate and possess political significance. Our survey data suggest that ordinary Islanders remain fundamentally committed to many aspects of their traditional identity. Their primordial attachment to the red soil of Prince Edward Island is manifested on a variety of indicators, and their concern over the burgeoning tourist trade is almost as evident. Moreover, these orientations display no sign of weakening over the quarter century we have been collecting data. Shifting Islanders away from their traditional sense of collective identity will be both difficult and highly contested. In the end, therefore, the transformation of Prince Edward Island's political orientations is not likely to parallel the process witnessed half a century ago in Quebec. There will be no abrupt shift to a new cultural consensus on Prince Edward Island. Indeed, rather than experiencing a quiet revolution, the much more likely eventuality for the Island is some variant of loud evolution.

# 12

# New Brunswick:
# The Politics of Language

That New Brunswick represents a distinctive social experiment is self-evident. Alone among Canadian provinces, New Brunswick has a substantial francophone minority (32 percent according to the 2001 census);[1] nowhere else in Canada (with the obvious exception of Quebec) does the corresponding figure exceed 10 percent. Thus, when the Canadian Constitution was patriated in 1982, only New Brunswick opted to entrench its bilingual character. Even though, as is revealed in Chapter 3, the two main language groups co-exist in both major parties, francophones and anglophones have traditionally been separated by a diagonal line running from Grand Falls in the northwest of the province to Sackville in the southeast. Most New Brunswick francophone communities have been located to the north and east of this invisible boundary and, at least until the 1960s, were both economically disadvantaged and politically marginalized relative to their anglophone counterparts to the southwest.

In such a setting, as we have already seen in previous chapters, the politics of language (and, by extension, of race, of culture, and of religion) are bound to be divisive. Anglophone and francophone participants in New Brunswick leadership elections behaved differently and differed in the political attitudes they held. Such divisions have long existed in New Brunswick politic more generally.

When successive administrations headed by Louis Robichaud, Richard Hatfield, and Frank McKenna sought to lessen the disparities in wealth and power between the two language groups, intercommunal tensions were frequently laid bare. Of course, some francophones cavilled at what they perceived to be the slow pace of social change and threw in their lot with the nationalist Parti Acadien, while some anglophones objected to what they perceived to be revolutionary changes in the province's socio-political fabric and turned to the Confederation of the Regions (CoR) party. Such infatuations generally proved to be fleeting. At the start of the twenty-first century, both francophone and anglophone New Brunswickers were largely supportive of the brokerage practices of the Liberal and Progressive Conservative parties.[2]

The partisan choices of French and English New Brunswickers have been extensively documented. Beginning with the wartime election of 1917, the former found a home in the Liberal party, while the latter were disproportionately found in the Conservative party. For the next half century, the Liberals consistently received between 15 percent and 20 percent higher vote shares in francophone than in anglophone counties. This ethnic polarization reached its peak in the 1970 provincial election (when the gap climbed to a remarkable 28 percent) but began to decline shortly thereafter. Since 1987, voting differences between English and French counties have been essentially negligible.[3]

That New Brunswickers no longer use voting to "express cultural loyalty"[4] does not imply, however, that the province's francophones and anglophones have become politically indistinguishable. On the contrary, as we shall discover, the two linguistic communities continue to differ in their general approach to political leadership as well as in their particular views on national and provincial issues (although Irish Catholics have occasionally managed to straddle this cleavage). Nor should such divergences be especially surprising. First, New Brunswick's francophones and anglophones have different interests on most matters pertaining to language (from the implementation of official bilingualism to the recognition of Quebec as a distinct society). Second, there have been long-standing differences in power and status between the two communities. Anglophones have not only been numerically preponderant (although their share of the provincial population has fluctuated from a high of 85 percent at Confederation to a low of 62 percent in the early 1950s), but they have also been economically and politically advantaged relative to their francophone counterparts.

Dominant majorities almost never regard politics from the same perspective as do subordinate minorities. The latter, for example, are likely to be particularly sensitive to any slights from members of the majority community. And such slights have never been entirely absent in New Brunswick.[5] During the First World War, for example, the *Gleaner* suggested that English-speakers would "put up a bitter fight" before they would countenance being "pitchforked into the position of serfs and servants for the Acadians."[6] P.J. Veniot, the first Acadian to accede to the premiership, had to endure repeated slurs (including a defamatory campaign initiated by members of the Ku Klux Klan). Noted one opposition organizer in a letter to his constituents: "the Premier we have today is a Roman Catholic and a Frenchman at that and we as Protestants want to put them out."[7] Nor did the province's second Acadian premier, Louis Robichaud, fare differently. In 1969, Robichaud's appearance before an angry crowd precipitated the shout "Get the Frog,"[8] while Robichaud's vigorous recruitment of francophone public servants led some Fredericton anglophones to dub the government's Centennial Building as the "Frog Pond."[9] Reference could also be made to Moncton major Leonard Jones' pointed refusal to hang a bilingual plaque in City Hall,[10] to the incendiary pamphlets of the Canadian Loyalist Society,[11] and to the eggs and abuse hurled by some anglophones during public information workshops on the Poirier-Basturache Report,[12] but the point has already been sufficiently documented. New Brunswick francophones could never be certain whether such hostility reflected the opinions of the silent majority of anglophones or whether they were merely the views of a few extremists.

Against such a backdrop, any minority group would be particularly vigilant about securing its place in society. As Table 12.1 makes clear, New Brunswick's Acadian community is no exception. A number of patterns are apparent on Table 12.1. First, the English and French of New Brunswick differ sharply on matters related to the province's linguistic regime; not surprisingly, the latter are strikingly more enthusiastic about protecting the linguistic changes made over the past four decades. Second, this cleavage transcends partisan affiliations. The 1997 data were taken from questionnaires completed by Progressive Conservative activists, while both the 1998 and 2002 data emerged from surveys of Liberal delegates. Yet the latter two samplings are indistinguishable from the former. There are obviously sharp differences of opinion on these matters in New Brunswick, but these divergences are not expressed in interparty politics (at least with respect to the province's two major parties).

Third, francophones and anglophones differ not only on those items of some tangible import (and the panoply of policies and institutions surrounding New Brunswick's official bilingualism manifestly falls into this category) but also on matters that are largely, or purely, symbolic in nature (such as the linguistic facility of provincial premiers or the presence of the Acadian flag in front of government buildings). Consider the latter issue. In 1884, at a gathering of Acadians from around the Maritimes, a communal flag was adopted (with a gold star superimposed on the traditional French tri-colour). One hundred years later, a Liberal backbencher proposed that New Brunswick honour this centenary by flying the Acadian flag on government flag poles for the remainder of the year. Anxious to solidify his party's nascent inroads in the francophone community, Conservative premier Richard Hatfield impetuously upped the ante by moving an amendment that the practice be made permanent, "where deemed appropriate."[13] Predictably, a firestorm of controversy ensued, with many anglophones claiming to feel slighted by the absence of any comparable recognition for their community. When Hatfield backtracked slightly on his commitment, it was the turn of Acadians to express outrage, although some cooler heads wondered if it was worth provoking an anglophone backlash over such a seemingly

*Table 12.1*

**New Brunswick leadership elections: language attitudes by language group**

| Value | Year | Language | Strongly agree (%) | Agree (%) | Disagree (%) | Strongly disagree (%) | N |
|---|---|---|---|---|---|---|---|
| NB should | 1982 | French | 6 | 19 | 43 | 32 | 97 |
| not expand | | English | 21 | 32 | 34 | 14 | 211 |
| bilingualism. | 1985 | French | 6 | 33 | 33 | 27 | 66 |
| | | English | 32 | 37 | 23 | 8 | 169 |
| Official | 1997 | French | 70 | 26 | 2 | 3 | 152 |
| bilingualism | | English | 11 | 30 | 32 | 19 | 392 |
| has been | 1998 | French | 75 | 21 | 3 | 1 | 281 |
| good for NB. | | English | 18 | 45 | 26 | 12 | 443 |
| | 2002 | French | 78 | 19 | 3 | 0 | 32 |
| | | English | 22 | 52 | 19 | 8 | 124 |
| NB should | 1997 | French | 95 | 5 | 0 | 0 | 153 |
| remain | | English | 31 | 39 | 17 | 14 | 394 |
| bilingual | 1998 | French | 93 | 6 | 0 | 1 | 286 |
| even if | | English | 38 | 41 | 12 | 9 | 456 |
| Quebec | 2002 | French | 91 | 6 | 3 | 0 | 34 |
| secedes. | | English | 44 | 41 | 9 | 6 | 127 |
| It is | 1997 | French | 76 | 19 | 3 | 3 | 153 |
| important for | | English | 25 | 44 | 25 | 6 | 401 |
| NB leaders to | 1998 | French | 73 | 21 | 4 | 2 | 286 |
| be bilingual. | | English | 25 | 48 | 20 | 8 | 459 |
| | 2002 | French | 59 | 35 | 6 | 0 | 34 |
| | | English | 27 | 61 | 11 | 2 | 119 |
| Could never | 1997 | French | 73 | 8 | 3 | 16 | 149 |
| vote for a | | English | 54 | 21 | 14 | 11 | 391 |
| CoR-type | 1998 | French | 71 | 7 | 6 | 15 | 282 |
| party. | | English | 62 | 18 | 12 | 7 | 448 |
| | 2002 | French | 82 | 6 | 3 | 9 | 33 |
| | | English | 68 | 15 | 12 | 5 | 123 |
| Both the | 1997 | French | 48 | 32 | 13 | 7 | 152 |
| NB and the | | English | 7 | 22 | 28 | 44 | 398 |
| Acadian flags | 1998 | French | 56 | 23 | 15 | 6 | 281 |
| should be | | English | 7 | 28 | 37 | 28 | 453 |
| flown in front | 2002 | French | 49 | 27 | 18 | 6 | 33 |
| of government | | English | 15 | 27 | 34 | 25 | 128 |
| buildings in NB. | | | | | | | |

inconsequential matter. Even former premier Louis Robichaud, a staunch defender of Acadian interests while in office, seemed bemused by Hatfield's initiative: "It's a heck of a nice flag. I have my own and I'm proud of it, but the premier should never have allowed it to fly on provincial buildings."[14] Twenty years on, the Acadian flag continues to be flown in front of most government buildings in the northeastern part of the province as well as at the Legislative Assembly and the Justice Building in Fredericton, and anglophones and francophones continue to disagree over the practice. Despite the objections of 60 percent of the former, over three-quarters of the latter endorse the policy.

Fourth, francophones are far more cohesive than are their anglophone counterparts in their approach to linguistic matters in New Brunswick. While the former tended to plump for a single response (typically "strongly agree"), the latter were more liberally scattered across the evaluative continuum. Thus, in one extreme case (the 1997 responses regarding whether New Brunswick should remain bilingual even if Quebec seceded), the standard deviation from the mean for French respondents was only 0.22, while the corresponding figure for their English counterparts was a whopping 1.00. Of course, one would anticipate that minority groups would be more likely than would majority groups to think and act as one; indeed, this is precisely the phenomenon that Bakvis and Macpherson uncovered in their analysis of Quebeckers' voting behaviour in Canadian federal elections.[15]

Finally, the format of Table 12.1 may exaggerate the degree of divergence between New Brunswick's francophones and anglophones. On most indicators, for the 1997, 1998, and 2002 samples, a majority of both groups endorse the linguistic/communal status quo. Admittedly, the size of that majority is invariably larger among the French respondents. Moreover, the nature of that majority agreement varies noticeably: francophones tend to strongly support existing practices, while the enthusiasm of anglophones is perceptibly more restrained. Nevertheless, but for the Acadian flag issue (and this exception underscores the potency of symbolic politics), the two groups do not find themselves ranged on opposite sides of a language policy barricade.

It has been suggested that "only a few extremists" are displeased with official bilingualism,[16] but the evidence from Table 12.1 indicates otherwise. Even within the leadership elections of parties that were avowedly brokerage in their orientation, between one-third and one-half of anglophones are apparently unhappy with official bilingualism, and, by definition, such numbers cannot be equated with "a few extremists." Is such opposition lodged in particular subgroups of the English community? Given their tendency to approach language matters en bloc (as well as their smaller sample sizes), it is unrewarding to disaggregate the francophone responses. Neither of these obstacles, however, exists with respect to anglophones. Thus, we can test, for example, Garland's proposition that, at least in rural Westmorland County, "open anti-French and anti-Catholic bigotry" was particularly common among Baptist adherents.[17] In fact, the evidence does not support Garland's contention. On the contrary, with respect to essentially all the indicators contained in Table 12.1, Baptist opinion is squarely lodged within the anglophone mainstream.

Similarly, some surveys have suggested that opposition to official bilingualism is concentrated principally among older anglophones.[18] Table 12.2, which displays the mean responses of various subgroups (the higher the score, the more supportive of official bilingualism), provides meagre confirmation for this thesis. In fact, but for a single exception, the linguistic perspectives of older and younger anglophones in New Brunswick are essentially similar. Nor does it seem to matter much whether an anglophone resides to the northeast or to the southwest of the aforementioned diagonal line across the province. There are fifteen counties in New Brunswick, and eight of them (Charlotte, York, Sunbury, Queens, Kings, St. John, Westmorland, and Northumberland) were settled by the first waves of United Empire Loyalists who arrived in the 1780s. Since only Westmorland and Northumberland lie on what is now the "French" side of the line, and since the Canadian Loyalist Society has been one of the most vituperative of the voices raised against the policy of official bilingualism (at one time dubbing it "senseless degenerate and ruinous"),[19] one might have surmised that anglophones in the southeast would have been particularly distressed by the language reforms of the past four decades. Again, however, the data are uncooperative. In fact, Table 12.2 reveals that English New Brunswickers who live in the province's southwest (and who thus reside in a county where the francophone share of the population does not exceed 10 percent) are, in fact, slightly more tolerant of the French language than are their counterparts to the northeast. Living in relatively close proximity with francophones, in other words, does not induce among anglophones any heightened feelings of linguistic tolerance. If anything, it seems to have the opposite effect.

What does serve to narrow the divisions between French and English is a bilingual capacity among the latter. This is hardly surprising. After all, according to the 2001 census, only 15 percent of New Brunswick's anglophones are bilingual. Thanks to the entrenchment of official bilingualism, this relatively small group enjoys a huge comparative advantage over their unilingual counterparts in the procurement of public-sector employment. Hence, on some indicators in Table 12.2, bilingual anglophones actually have opinions that are closer to those held by francophones than they are to those held by their linguistically challenged cohorts. The proportion of bilingual anglophones in New Brunswick has grown by approximately 3 percent over the past decade. Thus, creeping bilingualism could go some way to bridging

Table 12.2

**New Brunswick leadership elections: disaggregating Anglophone language attitudes (means: range of 0-3)**

| Value | Year | French All | English All** | Resident of SW county > 90% English | Resident of NE county < 90% English | Unilingual | Bilingual | Under 50 | 50 and over |
|---|---|---|---|---|---|---|---|---|---|
| Official bilingualism has been good for NB.[1] | 1997 | 2.62 | 1.42 | 1.45 | 1.35* | 1.36 | 2.03** | 1.39 | 1.54 |
| | 1998 | 2.69 | 1.69 | 1.68 | 1.69 | 1.64 | 2.13** | 1.64 | 1.84 |
| | 2002 | 2.75 | 1.87 | 1.93 | 1.84 | 1.86 | 1.91 | 1.92 | 1.64 |
| NB should remain bilingual even if Quebec secedes.[1] | 1997 | 2.95 | 1.87 | 1.92 | 1.73 | 1.82 | 2.39** | 1.90 | 1.90 |
| | 1998 | 2.90 | 2.09 | 2.14 | 1.93 | 2.05 | 2.39** | 2.02 | 2.21 |
| | 2002 | 2.88 | 2.24 | 2.27 | 2.20 | 2.21 | 2.38 | 2.31 | 1.91 |
| NB should not expand bilingualism.[2] | 1982 | 2.01 | 1.40 | 1.48 | 1.29* | – | – | 1.17 | 1.54* |
| | 1985 | 1.82 | 1.07 | 1.02 | 1.13 | – | – | 1.10 | 1.06 |

1 Strongly agree = 3 / agree = 2 / disagree = 1 / strongly disagree = 0
2 Strongly disagree = 3 / disagree = 2 / agree = 1 / strongly agree = 0
* = $\chi^2 < .05$
** = $\chi^2 < .01$
$\chi^2$ calculated from bivariate cross-tabulations.

the cleavage between French and English over language matters. Alas, the data in Table 12.2 also suggest that something more elemental is at work. If even that group of anglophones who are, in principle (although not necessarily, it must be admitted, in practice), advantaged by the institutionalization of bilingualism can offer up only lukewarm endorsements of the program, then it seems likely that they are moved, in part, by a primal disinclination to advantage "the other."

Linguistic divisions are also apparent in New Brunswickers' perspective on national unity. Over the past three decades, Canadians have witnessed two secessionist referenda in the province of Quebec and three rounds of mega-constitutional reform. All of these, both in New Brunswick and elsewhere, were principally perceived through the prism of French-English relations. As Table 12.3 makes clear, the two communities in New Brunswick differ sharply in their approaches to Canadian federalism. Despite constituting less than 3 percent of the country's population, New Brunswickers feel that residing in Canada's only officially bilingual province gives them a special role to play in matters of national unity. Admittedly, francophones are notably more pleased with this circumstance than are anglophones. Many anglophone New Brunswickers may also like the idea of punching above their weight, but they are apparently less enthused about the source of this distinctiveness than are francophones.

As it turned out, New Brunswick's premiers did play key roles in the first two mega-constitutional rounds of the 1980s (those that culminated in the success of the Constitution Act, 1982, and in the failure of the Meech Lake Accord). In the aftermath of the first Quebec referendum on separation, Prime Minister Trudeau proposed a constitutional reform package that raised the ire of most provincial premiers. Indeed, only Bill Davis of Ontario and Richard Hatfield of New Brunswick declined to join the court challenge initiated by their agitated brethren (famously dubbed "the Gang of Eight"), and both men helped promote the eventual compromise package (in which all but Quebec's René Levesque came onside). The upshot of these efforts was that New Brunswick's bilingual status was entrenched in Sections 16 through 20 of the Constitution Act, 1982 (although, even then, some Acadians grumbled that Hatfield's exuberant promotion of the French fact on the national stage was not always commensurate with his actions at home).[20]

New Brunswick's premier was to play an even more pivotal role in the Meech Lake negotiations. When Richard Hatfield signed the accord in early June 1987, he was heading a deeply unpopular administration that was already more than four years and seven months into its electoral term. Liberal leader Frank McKenna was openly critical of the accord, and, when his party swept all fifty-eight seats in the October 1987 election, McKenna claimed to have a mandate to seek changes to the document. Alas, Quebec's

*Table 12.3*

**New Brunswick leadership elections: national unity attitudes by language group**

| Value | Year | Language | Strongly agree (%) | Agree (%) | Disagree (%) | Strongly disagree (%) | N |
|---|---|---|---|---|---|---|---|
| Quebec | 1982 | French | 13 | 38 | 29 | 20 | 92 |
| should be | | English | 5 | 20 | 41 | 34 | 231 |
| recognized | 1985 | French | 26 | 39 | 22 | 13 | 54 |
| as a distinct | | English | 6 | 20 | 46 | 29 | 179 |
| society.* | 1997 | French | 29 | 32 | 14 | 25 | 108 |
| | | English | 13 | 29 | 27 | 32 | 439 |
| | 1998 | French | 36 | 27 | 17 | 20 | 278 |
| | | English | 12 | 28 | 22 | 38 | 445 |
| | 2002 | French | 31 | 22 | 29 | 19 | 32 |
| | | English | 12 | 26 | 29 | 34 | 121 |
| All provinces | 1997 | French | 44 | 27 | 20 | 10 | 113 |
| should be | | English | 60 | 30 | 10 | 1 | 447 |
| treated | 1998 | French | 45 | 34 | 16 | 6 | 285 |
| equally. | | English | 47 | 43 | 9 | 2 | 452 |
| | 2002 | French | 33 | 36 | 24 | 6 | 33 |
| | | English | 42 | 44 | 11 | 2 | 125 |
| As the only | 1997 | French | 62 | 31 | 6 | 2 | 118 |
| officially | | English | 18 | 51 | 25 | 7 | 449 |
| bilingual | 1998 | French | 59 | 35 | 4 | 3 | 281 |
| province, | | English | 22 | 56 | 18 | 4 | 452 |
| NB has a | 2002 | French | 50 | 44 | 6 | 0 | 34 |
| special role | | English | 26 | 55 | 17 | 2 | 127 |
| to play in | | | | | | | |
| matters of | | | | | | | |
| national | | | | | | | |
| unity. | | | | | | | |
| It is | 1997 | French | 15 | 11 | 31 | 43 | 112 |
| inevitable | | English | 6 | 17 | 45 | 32 | 440 |
| that Quebec | 1998 | French | 11 | 10 | 37 | 42 | 281 |
| will separate | | English | 8 | 11 | 52 | 30 | 440 |
| from Canada. | 2002 | French | 7 | 3 | 47 | 43 | 30 |
| | | English | 6 | 7 | 53 | 35 | 118 |

* In 1982 and 1985, this question was worded: "Quebec should have special recognition."

legislature had already ratified the Meech Lake Accord, and Premier Robert Bourassa had stipulated that Quebec would "not consider any proposed changes that [might] arise out of public hearings in other provinces."[21] Undeterred, McKenna proposed a lengthy list of amendments to Meech (including enhanced protections for the rights of women and Aboriginals, changes in the amending formula and in the nomination of Supreme Court justices, and fewer restrictions on the federal spending power). Of particular interest to McKenna were the sections dealing with language rights. Under Meech, the Quebec provincial government was to be given the power to "preserve and promote" its "distinct society." By contrast, while official language minorities were said to constitute "a fundamental characteristic of Canada," the role of the federal government and the other nine provincial governments was merely to "preserve" (and thus, by implication, not to promote) this attribute. For obvious reasons, McKenna could not acknowledge that governments should take a more active role on behalf of the French-speaking majority of Quebec than on behalf of the French-speaking minority of New Brunswick; accordingly, he urged that Meech be amended to ensure that the federal government be mandated to "promote" the interests of linguistic minorities.[22] For equally obvious reasons (i.e., such a change would provide constitutional grounds for the federal government to challenge Quebec's restrictive language laws), Premier Bourassa was completely unmoved by McKenna's arguments.

Thus began Meech Lake's three-year dance of death. Eventually, McKenna was joined by premiers Gary Filmon of Manitoba and Clyde Wells of Newfoundland in opposing the accord. Eventually, as well, McKenna grew concerned that the failure of Meech might precipitate the break-up of the country. With the constitutional clock winding down, McKenna ultimately chose to push the accord through the New Brunswick legislature (albeit accompanied by a companion resolution that suggested four specific ways, including the promotion of linguistic minority rights, by which Meech might be improved). Despite McKenna's repentance, the accord failed to pass the legislatures of either Manitoba or Newfoundland by the 23 June 1990 deadline. Surveying the wreckage, one senior minister from another province commented: "Here's the guy [McKenna] who essentially caused all this trouble and at the end of the day, his agenda was trivial."[23]

To what extent was McKenna constrained during this period by New Brunswick's Acadians? Logically, a move away from the bilingual vision of the Constitution Act, 1982, to the dualist understanding of the Meech Lake Accord might seem to be opposed to the interests of New Brunswick's francophones. Certainly, at the outset of the 1986-90 period, both the Société nationale des Acadiens and the Fédération des francophones hors Québec petitioned McKenna not to ratify the accord on just these grounds.[24] The reality, however, was somewhat more nuanced. Table 12.3, in fact, suggests that, before ratifying Meech, McKenna actually had more work to do in shoring up his English flank than his French flank. In the two surveys of party activists taken prior to Meech Lake, only one-quarter of anglophone respondents were in favour of granting Quebec any special constitutional recognition; the corresponding figure for francophones ranged from one-half to two-thirds support. Moreover, when McKenna did hold public hearings on the accord in 1989, most of the vitriol emanated from the anglophones. Almost all interveners (francophone and anglophone) recommended some reforms to the accord; unhappiness with the distinct society clause, however, led the Association of New Brunswick English-Speaking Canadians to call for the document's complete rejection.[25] The tableau was not without irony. Agitated anglophones were prepared to deny gains to "the other's" kin in a neighbouring province even if those gains would serve to undercut the legitimacy of future claims made by "the other" in New Brunswick.

In effect, identity trumped interest, just as it had for Acadians at the time of the first Quebec referendum. Canada without Quebec could not be advantageous to the remaining francophone minorities (especially since René Levesque had contemptuously ruled out the prospect of annexation to an independent Quebec: "We don't need a second Gaspé").[26] Nevertheless, the Société des Acadiens du Nouveau-Brunswick supported a conditional "oui" on the eve of the 1980 vote.[27] It is worth recalling, as well, that when the Meech Lake Accord was transmogrified into the Charlottetown Accord and put to a national referendum, francophones outside Quebec were one of the few groups to vote "yes." "French-Canadians outside Quebec like that province more than any other ethnic group did," notes one analysis. "Quebec just seemed less alien, and many still had ties of affinity to it."[28] Once again, the primal basis of identity politics is apparent.

Table 12.3 also permits us to contrast attitudes towards special status for Quebec held before and after the Meech Lake and Charlottetown accords. Somewhat surprisingly, the data suggest that at least anglophone New Brunswickers are now more supportive of such recognition than they were in the early 1980s. While the proportions who "strongly disagree" have not declined, there has been perceptible movement out of the more moderate "disagree" category. Moreover, Table 12.4 reveals that this pattern obtains for essentially all generational cohorts. Contrary to what one might have surmised, New Brunswickers of all ages have become somewhat more accommodating of special status for Quebec over the interval between 1982 and 1997. Admittedly, Table 12.3 also indicates backing for the notion of provincial equality to an extent that seemingly cannot be reconciled with the degree of support for a distinct society clause. Of course, ordinary New Brunswickers are not the only Canadians to have fallen prey to this contradiction: the English-speaking premiers did much the same when they crafted the otherwise forgettable Calgary Declaration in 1997. What is significant for our purposes is that the French and English of New Brunswick disagree on this measure as well: approximately one-quarter of the former take issue with what has seemingly become an article of faith for English-Canadians.

Finally, it is worth noting the absence of a linguistic cleavage on the indicator in Table 12.3, which is most explicitly analytical rather than evaluative. Within two years of the exceedingly close 1995 Quebec secession referendum, only one-quarter of the respondents from both language groups believed that Quebec would inevitably separate from Canada, and that proportion has subsequently tracked steadily downwards. New Brunswick's francophones may well be more fearful than anglophones of the consequences of Quebec separation, but they are no more inclined to believe that such an eventuality will ensue.

Aside from attitudes towards provincial and national issues, the data reveal several other ways in which New Brunswick's French and English differ (the latter, for example, are much more likely to arrive at a leadership convention undecided as to their choice). We address only three such differences in the remainder of this chapter. First, it is apparent from Table 12.5 that francophones are much less likely than are anglophones to be impelled by policy considerations when making their leadership choices. Given the sharp policy differences between the two groups (which we have already enumerated), this may be somewhat surprising. It is important to realize, however, that linguistic and constitutional issues aside, New Brunswick's French and English share views on most matters of public policy (from removing the Harmonized Sales Tax to banning VLTs). Of course, this does not mean that there is policy homogeneity in New Brunswick, merely that the divisions do not generally follow linguistic lines. Thus, francophones are more influenced than are anglophones by such factors as a candidate's personal characteristics or vote-winning abilities when making their selection. Again, this is perfectly consistent with what one would anticipate from a self-conscious minority: electoral success is seen to represent the best protection against the potentially capricious inclinations of the majority group.

Second, it is clear from Table 12.6 that francophone party activists have disproportionately plumped for the winning candidate; thus, they have been both more cohesive and more successful than have their anglophone counterparts. With respect to the former attribute, it is instructive that, while the anglophone vote has often been remarkably fractured, there have been no instances in which less than two-thirds of the francophone activists cohered around a single candidate. In fact, this phenomenon even occurred in 1982, when it was known that Doug Young's ancestors were linked to the 1875 death of Louis Mailloux[29] (the only Acadian to die in the dramatically dubbed Caraquet Riots). According to Bill Cross, such coherence is to be expected: "As a minority community, the New Brunswick Acadians appear well aware of the need to develop consensus among themselves if they are to have an influence in the broader political community."[30] As to "success," it is noteworthy that only in 1985, when a fair amount of their support was bled away to the candidacy of a fellow Acadian (Ray Frenette), were francophones

Table 12.4

**New Brunswick leadership elections: Quebec distinct society attitudes by language group**

| Year of birth | Year of election | Strongly agree (%) All | English | Agree (%) All | English | Disagree (%) All | English | Strongly disagree (%) All | English | N All | English |
|---|---|---|---|---|---|---|---|---|---|---|---|
| 1967-82 | 1982 | – | – | – | – | – | – | – | – | 0 | 0 |
|  | 1997 | 14 | 12 | 22 | 18 | 28 | 30 | 36 | 39 | 50 | 33 |
| 1963-67 | 1982 | 0 | 0 | 22 | 10 | 22 | 25 | 56 | 75 | 9 | 4 |
|  | 1997 | 14 | 18 | 32 | 18 | 27 | 29 | 27 | 35 | 22 | 17 |
| 1957-63 | 1982 | 0 | 0 | 29 | 30 | 50 | 55 | 21 | 15 | 24 | 20 |
|  | 1997 | 13 | 7 | 34 | 33 | 24 | 30 | 29 | 30 | 38 | 30 |
| 1952-57 | 1982 | 6 | 8 | 28 | 25 | 33 | 33 | 33 | 33 | 18 | 12 |
|  | 1997 | 14 | 14 | 39 | 31 | 25 | 28 | 23 | 28 | 52 | 36 |
| 1943-51 | 1982 | 7 | 2 | 28 | 25 | 39 | 42 | 26 | 32 | 87 | 60 |
|  | 1997 | 17 | 10 | 30 | 28 | 22 | 22 | 31 | 40 | 132 | 81 |
| 1933-42 | 1982 | 9 | 9 | 26 | 22 | 41 | 41 | 25 | 28 | 69 | 46 |
|  | 1997 | 16 | 13 | 33 | 31 | 21 | 24 | 30 | 33 | 131 | 98 |
| 1923-32 | 1982 | 12 | 10 | 24 | 14 | 36 | 41 | 28 | 36 | 58 | 42 |
|  | 1997 | 17 | 17 | 25 | 23 | 28 | 30 | 30 | 31 | 87 | 71 |
| Pre-1923 | 1982 | 7 | 4 | 19 | 13 | 33 | 38 | 41 | 45 | 58 | 47 |
|  | 1997 | 20 | 13 | 20 | 20 | 30 | 33 | 30 | 33 | 20 | 15 |

*Table 12.5*

**New Brunswick leadership elections: principal vote motivation by language group**

| Year | Language | Policy motivation (%) | Other motivation (%) | N |
|------|----------|-----------------------|----------------------|-----|
| 1982 | French   | 24 | 76   | 80  |
|      | English  | 33 | 67   | 201 |
| 1985 | French   | 25 | 75   | 73  |
|      | English  | 39 | 61*  | 181 |
| 1997 | French   | 23 | 77   | 79  |
|      | English  | 42 | 58** | 368 |
| 1998 | French   | 32 | 68   | 238 |
|      | English  | 44 | 56** | 346 |
| 2002 | French   | 12 | 88   | 25  |
|      | English  | 44 | 56*  | 96  |

\*  $\chi^2 < 0.5$
\*\* $\chi^2 < .01$

not at least 20 percent more likely than anglophones to join the camp of the eventual winner. Without the support, en bloc, of francophones, the victories of Doug Young, Camille Theriault, and, especially, Bernard Lord were far from certain. Indeed, had the French vote instead rallied to an equivalent extent around the candidacies of Joe Day, Norm Betts, and Greg Byrne, the first two of these gentlemen would have been leading after the first ballot by 9 percent and 21 percent, respectively, and Byrne would have secured an absolute majority.

Third, it is clear that, even aside from the friends and neighbours voting effect discussed in Chapter 5, the French and English of New Brunswick are prone to identify with, and to be supportive of, politicians from the same

*Table 12.6*

**New Brunswick leadership elections: vote for winning candidate by language group**

| Year | Francophone candidates | Winner | Francophones % | (N) | Anglophones % | (N) |
|------|------------------------|--------|----------------|-------|---------------|--------|
| 1982 | Frenette | Young | 70 | (112) | 46 | (249)* |
| 1985 | Frenette | McKenna | 68 | (81) | 84 | (189)* |
| 1997 | Lord | Lord | 67 | (125) | 25 | (356)* |
| 1998 | Theriault Richard | Theriault | 68 | (288) | 47 | (449)* |
| 2002 | – | D. Graham | 94 | (33) | 72 | (127)* |

\*  $\chi^2 < .01$

linguistic group. Table 12.7 provides a smorgasbord of evidence to this effect. Note, for example, that in 1982 it was Liberal francophones who were more likely to back the embattled Pierre Trudeau as national party leader. Three years later, John Turner's stewardship was similarly under siege; however, on this occasion, the party's anglophones were the more stalwart supporters. At the 1997 PC convention, activists were asked to assess the performance of nine prominent politicians. After allowing for partisan biases, the approval ratings of six of these individuals conform roughly to our expectations; that is, anglophones generally gave more favourable judgments about anglophone politicians, and francophones did likewise for politicians from their language group. The three exceptions to this tendency merit a closer look. In fact, the differential ratings of Richard Hatfield should not have been unexpected in light of Hatfield's determined outreach efforts to francophones. Indeed, Hatfield once quipped: "Actually, I'd just rather be premier of the Acadians."[31] Nor, upon reflection, are the assessments of Brian Mulroney especially surprising. Unlike all previous Tory leaders, Mulroney was perfectly fluent in French and his close association in the public's mind with the Meech Lake Accord and the Charlottetown Accord would, given our earlier discussion of attitudes towards the distinct society clause, have stood him in better stead among the francophones than among the anglophones of New Brunswick. In fact, only the approval ratings of Jean Chretien seem anomalous. Note that in both 1982 and 1985 the prospect of Jean Chretien as national party leader was regarded with more favour by francophones than by anglophones. Indeed, when Chretien did secure the Liberal leadership in 1990, he opted to enter the House of Commons via a by-election victory in the Acadian riding of Beausejour. Nevertheless, as the 1998 Liberal data confirm, francophone disaffection with the prime ministership of Jean Chretien was sufficiently intense to overcome the usual affinity derived from a shared language. Accounting for this finding is beyond the scope of this analysis, but it is undeniable that the Chretien government's early reforms to unemployment insurance were particularly unpopular in New Brunswick's northeast, at one point provoking riots in the community of Tracadie.

Our scrutiny of these deviant cases should not deflect us from the central truth of Table 12.7: the support of activists for those politicians with whom they share a tie of language. The final panel of Table 12.7 reinforces this point. Admittedly, we have opted not to display comparable data concerning national Liberal leaders. People are predictably reluctant to identify with political failures, and the modern pantheon of successful Liberal chiefs is top-heavy with francophones. In fact, our respondents would have had to harken back to Mackenzie King to consider the last anglophone federal Liberal leader who won a majority government. Thus, around 90 percent of the activists from both language groups identified principally with a

*Table 12.7*

___

**New Brunswick leadership elections: leadership attitudes by language group**

|  |  | English | | French | |
|---|---|---|---|---|---|
|  |  | *% agree (N)* | | | |
| 1982 | Pierre Trudeau should lead federal party in next election. | 21 | (241) | 38 | (106)* |
|  | If not Trudeau, who? Chrétien. | 7 | (141) | 16 | (70)* |
|  |  |  |  |  |  |
| 1985 | John Turner should lead federal party in next election. | 63 | (194) | 44 | (69)* |
|  | If not Turner, who? Chrétien. | 52 | (42) | 66 | (29) |
|  |  |  |  |  |  |
| 1997 | Approval for: | *Means: range of 0-3* | | | |
|  | Bernard Valcourt | 1.01 | | 1.43 | |
|  | Jean Chrétien | 0.92 | | 0.76 | |
|  | Jean Charest | 2.09 | | 2.35 | |
|  | Brian Mulroney | 1.32 | | 1.48 | |
|  | Richard Hatfield | 1.68 | | 2.18 | |
|  | Frank McKenna | 1.39 | | 1.06 | |
|  | Elsie Wayne | 1.85 | | 1.66 | |
|  | Alexa McDonough | 1.16 | | 1.04 | |
|  | Preston Manning | 0.99 | | 0.38 | |
|  |  |  |  |  |  |
| 1998 | Jean Chrétien should lead federal party in next election. | *% agree (N)* | | | |
|  |  | 53 | (441) | 41 | (279)* |
|  |  |  |  |  |  |
|  |  | *% strongly agree (N)* | | | |
|  | Frank McKenna was right to resign. | 25 | (454) | 42 | (280)* |

| 1998 and 2002 | Provincial leader with which greatest affinity felt: | 1998 | 2002 | 1998 | 2002 |
|---|---|---|---|---|---|
|  | Frank McKenna | 72 | 71 | 48 | 48 |
|  | Louis Robichaud | 16 | 19 | 39 | 48 |
|  | Other | 12 | 11 | 13 | 3 |
|  |  | (440) | (119) | (279)* | (29) |

* $\chi^2 < .01$

___

francophone national leader. With respect to provincial Liberal leaders, however, the data are much more instructive. Both the 1998 and the (admittedly much smaller) 2002 samplings revealed that English New Brunswickers were particularly enamoured with Frank McKenna, while their French counterparts were far more likely to identify with Louis Robichaud. Even among the lesser-regarded leaders, a similar pattern obtained. Among the nine activists who declared a close affinity with Joe Daigle, six were francophones, while of the twenty-five respondents who identified with Robert Higgins, all were anglophones.

This chapter demonstrates the continuing power of language to animate New Brunswickers. True, this power has not been expressed at the ballot box since CoR's meteoric rise to prominence in the 1991 campaign. In fact, in the three subsequent provincial elections, the link between language and vote has been insignificant – a testament to the capacity of political elites to sublimate, rather than synthesize, the divergent views of francophones and anglophones. Even among those who share a particular partisan commitment, the cleavage between French and English is starkly apparent. Small wonder that, as the appendix to this book details, Frank McKenna and Ray Frenette tried to reach a pre-convention accord in 1985 to keep linguistic issues off the table. The presence of these divisions among partisan activists is indicative of their relevance in the wider polity. While it is true, as we point out in Chapter 3, that voters in leadership elections do not constitute a miniature replica of the provincial electorate, the fact that divisions exist in both parties, and that controlling for demographic features does not alter the francophone opinion on a range of linguistic matters, provides us with confidence that these divisions are not restricted to leadership elections. Whether construed as premodern tribalism or postmaterial identity politics, these deep differences display no signs of abating.

# 13
# Nova Scotia: The Challenge of Social Democracy

Leadership elections in Nova Scotia do not demonstrate either the celebration of rural society, as in PEI, or the linguistic dimensions of New Brunswick. However, our analysis of Maritime leadership elections highlights a feature of Nova Scotia politics that is not replicated in the remainder of the region. What stands out in Nova Scotia is the special role played by the New Democratic Party. Although the NDP has been prominent in our discussion of leadership politics in Nova Scotia, we have no data on the New Brunswick wing of the party and scarcely more on the PEI New Democrats. In some ways, this pattern mirrors the wider fate of the party in the Maritimes. Prince Edward Island has provided particularly desolate terrain for CCF and NDP candidates, with vote totals customarily in the single digits in percentage terms and barely more than that as an absolute tally. In the 2003 provincial election, for example, the New Democratic candidate in the riding of Tignish-DeBlois received only twenty votes. When, in 1973, Aquinas Ryan achieved the previously unprecedented total of 14.9 percent in the riding (losing his deposit, but only just!), the party's joy was unconstrained. To those attending Ryan's election night soiree, it "seemed as if the party had won the election, so intense was the enthusiasm."[1] Indeed Dr. Herb Dickieson's 1996 victory in West Point/Bloomfield constitutes the CCF-NDP's sole triumph in either the federal or provincial arenas on PEI.

In New Brunswick, the party's electoral record is only marginally better. Only four CCF-NDP candidates have ever won elected office – Robert Hall (1982) and Elizabeth Weir (1991, 1995, 1999, 2003) at the provincial level and Angela Vautour (1997) and Yvon Godin (1997, 2000, 2004, and 2006) at the national level. As the above dates suggest, the party's fortunes have, at least federally, improved somewhat of late. In the three federal and three provincial elections immediately prior to 1994, the NDP managed to average, respectively, 9 percent and 10 percent of the popular vote; these figures have changed to 18 percent and 9 percent for the four federal and three provincial votes since 1994. Even so, the NDP remains only a marginal player on the New Brunswick stage.

One of the major stories in Maritime politics over the past fifteen years has been the emergence of the NDP as a major contender for power in Nova Scotia. However, even before this, the status of the CCF and the NDP was much more significant in Nova Scotia than it was in New Brunswick or PEI. Nova Scotians actually elected CCF candidates, and in 1945, thanks principally to the ineptitude of the Progressive Conservatives, the CCF became the official opposition at Province House. The NDP, as well, enjoyed regular, if modest, success through its first three decades of existence before vaulting to prominence in 1997. In that year's federal election, the NDP won a plurality of the vote and a majority of the seats in Nova Scotia, while in the provincial campaign the following year they tied the Liberals for first place with nineteen elected MLAs. Since then, the NDP's support has ebbed only slightly; thus, it remains a major player in Nova Scotia politics.

In its almost seven decades of existence, the Nova Scotia CCF-NDP has undergone two key metamorphoses. The first occurred in 1980, when it changed from Cape Breton-centric to Halifax-centric. The second was the aforementioned shift of 1997 from minor to major party. Fortunately, our data provide some purchase on both these transformations, and in this chapter we discuss in detail the nature of these changes.

That the Nova Scotia CCF-NDP was, at the outset, a creature of Cape Breton is indisputable. Long before 1938, when the Island branch of the United Mineworkers of America made the "spontaneous and unexpected" decision to affiliate with the fledging CCF,[2] Cape Breton had been a hotbed of working-class radicalism. The discovery of huge coal seams, combined with the ready availability of iron ore from Newfoundland, propelled an economic boom that attracted tens of thousands of immigrants to the Island at the turn of the twentieth century.[3] In fact, prior to the First World War, Cape Breton was producing over half of Canada's coal and almost a third of its pig iron.[4] Not surprisingly, this explosive growth was accompanied by turbulent industrial relations culminating in the "epic struggle" of 1925 between striking miners and a British Empire Steel Company (BESCO) management team determined to ratchet down labour costs.[5] Politically, the workers of Cape Breton County elected four Labour MLAs in the 1920 provincial election and, on several occasions thereafter, almost sent J.B. McLachlan ("the region's most vigorous, not to say notorious exponent of labour radicalism")[6] to represent them in Halifax and Ottawa (initially for the Independent Labour Party [ILP] subsequently for the Communist Party of Canada [CPC]).

Thus, although the CCF was not established in Nova Scotia until 1939 (later than every province save Prince Edward Island), in industrial Cape

Breton it hardly represented a dangerous departure from past practices. From the outset, the new party enjoyed considerable electoral success on the Island. Despite not nominating a candidate until twelve days prior to the vote, the CCF triumphed in a by-election in Cape Breton Centre in December 1939. Two years later, the CCF provided "one of the surprises"[7] of the provincial election when three of its six candidates proved victorious. In 1945, the CCF, campaigning under the slogan "jobs for all,"[8] actually became the official opposition at Province House when its two-member contingent exceeded by two the total won by the hapless Tories. And, at the federal level, the electors of Cape Breton South sent CCF icon Clarie Gillis to Ottawa in 1940 for the first of his four successive victories.

Three points in particular need to be stressed about the early years. First, as Table 13.1 makes clear, the Nova Scotia CCF of the 1940s was overwhelmingly centred in Cape Breton. True, in both 1945 and 1949, the party actually received more votes on the mainland than in Cape Breton. Nevertheless, off the Island, the CCF candidates routinely lost their deposits and the party was regarded as both exotic and irrelevant. Second, the advent of the CCF marked, if anything, "a shift to the right in Cape Breton labour politics."[9] In fact, the CCF members at Province House "were for the most part not radical. They did not aggressively pursue nationalization or speak combatively of replacing capitalism; they represented, in a fairly straightforward way, the labour interest."[10] Of course, even with these moderate platforms, Liberal spokespersons tried to tar CCF candidates with the brush of extremism. Thus, one MP wondered in the face of "what the Russians were doing to the hapless Finns ... how any Christian person could vote for a party whose sympathies were undoubtedly communistic,"[11] while a Liberal MLA bemoaned the activities of the Nazis and asked CCF legislators "how far their leaders intend to go."[12] Third, from the outset, the CCF was riven by tensions between Cape Breton and the mainland. As national party secretary, David Lewis quickly discovered "the difficulty in persuading the Cape Bretoner to accept a person from the Nova Scotia mainland as his spokesman."[13] In fact, when Lewis proposed the transfer of the provincial office from Glace Bay to Halifax, "imprecations rained on [him] from almost every leading CCF person on Cape Breton,"[14] and the plan was abandoned, at least temporarily. Fuelling these animosities were not only the dramatically differing electoral circumstances of the two wings but also the divergent social bases. In Cape Breton, "CCF support came almost exclusively from the trade union movement, whereas the Halifax CCF clubs drew their membership from reform-minded members of the middle class, from the Halifax universities and from the Protestant clergy."[15] Not that such sectional animosity was peculiar to the CCF. Even Conservative MLAs from Cape Breton have introduced secession resolutions at Province House,[16] while in pre-

Confederation times, one candidate secured 394 of 401 votes in a Sydney poll with the simple slogan of "Down with Nova Scotians."[17]

The 1950s were a time of retreat for the Nova Scotia CCF. In 1945-47, the party had 1,697 members and an annual budget of over $10,000; ten years later, the corresponding figures were only 191 members and a $1,000 budget. One observer traces the party's decline to the disastrous coal miners' strike of 1947; shortly thereafter, the United Mine Workers's pro-CCF daily newspaper (the *Glace Bay Gazette*), shut down and enthusiasm for the party began to wane perceptibly.[18] The CCF was also in full retreat elsewhere in Canada, so attributing too much of the blame to local factors would seem unwise. By 1956, the party had plummeted to 11 percent of the vote in Cape Breton (although, amazingly, it managed to retain Cape Breton Centre) and 3 percent provincewide. At the federal level, Clarie Gillis – despite being variously described by a sympathetic biographer as "a champion of his own community, province and region," as "one of the best orators in

*Table 13.1*

**Nova Scotia elections: CCF-NDP candidates elected by region**

| Federal election year | MPs | | Provincial election year | MLAs | |
|---|---|---|---|---|---|
| | Cape Breton | Mainland | | Cape Breton | Mainland |
| 1940 | 1 | 0 | 1941 | 3 | 0 |
| 1945 | 1 | 0 | 1945 | 2 | 0 |
| 1949 | 1 | 0 | 1949 | 2 | 0 |
| 1953 | 1 | 0 | 1953 | 2 | 0 |
| 1957 | 0 | 0 | 1956 | 1 | 0 |
| 1958 | 0 | 0 | | | |
| 1962 | 1 | 0 | 1960 | 1 | 0 |
| 1963 | 0 | 0 | 1963 | 0 | 0 |
| 1965 | 0 | 0 | | | |
| 1968 | 0 | 0 | 1967 | 0 | 0 |
| 1972 | 0 | 0 | 1970 | 2 | 0 |
| 1974 | 1 | 0 | 1974 | 3 | 0 |
| 1979 | 1 | 0 | 1978 | 4 | 0 |
| 1980 | 0 | 0 | | | |
| | | | 1981 | 0 | 1 |
| 1984 | 0 | 0 | 1984 | 0 | 3 |
| 1988 | 0 | 0 | 1988 | 0 | 2 |
| 1993 | 0 | 0 | 1993 | 0 | 3 |
| 1997 | 2 | 4 | 1998 | 3 | 16 |
| 2000 | 0 | 3 | 1999 | 1 | 10 |
| 2004 | 0 | 2 | 2003 | 2 | 13 |

the House," as "a towering figure," and as "one of the few Canadian names fit to be included in a list that includes Keir Hardie, Jimmy Maxton, Ernie Bevin, Nye Bevan and Eugene Debs"[19] – saw his seventeen-year stretch as an MP end ignominiously when he finished third in the 1957 election. Clearly, the CCF experiment had run its course; when the party morphed into the NDP, Nova Scotia organizers were apparently confident that electoral victory "lay just around the corner."[20]

As it turned out, this hope was misplaced. The founding convention of the Nova Scotia NDP was held in October 1962. For the remainder of the decade, as Table 13.1 and Table 13.2 make clear, the party was blanked at both the federal and provincial levels, and its share of the provincial vote hovered around 5 percent. During this time, the party was led for the first time by someone from the mainland – Dalhousie political scientist J.H. Aitchison. In the 1967 election, Aitchison opted to run not in Halifax but in Glace Bay, where he achieved the modest distinction of being the only NDP candidate provincewide not to forfeit his deposit. "I think that in the final analysis" complained Aitchison after the election, "that it was the power of money that beat me in Glace Bay."[21]

Mainland New Democrats had been convinced in 1962 that electoral growth could not be achieved without breaking Cape Breton's seemingly dynastic control of the party leadership. Although Aitchison's tenure as party steward (he did not officially become leader until 1966) was hardly an unqualified success, most mainlanders lined up behind yet another Dalhousie social scientist (economist Keith Jobson) at the 1968 leadership convention. Yet, by a margin of only four votes (out of 156), transplanted Cape Bretoner Jeremy Akerman reclaimed the leadership for the Island.

Three points must be made about Akerman's twelve-year stint as leader. First, it was a time of modest electoral recovery. Table 13.1 reveals that, after having been shut out in the previous two provincial elections, NDP representation grew to two, then three, then four MLAs (all from Cape Breton) under Akerman's stewardship. As well, Table 13.2 indicates that, after achieving little growth in 1970, the NDP's share of the provincial vote effectively doubled in 1974. Much of this gain was achieved on the mainland, where, thanks to Akerman's insistence on running candidates in every riding, the party enjoyed a double digit support level for the first time. In fact, in 1978, the party enjoyed a breakthrough of sorts, when Austin Sutton in Pictou Centre became the first mainland New Democrat to finish second. Finally, it is worth noting that, over this period, the electors of Cape Breton East Richmond twice sent New Democrat Father Andy Hogan to serve as their representative in Ottawa.

Second, these electoral gains were achieved without significantly diluting party dogma. While it is conventional wisdom to regard Akerman as a pragmatic moderate,[22] his rhetoric on the campaign trail would seem to indicate

*Table 13.2*

**Nova Scotia elections: CCF-NDP popular vote by region**

| Year | Cape Breton CCF/NDP | Mainland CCF/NDP | Nova Scotia (%) | Cape Breton (%) | Mainland (%) |
|---|---|---|---|---|---|
| 1941 | 18,322 | 261 | 7 | 31 | 0.1 |
| 1945 | 18388 | 21,249 | 14 | 33 | 9 |
| 1949 | 15,295 | 18,741 | 10 | 26 | 7 |
| 1953 | 17,576 | 6,084 | 7 | 23 | 2 |
| 1956 | 8,417 | 1,515 | 3 | 11 | 1 |
| 1960 | 16,730 | 14,781 | 10 | 20 | 6 |
| 1963 | 10059 | 4,017 | 5 | 13 | 2 |
| 1967 | 9,944 | 7,929 | 6 | 24 | 3 |
| 1970 | 15,410 | 9,849 | 7 | 18 | 4 |
| 1974 | 23,043 | 36,316 | 15 | 24 | 12 |
| 1978 | 25,586 | 38,393 | 15 | 25 | 12 |
| 1981 | 13,750 | 62,539 | 18 | 15 | 19 |
| 1984 | 7,083 | 58,793 | 16 | 8 | 18 |
| 1988 | 13,400 | 60,638 | 16 | 14 | 16 |
| 1993 | 12,366 | 72,876 | 17 | 15 | 18 |
| 1998 | 31,566 | 123,796 | 35 | 38 | 34 |
| 1999 | 26,984 | 102,490 | 30 | 34 | 29 |
| 2003 | 19,057 | 107,422 | 31 | 26 | 32 |

*Note:* Due to incomplete data, the year 1949 does not include the ridings of Inverness and Antigonish.

otherwise. Consider, for example, the 1974 election. Aside from standard social democratic fare (reducing political patronage, expanding the welfare state, and so on), the NDP pledged to introduce public auto insurance, rent controls, public housing, interest rate rollbacks, and a land registry. What is significant in the present context is the language employed by Akerman in defence of these commitments. According to the NDP leader, land developers had to be "curbed,"[23] there had been an "erosion of sovereignty" as Nova Scotia land was "gobbled up by non-residents,"[24] mortgage and insurance companies were engaged in "exploitation and profiteering,"[25] finance companies were "parasites" who were "ripping off" the public and "getting fat" at their expense,[26] and AVCO corporation was a "leading corporate leech."[27]

Third, Akerman's leadership was plagued by chronic internal bickering. The customary tensions between the Cape Breton and mainland wings of the party (rooted principally in differences of region and of class) were magnified by personality conflicts and by disagreements over the appropriate locus of party authority. Throughout this period, all of the legislators and most of the members (73 percent at one point)[28] were from Cape Breton; in contrast, the provincial executive was top-heavy with mainlanders. In 1978, for example, eleven of the fourteen executive members, including the president, came from the mainland.[29] During Akerman's stewardship, the parliamentary and extra-parliamentary wings clashed over a number of issues (such as supplementing the leader's salary and accepting corporate donations), and each was convinced that it should have the final authority over these matters. Not surprisingly, the Cape Breton contingent of MLAs was intent on improving the NDP's electoral fortunes; in contrast, according to Paul MacEwan, the executive was dominated by idealists who were "disinterested in power, and obsessed with 'ideals.' They liked losers because they themselves were losers."[30] Of course, a more sympathetic observer would suggest that the executive was simply protecting both the traditional social democratic principles of intraparty democracy and the specific provisions of the NDP's constitution.[31] This internecine cauldron was further disturbed by intractable interpersonal conflicts. To the mainlanders, Akerman was both "egotistical" and of "suspect integrity," while the judgment on his "xenophobic" and "bombastic" sidekick Paul MacEwan "was even harsher."[32] For their part, the Cape Bretoners cared little for the "Halifax pipe-puffers"[33] whose "idealism" they found to be "bigoted, bristling and irreconcilable."[34]

The reinforcing nature of these cleavages left few opportunities to build bridges between the two camps. Matters ultimately came to a head in May 1980 when Akerman resigned the party leadership to accept a patronage position from John Buchanan's Tories (but not, it has been alleged by Alexa McDonough, before earning his job by refusing to embarrass the Conservatives over the Rollie Thornhill scandal).[35] Alarmed by even the prospect of a MacEwan bid for the leadership (and paralytic at the possibility it might succeed), the provincial council expelled the renegade MLA for Cape Breton Nova in July 1980. After all, notes one apologist for the party establishment: "It did not make sense to allow MacEwan the opportunity to stick around to pick away at the scab."[36]

Inevitably, the party's November 1980 leadership convention was profoundly shaped by the controversial departures of Akerman and MacEwan. As detailed in the appendix to this book, the three candidates (Buddy MacEachern, Alexa McDonough, and Len Arsenault) all carved out distinctive positions on the matter. MacEachern served as a MacEwan surrogate: a blunt, Cape Breton trade unionist who believed that the NDP's extra-parliamentary wing should defer to its elected MLAs. McDonough's persona was markedly different: a young, unelected, articulate female Halifax professional intent on securing the party's socialist soul. In a quote that bears repeating, she advised delegates: "We will hold our members to our principles and policies and unlike the other major parties we are prepared to commit near electoral suicide to enforce those policies."[37] Finally, Len Arsenault positioned himself as the compromise candidate: a Cape Bretoner who was also a middle-class professional, an elected MLA who was also respectful of the supremacy of the party's extra-parliamentary wing. McDonough's smashing victory (with just fewer than three-quarters of the votes on the first ballot) heralded a dramatic shift in the nature of the Nova Scotia NDP.

Our survey of the delegates to the 1980 leadership convention affords some purchase on these intraparty tensions. Two caveats, however, must be registered. First, it is likely that many long-standing members from Cape Breton had already fled the party in the months preceding the November 1980 convention. One observer notes that, after the party council had formally expelled MacEwan from the party, many of the Cape Bretoners present had followed the maverick MLA "out of the room, and out of the NDP."[38] Thus, our data likely underestimate the extent of the Cape Breton-mainland conflict that had been simmering over the previous decade. Second, we take some comfort in the close fit between actual vote totals and those reported in our surveys. Nevertheless, Table 1.2 reveals that Buddy MacEachern's figures constitute a significant exception to this generalization as, despite receiving 13 percent of the first ballot votes, he was the choice of only 6 percent of those surveyed. Given that MacEachern embodied the traditional verities associated with the Cape Breton wing of the party, the relative disinclination of his supporters to complete the questionnaire is unfortunate. Once again, the likely impact of the deviation is to diminish the actual cleavage between Cape Bretoners and mainlanders.

Even so, Table 13.3 provides some insight into this division. Perhaps not surprisingly, Cape Breton delegates were far more likely than were their mainland counterparts to be both native Nova Scotians and long-standing party members. Indeed, it is indicative of the NDP's disconnect from contemporary Nova Scotia that, at a time when over 80 percent of provincial residents were native bluenosers (a figure that admittedly includes the relatively static population of Cape Breton), almost half the party's mainland delegates were "come from aways." The sharp regional cleavage is also apparent in the voting pattern. Only one mainlander in eight opted for a sitting MLA as leader; the rest preferred a candidate who may have been defeated in her only two attempts to secure elected office but who had the key qualification of not being a Cape Bretoner. Finally, Table 13.3 reveals that even those Cape Bretoners who had not already left the Nova Scotia NDP over the MacEwan affair had significantly different views about the appropriate balance of power between the trade union movement, the elected MLAs, and the extra-parliamentary wing.

Alexa McDonough would contest four provincial elections during her sixteen-year tenure as party leader. During that period, there was a barely perceptible increase of one to three percentage points from the 15 percent share of the popular vote secured by Jeremy Akerman in both the 1974 and 1978 campaigns. What did change dramatically was the distribution of that

*Table 13.3*

**Nova Scotia NDP leadership election, 1980: selected attributes by region**

|  |  | Cape Breton (%) | Mainland (%) |
|---|---|---|---|
| Born and raised in Nova Scotia | Yes | 83.7 | 53.6** |
| Joined the party | Since 1979 | 16.3 | 32.7 |
|  | Before 1963 | 27.9 | 14.9* |
| Voted for | Len Arsenault | 30.2 | 10.1 |
|  | Alexa McDonough | 48.8 | 87.5 |
|  | Buddy MacEachern | 20.9 | 2.4** |
| Individual MLAs should have more say in determining party policy than the individual members of the General Council or Executive. | Agree and strongly agree | 32.6 | 16.1* |
| Party hierarchy has lost contact with the grassroots of the party. | Agree and strongly agree | 41.9 | 17.9** |
| Labour unions should have more say in determining the policy of the party. | Very strongly agree and strongly agree | 30.2 | 15.5 |
|  | N | 43 | 168 |

* $\chi^2 < .05$
** $\chi^2 < .01$

vote. As Table 13.2 reveals, there had never been a provincial election before 1981 in which the NDP's share of the popular vote in Cape Breton was less than double what it received on the mainland. Under Alexa McDonough's leadership, however, the party always won a greater proportion of votes on the mainland than it did on Cape Breton. Thus, in 1981, McDonough's spirited attacks on the Buchanan government's record in health care, fiscal management, labour relations, and offshore resources obviously resonated with many mainland voters. The NDP not only elected its first ever mainland MLA but also outpolled the Liberals in the metropolitan Halifax area. "The triumph of Mrs. McDonough in Halifax Chebucto," gushed one observer "must rank as the biggest step forward in the party's history." [39] Perhaps, but the continuing fallout from the Akerman-MacEwan controversy decimated the NDP in its traditional Cape Breton strongholds. MacEwan easily won re-election as an independent in Cape Breton Nova (with the unfortunate Tony Gale receiving fewer votes than any other NDP candidate in the province), and the party was trounced in the other three ridings it had secured in 1978. Thus, for the first time in over a decade, the NDP failed to reach the two-member benchmark required for recognition as an "official" party in the Nova Scotia legislature.

New Democrats must have hoped that Cape Breton's estrangement from the party was to be only temporary. Shortly after the 1981 election, Alexa McDonough professed to be "heartbroken about [the results in] Cape Breton ... They are the soul of the NDP."[40] But no rapprochement was possible, with Paul MacEwan, egged on by the governing Tories, waging a personal vendetta against Alexa McDonough at the legislature. Again, New Democrats must have hoped that "in time, the relentless viciousness of his assault [would] nauseate even his own constituency."[41] Such was not to be the case. Soon, MacEwan had launched the Cape Breton Labour Party (CBLP) to promote provincial status for the Island and to combat "the exploitation of Cape Breton by Halifax and the Nova Scotia mainland and the denial of equality to Cape Bretoners."[42] In the 1984 election, MacEwan was returned with his largest majority ever, and with CBLP candidates finishing second in Cape Breton Centre and third in Cape Breton East, his upstart party had outpolled the NDP on the Island.[43] For her part, Alexa McDonough campaigned vigorously for tax reform, pay equity, improved daycare, and more effective economic development, and she was rewarded, as Table 13.1 makes clear, with two additional seats on the mainland. Exulted McDonough: "I do not intend to stand alone anymore."[44] The remaining twelve years of McDonough's stewardship represented a holding pattern for the Nova Scotia NDP. MacEwan soon folded up the CBLP,[45] but he won re-election as an independent in 1988 and as a Liberal in 1993 (with an astonishing 82 percent of the vote). In the absence of the CBLP, the NDP was able to recover some of its lost support on the Island, but not enough to secure representation at Province House. On the mainland, the party was hurt when Kings South MLA Bob Levy accepted a judgeship from the Buchanan government immediately prior to the 1988 vote. After falling back to two seats in that election, they returned to three MLAs in 1993.

By 1995, Alexa McDonough had moved on to the national leadership of the NDP. The 1996 convention that elected Robert Chisholm as her successor was relatively uneventful; it attracted few delegates and little media attention. After all, the Nova Scotia NDP was then experiencing a form of "free-floating failure,"[46] and its reputation as a fringe party seemingly ensured that it would remain in that unhappy state. Nevertheless, 92 percent of the delegates surveyed at the 1996 convention believed that the NDP had "a bright future" in Nova Scotia. As it turned out, these seemingly misguided souls were soon proved correct. With a native daughter at the helm, and with the federal Liberals tilting to the right, the NDP won an unprecedented six seats in Nova Scotia in the June 1997 federal election (sweeping both metropolitan Halifax and Cape Breton) with 30 percent of the provincial vote.[47] Five months later, they built on this success by garnering 33 percent of the vote in a round of four provincial by-elections and electing Helen MacDonald in Cape Breton-The Lakes.

Having thus shed their reputation as a party of losers, the Nova Scotia NDP entered the March 1998 provincial election with unusually elevated expectations. The party received some criticism for not costing its various election promises,[48] but otherwise it presented itself as a model of fiscal rectitude. At the campaign's outset, Chisholm claimed: "We would not add a red cent to the operating deficit of the province of Nova Scotia."[49] Aided by a bumbling campaign by the Liberal government, the NDP was largely able to defuse charges that it stood for "risky, doctrinaire, tax-and-spend adventurism."[50] Suitably reassured, the electorate rewarded the NDP with 35 percent of the vote and nineteen seats. Only compared to these stratospheric totals could the 1999 results (30 percent of the vote and eleven seats) possibly be construed as a disappointment. Nevertheless, many party members felt that a historic opportunity to win government in Nova Scotia had eluded them, and some of the blame inevitably fell on Robert Chisholm, not only for his cautious "front-runner's" campaign but also for his seeming duplicity over a 1978 DUI conviction. Shortly after, Chisholm resigned as party leader.

Thus, one might have surmised that the Nova Scotia New Democrats who gathered in July 2000 to select a new leader would have had a different political outlook from those who had anointed Robert Chisholm four years previously. In the interim, the Nova Scotia NDP had enjoyed unprecedented electoral success in both the provincial and federal arenas. No longer was the prospect of an NDP government at Province House a risible delusion.

For a century or more,[51] students of left-wing political movements have noted their tendency to moderate, or "deradicalize,"[52] with time and, especially, with greater proximity to power. Did the Nova Scotia NDP undergo such an ideological metamorphosis as it vaulted from minor to major party status? In contrast to their liberal and conservative counterparts, social democratic parties customarily prefer the state, rather than the market, to allocate goods and services; in fact, in Chapter 8 we detect precisely this pattern. What is important for our present purposes, however, is whether the Nova Scotia NDP's distrust of the market ebbed after 1996, especially given the increasingly mainstream character of many neoliberal nostrums. Fortunately, our surveys included several questions that tap into this dimension, and these are summarized in Table 13.4. The data suggest the party tracked towards the political centre both initially (between 1996 and 2000) and subsequently (between 2000 and 2002). While the NDP's ideological profile could still be readily distinguished from those of their Liberal and Conservative

*Table 13.4*

## Nova Scotia NDP leadership elections: indicators of deradicalization

| % | | 1996 | 2000 | | | 2002 | | |
|---|---|---|---|---|---|---|---|---|
| | | All | All | Members for 2 years or less | Members for 3+ years | All | Members for 5 years or less | Members for 6+ years |
| Describe political views as: | Left | 48 | 39 | 20 | 41** | 32 | 26 | 35** |
| Social programs should remain universal. | Strongly agree | 87 | 80 | 70 | 82 | 77 | 69 | 83** |
| Foreign investment should be regulated. | Strongly agree | 56 | 46 | 35 | 48 | 46 | 33 | 51** |
| Labour unions are essential in Canadian life. | Strongly agree | 64 | 48 | 47 | 47 | 40 | 32 | 46** |
| Free trade with US has been good for Nova Scotia. | Strongly disagree | 62 | 34 | 9 | 34 | 39 | 34 | 41* |
| Most modern-day social problems will not be solved until government gets less, rather than more, involved in society. | Strongly disagree | 49 | 40 | 23 | 42 | 30 | 27 | 32 |
| Nova Scotia should always have a balanced budget. | Agree and strongly agree | 26 | 33 | 46 | 32 | 37 | 42 | 36 |
| N | | 159 | 306 | | | 497 | | |

* $\chi^2 < .05$
** $\chi^2 < .01$

opponents, it had become demonstrably more moderate than it had been prior to the party's ascension to major party status.

Was this ideological evolution driven principally by addition or by conversion? In other words, did the Nova Scotia NDP add fresh recruits who were more centrist in their orientations or were long-standing members moderating their views? As Table 13.4 makes clear, the former process was certainly at work. In fact, on none of the fourteen points of comparison were recent party members offering views to the left of their more experienced cohorts, and in many instances the gap was statistically significant. Yet Table 13.4 also reveals that party veterans were undergoing some measure of deradicalization. Of course, these two phenomena did not likely occur independently. In other words, centrist recruits joined the NDP as the party shifted in their direction, while long-standing members moderated their views as they interacted with the newcomers.

As for the long-standing cleavage between members from Cape Breton and those from the mainland, it has been much less apparent in more recent soundings than it was in the 1980 survey. Even so, Table 13.5 reveals that this gap has not been entirely eradicated. Despite their relatively small numbers, Cape Breton members of the NDP were significantly more enthusiastic than were the mainlanders about maintaining organized labour's voice in the party.

The Nova Scotia NDP entered the 2003 provincial election with both a legitimate prospect of winning and a more centrist ideological profile. In some measure, the party campaign reflected this novel circumstance. For one thing, the NDP began to experiment with attention-getting electoral gimmickry. On one occasion, party leader Darrell Dexter offered free airline tickets to British Columbia or Manitoba to his opposition counterparts so that they could experience first-hand the virtues of a public auto insurance system. In another instance, Dexter donned the persona of a game show host and asked reporters to match up party leaders and their quotes on

*Table 13.5*

**Nova Scotia NDP leadership election, 2002: selected attributes by region**

|  |  | Cape Breton (%) | Mainland (%) |
|---|---|---|---|
| The voice of the trade union | Strongly disagree | 2 | 5 |
| movement must remain | Disagree | 15 | 25 |
| strong in the councils of the | Agree | 30 | 50 |
| NDP. | Strongly agree | 52 | 20 |
|  | N | 46 | 400* |

* $\chi^2 < .01$

insurance rates.[53] These stunts may have been almost unspeakably lame (after all, journalists were awarded "prizes" of NDP campaign buttons for correct responses), but they still represented a significant departure from the more earnest campaigns of the past. As well, the party's seven-point platform in the 2003 campaign reflected its new circumstance. True, five of the planks emphasized traditional social democratic shibboleths: student debt relief, classroom resources for those with special needs, reduced health-care waiting lists, and the like. What is significant in the present context is that one of the commitments was to a balanced budget, while another was to tax relief (removing the HST from heating oil and electricity).[54] In the words of Darrell Dexter, there are "some areas where the tax man ought not to be."[55] In fact, such was the eagerness to shed its image as the party of high taxation that, unlike the Liberals, the NDP did not promise to repeat the Hamm administration's rash (and likely unsustainable) 10 percent cut in provincial income tax rates. In the end, the Nova Scotia New Democrats won 31 percent of the vote and fifteen seats in 2003. For the third succes-sive election, they had secured official opposition status at Province House.

Thus, the New Democratic Party of Nova Scotia entered the new millen-nium in circumstances vastly different from those facing their counterparts in New Brunswick and Prince Edward Island. During the previous two dec-ades, it switched its ideological and electoral centre of gravity from Cape Breton to metropolitan Halifax and also vaulted from minor to major party status. The obvious question to consider is whether there were any linkages between these two phenomena.

At first blush, it seems implausible to suggest that there was any electoral advantage to be gained by the expulsion of Paul MacEwan and the subse-quent collapse of the NDP vote in its long-standing Cape Breton heartland. Yet Tables 13.1 and 13.2 reveal that, although the NDP's legislative contin-gent plunged from four representatives to one, its share of the provincial vote did not decline in the 1980s as ballots lost in Cape Breton were essen-tially recouped on the mainland. Moreover, it is worth recalling that, from 1937 to 1980, the CCF-NDP's electoral bedrock had been found among the coal miners and steel workers of industrial Cape Breton. At one time, there were seventeen thousand miners labouring in the Island's collieries;[56] today, there are none. Likewise, there were once six thousand workers employed in Cape Breton's steel industry.[57] Once again, there are none at present. It can hardly be advantageous for a political party to hitch its electoral wagon to a demographic in dramatic decline. The Newfoundland Liberal Party, for example, needed to transcend its immediate post-Confederation base in iso-lated outport communities in order to remain electorally competitive in the modern period. Had they not undergone a similar metamorphosis, it is dif-ficult to imagine that Nova Scotia's New Democrats would today be cred-ible contenders for power. Not that those who precipitated the party's transformation in 1980 deserve any particular credit for political far-sightedness; on the contrary, petty and parochial quests for advantage and retribution were rarely far from the surface. Even so, the NDP has now established a beachhead on the Maritime coast that will not readily be rolled back.

Our analysis of leadership selection in Nova Scotia identifies and highlights the stronger role played by the New Democratic Party in provincial politics. In this chapter, our examination of NDP elections sheds light on the regionalism and pragmatism that marks Nova Scotia politics more generally. We see the Cape Breton/Halifax rivalry not only as a historic part of NDP history but also as an ongoing indication of the strength of regionalism within Nova Scotia – a regionalism we also saw in candidate support patterns in other parties. We also see New Democratic voters moving closer to the political centre, perhaps in the realization that, in this direction, lies the path to power.

# 14

# The End of the Affair? Political Scientists and the Delegated Convention

Since before Confederation, the electorate charged with the responsibility of choosing Canadian political party leaders has progressively widened – from the representative of the Crown, to members of the legislative caucus, to delegates at a leadership convention, and, most recently, to all party members. This latest method was first employed in Canada by the Parti Quebecois in 1985 (four years after it had been introduced by the British Social Democrats). Since that date, many federal and provincial parties have experimented with some form of all-member vote. Most now permit individual members to cast leadership ballots, often at a time and usually at a place far removed from the hubbub of the convention floor. Thus, the Manitoba Liberals employed an all-member postal ballot in 1993, while the 1993 British Columbia Liberals utilized telephone voting, and the 1992 Alberta PCs relied on riding-based ballot boxes. Other parties have attempted to marry the traditional leadership convention to some form of all-member vote. The first ballot results at the 1991 Ontario Liberal convention were tied to an all-member primary, while the 1996 PEI Liberals employed the simple expedient of holding a convention to which all party members were invited. By the end of the twentieth century, therefore, the traditional delegated leadership convention had been largely uprooted from the Canadian political scene. Not all observers have welcomed this transformation. In fact, the response from the academy has been remarkably cool. Canadian political scientists have compiled a long list of perceived problems associated with the all-member vote. In no particular order, these include the increased likelihood that money will play a decisive role in the outcome, that substance will be sacrificed to image, that interests outside the party will hijack the process, that lengthy experience in party affairs will be discounted, that activists will have less reason to participate in the day-to-day affairs of the party, that intraparty accommodation will be rendered more difficult, that it will be more difficult to get rid of party leaders, and so on.[1]

Political scientists are typically a contentious lot. On the subject of the universal ballot, however, the balance of opinion is overwhelmingly tipped in the negative direction. George Perlin, for example, has itemized a number of the faults associated with all-member votes and has concluded that Canadian parties would be wiser to reform the delegated convention than to abandon it.[2] Similarly, Peter Woolstencroft has suggested that, with the adoption of the universal ballot, "the goals of democracy [have been] undermined by the reforms of democracy,"[3] while Heather MacIvor has lamented that despite "a number of serious drawbacks," it may be "impossible for parties to resist this reform."[4] As for Keith Archer and David Stewart, their analysis of the 1994 Alberta Liberal leadership selection led them to question whether the proceedings had been an "electronic fiasco."[5] Leonard Preyra suggests that all-member votes might appear to represent an improvement over the traditional delegated convention, but "at the operational level a huge chasm in expectations and outcomes remains."[6] According to Patrick Malcomson, proponents of some form of direct leadership election are relying on a series of "rather dubious assumptions." Admittedly, the universal ballot is "in vogue" in Canada; but, advises Malcomson, "its popularity is not necessarily a measure of its wisdom."[7] John Courtney, one of Canada's foremost students of leadership politics, is largely disapproving of the all-member vote as a mechanism for choosing leaders. In his comprehensive book on leadership selection, *Do Conventions Matter?*, he dismisses universal ballots as "mail-order leadership" and closes his book with this warning: "Yet the alleged benefits of universal voting may in the long run be more ephemeral than its proponents claim. The switch could ultimately prove problematic for the health of local political organizations and the larger political community in Canada."[8]

Initially, party activists shared this academic suspicion of the universal ballot. Table 14.1 reveals that, at the outset of the 1980s, and irrespective of province and of party, Maritime activists endorsed the convention method of selecting a party leader. For every activist who rejected the convention method during the early 1980s, there were ten on the affirmative side. The Pequiste experiment with the all-member vote in 1985, however, may have had repercussions outside Quebec as the monolithic character of opinion on this subject began to erode in the 1985 and 1986 samples. Even so, a clear majority of activists continued to endorse the convention system of leadership selection.

Much the same message can be gleaned from Table 14.2, which details support for the universal ballot. Again, the 1980 Liberal sample was characterized by a general disinterest in the all-member vote: only 20 percent of the respondents were supportive. In the succeeding years, however, enthusiasm for this reform grew steadily, from 20 percent in 1980, to 30 percent in 1981 and 1982, to 40 percent in 1985 and 1986, to 50 percent in 1988 and 1991, to 70 percent in 1993, to 80 percent in 1996, and, finally, to over

*Table 14.1*

**Maritime leadership elections: support for convention vote for selecting leaders**

| % | NS NDP 1980 | NS Liberal 1980 | PEI Liberal 1981 | PEI PC 1981 | NB Liberal 1982 | NB Liberal 1985 | NS Liberal 1986 |
|---|---|---|---|---|---|---|---|
| Strongly agree | 23.1 | 27.9 | 23.2 | 36.0 | 16.1 | 20.8 | 18.9 |
| Agree | 59.6 | 57.9 | 62.5 | 48.8 | 60.7 | 53.3 | 47.9 |
| Disagree | 6.0 | 5.3 | 3.6 | 5.4 | 8.5 | 15.3 | 17.4 |
| Strongly disagree | 1.9 | 1.6 | 1.2 | 0 | 3.0 | 1.1 | 4.9 |
| No opinion | 9.4 | 7.3 | 9.6 | 9.8 | 11.8 | 9.5 | 10.8 |
| N | 192 | 437 | 168 | 203 | 366 | 274 | 943 |

90 percent in 2002. Rarely does data march in such a straight line. Unfortunately, Tables 14.1 and 14.2 are not entirely comparable as the time-series data in the former ceases in 1986. Even so, at least some respondents apparently perceived no inherent contradiction between the delegated convention and the all-member vote. The portion of the sample that embraced the latter was, on average, approximately 20 percent larger than was the group that rejected the former. Assuming that this does not simply constitute a response-set bias (i.e., a tendency to agree rather than to disagree with proffered statements), at least some Maritime activists believed that the typical leadership convention could be expanded to include all party members. This, in fact, is essentially the method now employed by all PEI parties to select their leaders: a convention is held (presumably in Charlottetown) at which all party members are eligible to vote. Only the small scale of Maritime politics makes such a synthesis possible. In fact, even in New Brunswick, the Conservatives had to backtrack from a similar plan in 1997, when objections were raised that northern New Brunswickers would have to drive too far to attend an open convention in a southern metropolis. In the larger Canadian provinces and, especially, at the national level, the contradictions between the convention method and the universal ballot are likely to be irreconcilable.

The message to be gleaned from Tables 14.1 and 14.2 is unambiguous. Note that ambivalence towards the universal ballot has dropped sharply (from one-fifth of the sample at the outset to less than one-twentieth at the conclusion). Similarly noteworthy is the shift in intensity of support. Prior to 1993, it was more usual for respondents to "agree" rather than to "strongly agree" with all-member votes. Subsequent to that date, the pattern has, without a single exception, been reversed. In short, a steadily increasing proportion of activists, irrespective of party or province, have wished to see the delegated convention superseded by the universal ballot.

Not surprisingly, Maritime parties have been steadily changing their leadership practices to conform to this shift in popular values. At the outset of our study, all of the region's political parties selected their leaders through delegated conventions. In 2005, the New Brunswick NDP finally turned to the universal ballot to replace Elizabeth Weir after her seventeen-year tenure as leader. Of course, some Maritime parties have been slow to embrace this reform.[9] Notwithstanding the emerging regional consensus, the New Brunswick Liberals in 1998 and the Nova Scotia NDP in 2000 both opted to elect their leaders in delegated conventions. Yet, as Table 14.2 indicates, these decisions were, in both cases, out of step with the responses of a clear majority of surveyed party activists. In fact, Table 14.2 may even underestimate the elite-mass disjuncture since it necessarily excludes the opinions of those party members who were not selected as convention delegates and who might, as a result, have been expected to be particularly enthusiastic about the universal ballot.

Was there wisdom in the conscious decisions of the 1998 New Brunswick Liberals and the 2000 Nova Scotia New Democrats to be policy laggards? Were their leadership contests models of deliberative democracy? As we shall see, such questions cannot easily be answered in the affirmative. Admittedly, Nova Scotia's New Democrats may have had valid reasons to resist the trend towards the universal ballot, given that they have traditionally situated their leadership selection process within the context of a policy convention. The latter requires participants to be directly engaged in the proceedings, to hear opposing views and to deliberate on their respective merits before signifying a preference. All-member leadership votes, by contrast, rarely demand and often prohibit this high level of involvement. Thus, as long as the discussion of public policy was regarded as central to any gathering of Nova Scotia New Democrats, the universal leadership ballot was unlikely to be employed. Even so, it is worth noting that the final occasion on which the party relied on a delegated convention to select its leader was hardly a success. Elected on the third ballot of the 2000 convention, new leader Helen MacDonald was without a seat in Province House. Alas, she suffered an ignominious defeat in a Cape Breton North by-election the following March (finishing last), and the caucus was soon in open revolt. Less than a year after winning the post, Helen MacDonald resigned as leader; at the subsequent annual convention, party delegates overwhelmingly opted to choose their next leader by the one member-one vote system.

In some respects, the case of the 1998 New Brunswick Liberals is the more interesting of the two leadership selection laggards (see the appendix to this book for a complete discussion of this contest). At their 1997 biennial convention, a simple majority of delegates had, in fact, voted in favour of

*Table 14.2*

**Maritime leadership elections: support for all-member vote for selecting leaders**

| % | NS Lib 1980 | NS NDP 1980 | PEI Lib 1981 | PEI PC 1981 | NB Lib 1982 | NB Lib 1985 | NS Lib 1986 | PEI PC 1988 | NS PC 1991 | PEI Lib 1993 | PEI Lib 1996 | NB PC 1997 | NB Lib 1998 | NB NDP 2000 | NB Lib 2002 | PEI NDP 2002 | NS NDP 2002 | NS Lib 2002 | PEI Lib 2003 |
|---|---|---|---|---|---|---|---|---|---|---|---|---|---|---|---|---|---|---|---|
| Strongly agree | 6.6 | 7.5 | 10.9 | 11.8 | 10.9 | 15.0 | 17.3 | 25.7 | 21.6 | 37.2 | 51.2 | 56.7 | 39.5 | 32.7 | 41.5 | 55.3 | 47.3 | 60.3 | 64.5 |
| Agree | 13.5 | 19.8 | 19.0 | 19.7 | 20.2 | 27.2 | 24.1 | 24.7 | 25.9 | 33.5 | 33.7 | 30.5 | 31.2 | 30.4 | 36.0 | 38.3 | 42.5 | 28.5 | 21.8 |
| Disagree | 54.2 | 36.8 | 42.3 | 34.5 | 43.4 | 35.4 | 35.4 | 27.4 | 33.8 | 19.7 | 7.9 | 4.9 | 20.4 | 25.5 | 12.2 | 0 | 4.8 | 7.3 | 4.0 |
| Strongly disagree | 14.0 | 14.2 | 9.5 | 12.8 | 13.4 | 10.9 | 12.1 | 13.3 | 15.4 | 7.0 | 4.1 | 3.2 | 6.1 | 5.2 | 3.7 | 4.3 | 1.0 | 2.6 | 2.0 |
| No opinion | 11.6 | 21.7 | 18.5 | 21.2 | 12.1 | 10.9 | 11.0 | 8.9 | 3.3 | 2.5 | 3.0 | 4.7 | 2.6 | 6.2 | 5.7 | 2.1 | 4.4 | 1.3 | 7.7 |
| N | 437 | 212 | 168 | 203 | 366 | 274 | 943 | 248 | 1,230 | 968 | 365 | 593 | 773 | 306 | 164 | 47 | 497 | 151 | 248 |

introducing the universal ballot for future leadership contests. Since the party constitution requires such amendments to be passed by a two-thirds majority, however, the motion was lost.[10] As a compromise, the party executive decided to double constituency representation; at the next leadership convention, Liberal riding associations would be eligible to send as many as seventy-five delegates. In the words of Steve MacKinnon, the executive director of the New Brunswick Liberal Association: "The issue that was determined here was that the party threw open its doors to more youth, more women and more grassroots people from all over the province. This means that every delegate, every Liberal in New Brunswick, that wishes to attend the convention will be able to do so."[11] Unfortunately, this optimistic scenario failed to materialize.

On the contrary, most of the ills associated with delegated conventions were visited on the New Brunswick Liberals in the winter and spring of 1998. Ken Carty has persuasively argued that leadership conventions were transformed in the twenty-six years between the 1967 election of Robert Stanfield as PC national leader and the 1993 elevation of Kim Campbell to that same position. In essence, Carty claims that, over this interval, the effective point of decision (at least for national parties) became progressively further removed from the actual convention ballot as candidates took rational advantage of the institution's incentive structure. Thus, while the contests of the 1960s were won at the convention proper, those of the 1970s, the 1980s, and the 1990s were decided, respectively, at the campaign, the delegate selection, and the pre-contest stages.[12] A number of negative attributes have been associated with this metamorphosis of the delegated leadership convention, all of which descended upon the Liberal party of New Brunswick.

### Pre-Contest Intimidation

The need to compete vigorously for constituency delegates in all fifty-five provincial riding associations favoured those candidates with well-established machines. For almost two years prior to Frank McKenna's resignation, Minister of Economic Development Camille Theriault had been running a "stealth" campaign for the party leadership. According to his manager, Jack MacDougall, Theriault was not initially regarded in the party as leadership material. Thus, even before McKenna's departure, the Theriault team sought to alter that perception. In MacDougall's words:

> We had to identify in each of those ridings who some of the key people were. Camille came to me because I was a field worker with the party; I knew who the "players" were. If we could get these ten people, they are opinion leaders within that association. They should create a sense that you are a "player."[13]

The strategy obviously worked. Media reports after McKenna's resignation referred to "the Theriault juggernaught"[14] and labelled the minister of economic development as the "frontrunner-presumptive."[15] To some observers, Theriault's palpable eagerness to vault from the starting blocks was a tactical mistake, especially when the party chose in October 1997 to delay the convention until May 1998. According to columnist Don Richardson, the Liberals had thus guaranteed that the leadership race would not "start in earnest until February, or perhaps later. There is no longer any advantage to declaring one's intentions now; in fact, there are distinct disadvantages to being tagged as the early front-runner (as Camille Theriault is doubtless discovering)."[16] Even in late January 1998, such sentiments were still being articulated. According to prominent Liberal Art Doyle, Jr., it was not too late at that time for a new candidate to enter the race. "In political terms," observed Doyle, "three months is a lifetime away and there's tons of time to get an organization going."[17] After all, had not the then unknown Frank McKenna swept to victory in the 1985 Liberal leadership race despite entering the contest only five weeks prior to the vote? What such analyses overlooked was the manner in which delegated conventions had changed over the preceding thirteen years. Serious candidates now recognized the salutary effects of a pre-contest flexing of organizational muscles: wavering activists could be induced to climb on an apparently winning bandwagon, and wavering candidates could be intimidated to stay out of the fray. Knowing this, the Theriault camp organized a large public rally in January 1998 in advance of their candidate (or any other) officially entering the race. At the time, Finance Minister Edmond Blanchard was widely regarded as a worthy successor to McKenna – a francophone centrist whose appeal crossed ethnic lines. According to Jack MacDougall:

> Before the meeting, someone came up to me and said there are a couple of Edmond Blanchard people here. Should we kick them out? I said: "No. Put them front and centre. I want them there. I want them to know what we have got" ... So critical was the exercise that Blanchard (who at that point was the number one guy, the Minister of Finance, a tremendous guy who oozed credibility) announced that morning in Saint John to a house of 25 people that he was going [to enter the race] and that night he changed his mind. I know those two guys went back and told him that these guys are rolling, big time.[18]

In this case, pre-contest pressure manifestly served the interests of the Theriault organization as, citing unspecified health concerns, Blanchard opted out of the race. Whether such intimidation served the interests of either the Liberal party or the people of New Brunswick is, however, far more problematic.

## Packing Meetings and Slate Politics

At national leadership conventions in the 1960s and 1970s, constituency delegates were not typically elected as part of a slate pledged to back a particular candidate; on the contrary, most arrived at the convention unencumbered with binding commitments. More recent national contests, however, had reversed this pattern as slate politics had become the norm and unattached delegates had become the exception. So it was with the New Brunswick Liberal Party in 1998. Sixty percent of the respondents in our survey acknowledged being elected as part of a candidate slate. Again, it was Camille Theriault who took the fullest advantage of convention rules. The first delegation selection meeting was held on 2 February 1997 in Moncton East. Recalled riding association president Steve Campbell:

> [Mr. Theriault] was better at it, being early off the mark and very organized and aggressive ... The others were not prepared and scrambled throughout the hall telling their supporters who among the nominated delegates were sympathetic to their candidate, with little success. The prepared candidate elected most of his supporters.[19]

Interestingly, the Theriault camp never strove to secure a full slate of sympathetic delegates, even where their organizational strength might have permitted; instead, they opted for partial slates of fifty committed delegates from each constituency. Theriault was thus able to avoid some of the backlash that would inevitably have ensued had his team tried, for example, to block the mother of fellow candidate Greg Byrne from securing delegate status.[20]

Somewhat surprisingly, those delegates elected as members of a slate tended to be more urban, more educated, and of higher income than did their non-affiliated counterparts. As well, the former group tended to have less party experience than did the latter. Fully 42 percent of the independent delegates had been Liberal members for more than twenty-five years; for those elected on slates, the corresponding figure was only 27 percent. Even so, neophyte Liberals did not play a direct role at the May 1998 convention. Less than 4 percent of the surveyed delegates had been party members for less than one year. Where "instant members" proved to be decisive, however, was in the election of delegate slates at the constituency level. Camille Theriault's campaign manager, Jack MacDougall, subsequently boasted about his team's ability to pack delegate selection meetings:

> There were some ridings where MLAs and cabinet ministers supported other candidates and we beat them in their own riding, because we went out and signed up new people. These people are just as powerful as members who have been around for 30 or 40 years ... In fact, I remember one cabinet

minister commenting to me she was astonished; she had 60 people picked out to support the other candidate, but when she showed up, she saw about 200 people there and she said: "Oh my goodness, there are an awful lot of instant members here." I said, "Well, they all are."[21]

Thus, the process used to select convention delegates was an exercise not of deliberative democracy but, rather, of organizational muscle. Those who wished to pass judgment on the qualities of potential delegates were swept aside by a disciplined and unreflective phalanx of instant members recruited for the sole purpose of sending a committed slate to the convention at Saint John.

**The Irrelevant Convention**
The New Brunswick Liberal leadership convention was held on the week-end of 1 May 1998. The final delegate selection meeting, however, was held on 29 March in the riding of Nepisiquit. The intervening five weeks should have been a time for Liberals to deliberate and debate about the merits of the three candidates; instead, an eerie silence descended on the campaign. Admittedly, five leadership forums were held in the month of April. Front-runner Camille Theriault was intent, however, on doing nothing that might dislodge the 55 percent to 60 percent of delegates he claimed to have se-cured at the constituency stage. "These debates are fraught with peril for a front-runner," acknowledged Jack MacDougall at the time. "We have got to be very careful not to say or do something stupid in one of these."[22] When their candidate successfully cleared that rather unambitious hurdle, the Theriault organization was able to devote all its energies to delivering its slate delegates to the convention. As for Theriault himself, he seemingly came to regard the convention vote as a mere formality. Conciliatory bou-quets of praise were repeatedly offered to his two rivals for the job,[23] and, in a surprising display of confidence, Theriault called Allan Rock in the final week of the campaign to warn the federal health minister that, as premier, he would not stand for further cuts in transfer payments.[24] As it turned out, Theriault's certainty was not misplaced. Only 20 percent of surveyed delegates claimed to have decided in the final seven days preced-ing the vote (and one-third of these individuals had been elected on can-didate slates). Bernard Richard was widely acknowledged as having delivered the most effective speech at the convention, but there was too small a pool of unattached delegates for his efforts to matter. Indeed, one reporter at the convention wandered the floor of Saint John's Harbour Station for over two hours prior to the speeches before locating an un-committed delegate.[25] Ultimately, Theriault's first ballot total of 56 percent of the votes conformed exactly to his organization's post-delegate selection calculations.

Was the New Brunswick Liberal party hurt by its idiosyncratic retention of the delegated convention? It is true that Camille Theriault led the twelve-year-old Liberal administration to a crushing defeat in the 1999 provincial election. On the other hand, the electoral defeats of fellow Liberals Russell MacLellan in Nova Scotia and Keith Milligan in PEI, both of whom assumed the leadership of their party (and, thus, the premiership of their province) by means of a universal ballot, suggest the need for interpretive caution. Even so, there were early indications that Theriault was not necessarily the best choice to lead the New Brunswick Liberals into electoral battle. An early March poll, for example, revealed Bernard Richard to be the preferred choice for Liberal leader among the general public.[26] One month later, a survey of provincial Liberal voters put the three candidates in a virtual dead-heat.[27] Theriault was not necessarily the most appealing candidate; he was simply the best organized. Yet electing leaders based strictly on their ability to exploit the incentive structure of a delegated convention is not likely to serve the long-term interests of any political party.

Nor should democrats of any political persuasion have been enthused by the shenanigans described in the previous pages. Yet in mid-campaign, Barry O'Toole, a political scientist at St. Thomas University, suggested that the New Brunswick Liberals were "right to stick with the current system." After all, the "people who are delegates are interested in politics" and they will be able to partake "in that valuable consensus exercise which inevitably occurs when the final vote looms in the convention hall."[28] O'Toole's opinions again highlighted the disjuncture between the students and the practitioners of party politics; the former have tended to reject the all-member vote, even as the latter have moved to embrace it.

Admittedly, there may be some wisdom in the academy's rejection of the universal ballot; certainly, some of what has transpired at recent all-member votes lends credence to their earlier warnings. Nevertheless, it cannot be denied that the academy's position lends itself to some uncharitable interpretations. Political scientists gravitate towards different areas of the discipline for both ideological and psychological reasons (although other forces are also at play). Those drawn to the study of leadership and of authority, it might well be suggested, have been especially likely to have a conservative's suspicion of the universal ballot. Alternatively, it might be advanced that political scientists have been protecting their vicarious participation in a process imbued with great drama and excitement. All-member votes, as Daniel Latouche has suggested, can lack a sense of place, spontaneity, and spectacle.[29] With the universal ballot becoming standard practice, many students of leadership politics might be missing the theatrical qualities inherent in a traditional delegated convention. Finally, it might also be alleged that political scientists have been protecting sunk scholarly costs.

Alan Cairns once observed that the discipline of political science was slow to respond to the post-Charter constitutional reality:

Political science students of the constitution have built up sophisticated expertise and extensive intellectual capital around the twin concerns of parliamentary government and federalism, the primary institutional components of the Canadian constitutional order since 1867. Both have attracted sympathetic scholarly attention from political scientists ... Retooling, therefore, requires overcoming what Veblen called the trained incapacity of experts to respond to new challenges for which their expertise has diminished relevance ... The mainstream political scientists' version of the biographer's disease of identifying with their subjects is to become committed to the defence of the institutions they have long and lovingly studied.[30]

Those political scientists who had "long and lovingly studied" the delegated leadership convention might have been particularly resistant to its potential extinction. These charges, if valid, would raise questions regarding the academy's role in the debate over reforming the leadership selection process.

Political parties in the Maritimes and elsewhere in Canada have seemingly decided that employing a more open model of leadership selection effectively trumps other considerations. This does not mean that many of the ills previously visited upon delegated conventions (such as the use of organizational muscle) have not reappeared in a slightly altered guise with the universal ballot. Nevertheless, with approval rates among party activists now pushing into the 90 percent range, the universal ballot is highly popular. Its pre-eminence is not completely unchallenged, however, and although fresh reform impulses may well seek to widen (perhaps through provincewide leadership primaries), rather than constrict, the leadership electorate, there remain elements within the parties that prefer conventions and the media attention garnered by these spectacles. Indeed, as they moved to replace John Hamm as their leader in 2006, the Nova Scotian Conservatives found the potential publicity of a traditional convention irresistible. Their Liberal counterparts made a similar decision to return to a convention when they chose a new leader in 2007. The choice of leadership selection methods remains in flux.

# 15
# Conclusion

We began this study by pledging to consider the impact on Maritime leadership conventions of four key variables: time, method of election, party, and province. As the preceding pages have attested, convention processes and outcomes have been profoundly shaped by all four of these factors. Yet other forces have also been at play, and the appendix that follows this chapter presents some of the more idiosyncratic sources of variation. Even when the same party in the same province employed the same election process twice in a relatively brief time frame, the outcomes were generally quite different. For the Prince Edward Island Liberals, for example, the 1978 leadership contest was significantly shaped by the facts that the party was still in office, that one of the candidates was the interim premier, and that the other, not surprisingly, opted to run on a populist platform. Three short years later, however, the context was notably different. The Island Liberals were now out of power and were obliged to consider not only the impending outcome of a Conservative leadership convention but also the clear resemblance of one of the candidates to party icon Alex Campbell. Similar observations can be made with respect to the New Brunswick Liberals. In 1982, the party feared that it would never be able to dethrone Conservative premier Richard Hatfield, and the caucus putsch of former leader Joe Daigle cast a long shadow over the proceedings. Three years on, however, the New Brunswick Liberals were supremely confident that they would topple the Hatfield regime, and neither Joe Daigle's fate nor the appropriate relationship between caucus and the rank-and-file membership were much mentioned.

The appendix also alerts us to the distinctive and, at times, decisive role played by the key actors in our convention dramas – the candidates themselves. The seventy-five men and women who contested our twenty-five leadership conventions manifested a wide array of attitudes, motivations, and skills. Some (such as Doug Young) were openly ambitious; others (such as Angus MacLean) seemed to seek their party's leadership either reluctantly or as an after-thought. Some of the aspirants had the set of interpersonal skills normally associated with successful politicians; thus, Mel Gass, Rollie Thornhill, and John MacDonell were variously described as folksy, charming, and likeable. In contrast, Jim Lee was seen as a cold fish, Donald Cameron as thin-skinned, and Pat Binns and Jim White as painfully shy. Some candidates (such as Frank McKenna) ran error-free campaigns; others (such as George Hawkins) seemed to lurch from one crisis to the next. Finally, some (such as Bernard Richard, Barry Clark, and Alan Buchanan) delivered terrific convention speeches; others (such as Ray Frenette and Bernard Lord) did not. Each of our candidates, in fact, constituted a particular melange of character, personality, and ability, and it would be the rare voter who entirely discounted such attributes. Teasing out the precise linkages, however, is difficult. Some of the impacts only registered unconsciously, while others were likely suppressed by respondent reactivity. Worse yet, some candidate attributes (such as Fred Driscoll's intelligence or Donald Cameron's Puritanism) were likely to elicit both positive and negative responses (perhaps even from the same voter!). Even so, we are confident that convention outcomes cannot be fully explained without recourse to the range of candidate idiosyncrasies detailed in the appendix. At the outset of our analysis, we observed that leaders matter; at its close, we must note that candidates matter as well.

Our four key variables (time, method of election, party, and province) have had a more generalized impact on the twenty-five leadership contests under scrutiny. Of these, the most pervasive has been the influence of province. Admittedly, Nova Scotia, New Brunswick, and Prince Edward Island have numerous characteristics in common. By Canadian standards, all three provinces are small, rural, devout, economically backward hinterlands that were largely by-passed by the twentieth-century waves of immigration that helped to fill up the remainder of the country. In their politics, the three provinces have seemingly shared an affinity for partisan stability, for policy conservatism, for patronage practices, and so on. Like most stereotypes, the supporting evidence is not particularly compelling under close scrutiny.[1] Nevertheless, other Canadians (both inside and outside the academy) have typically found it convenient to group Nova Scotia, New Brunswick, and Prince Edward Island into a single region: the Maritimes.

Lost in such groupings, however, are the unique features of each province. Repeatedly, in our analysis, these distinctive provincial attributes permeated the selection of party leaders.

Of course, Chapters 11 through 13 focused on political phenomena unique to each of the three Maritime provinces. Only a surrealist would wish to consider Nova Scotia and the garden myth, for example, or the rise of the NDP in New Brunswick, or the politics of language on Prince Edward Island. But even when all these provinces could plausibly be grouped as one, obvious differences emerged in the analysis. Only in New Brunswick was there not typically a religious basis to friendship; as well, only in that province did businesspeople and lawyers monopolize the leadership fields. Prince Edward Island was also readily distinguishable on several dimensions – from its distinctive marriage of the all-member vote to a traditional convention setting, to the greater durability (in both age and partisan attachments) of its electors, to the relative slowness with which Island voters came to a decision. As for Nova Scotia, neither of the other two Maritime provinces had any analogue for the fierce localism of Cape Bretoners – apparent in the strength of the neighbourhood effect for Cape Breton candidates and in the chronic distrust of the mainland through much of the history of that province's CCF-NDP.

Admittedly, an appreciation for these interprovincial differences may largely be a matter of perspective. Differences between nations that John Glenn once regarded, from the floor of the US Senate, to be highly salient must have seemed much less significant in his previous incarnation as an astronaut. So it is with differences in the Maritimes. Others may regard the interprovincial dissimilarities sketched in this book as matters of nuance, as only minor variations within an overarching conformity. To us, however, these differences are of an altogether different order of magnitude and speak to the existence of fundamentally distinctive political experiences in Prince Edward Island, New Brunswick, and Nova Scotia.

That we should find such sharp interprovincial variation in leadership politics in the Maritimes speaks volumes about the centrifugal tendencies inherent in federations. Prince Edward Island, New Brunswick, and Nova Scotia manifestly share some socio-economic characteristics. Yet, contrary to what is assumed by many advocates of Maritime Union, the political boundaries that separate these three provinces are not superstructural ephemera; rather, they have created three different political communities, each with their own histories, symbols, perceptions, and identities.[2] Our leadership surveys have provided a window through which we have been able to regard these distinctive communities. Similar cross-provincial studies elsewhere in Canada would undoubtedly heighten our appreciation of these "small worlds."

Partisan differences also jumped out of the data on a host of occasions. Admittedly, few would have been surprised by the gap that frequently emerged between the NDP, on the one hand, and the Liberals and Conservatives, on the other. To take but five examples, New Democratic electors were distinctively left-wing, were less likely to declare a religious affiliation, were more hostile to patronage practices, were more likely to have at one time supported a different party, and were more likely to have the opportunity to vote for a woman candidate. Throughout much of the twentieth century, each of these five attributes would arguably have placed the NDP some distance from the political mainstream in Prince Edward Island, New

Brunswick, and Nova Scotia. Entering the twenty-first century, however, there is some evidence that, for all of these attributes, the gap has narrowed considerably. We saw in Chapter 13, for example, that the NDP (at least in Nova Scotia) has recently tracked towards the political centre on a range of matters (including ideological self-placement). We saw in Chapter 8, as well, that NDP activists have become increasingly resigned to the inevitability of patronage practices. There has also been some evolution from the other direction. We know, for instance, that residents of the three provinces are growing less devout: between 1985 and 2003, the percentage of Maritimers attending church at least once a month dropped from 54 percent to 38 percent, while attendance at least once a week slid from 36 percent to 25 percent. Given that the Maritime provinces have a reputation for being Canada's "Bible Belt," it is worth noting that the corresponding figure for the rest of English Canada is only marginally lower at 20 percent.[3] We also know that Maritimers have grown more accustomed to women in positions of political prominence. Prince Edward Island did not elect its first female MLA until 1970, but a 1993 formal portrait of the province's premier, the leader of the opposition, the speaker, the deputy speaker, and the lieutenant-governor displayed only female faces.[4] Finally, we know that partisan consistency is no longer a Maritime hallmark: of those Maritimers who voted for one of the four major parties in the 1993 federal election, only 59 percent voted the same way in 1997, while the corresponding figure for the rest of English Canada was 67 percent.[5] Nor was this result particularly anomalous. In the 2000 national election, 70 percent of Maritimers and 66 percent of those in the rest of English Canada cast ballots consistent with their previous vote.[6] On some matters, the mainstream has moved towards the New Democratic Party, while on others, the New Democratic Party has moved towards the mainstream. As a result, supporting the NDP in Prince Edward Island, New Brunswick, and Nova Scotia is no longer a badge of social marginality.

Also interesting were the differences between the two old-line parties themselves. That both the candidates and the electors of the Liberals and Conservatives would have distinctive religious profiles (with Catholics disproportionately located in the Liberal parties of Nova Scotia and New Brunswick and among the Conservatives of Prince Edward Island) is not particularly surprising and attests to the continued relevance of religion in regional politics. That Grits and Tories could be distinguished on ideological grounds, however, is significant. In Chapter 8, we discovered that Liberal and Conservative electors differed in their ideological self-placement (with the former tilting to the centre-left and the latter to the centre-right). Nor was this a hollow distinction. On a range of matters (including the role played by trade unions, the centrality of the market, the benefits of free trade, and the expansion of provincial powers), Liberal and Conservative views were significantly different. Thus, even leaving aside the New Democratic Party, elections in the three Maritime provinces are more than merely contests between the "ins" and the "outs," between those who have been dispensing and receiving patronage and those who would like to do so.

The preceding pages have also underscored the importance of changes in the method of leadership election. It is clear that moves to the universal ballot have done much more than merely increase the number of electors. All-member votes have been marked by differences in the social composition of the electorate (with a dramatic rise in the proportion of older voters), in the dynamics of decision making (with voters more frequently coming to decisions well in advance of the convention), and in the competitiveness of the race (with contests increasingly being settled on an initial ballot). Those inside the academy have long realized that institutional rules are not neutral and that changes in these rules will always advantage some social actors and disadvantage others relative to the status quo. The appendix highlights the fact that some candidacies (such as those of Paul Duffie [for the New Brunswick Liberals in 2002] and Dennis James [for the Nova Scotia Liberals in 2002]) were aborted in mid-contest. Both of these individuals, it seems clear, were disadvantaged by the particularities of the all-member vote and would have had better prospects for success under a delegated convention regime. It is surprising, therefore, that the decision either to adopt or to retain the universal ballot has engendered relatively little controversy in the Maritime parties under scrutiny.

There would seem to be three possible answers to this riddle. First, it may be that those Maritime candidates whose interests would be harmed by an all-member vote had not penetrated the rule-making body at the time of decision. While some aspirants, such as Camille Theriault, plotted their leadership campaigns for years ahead of the vote, it cannot be denied that others, such as Angus MacLean or Hinrich Bitter-Suermann, entered their contests without much advance strategic planning. Second, it may be that such penetration had occurred, but there was uncertainty about how the candidates would be affected by the adoption or retention of an all-member vote. Institutional change invariably produces some unanticipated consequences; impacts that seem obvious in retrospect are rarely as self-evident at the outset. Third, even if candidates had penetrated the decision-making body and were conscious that their interests would be adversely affected by the universal ballot, it may be that they were constrained from articulating same by a widespread adherence to the democratic ethos. We saw in Chapter 14 that party activists are now overwhelmingly supportive of giving every member a vote in leadership contests. Arguments to the contrary would generally have been regarded as elitist and regressive. Under such circumstances, the rhetoric of democracy may have been so potent as to stifle the articulation of mere interest.

Changes over time (aside from those directly associated with changes in the method of leadership election), have also been readily apparent throughout this study. Three are worthy of note. First, attitudes towards the universal ballot itself changed dramatically over time, irrespective of party or province. Second, in the initial years covered by our study, leadership candidates were drawn disproportionately from the ranks of lawyers or those with extensive political experience (or both); these attributes have been much less evident in the more recent contests. Third, as both candidates and voters, women became far more prevalent in the later years of our study.

These temporal changes should come as no surprise. Since our study commenced in 1971, liberal egalitarian values have grown ever more prominent in Canadian political discourse – a change reflected in, and accelerated by, the entrenchment of the Charter of Rights and Freedoms. This concern for individual rights and equality of opportunity has taken many forms over the past three decades, including a heightened enthusiasm for participatory democracy, populism, and liberal feminism. Inevitably, such ideas influenced party activists and candidates alike, and the aforementioned changes in Maritime leadership contests over time can be directly linked to this evolution in the cultural backdrop.

In 1976, Stephen Clarkson opined that further research on Canadian leadership conventions might not be "of any interest."[7] Yet even after completing this study, we are aware that much still needs to be learned about the phenomenon, both in the Maritime provinces and elsewhere in Canada. How will new forms of information technology influence the campaigns of leadership candidates and the choices of leadership electors? How will leadership selection be altered should Canadians continue to manifest "a serious public thirst ... for maintaining and extending the spaces of democratic politics?"[8] What happens if the provincial state further extends its regulatory reach into contests that used to be regarded as the private, internal affairs of political parties? Will the pressing social need to engage young people in the political process affect either the composition of leadership electorates or the profiles of victorious candidates? Thirty years on, Stephen Clarkson's doubts about the efficacy of future research in the field still seem ill-founded. Much important work remains to be done.

Our analysis of twenty-five leadership elections also permitted us to look at questions regarding the support for fringe candidates and the impact of the endorsements made by defeated candidates that could not be examined within the context of a single election. We found that supporters of fringe candidates were less likely to be motivated by the traditional triggers of policy and patronage, made up their minds later, and were more likely to be affected by speeches. Unfortunately, for fringe candidates, these sorts of voters are generally in short supply. With respect to candidate endorsements, we found that voters moved disproportionately in the intended direction, but this movement reflected individual preferences as much as it did candidate cues.

Interweaving our four key variables has permitted us to construct a complex tapestry of Maritime leadership conventions. Such a project, however, inevitably draws one's eye to matters of difference, as the interplay of province, of party, of time, and of method of election generates seemingly singular outcomes. Two concluding observations, however, should serve to mitigate this tendency. First, much of the variation introduced by three of our four key variables (party, time, and method of election) has hardly been unique to the Maritime provinces. Elsewhere in the country, women are also playing a more prominent role in leadership contests, political experience is less essential for leadership aspirants, Liberal and Conservative activists have ideologically distinctive profiles, and so on. Dissimilarities rooted in the political cultures and social structures of individual provinces are, of course, another matter. We might conclude, therefore, that, while the differences between the leadership politics of Nova Scotia, New Brunswick, and Prince Edward Island are at least comparable to those that exist between any other three Canadian provinces (say, British Columbia, Ontario, and Quebec), the leadership processes and outcomes of all six would have much in common.

Second, while the interplay of our four key variables has sensitized us to differences in leadership politics in the Maritimes, a few phenomena have transcended this force. We saw, for example, that, irrespective of province, party, time, and method of election, Maritime leadership electors have been politically engaged, that they have been, in all instances, active partisans rather than detached tourists. Religion continues to be associated with candidate choice in the region, albeit perhaps not as strongly as in the past. In any event, the religious patterns displayed generally reflected a version of "bonding" social capital[9] and rarely intruded when such electoral cues were not primed by the presence of candidates from both Catholic and Protestant traditions. Even more omnipresent has been the neighbourhood effect. Given prior research on this topic, we anticipated the existence of a link between a voter's home turf and his or her candidate preference. Early in the book, our expectations on this subject were completely confirmed. In subsequent chapters, however, the ubiquity of this phenomenon became more fully apparent. The neighbourhood effect was shown to have existed for both serious and fringe candidates, for example, and to have been central to the factionalism in the Nova Scotia CCF-NDP. As long as future Maritime leadership electors are animated by this pervasive localism, they will continue to make "conventional choices."

# Appendix:
# Leadership Election Profiles
# for Nova Scotia, New Brunswick,
# and Prince Edward Island

## Nova Scotia

### Progressive Conservatives: 1971, 1991, and 1995

*6 March 1971*

When Nova Scotia Tories gathered in Halifax in early 1971 to elect a new leader, few Nova Scotians paid much heed. Two days previously, Prime Minister Trudeau had shocked the nation with a secret wedding. Moreover, Gerald Regan's Liberals had just ended fourteen years of Conservative provincial rule and were still in their honeymoon phase with the electorate. Surveying the prospect of an extended stay in opposition, the party's "three acknowledged front-runners" (Annapolis Valley MP Pat Nowlan, former minister of finance T.J. McKeough, and former party president Finlay MacDonald) had all declined to enter the contest.[1] As a result, the Conservatives were left with three leadership candidates in their thirties: former fisheries minister John Buchanan, former education minister Gerald Doucet, and Dartmouth mayor Rollie Thornhill. Buchanan subsequently provided a peculiar rationale for his decision to run: "I'd never run for the leadership before and I was curious as to what it would be like."[2] Dissatisfaction with the field led many to speculate, even on the eve of the voting, that a more prominent Tory was poised to accept a leadership draft. In the words of one commentator, "rumours flew as fast as bottle tops in the hospitality suites" and at the sold-out four-dollar-per-plate convention dinner.[3] Such speculation proved to be baseless: no last-minute candidate came forward.

The initial part of the campaign was distinguished by John Buchanan's extravagant rhetorical attacks on the fledgling Regan administration. At one point, Buchanan claimed that the new premier's "arrogance in attempting to put the spotlight on himself personally for his own political purposes has never been rivalled in the political history of this province."[4] Doucet and Thornhill were not reluctant to criticize the Liberal government but were less prone to such hyperbolic flourishes. Doucet, for example, justified his entry into the race on the straightforward grounds that the Regan administration was doing "a bum job."[5] Aside from the predictable attacks on the Liberal government, the three candidates also stressed the importance of party renewal and of attracting young people into politics (an unsurprising emphasis given that upwards of 30 percent of the convention delegates were under thirty years old). In fact, one analyst suggested that the "lack of basic disagreement" between candidates ensured that the campaign would be akin, in the vernacular of the day, to "a giant party love-in."[6] Nevertheless, the discerning delegate would have been able to detect some policy differences between Doucet and the other two candidates. Early in the campaign, Doucet had signalled his receptivity to new approaches. "A party can only live by growing," claimed Doucet. "Intolerance of new ideas brings its death, not that new ideas are always good, but I prefer the errors of enthusiasm to the indifference of wisdom."[7] True to his word, Doucet was far more open-minded than was either Buchanan or Thornhill about the potential benefits of Maritime Union, of legalizing marijuana, and of government auto insurance.[8]

Nevertheless, few delegates would have disagreed that the campaign "had been painted various shades of dull,"[9] especially with the candidates all arriving for the policy bear-pit session wearing similar grey suits. Buchanan and Doucet were adjudged by the media to be the front-runners; the latter had the support of a majority of the provincial Tory caucus who had declared a preference, while the former was the favourite among federal Conservative MPs. When Thornhill failed to gain much ground in the convention preliminaries, his first ballot elimination was assured. Thus, in the party's

"Alas, that I may choose only one when all three are so lovely."

ROBERT CHAMBERS / *CHRONICLE-HERALD,* 5 MARCH 1971, 6

first contested convention since Robert Stanfield's one-ballot victory in 1948, John Buchanan picked up almost three-quarters of Thornhill's supporters and overcame Doucet's slender first ballot lead.

|  | 1st ballot | 2nd ballot |
|---|---|---|
| Buchanan | 242 | 391 |
| Doucet | 282 | 341 |
| Thornhill | 212 | |

### 9 February 1991

"Life was so much easier twenty years ago." These words from a Kenny Rogers tune floated around the Halifax Metro Centre as Tory delegates celebrated two decades of John Buchanan's stewardship of the party. And perhaps it was easier at the start rather than at the end of Buchanan's political career to employ deficit financing and party patronage. Certainly, the four men who aspired to succeed Buchanan (and interim leader Roger Bacon) were under some pressure to refashion the traditional model of governance in Nova Scotia. Five months earlier, beset by scandals and plummeting towards single-digit support in the polls, Buchanan had abandoned Province House for a sinecure in the Canadian Senate. Somewhat surprisingly, for a party in such obvious need of renewal, only one candidate emerged from outside the Tory caucus. Despite being the oldest candidate at fifty-seven, the former president of the Technical University of Nova Scotia, Clair Callaghan, was the closest thing to a "fresh face" in the leadership race. In Callaghan's only previous political foray, he had been narrowly defeated by NDP leader Alexa McDonough in the 1988 provincial election. Without money, without a network of supporters, and without a distinctive policy profile, the highlight of Callaghan's candidacy was destined to be his mid-campaign wedding.

The leadership contest was thus effectively left to three cabinet veterans, each with a particular set of strengths and weaknesses: fifty-four-year-old Rollie Thornhill, forty-four-year-old Tom McInnis, and forty-three-year-old Donald Cameron. The latter had the backing of many federal heavyweights and thirteen of the sixteen Tory MLAs who had expressed an allegiance,[10] but a stranger "establishment" candidate would be difficult to uncover. A dairy farmer and five-term MLA, Cameron had long been regarded as a quixotic figure for his virulent hostility to party patronage. His refusal to fire Liberal highway workers in Pictou East when the Tories returned to power in 1978 was to earn him plaudits from *Globe and Mail* columnists,[11] but it outraged local Tory place-hunters and befuddled his boss. An eight-year exile to the backbenches only stiffened Cameron's Puritan resolve, and when the soft moral underbelly of Buchananism became exposed in the late 1980s, the former tilter at windmills suddenly found himself at one with the sentiments of many Nova Scotians. Nor did Cameron's convictions on this matter waver during the course of the campaign. Repeatedly, he stressed that anyone who supported him in the hope of receiving a patronage plan was "in for a rude shock."[12] To emphasize the point, Cameron insisted that avowed Liberals were eligible to provide some of his campaign services,[13] and, despite having the largest war-chest, he refused to dole out any free drinks at his hospitality suites.[14]

Cameron's other campaign shibboleth was fiscal probity. Repelled by the profligacy of previous administrations, Cameron insisted that "we must start living within our means"[15] and that "there is no question that we have to make the government smaller and to consolidate services."[16] To demonstrate his commitment to these principles, Cameron pointedly refused, at the campaign's outset, to authorize a $3 million bailout of a Lockeport fish plant. Even at the costs of hundreds of jobs, Cameron averred: "It is unwise to use tax dollars to find short-term answers."[17]

Moreover, Cameron also had to overcome the perception that he was extraordinarily thin-skinned. Hence, Liberal MLA John MacEachern asserted that Cameron had "the shortest fuse of anybody I've met in my political life, and when he's fused off he's out of control."[18] Cameron's response to an unflattering report on the CBC's *Fifth Estate* was certainly consistent with this contention. According to Cameron, the report was nothing more than a "smear" campaign, a "hatchet job" undertaken by "sleaze buckets."[19]

Tom McInnis' candidacy shared many attributes with that of Donald Cameron. Hence, McInnis' willingness as attorney general to accept all eighty-two recommendations from the Marshall inquiry on reform of the provincial justice system had also earned him a reputation as something of a "white knight." As well, McInnis shared Cameron's enthusiasm for downsizing the provincial state. He promised a balanced budget within two years[20] and was a forceful advocate of privatizing Crown assets (including liquor stores).[21]

But McInnis' candidacy was dogged by a distinctive set of problems. Despite being a veteran of five ministerial portfolios, only one member of caucus (Ken Streatch) was in his camp. Apparently, some of his colleagues regarded his "Mr. Clean act" after the Marshall report "as shameless and unseemly positioning for a leadership bid."[22] Regarded as something of a dandy for his "spit-polished cowboy boots and stylish hair,"[23] McInnis was dogged by the allegation that he was neither a deep thinker nor a hard worker.[24]

As for Thornhill, his candidacy was of an entirely different order. Unlike the other two serious candidates, Thornhill was both "charming and shrewd."[25] As well, only Thornhill was pro-choice on abortion,[26] only Thornhill was opposed to the privatization of SYSCO,[27] and only Thornhill did not worship at the altar of fiscal rectitude. Just "blatant" patronage needed to be eliminated, according to Thornhill, and no immediate action needed to be taken to reduce the provincial deficit.[28]

Thornhill was bedevilled, however, by a personal financial scandal. In the mid-1970s, he had invested heavily in a Newfoundland hotel (with the eerily appropriate name of "The Albatross"). When that venture failed, Thornhill was left with $140,000 in personal debts. When the Conservatives were victorious in the 1978 provincial election, Thornhill was named to the cabinet as minister of development, and a number of banks agreed in November 1979 to write off three-quarters of his debt. Even before that time, there is evidence that at least one bank manager "felt it was good to be nice to Mr. Thornhill, as it would possibly help his position within the community as a banker to obtain business for the Royal Bank."[29] Not surprisingly, the opposition parties objected to Thornhill's preferential treatment and claimed that "a form of influence-peddling had taken place."[30] Over the next decade, there were a number of Byzantine developments in the case. The initial RCMP recommendation that a charge be laid against Thornhill was squelched by Attorney General Harry How and his deputy, Gordon Coles, but the matter resurfaced periodically until the January 1990 release of a royal commission report, which noted that Thornhill, among others, had benefited from the existence of a two-tiered system of justice in Nova Scotia.[31] With the RCMP re-examining the file, Thornhill's leadership ambitions depended on "how much carving this old carcass can stand."[32] Surprisingly, Thornhill concluded that he could shrug off the rumours of impending police action[33] and announced his intention to spend up to

BRUCE MACKINNON / *CHRONICLE-HERALD,* 12 FEBRUARY 1991, A6

Reprinted with permission from The Halifax Herald Limited

$150,000 on his leadership bid before noting wryly: "I don't plan to borrow any from the banks."[34] The innuendos about influence-peddling were to dog Thornhill's campaign and were not put to rest by the belated release of a letter from John Buchanan, who claimed to have been fully apprised of Thornhill's bank settlement.

The actual campaign was generally regarded as a lacklustre affair,[35] and the only dramatic moment of the three all-candidates debates came in Truro, when the moderator interrupted the proceedings to announce that war had broken out in the Persian Gulf.[36] As anticipated, the three front-runners were remarkably close after the first ballot. Clair Callaghan mysteriously declined to be the king-maker, and the second ballot was so tight that a full recount was required. Notwithstanding Thornhill's earlier slip that he planned to meet any police charges with "conviction,"[37] McInnis was ultimately dropped from the third ballot. The final showdown between Thornhill and Cameron offered Tory delegates a stark choice between maintaining and repudiating Buchananism. With the understandable reluctance that came from thirteen uninterrupted years in power, they opted for the latter.

|  | 1st ballot | 2nd ballot | 3rd ballot |
|---|---|---|---|
| Donald Cameron | 754 | 801 | 1,201 |
| Rollie Thornhill | 736 | 775 | 1,058 |
| Tom McInnis | 680 | 762 | |
| Clair Callaghan | 178 | | |

### 28 October 1995

"Three white guys you don't know – none from the O.J. Simpson jury – want to be premier of Nova Scotia."[38] Such was the dismissive tone that characterized much of the media coverage of the 1995 Tory leadership race. Although the Conservatives had ruled the province from 1978 to 1993 (principally under John Buchanan), they sank precipitously in public esteem over their final years.[39] Elected as leader (and premier) in 1991 after the interim stewardship of Roger Bacon, Donald Cameron had been unable to reverse the decline, and the Conservatives were hammered by an angry electorate in 1993. Cameron's subsequent departure for a patronage appointment in New England (a move that struck most observers as inconsistent with Cameron's frequent attacks on place-hunting) only deepened public disenchantment with the Tories. The 1995 leadership convention, then, was seen by many Conservatives as an opportunity for party renewal. One change was the abandonment of the traditional delegated convention in favour of an all-member vote system. True, the Conservatives did not use MT&T's vaunted computer voting system. The technical glitches that had bedevilled the Nova Scotia Liberals in 1992 had apparently been solved, and subsequent trials in British Columbia and Saskatchewan had worked well. Yet, for a party with $100,000 debt (and another $400,000 effectively off-loaded to the provincial constituency associations), the estimated $130,000 price tag for the MT&T system was "just too expensive."[40] Instead, the Conservatives opted for a lower-tech system (banks of telephone operators would manually record votes after callers provided PINs) at one-third of the cost.

Three candidates entered the race: fifty-six-year-old freshman Pictou MLA John Hamm, forty-four-year-old Windsor lawyer Jim White, and forty-eight-year-old Halifax architect Michael MacDonald. Hamm was the first to enter the race and was instantly tagged as both the front-runner and the establishment candidate. Four of the five Tory MLAs who declared their support were in Hamm's camp, as were most of the senior Conservatives in the extra-parliamentary wing.[41] Yet Hamm's candidacy was not without problems. For one, even without the laryngitis he contracted during the campaign, his oratorical skills were rather limited. While one editorialist characterized Michael MacDonald as an "engaging speaker" and Jim White as a "forceful orator," John Hamm was depicted as "speak[ing] haltingly."[42] Indeed, in his first months in the legislature, Hamm spoke not at all: immobilized by a neck collar after back surgery, he could only sit and listen to the debates of others.[43] Moreover, Hamm was somewhat tainted by his close association with Donald Cameron. The ex-premier had recruited Hamm to run in the 1993 election, and the links between the two were obvious. Both shared a Pictou County heritage, both embraced a type of Puritan ethic, and both even employed the same operatives to run their leadership bids. As one observer noted, there was "a bull's-eye painted on Tory frontrunner John Hamm's forehead, and it [had] Don Cameron's face on it."[44]

Unfortunately for Jim White and Michael MacDonald, their candidacies were also not without blemishes. Most notably, neither had a seat in the legislature. For an impoverished organization, this inevitably raised "the bake sale factor" since the Conservative party, rather than the taxpayers of Nova Scotia, would be on the hook for the leader's salary.[45] Jim White attempted to defuse this issue by suggesting that his extensive business contacts would permit him to raise the additional funds necessary to cover his salary, but interim leader Terry Donahoe expressed public doubts about this plan. "I would be concerned," noted Donahoe, that "there isn't a lot of new cash out there to be raised."[46] Moreover, neither White nor MacDonald was able to carve out an ideologically distinctive profile. Like Hamm, they embraced the usual assortment of conservative goals: a smaller government and a reduced debt but no indiscriminate cutting of programs, a social welfare regime that helped the needy but was not a life-long entitlement, an economic development program that was administered in a more business-friendly fashion, and so on. As MacDonald acknowledged at one leadership forum, "I think you'll find that the three of us aren't all that different on policy."[47] MacDonald could be distinguished, however, by the incendiary quality of his attacks on the party brass. "They are scared witless in John Hamm's corner," alleged MacDonald, "wondering what's going to happen to them if I win ... The blue suits are terrified!"[48] As for White, he centred his campaign around the need for policy renewal based on traditional conservative principles. Described by one observer as "painfully shy," White was not a particularly effective campaigner, and the only party notable in his camp was MLA Brooke Taylor.

At the convention, it became apparent that the Tories had failed to revitalize the party. True, they were able to celebrate a surprising by-election victory for the Conservative candidate in Cape Breton West. Otherwise, there was little good news to be found. Of the seven thousand party members, less than half bothered to pay the fifteen-dollar registration fee to vote by phone (or the forty-dollar stipend to attend the convention). Despite the move to a universal ballot, in other words, the number of votes cast was comparable to the total from the delegated convention four years previously. And party members in the northwestern section of the province, with access only to the CBC English-language feed from New Brunswick, were unable to follow the proceedings on television. Worse yet, the Tories had the misfortune to schedule their convention only two days prior to the second Quebec referendum on separation. With the fate of the country seemingly up in the air, even diehard Conservatives were understandably disengaged from the relatively picayune task of selecting a new leader.[49] "The

Reprinted with permission from The Halifax Herald Limited

BRUCE MACKINNON / *CHRONICLE-HERALD*, 27 OCTOBER 1995, D1

campaign was a yawn," as one summary put it, "and the convention a dis-traction."[50] Perhaps the only suspense was whether Hamm would go over the top on the first ballot and thus avoid a potential gang-up by the two "outsider" candidates. In fact, he did so with ninety-nine votes to spare and, in the process, delighted party organizers who had only booked the convention ballroom until 5:00 PM and had thus run the risk of having any second-ballot activities bumped by an incoming wedding party.[51] Not every-one was pleased with the outcome. John Hamm "could benefit from a basic civics course," groused the *Chronicle Herald* in its post-convention editorial. "The man has some growing to do, if he really wants to make it to the pre-mier's office."[52] For a party striving to shed a reputation for pork-barrelling, it was at least symbolically unfortunate that the Nova Scotia Tories in the 1990s turned for leadership initially to Roger Bacon and subsequently to John Hamm.

| | |
|---|---|
| John Hamm | 1,594 |
| Jim White | 1,107 |
| Michael MacDonald | 284 |

## Liberals: 1980, 1986, 1992, and 2002

### 8 June 1980

After fifteen years as leader of the provincial Liberals (eight as premier), Gerald Regan successfully jumped into federal politics in the February 1980 election. Given that Nova Scotians in the previous century had never de-feated a government after only a single term in office, and given that John Buchanan's Tories were only two years into their initial mandate, Regan's successor seemed destined for a lengthy sojourn as leader of the opposition. Nevertheless, four candidates entered the contest: fifty-three-year-old Fraser Mooney (a pharmacist and MLA for Yarmouth), forty-one-year-old Sandy Cameron (a farmer and MLA for Guysborough), thirty-five-year-old Vince MacLean (a history teacher and MLA for Cape Breton South), and thirty-six-year-old Ken MacInnis (a marine lawyer and failed federal candidate). Only MacInnis lacked extensive experience in political office, as the other three candidates had all served as cabinet ministers. MacInnis claimed, how-ever, that his status as a neophyte would facilitate party renewal. In his words, it was a "distinct advantage" not to have been a member of the Regan administration.[53]

On most policy issues, the candidates spoke as one. Certainly, they all genuflected before the totem of grassroots democracy. Hence, Mooney called for party policy to emerge "from the poll and constituency level";[54] MacLean told delegates the Liberals "must have a leader accountable to you, the pol-itical wing of the party";[55] and Cameron promised to constitutionalize an open party with such reforms as a leader's policy advisory committee, travelling caucus meetings, and the like.[56] Finally, Ken MacInnis was also anxious to don the mantle of populist tribune. "There is a feeling among Liberals outside Halifax," observed MacInnis, "that the party is being run by a narrow group of advisors in Halifax." The Liberals must regain the "common touch," concluded MacInnis, and become a "party of the people."[57]

Control of offshore oil was the only issue to provide a spark in an otherwise lacklustre campaign. In the weeks preceding the convention, Premier Buchanan had introduced a series of bills predicated on the assumption that offshore resources were exclusively within provincial jurisdiction. The official Liberal position (and that of Cameron, MacLean, and Mooney) was that Buchanan was being unnecessarily confrontational, that Nova Scotia would be better off negotiating favourable terms with the Trudeau government than goading Ottawa into a winner-take-all court case. As Sandy Cameron was Liberal energy critic, his views on this subject received extensive media attention.[58] Curiously, Ken MacInnis was one of the harshest critics of the Conservative position, even though, like Buchanan, and unlike his three competitors for the leadership, MacInnis believed that Nova Scotia should exercise all control over, and receive all revenues from, the offshore. Where he differed from the premier, as MacInnis repeatedly reminded delegates, was that he held a degree in marine law and was thus able to "take an intelligent position."[59] Perhaps, but this was the same candidate who foresaw an immediate offshore El Dorado of such proportions that it would bestow on the Buchanan administration "an awesome patronage capability." The Liberals must win the next election, warned MacInnis, before burgeoning offshore revenues "provide the Tories with the potential of crushing all opposition ... We have no desire to return to the dark days of the 1960s."[60]

At the convention, each candidate played to his or her perceived strengths. Hence, Vince MacLean suggested that there was "no place in opposition for a statesman" and that the new leader "must be prepared to take a tough and aggressive approach."[61] In contrast, the oldest candidate, Fraser Mooney, stressed the need for "maturity, ingenuity, and experience." From his perspective, the new leader had to "appreciate the party's history" and be "prepared to continue the tradition."[62] Nevertheless, it was Sandy Cameron who led after the first ballot. The MacLean camp, which was reportedly "stunned" by Cameron's vote total, received a boost when the eliminated Ken MacInnis pledged his support on the inexplicable grounds that the two candidates had "similar positions on the major issues."[63] Even so, MacLean narrowed the gap by only a single vote after the second ballot. With Fraser Mooney releasing his delegates to vote as they wished, Cameron's triumph on the third ballot was secured. In typically understated terms, Cameron told the cheering throngs: "I suppose this must be a greatest day of my life."[64]

|               | 1st ballot | 2nd ballot | 3rd ballot |
|---------------|------------|------------|------------|
| Sandy Cameron | 340        | 412        | 558        |
| Vince MacLean | 244        | 317        | 356        |
| Fraser Mooney | 192        | 187        |            |
| Ken MacInnis  | 138        |            |            |

### 22 February 1986

In the early part of 1986, the Nova Scotia Liberal party was adjudged to be "dangerously close to the borders of political ignominy."[65] In three successive elections (two with Sandy Cameron as leader), they had been hammered by John Buchanan's Conservatives. In the most recent debacle, Cameron had been personally defeated in his Guysborough riding, the party had slipped to third place (behind both the Tories and the NDP) in the metropolitan Halifax area, and only a corporal's guard of six dispirited MLAs had been returned to Province House. That the Liberal leadership race that emerged out of this political context was disputatious and mean-spirited cannot have been a surprise.

Two candidates contested the leadership: Vince MacLean and Jim Cowan. MacLean had a wealth of political experience. The former history teacher had spent twelve years in the legislature, had been a cabinet minister in the last Regan administration, had come close to winning the 1980 leadership convention, and had served as interim leader for eleven months after Cameron's resignation. Cowan, by contrast, had never sought elective office (although, win or lose, he had pledged to run for the party's nomination in Halifax Citadel). Cowan had, however, been the Liberal party president until resigning in order to seek the leadership. Both candidates attempted to put the best spin on their respective political background. Cowan's convention speech pointedly insisted that the Liberals "must not become the party of old ideas and yesterday's men."[66] The Liberals needed a new look, echoed Cowan confidante Guy Brown, not "leftover faces" from the days of Gerald Regan.[67] MacLean's speech to the convention, on the other hand, emphasized the virtues of "experience." "Nova Scotians won't buy a car without looking under the hood," he claimed. "And this party cannot afford a leader who has not been out of the showroom."[68] While automobile buyers might cavil at the notion that a used car was preferable to a new model, the gist of MacLean's message was apparent. Ironically, Cowan might claim to have the fresher face, but, at forty-three, he was a year older than MacLean.

The two candidates could not be distinguished on policy grounds. Early in the campaign, MacLean had released detailed position papers on both policy reform and party renewal. Neither contained anything particularly novel, but MacLean believed that standing for something positive might help dispel his image as a confrontational street fighter. Moreover, he claimed to have a responsibility to show delegates where "Vince MacLean wants to take the party and how he wants to rebuild it."[69] By contrast, Jim Cowan felt no such obligation. In his view, party policy should be developed in concert with the rank-and-file members rather than being "dictated" by the leader.[70] In any case, both candidates gave similar answers at the convention's bear-pit sessions: government waste needed to be eliminated, more jobs needed to be created, the government's offshore oil company needed to be sold, and so on. Only in the area of party strategy did the two candidates disagree. While Cowan wanted to counter what he perceived to be the growing appeal of the NDP, MacLean urged delegates to remember that Buchanan's Tories were the real enemy. The Liberal party, according to MacLean, should concentrate on "the big game, not rabbit tracks."[71]

What did develop was a campaign marked by extravagance, misrepresentation, and questionable practices. No limit was placed on expenditures. At the convention alone, both candidates were estimated to have spent over $200,000 on such democratic essentials as huge black light signs, red quartz watches for all, and, of course, free alcohol in the ubiquitous hospitality suites.[72] Seeking a bandwagon effect, both candidates released a variety of in-house "polls" that purported to demonstrate how well they were doing.

At his final pre-convention rally in Cape Breton, MacLean was able to draw all the Island's federal and provincial riding association presidents as well as all ten of the defeated provincial candidates from the preceding election. "Of the 374 Cape Breton delegates," crowed MacLean, "none has declared his or her support for Mr. Cowan."[73] The riposte from the Cowan camp was that MacLean would, as in 1980, fall victim to the "Flora syndrome," that delegates would enter the voting booths wearing Vince buttons but would cast their ballots for Cowan.

At many of the delegate selection meetings, slate politics were the order of the day. Moreover, the absence of a residency requirement permitted candidates to bring in outside supporters to be chosen as delegates; thus, many of those elected from the riding of Halifax Eastern Shore were workers from MacLean's office. A Cowan appeal was disallowed by the convention's credentials committee. As MacLean blandly observed, "we just adhere to the rules."[74] Other disputes arose over the propriety of funnelling campaign contributions through constituency offices in order to issue tax receipts and over Cowan's assumption of the past-president position (and automatic delegate status) after resigning as party president in order to contest the leadership. Cowan's action had the effect of bumping his immediate predecessor, Wilf Moore, from his post as past president. An incensed Moore claimed: "I wouldn't support [Cowan] for dogcatcher."[75] At the convention, even the legality of MacLean's nomination was challenged. Convention rules required a candidate to indicate his or her consent to be nominated, but MP David Dingwall omitted this detail in his nomination speech for MacLean. The Cowan camp thus urged the party to avoid the "embarrassment" of ending the convention with a leader who had not been legally elected.[76]

Ultimately, this manoeuvring was of no account. MacLean's success in the trenches at the delegate selection stage had secured his victory more than a month prior to the convention. In retrospect, noted one prominent Liberal, Cowan would have been better off had he used his position as party president to reform the leadership process to his advantage.[77]

| | |
|---|---|
| Vince MacLean | 1,082 |
| Jim Cowan | 721 |

### *20 June 1992*

In the 1988 provincial election, the Nova Scotia Liberal Party came within four thousand strategically placed votes of upsetting John Buchanan's Conservatives.[78] Shortly thereafter, the Tory government began to collapse under the weight of its mismanagement of the people's affairs, and Liberal leader Vince MacLean seemed destined for the premier's office. Yet revelations that MacLean's salary was being secretly augmented by monies from the notorious Liberal trust funds (many of which were illegally gathered through "toll-gating" in the 1970s) raised doubts about the leader's ethics, and his inept handling of the subsequent controversy confirmed concerns about his judgement. At the 29 February 1992 annual meeting of the Nova Scotia Liberals, Vince MacLean received only 51.4 percent support in a leadership review vote. Four days later, he resigned.

Despite the party's high standing in the polls, no one from the twenty-one-member Liberal caucus chose to enter the leadership race. First into the contest was lawyer George Hawkins, whose dogged insistence on airing the trust fund issue had earned him the sobriquet "Halifax's south-end Jeremiah."[79] Given Hawkins' age ("I am 67 years old and that's damn old. I'm old, let's be straight out."),[80] his poor organization,[81] and the coolness with which whistle-blowers are customarily regarded, it is not surprising that Hawkins' campaign failed to gather any momentum.

Two other outsiders (forty-four-year-old unemployed Digby electrician John Drish and forty-eight-year-old Bedford marine lawyer Ken MacInnis) also entered the fray. A former conscientious objector to the Vietnam War, Drish had emigrated from the United States in the mid-1970s. Without significant resources and with a penchant for offbeat causes (land ferries, a Nova Scotia university of global learning), Drish's candidacy was doomed from the outset. As for MacInnis, he had finished last in the 1980 Liberal leadership race, and his stolid insistence on the virtues of economic self-sufficiency and rural revival ensured that his vote total in 1992 would not be appreciably different. The three minor candidates had no backing from among the twenty-one members of the provincial caucus. Admittedly, MacInnis had dismissed the Liberal MLAs as "baggage," while Hawkins had denounced them as "mobsters, thugs, and thieves."[82] Whether such comments were the cause or the consequence of the lack of caucus support is unclear.

From the outset, John Savage and Donald Downe were the race's acknowledged front-runners. Of the seventeen MLAs who expressed a preference, eleven, including most of the MacLean loyalists, were with Savage; the other six, including most of the MacLean dissidents, were with Downe. Yet, even with Savage claiming to be "a good friend" of the ousted leader,[83] this was much more than a revisitation, by proxy, of the February review vote. In both their backgrounds and their ideologies, Savage and Downe provided a stark contrast to delegates. For one thing, Savage was almost twenty years older than his rival, a fact that Downe highlighted by leading attendees at an all-candidates debate in a rendition of "Happy Birthday" on the occasion of Savage's sixtieth birthday. As well, Savage was a Roman Catholic, Downe a Baptist deacon. Furthermore, Savage was a profoundly urban individual: he had been mayor of Dartmouth for the previous seven years and was the past president of the Union of Nova Scotia Municipalities. Downe, by contrast, was a prosperous poultry farmer with previous executive experience in the Nova Scotia Federation of Agriculture, the Canadian Federation of Agriculture, and the Maritime Farm Council.

Perhaps not surprisingly, the two favourites offered different policy prescriptions to the voters. On the one hand, there was John Savage, who opposed the privatization of Nova Scotia Power Corporation (unless there were stringent guarantees with respect to purchase of Devco coal), repeatedly stressed his hostility to user fees for medical care, urged greater student aid, and trumpeted his belief in "social policies."[84] Nor should such positions have come as a surprise. As mayor of Dartmouth, he had walked for Africa, hosted victims of apartheid, heightened awareness of Third World poverty, and so on. While Savage acknowledged the importance of getting the provincial debt under control, he offered no quick or easy solutions to the problem. According to Savage, "making society better" was the main reason for his involvement in politics.[85] When he announced his candidacy, Savage stressed that he had an understanding of business but that he had "always been ... regarded as left of the centre."[86]

A clear contrast was offered by the candidacy of Don Downe. Downe indicated a sympathy (at least early in the campaign) for the privatization of the Nova Scotia Power Corporation (NSPC), supported restructuring the educational system as a cost-saving measure, upbraided the Conservative government for new hospital construction, and stressed the importance of deficit reduction.[87] Repeatedly, Downe emphasized that the "government cannot and should not be expected to do it all,"[88] that Nova Scotians are "taxed to death,"[89] and that "we must foster through initiatives an attitude less reliant on government and more reliant on the individual."[90] This was clearly not to be a contest between Tweedledum and Tweedledee.

Perhaps to deflect attention from the recent squabbles over Vince MacLean and the tainted trust funds, the party opted to elect the new leader through an automated tele-vote of all party members. "We're rather enthusiastic about it," noted party president John Young, "because we think that it's going to allow for the first time, all Liberals to join in – not just the establishment, not just the executive, not just key personnel, but everybody."[91] Accordingly, there were no delegate selection meetings; instead, the party organized ten all-candidate meetings throughout the province. The Westray mine disaster of 9 May did cause the postponement of several meetings, but, in the end, they all took place. The rules for voting were quite simple. All persons who, by 15 April, were members of the party were entitled to register to vote by telephone. Those who wished to vote from home paid a fee of twenty-five dollars, and those who wished to attend and also vote by phone from the Metro Centre in Halifax were charged forty-five dollars.

There were just under seventeen thousand members eligible to participate, but by the first deadline, 15 May, only six thousand had paid their fees; thus, the deadline was extended to 5 June, the opening night of the convention. "Our guiding principle has been to ensure the broadest possible participation," noted party president John Young, "so we're prepared to make the bureaucratic adjustments."[92] Even then, only 7,451 (or 45 percent of eligible party members) had registered to vote on 6 June.

Perhaps seduced by MT&T's apparent technological wizardry, the Liberals bragged about being on the cutting edge ("Historically, ballots were counted by hand. Now it can be done in 10 minutes")[93] and failed to provide any backup. "If it blows up on the launch pad," commented John Young, "it blows up on the launch pad."[94] In fact, the system did not get off the ground. There was a breakdown in the computer software and no backup system was in place on 6 June. After seven hours of futile attempts to fix the problem, the party cancelled the vote. To make matters worse, a cellular telephone conversation between a panicky MT&T employee in Halifax and the Montreal computer centre concerning the running vote total was picked up on a scanner and broadcast by the CBC. Although these numbers were subsequently claimed to be merely a record of the attempts to vote rather than actual votes (and some people were rejected by the computer as many as eighty times before giving up in frustration), they seemed to confirm the expectations of most pundits that Dartmouth mayor John Savage (at 44 percent) and Bridgewater farmer Donald Downe (at 39 percent) were well ahead of the other three candidates. Ken MacInnis, apparently far back at 14 percent, threatened legal action on the grounds that the unauthorized release of those irrelevant totals had irreparably damaged his candidacy.

BRUCE MACKINNON / CHRONICLE-HERALD, 9 JUNE 1992, B1

Reprinted with permission from The Halifax Herald Limited

On 7 June it was not clear who was more embarrassed by the previous day's fiasco – MT&T or the Nova Scotia Liberal party. Conservative premier Donald Cameron confessed to having had a "few laughs" when the phone system crashed, while New Democratic leader Alexa McDonough gloated: "Sometime in the political arena we're accused of taking politics too seriously. Well, I want to tell you I didn't take it very seriously on Saturday."[95] With the leadership contest in a state of limbo, the party, somewhat surprisingly, decided to give tele-democracy a second chance. Convinced by several test runs that they could prevent another malfunction, MT&T agree to pay the Liberals $100,000 in compensation, waive any fees associated with the vote, establish a backup manual system, and post a $350,000 performance bond.[96] On 20 June the system worked perfectly not once but twice. With Savage and Downe far ahead after the first ballot, the stage was set for a showdown between the left and right wings of the Liberal party. Ultimately, John Savage was narrowly elected on the second ballot and, within a year, became premier of Nova Scotia.[97]

|  | 1st ballot | 2nd ballot |
|---|---|---|
| John Savage | 3,312 | 3,688 |
| Donald Downe | 2,832 | 3,311 |
| Ken MacInnis | 755 | |
| John Drish | 60 | |
| George Hawkins | 39 | |

## 13 April 2002

Choosing Russell MacLellan as party leader in 1997 to replace the surprisingly unpopular John Savage[98] did little to revive Liberal fortunes. Under MacLellan's stewardship, the party could only form a minority government after the 1998 election, and one year later it was reduced to just eleven of the fifty-two seats in the provincial legislature (centred principally in the Liberals' Cape Breton redoubt). When MacLellan took his leave in 2000, Clare MLA Wayne Gaudet was made interim leader, while the party made desultory plans for a leadership convention.

After some false starts, the Liberals settled on an April 2002 date and, as in 1997, four candidates came forward. Yet, unlike 1997 (when two MPs and two MLAs had squared off), in 2002 none of the candidates had ever held elected office. Indeed, only Dennis James, a forty-year-old Truro lawyer, had particularly deep Liberal roots, having been, at various times, president of the Young Liberals, vice-president of the provincial party, defeated federal candidate, and chief of staff under John Savage. James was burdened, however, by a distinct shortage of charisma. One commentator suggested that he was too solemn on the campaign trail ("I'm talking never-smiles-at-the-crowd, dry-as-dust solemn") and concluded that his performance might be improved with the judicious use of a defibrillator.[99] As well, James had been one of the architects behind the Liberals' lacklustre 1999 campaign. "Do you think Angus L. Macdonald would have run an election like the last one in Nova Scotia?" one of his rivals pointedly asked.[100]

Even so, James' extensive network of Liberal connections might have propelled him to the leadership if the franchise had been restricted to the six thousand Nova Scotians who were paid-up members of the Liberal party at the commencement of 2002. Alas, that total ballooned to twenty-one thousand during a frantic sign-up period. With the James camp responsible for only 1,200 (or less than 10 percent) of the new members, and with Cape Bretoners suddenly constituting 40 percent of the party's membership, James realized his leadership bid was futile and quit the race. As an emotional James put it, his camp had "come to Jesus meeting, and he spoke to us and said it was time to move on."[101]

James' departure left three party neophytes to contest the leadership: forty-year-old Danny Graham, who had been raised in Sydney but was now a Halifax lawyer; forty-one-year-old Francis MacKenzie, another former Caper with experience as both a bureaucrat and a businessman; and fifty-eight-year-old Bruce Graham, a broadcaster and novelist residing in rural Hants County. The latter was entirely without a party network (although he did have the mercurial MLA Brian "Crusher" Boudreau in his corner) and, in fact, had only taken out his Liberal membership in December 2001. Not surprisingly, given his background as a wordsmith, Bruce Graham proved to be an adept public speaker. Commenting on the fact that stores were closed on Sunday, while casinos were open, Graham wryly noted that Nova Scotia was "one of the few places where you can lose your shirt, but you can't buy one."[102] At times, Graham was too blunt in his pronouncements. With respect to offshore gas, he complained that, by setting conditions on the resource's exploitation, the Nova Scotia government was acting like "a tinpot dictatorship."[103] And on the issue of patronage, Graham unwisely eschewed the doublespeak favoured by other candidates. Rather than refer in code to the unfairness of discriminating against fellow Liberals, Graham brazenly stated: "I think patronage will always be a part of politics. It's not a bad thing. It has its place in politics just like everything else."[104] While Graham's tirades against a cloistered establishment in Halifax resonated effectively with many rural Liberals, few agreed with Graham's analysis that the party was in "desperate shape"[105] and that, without major reform, "we don't have a hope in hell."[106] Relegated to this role of Cassandra, Graham had little hope of becoming, after Ralph Klein, the second reporter from CFCN in Calgary to be elected premier.

At the outset of the race, Francis MacKenzie's prospects seemed similarly bleak. MacKenzie had briefly worked as the head of the investment and trade division of the provincial Department of Economic Development before moving into the private sector. As such, his public profile had been largely restricted to his role in the ill-fated decision to grant $200,000 to MacTimber four months before the company folded. Those who dismissed him as a "dark horse," however, were reminded by MacKenzie that, at the racetrack, favourites win less than 40 percent of the time,[107] and it soon became apparent that MacKenzie's backers were prepared to wager significant dollars on his success. MacKenzie's name recognition was quickly enhanced with glossy promotional material and large ads in local media outlets. Moreover, on at least one occasion during the all-candidates tour of the province, MacKenzie eschewed the overland route and chartered a plane for his entourage. Having such deep pockets obviously facilitated his recruitment drive, but MacKenzie's campaign was soon ensnared by allegations of vote-buying. A volunteer at a Glace Bay food bank complained to the media that a MacKenzie operative, John Marr, had offered to waive his membership fees and pay him twenty dollars after he had cast his ballot.[108] For his part, MacKenzie denied any wrongdoing ("Show me what's been violated here")[109] since the alleged miscreant had no official campaign position. Liberal headquarters was initially disinclined to investigate the incident. As President Ed Kinley observed, "We don't have a KGB in the party."[110] Nevertheless, a party probe headed by Robert Samson was established after Bruce Graham lodged an official complaint over the matter. When Marr declined to reveal who had asked him to sign up new members, however, the matter was deemed to be closed. "There has been no breach of the rules," blustered Samson.[111]

On the campaign trail, MacKenzie was distinguished by his "bombastic and unpredictable" speeches[112] and his "one-trick pony" approach to policy.[113] MacKenzie's penchant for unscripted remarks occasionally got him in trouble. At one point, for example, he joked that ineffective MLAs should be machine-gunned![114] Yet, irrespective of the topic, MacKenzie's remarks invariably returned to the matter of economic growth. In his view, any and all social ills (from cleaning up the Sydney Tar Ponds to maintaining shelters for battered women) could only be ameliorated with a robust economy, and the provincial government had an overarching imperative to achieve same. "We need a salesman," MacKenzie intoned, "not a statesman."[115]

The final candidate, Danny Graham, at least came from a prominent Liberal family. His father, Al, was an influential Liberal senator and his brother, Jack, was a prominent party operative. During much of Wayne Gaudet's tenure as interim party leader, Danny Graham had been in Ottawa on secondment to the federal Department of Justice. Yet his supporters on the provincial executive were able to delay the date of the leadership convention until Graham's twenty-four-month contract was completed and he had decided, after some initial misgivings, to contest the leadership. Danny

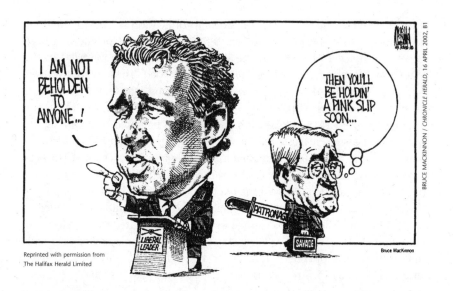

Reprinted with permission from
The Halifax Herald Limited

Graham had a plurality of the Liberal MLAs in his camp as well as the backing of the executive of the provincial youth wing. Unlike both Bruce Graham and Francis MacKenzie, Danny Graham did not believe that the Nova Scotia Liberal party was in a particularly dire circumstance. "We don't need deconstruction," he claimed. "We need remodelling."[116] On policy matters, Danny Graham was cautious, emphasizing the need for both fiscal responsibility and social justice. He did not prove to be a particularly polished public performer. In one commentary, he was adjudged to be "wooden and stilted";[117] in a second, it was suggested that he would benefit from the services of a voice coach.[118] Fortunately, Graham had a first-rate organization, and his operatives were responsible for almost half of the approximately sixteen thousand new memberships sold during the campaign.[119]

Around eleven thousand Liberals cast preferential ballots in advance polls one week prior to the convention. With fewer than one thousand registering to vote at the convention, the turnout level would be under 60 percent (even though the party had, after some criticism, dropped the twenty-dollar fee for casting an advance ballot). While media reports speculated about a "coronation" for Danny Graham, both his opponents remained upbeat. Bruce Graham assured listeners that he was in second place and well positioned to win on a second ballot, while Francis MacKenzie crowed that his campaign had enjoyed "a monster day" at the advance poll.[120]

In fact, Danny Graham won easily on the first ballot. "That's a lot of miles and a lot of community-hall speaking for 800 votes," observed a downcast Bruce Graham, while an equally disappointed Francis MacKenzie blamed his defeat on unfair media coverage of the vote-buying scandal ("Once the toothpaste is out of the tube, you can't put it back in").[121] Danny Graham may have been the "establishment candidate,"[122] but he sounded discordantly defiant in his victory address. "I'm not beholden to anyone," he trumpeted. "There were some people who didn't stay with our campaign because ... we couldn't come to terms."[123] With the party well ahead in the polls and an election expected within a year, fresh Liberal blood-letting over patronage was on many people's minds.

| Danny Graham | 6,846 |
| Francis MacKenzie | 3,855 |
| Bruce Graham | 835 |

## New Democrats: 1980, 1996, 2000, and 2002

### *16 November 1980*

The Nova Scotia New Democratic Party was in some disarray when it gathered in the late fall of 1980. In his twelve-year stewardship, Jeremy Akerman had taken the party from 6 percent of the provincial vote and zero seats to 15 percent of the vote and a caucus of four. Nevertheless, Akerman claimed to be "uncomfortable" with many party positions and "out of sympathy" with several senior members of the party's extra-parliamentary wing. Sensing a chance both to neutralize a respected adversary and to undercut the NDP's electoral prospects, Conservative premier John Buchanan offered Akerman a plum posting in the civil service. In May 1980, Akerman resigned his leadership and was later appointed as Nova Scotia's executive director of intergovernmental affairs. At the same time, a second member of the provincial caucus, Cape Breton Nova MLA Paul MacEwan, was also making headlines. MacEwan had made a number of intemperate remarks over the years, but in the spring of 1980 he took his inflammatory rhetoric to a new level with his charge that the NDP organization was riddled with Trotskyites. In response, the NDP general council convened a hearing and expelled MacEwan from the party, although, somewhat perversely, MacEwan continued to sit as a member of the NDP's legislative caucus.

The turbulent events of 1980 had exposed a deep fissure in the Nova Scotia NDP, a divide deepened by overlapping cleavages of region, class, and ideology. On the one side were working-class Cape Bretoners devoted to the interests of organized labour; on the other side were middle-class Haligonians who wished the party to be more clearly animated by socialist principles. That the former faction had enjoyed extensive electoral success, while the latter had yet to elect even a single MLA, did nothing to ease the intraparty tensions.

It was inevitable that the race to succeed Jeremy Akerman would put these divisions on public display. Three candidates came forward: Cape Breton

Centre MLA Len Arsenault, Cape Breton North MLA Buddy MacEachern, and Alexa McDonough, a twice defeated federal candidate in Halifax. At one extreme was Buddy MacEachern. A six-year MLA and a former trade unionist, MacEachern observed that a "working-class party" required a working-class leader[124] and insisted that the NDP needed to forge a much closer relationship with organized labour rather than becoming "a party of the elite."[125] Moreover, MacEachern was a staunch defender of Paul MacEwan and had, in fact, cast the decisive vote that had permitted the embattled MLA to remain in the party caucus after his expulsion by the general council. In MacEachern's eyes, the NDP needed to forget its "holier-than-thou attitude"[126] and remember that the electorate, rather than the party, was supreme. Only in places such as China and the Soviet Union, he warned, was party supremacy taken to be axiomatic.[127]

The candidacy of Alexa McDonough was animated by a quite different set of impulses. On the MacEwan affair, McDonough was outraged that the maverick MLA had managed to remain in the NDP caucus. In one particularly revealing remark, she noted: "We will hold our members to our principles and policies, and unlike the other major parties we are prepared to commit near electoral suicide to enforce those policies."[128] McDonough made few concessions to pragmatic politics, although she did emphasize that the NDP would be advantaged by having a leader from the mainland.[129] Her convention speech attacked the traditional parties and "reactionary governments" who refused to use the state to redistribute society's resources "based on human needs, human rights, and human dignity." New Democrats, she emphasized, "believe in using public policy to enforce co-operative obligations" and, if elected, would achieve "a level of economic and social democracy not previously attained in this country."[130]

Attempting to find a middle ground between McDonough and MacEachern was Len Arsenault. Like the latter, Arsenault emphasized that the party leader must have a seat in the legislature and that the NDP must never be allowed to relapse to the status of a "glorified debating society."[131] But, like McDonough and unlike MacEachern, Arsenault had accepted the party position on Paul MacEwan and had voted to expel the renegade MLA from caucus. Although Arsenault acknowledged that he had been in third place at the campaign's outset, media reports suggested that he had been "steadily gaining support in all areas."[132] In fact, one observer suggested that Arsenault's momentum was such that he might be entering the convention "as a slight favourite in a close race."[133]

As it turned out, such prognostications were badly wrong. Buddy MacEachern's leadership prospects dimmed perceptibly when a resolution requiring that a member of the NDP caucus also be a member in good standing of the party easily surpassed the two-thirds support level necessary for

constitutional amendments.[134] But Len Arsenault's backing proved to be equally thin, as Alexa McDonough became the first woman to be elected leader of a Canadian political party. McDonough's triumphant victory, gushed one commentator, "skyrockets her profile to a level that makes her a dominant figure in the province's political arena."[135]

| Alexa McDonough | 237 |
| --- | --- |
| Len Arsenault | 42 |
| Buddy MacEachern | 41 |

### 30 March 1996

The 1995 federal New Democratic Party leadership convention begat the Nova Scotia New Democratic leadership contest of 1996. Although the party's constitution mandates an automatic leadership vote at every annual meeting, Alexa McDonough's surprising departure for the national stage precipitated the first de facto leadership contest in sixteen years. Under McDonough's stewardship, much had changed for the Nova Scotia New Democratic Party; most notably, the party's organizational, electoral, and ideological centre of gravity had shifted dramatically from Cape Breton to the mainland (and, in particular, to Halifax). But there was at least one obvious constant: the New Democratic Party seemed no closer to winning power at the end of McDonough's watch than it had been at the start.

One possible candidate to succeed McDonough was long-time Sackville MLA and interim leader John Holm, but health considerations may have closed off this option. In fact, like former party stalwarts Jeremy Akerman and Bob Levy, Holm was almost induced during the campaign to accept a patronage posting (in this instance, to the provincial Utility and Review Board), before being repelled by the transparently partisan motivation that underlay the offer of appointment.[136] It was thus left to the only other incumbent MLA, thirty-seven-year-old union organizer Robert Chisholm, to seek the leadership. Chisholm had first entered the legislature in 1991 in a by-election necessitated by John Buchanan's appointment to the Canadian Senate. In the 1993 provincial election, Chisholm had retained his Halifax Atlantic seat by only twelve votes, but after five years of experience at Province House, the telegenic MLA was widely touted to be the logical successor to McDonough.

With Chisholm the only entrant by the 19 January 1996 deadline, it appeared that he would be acclaimed as party leader. On 9 February, however, Yvonne Atwell, a fifty-three-year-old social activist and manager of the African Canadian Employment Clinic announced her intention to seek the New Democratic Party leadership. Given that the party constitution permits nominations from the floor, the New Democratic Party brass decided to accept Atwell's "late" candidacy. Atwell had an unconventional leadership resumé: she acknowledged that she had not been an active party member and that in 1993, in her only prior electoral venture, she had finished last in a field of four as the New Democratic Party candidate for Preston. Atwell later justified her candidacy thusly: "Part of the reason I did that – knowing that I would not win – was to 'up' my profile, so that people around the province would begin to know who I was, and to get some experience speaking, talking to people and just getting to know the communities."[137]

Walter Young once characterized Canadian social democracy as both political party and social movement.[138] The candidacies of Chisholm and Atwell epitomized this duality. Chisholm's emphasis on electoral and legislative politics contrasted clearly with Atwell's commitment to citizen engagement. As Atwell noted when she declared her candidacy: "If the NDP is to be a vital and relevant force, it must abandon the traditional approach to politics that treats people as mere spectators on the stage of history, to be trotted out as voting cattle on election day."[139]

The leadership campaign was a relatively lifeless affair. The two candidates did not engage in a series of debates, and media coverage of the race (owing both to the New Democratic Party's minor status in provincial politics and to the near certainty of a Chisholm victory) was essentially non-existent. At the convention, the different emphases of the two leadership aspirants were readily apparent. Only the Chisholm camp deployed the customary array of banners and placards in support of its candidate. "As a party that takes a strong stand on environmental issues," groused Atwell, "it makes no sense to waste scarce resources by putting papers on sticks and making a lot of noise."[140] Atwell did, however, enliven the proceedings with an unconventional speech. A good portion of her remarks was directed at the voters of Preston; incumbent Liberal MLA Wayne Adams was vilified amid predictions that the New Democratic Party candidate (presumably Yvonne Atwell) would take the riding in the next election.[141] Even more unusually, Atwell regaled the assembled delegates with a recitation of what she perceived to be the failures of at least some of them:

> Prior to joining the race for the leadership, I had always felt that the NDP was justified in assuming the moral high ground because of what the party stands for. Looking back, I have to say that I no longer hold a romanticized view of the party. In the short space of two months, I've experienced racism, sexism, and, yes, classist attitudes from members of this party. These views have no place in our society and certainly no place in a party committed to social democratic principles.[142]

Atwell's speech was well received but not all delegates were persuaded by her message: "That's crap," seethed one labour delegate.[143]

The actual vote totals were not surprising, as Chisholm won easily on the first ballot with just under 80 percent of the total. In his acceptance speech, Chisholm pledged to take the convention's message of party unity to the "Dr. Johns" (Savage and Hamm), and in a convoluted railway metaphor he alluded to the impending arrival of a locomotive: "We're going to lead that freight train right through Nova Scotia. Nova Scotians are going to jump on by the carload and we're going to run her right into the legislature and shove those suckers off the track."[144] Whatever transportation experts might make of this imagery, the editorial team of the *Chronicle-Herald* were clearly unimpressed with Chisholm's determination to send "huge numbers" of New Democrats to Province House. Under the heading "A Leader Too Much in a Hurry," the editors urged Chisholm to take "a more even-handed glimpse" of New Democratic Party fortunes. "Mr. Chisholm faces a tough road already," they concluded, "without dreaming in technicolor about driving the Liberals from office and taking control."[145]

| Robert Chisholm | 201 |
| Yvonne Atwell | 59 |

**15 July 2000**

Reprinted with permission from The Halifax Herald Limited

The NDP 2000 convention is described in Chapter 2.


**2 June 2002**

In 2000, Nova Scotia's New Democrats elected Helen MacDonald as party leader even though, alone among the three principal contenders, she lacked a seat in the provincial legislature. This collective gamble backfired when, in March 2001, MacDonald was defeated in a Cape Breton North by-election. With a caucus revolt imminent, MacDonald resigned in April 2001 rather than meet with six of the insurgents (theatrically dubbed "the Cyanide Six"). MLA Darrell Dexter was confirmed as MacDonald's replacement two months later, while plans were made for a full-fledged leadership convention in 2002.

Only two candidates entered the race; not surprisingly, both were sitting MLAs. John MacDonell (Hants East), a forty-five-year-old former teacher and part-time farmer, was first to declare, followed shortly thereafter by the incumbent Dexter (Cole Harbour–Dartmouth), a forty-three-year-old lawyer. Both men had been first elected in 1998 and both had retained their seats in 1999. Dexter was immediately dubbed the "establishment candidate" and was assumed by most observers to be well in the lead. He had performed ably in his first year as leader and had an impressive phalanx of supporters, including six of the nine other members of the provincial caucus, such prominent trade union leaders as Rick Clarke and Larry Wark, and party godmother Alexa McDonough. MacDonell did have the support of three of his caucus cohorts; however, whereas Dexter was able to list the names of 375 adherents from around Nova Scotia on his website, the comparable list on MacDonell's home page numbered only thirty.[146]

As befitted his status as a relatively unknown underdog, MacDonell ran the more aggressive campaign. At the outset, he attacked Dexter for reneging on a commitment (allegedly made when he became interim leader) not to contest the convention. For his part, Dexter categorically denied making such a pledge, and his version of events was vehemently supported by then caucus chairman Bill Estabrooks. "I will swear on a stack of Bibles 10 feet thick," asserted Estabrooks, "that was not a condition."[147] With no member of caucus coming forward to substantiate his claim, MacDonell dropped the matter, but the undercurrent of nastiness was reinforced a few days later when details of Dexter's twenty-five-year-old conviction for impaired driving were faxed anonymously to local media outlets.[148]

On substantive matters, the two candidates differed little. The party organized seven leadership forums in different parts of Nova Scotia, but attendance at these gatherings was spotty, ranging from a high of one hundred in Halifax to lows of twenty-five and twenty in Stellarton and Yarmouth, respectively. Given that there was "virtually no disagreement on issues," generating enthusiasm for the race was difficult.[149] In fact, at the Truro forum, it was observed that Dexter and MacDonell each "nodded in polite agreement every time the other trotted out solutions to the province's economic and social woes."[150] Both candidates opposed tax cuts, favoured more spending on health care, endorsed a tuition freeze for universities (although MacDonell would have rolled back tuition an additional $1,500 before instituting a freeze), called for a new deal on the offshore, and so on. Both saved their strongest criticisms for John Hamm's Tory government, which, they claimed, was misguidedly attempting to balance the province's books with cuts to essential social programs.

Nevertheless, there were a variety of ways in which the two candidates could be distinguished. First, Dexter had far deeper roots in the party, having worked on provincial campaigns for almost a quarter-century. MacDonell, by contrast, was a relative newcomer, having only joined the NDP in 1993. Second, MacDonell seemed to possess the more attractive public persona. One media report characterized him as "very likeable,"[151] while another praised his "engaging animation"; Dexter, on the other hand, was depicted as a "solid, conscientious plodder."[152] Third, the continuing reverberations from the Helen MacDonald putsch affected the two candidates quite differently. Dexter had been largely aloof from the caucus plots against the former leader; after the shocking by-election loss, he had favoured giving MacDonald more time to deliberate on her leadership future.[153] MacDonell, in contrast, had been one of the notorious "Cyanide Six." For the seven hundred party members from Cape Breton, many still seething about the unseemly ouster of one of their own, 2 June promised to be pay-back time.

Finally, the two candidates differed over future electoral strategy. While the NDP had been able to win substantial numbers of seats both in metropolitan Halifax and in Cape Breton, its support elsewhere in the province had always been patchy at best. As one of the few New Democratic candidates successfully able to buck this trend, MacDonell saw his leadership as pivotal to a New Democratic breakthrough in the rural mainland. "We've got to expand that rural base," he declared at his first press conference: "We need the seats in rural Nova Scotia."[154] While Dexter might protest he had spent a good portion of his life in rural Queens County, it was clear that a Dexter victory would be more likely to reconfirm the party's bases in Halifax and Cape Breton.

For the first time, the Nova Scotia NDP employed a universal ballot to select its leader, and party membership jumped from 2,200 to 3,900.[155] MacDonell's organization in Hants East was particularly busy, selling three hundred new memberships in that constituency alone. Yet, the party managed to avoid any hint of the vote-buying scandals that were at that time plaguing the provincial Liberal leadership race.

Dexter was serenely confident entering the final weekend. "I'm going to a convention where I have a lot of friends," he intoned, "I'm going to let Sunday take care of itself."[156] With most of the ballots already cast and tabulated, an air of anticlimax lingered at the convention. Unusually for an all-member vote, the participation rate was well over 80 percent. Having already won a hockey pool and a party raffle for ninety dollars' worth of lobsters, Dexter completed his weekend with an easy first ballot triumph.

| | |
|---|---|
| Darrell Dexter | 2,006 |
| John MacDonell | 1,181 |

## New Brunswick

### Progressive Conservatives
The leadership contest of 1997 is described in Chapter 2.

### Liberals: 1982, 1985, 1998, and 2002

#### *27 February 1982*
The New Brunswick Liberals who gathered at the Aitken Centre in Fredericton in February 1982 were a fractious and ill-tempered bunch. The party had been out of office for twelve years after three successive defeats to the Conservatives under Richard Hatfield. With another provincial election widely predicted to occur sometime in 1982, anxious Liberals began to wonder whether incumbent leader Joseph Daigle had the ability to oust the Tories. A leadership review vote at the party's biennial convention in the spring of

1981 had solved nothing. The endorsement of Daigle's leadership had been lukewarm: only 69 percent had opted against a review (which means he had 2 percent more support than Joe Clark was to receive in his infamous leadership review vote later that same year). With Daigle apparently staying on, his fellow Liberal MLAs decided to force the issue. In November 1981, twenty-three of the other twenty-six members of the Liberal caucus voted that they had lost confidence in Daigle as party leader. This apparent putsch raised interesting constitutional questions for the New Brunswick Liberal party. What precisely were the lines of authority and accountability between leader, caucus, and convention? Daigle might have chosen to argue that, as he had been elected leader by the party rank-and-file, only they could force his removal. Such a posture might well have precipitated a debilitating internal squabble, however, and Daigle opted to resign instead. Ten weeks later, he was appointed to the Court of Queen's Bench of New Brunswick.

In the ensuing campaign, it was inevitable that the Daigle affair would be prominently featured. The four candidates (MLAs Doug Young, Ray Frenette, and Allan Maher, and lawyer Joe Day) had remarkably similar views on most public policy questions. All were in favour of removing tolls from the Saint John Harbour Bridge, all preferred to look for alternatives to spruce budworm spraying, all wanted to stop funding abortions on demand, all supported official bilingualism, all hoped to institute provincewide kindergarten, all believed that natural gas distribution rights should not be given to the New Brunswick Electric Power Commission, and so on.[157] The candidates could, however, be clearly differentiated on a constellation of matters relating to party leadership. Young and Frenette had been among the caucus rebels, and, indeed, Young was widely suspected to have been the ringleader. Ironically, Young had helped Daigle secure the leadership in 1978: when Young had been dropped after the second ballot, he had delivered his delegates to the Daigle camp. At a series of all-candidates meetings around the province, many Liberal activists pilloried Young and Frenette for their disloyalty to Daigle and for usurping the authority of the membership in matters of leadership. In response, Frenette claimed that he had not actually "short-circuit[ed] the supremacy of the party" since, after the nonconfidence vote, Daigle had options other than resignation. In any case, deadpanned Frenette, Daigle was to blame for not having "put his foot down" on the dissidents earlier.[158] As for Young, he suggested that loyalty to the leader was important but that so, too, was loyalty to tradition, to the party, and to oneself.[159] From Young's perspective, Daigle had failed to respect the party "tradition" that leaders must resign after even a single electoral defeat. Besides, noted Young, if the caucus rebels had erred in their judgment, why was there no evidence of a "draft Daigle" campaign among the Liberal rank-and-file?[160]

For Frenette and, especially, for Young, there was only one issue in the leadership campaign: "After 12 years in Opposition, who can win the next election? That's what it's all about."[161] Both men engaged in coded attacks on the lifestyle of Richard Hatfield. On more than one occasion, Frenette urged Liberals to help send the premier "into total retirement to pursue his hobby of collecting dolls."[162] As for Young, he frequently recounted that he had been unmarried at the time of his initial leadership bid in 1978 and had been told that people "were leery of bachelors because of Premier Hatfield's marital status." Since then, Young had gotten married and fathered one child, with a second on the way. "I really did listen to you," he told Liberal delegates, "and I am really working on it."[163]

In contrast, Allan Maher and Joe Day took a different approach to the leadership question. Maher had been one of only three caucus members to indicate their confidence in Joe Daigle. He believed not only that Daigle could win the next election but also that caucus should not usurp the authority of the party membership. Pointedly, Maher characterized himself as "the responsible candidate."[164] Day's position on the issue was even stronger. Although he emphasized that he was "not running an anti-caucus campaign,"[165] Day trumpeted the virtues of "trust, loyalty, and democracy." "If we don't have rule by the majority, we have tyranny," proclaimed Day. "If the majority wants something and a small group decides something else," then the New Brunswick Liberals were no different from a communist government.[166] In a clear dig at front-runner Doug Young, Day claimed that the Liberals must stand for the principles of "equality and justice"[167] and reject the view "that winning is everything and that we sacrifice anything to win."[168] Even the issue of the leadership review mechanism sharply divided the candidates. For Young, the procedure was "not of much value to the party"; for Day, by contrast, it constituted "an essential part of a democratic party."[169]

Entering the convention, Doug Young was clearly the front-runner. Twenty-one members of the Liberal caucus were in his camp, and he had been appointed interim leader after Daigle's resignation. When queried about the propriety of serving as interim leader while seeking the party leadership, Young made the rather fine distinction that he was the interim leader of the caucus of the Liberal party.[170] The other candidates, by contrast, struggled to put the best spin on their lack of caucus adherents. Hence, Frenette rather feebly assured delegates that the MLAs who were not backing him were "not against him,"[171] while Maher, equally feebly, proclaimed his absence of caucus support to be "useful because it means that at least I won't owe any of them anything when it's all over."[172]

Ultimately, the delegates had a clear choice between contrasting leadership styles. Joe Day was widely perceived to be a "Nice Guy of the Bob Higgins or Joe Daigle variety." Doug Young, on the other hand, was seen to

Provincial Archives of New Brunswick, Josh Beutel fonds, MC2806-914

be a "go-for-the-jugular Tough Guy."[173] In a single ballot, the New Brunswick Liberal rank-and-file signalled their clear preference for the latter.

| | |
|---|---|
| Doug Young | 1,324 |
| Joe Day | 811 |
| Ray Frenette | 308 |
| Allan Maher | 160 |

### 4 May 1985

When the New Brunswick Liberals convened in the spring of 1985, they
were in surprisingly good spirits, considering they had lost four successive
elections under four different leaders to Richard Hatfield's Progressive Conservatives. A series of well-publicized scandals had ensnared the Tory premier, and few Liberals doubted that the next provincial campaign would
catapult their party into power. Even so, only two candidates contested the
Liberal leadership: thirty-seven-year-old Chatham lawyer Frank McKenna
(first elected in 1982) and forty-eight-year-old Moncton businessman Ray
Frenette, who had served as an MLA for eleven years and as interim party
leader for eighteen months after Doug Young's resignation (and had, in
fact, been initially backed by McKenna for the leadership). For Frenette,

this was his second run for the leadership; he had finished a distant third at the 1982 convention.

The two candidates could obviously be distinguished on the basis of language and ethnicity. Although he had tried to learn French in the months prior to the convention, McKenna was essentially a unilingual Anglophone. Frenette, by contrast, was a fluently bilingual Acadian. This difference could not have been lost on delegates in a province where ethnic tensions have been an endemic feature of the political landscape[174] and where the government had just released a highly contentious document (the Poirier-Bastarache Report) calling for the decentralization of public services into two unilingual enclaves. Nevertheless, both candidates attempted to downplay the language issue. In fact, at the campaign's outset, Frenette had called on McKenna to establish a joint stance on the matter and thus minimize intraparty acrimony.[175] No such modus vivendi was actually reached, but both emphasized their happiness with the bilingual status quo (although in a construction that may have been coded to reassure nervous Anglophone delegates, McKenna generally noted: "I also respect the right of being unilingual").[176] At the symbolic level, Frenette's ethnicity seemed to work to his disadvantage. Although the last Liberal premier (Louis Robichaud) had been a francophone, one prominent columnist suggested that Frenette's Acadian background was an "albatross."[177] With a backlash building in English New Brunswick against the incremental expansion of French language rights, some Liberal delegates speculated openly about the public's perception that the party needed an Anglophone leader.[178]

With Frenette and McKenna indistinguishable on matters of substance (indeed, the former was to claim in his convention address that there was "really no difference" between the candidates over policy),[179] considerations of image rose to the forefront. In fact, even the physical stature of the two candidates provoked comment. At one point, the vertically challenged McKenna felt compelled to mention that Liberal icon Louis Robichaud had also been somewhat diminutive.[180] The image battle was principally fought, however, over the relative benefits of youth versus experience. On the one hand, McKenna repeatedly emphasized the need for party renewal. Future Liberal success would be dependent upon attracting new people with fresh ideas; McKenna urged Liberals to "face the challenge of blowing the cobwebs out of the halls in order to win the next election."[181] McKenna's campaign icon, a tricoloured rainbow, symbolized the candidate's commitment to "retrofit" the party; the broad band of Liberal red was augmented with stripes of New Democratic yellow and Tory blue.[182]

In contrast, Frenette stressed, in progressively more strident terms, the virtues of political experience. At the outset, Frenette was content to emphasize his own ostensible virtues. On one occasion, he noted the need for "experience and a proven track record";[183] at another meeting, he suggested his "best attributes" were "the political smarts" acquired over eleven years experience in the legislature.[184] In mid-campaign, Frenette began to patronize McKenna by suggesting that, while his opponent had the capacity "some day" to become provincial premier, New Brunswickers needed an experienced alternative to Richard Hatfield "now."[185] At the convention, the barbs from the Frenette camp became even more pointed. In moving Frenette's nomination, Joe Boyce informed delegates that he had attended too many leadership conventions where the party had been intoxicated by the "energy and vigour of youth." Alas, noted Boyce, Liberal delegates had, in the past, acted like drunken sailors, and "the morning after had been a very painful awakening."[186] Frenette's speech was even more forceful. The previous two Liberal conventions, noted Frenette, had elected young lawyers (Joe Daigle, Doug Young) with exactly three years of prior service as MLAs. In subsequent general elections, however, "the people of New Brunswick chose experience" and elected Richard Hatfield and the Tories. "Not one of those young and inexperienced lawyers was able to follow through and get the job done," argued Frenette. "How often do we as a party need to be given a message?"[187]

Yet, ironically, it was the neophyte, Frank McKenna, who ran an error-free campaign, while the veteran, Ray Frenette, seemed to blunder repeatedly. For example, Frenette was surprisingly slow to enter the race and did so only after musing publicly that the party would benefit from having "a new face" as leader.[188] Less than two weeks before the convention, Frenette overreacted to a CBC-commissioned poll showing McKenna with a seventeen-point lead among decided delegates. After denouncing the poll (and the pollster), Frenette threatened to withdraw from the contest if soundings within his organization generated similar numbers. Not surprisingly, many of Frenette's supporters reacted with "bewilderment and even anger" to this announcement.[189] Having damaged his credibility and discouraged his backers,[190] Frenette re-entered the fray armed with fresh polling data that purportedly confirmed the credibility of his candidacy – a perplexing manoeuvre, given Frenette's earlier insistence that his threat to quit the race had been designed as a "shocker" to prevent the race from being effectively decided by "private polls."[191] Finally, Frenette angered many Liberal delegates with his pointed attacks on McKenna's future "winnability" at the convention. Although he had previously claimed to prefer a contest that was "dull and united" rather than "spirited and divided"[192] (and, in fact, one observer compared the candidates to "old-time duellists" who deliberately shot wide of the mark),[193] Frenette's convention speech was bluntly critical of his opponent. A McKenna victory, Frenette claimed, would be giving the Tories another five years in office.[194] While the McKenna people booed and shook their fists, many Frenette delegates either sat on their hands or promptly donned McKenna badges. Art Doyle, a senior member of the Frenette camp, estimated that the speech, written under the direction of an operative imported from Toronto, cost Frenette at least two hundred votes. Concluded Doyle: "The speech was a disgrace and an embarrassment."[195]

McKenna had come to the convention with the declared support of 42 of the 58 constituency association presidents and with the backing of 6 of the 10 MLAs who had indicated a preference.[196] With the Frenette campaign misfiring badly, there seemed every prospect of a McKenna rout. Realizing that the contest was effectively over, the McKenna team became more magnanimous to its foe. Hence, although McKenna workers had claimed all of the preferred signage locations in the Moncton Coliseum for their candidate, they graciously ceded many of these to the Frenette people.[197] Indeed, some McKenna supporters were apparently prepared to help Frenette save some face by padding his floor demonstration.[198] McKenna's speech to the assembled delegates was an opaque paean to "the politics of optimism."[199] There were certainly no references to the crushing Liberal defeats in two by-elections held during Frenette's interim stewardship of the party. Nor were delegates reminded of Frenette's key role in the controversial caucus coup against former leader Joseph Daigle. Without taking the gloves off, McKenna cruised to an easy victory.

|  |  |
|---|---|
| Frank McKenna | 1,901 |
| Ray Frenette | 847 |

Provincial Archives of New Brunswick, Josh Beutel fonds, MC2806-1905

JOSH BEUTEL / TELEGRAPH-JOURNAL, 6 May 1985, 10

**2 May 1998**

On 13 October 1987, Frank McKenna led his Liberal party to the first of three successive majority triumphs. At the time, few paid much heed when the incoming premier mused that a decade on the job would be ample. Ten years to the day later, however, McKenna opted, at the relatively young age of forty-nine, to resign as premier. For most New Brunswickers, this was uncharted territory; not since the Second World War had a provincial government changed leaders in mid-term. Unanimously, the Liberal caucus decided that the interim leader and premier would be Ray Frenette (an embittered loser at the party's two previous leadership conventions but at this point, a respected elder statesman). A leadership convention was scheduled for the following May, and, bucking regional and national trends, the New Brunswick Liberals chose to eschew the all-member ballot in favour of a traditional delegated contest.

With the premiership as the immediate prize, a strong field was anticipated. First to declare was Economics Development Minister Camille Theriault, a forty-three-year-old businessman from Baie Sainte-Anne. A ten-year veteran of the legislature, Theriault's leadership ambitions were an open secret in the party; for several months prior to McKenna's retirement announcement, Theriault had been conducting a "stealth campaign"[200] – collecting money, securing endorsements, building an organization, and so on. At Theriault's "flawlessly produced" campaign kick-off, Theriault pledged to introduce a "third wave" of New Brunswick liberalism in which government would reinvest in the social welfare of its people.[201]

Many had anticipated that Minister of Finance Edmond Blanchard would enter the race. Blanchard had many political assets: he was near the party's ideological mid-point, he had a reputation for integrity, and, as a fluently bilingual Acadian with apparently widespread support among anglophone voters, he easily bridged New Brunswick's linguistic divide. Yet, after a well-attended rally designed to gauge the level of enthusiasm for his candidacy, Blanchard shocked backers by announcing that, for health concerns that were unspecified (and, some whispered, unspecifiable), he would not contest the leadership. According to one observer, Blanchard's impressive list of credentials did not happen to include a "burning desire" to be premier; thus, his campaign was "a mirage: all organization and no candidate."[202]

With Blanchard out, Bernard Richard, the forty-six-year-old minister of education and Shediac lawyer, was suddenly in. Richard's putative candidacy had floundered in the preceding months, but Blanchard's departure suddenly freed up many party operatives who were looking for an alternative to Camille Theriault. In his youth, Richard had been a candidate for the Parti Acadien (securing a paltry 273 votes in the 1974 provincial election).

Reborn as a Liberal, however, Richard had become an electoral juggernaut, winning his Shediac riding in 1991 and 1995 with 73 percent and 81 percent of the vote, respectively. Nevertheless, some Liberals wondered whether anglophone New Brunswickers could countenance a premier with a background as a strong Acadian nationalist. Richard acknowledged this to be a "fair" question,[203] but he insisted that, just as in the 1990s, his political activities in the 1970s had been animated by a straightforward commitment to "social justice and linguistic equality."[204]

The final candidate to enter the race was thirty-six-year-old Fredericton lawyer, Greg Byrne. Unlike both Theriault and Richard, Byrne had a relatively skimpy political résumé, having been elected as a freshman MLA in 1995 and promoted in 1997 to the junior cabinet post of minister of state for mines and energy. Derided at the outset as "the token anglophone candidate," Byrne had to struggle against the perception that he was only in the race to secure a more prestigious cabinet posting and to heighten his profile for a future leadership bid. Unlike the other two candidates, Byrne was not bilingual; nevertheless, under the tutelage of Frank McKenna's former language coach, the quality of Byrne's spoken French improved from "laboured"[205] to "respectable" over the course of the campaign.

In deciding upon their campaign platforms, the three candidates operated under similar constraints. First, they had all contributed to recent government decision making and, thus, could not legitimately distance themselves from the McKenna legislative record; they were, in any case, under orders from interim premier Frenette not to do so.[206] Second, they all recognized that Frank McKenna remained the most popular politician in the province and that the only certain method to elicit a positive audience response was to praise the former premier; only the most subtle moves to some form of "post-McKennism" were possible. Third, and despite the foregoing, there was an apparent consensus among Liberals that New Brunswickers deserved some sort of social dividend for the previous years of fiscal rectitude; thus Theriault, Richard, and Byrne spoke as one about the importance of injecting fresh monies into education, health care, and the like. The combined impact of these constraints was a "bland" campaign in which the three candidates "seemed to be reading from the same page book."[207] Greg Byrne might call upon Liberals to "balance our books with our hearts,"[208] but both Theriault and Richard were given to uttering similarly imprecise pieties. Nor was the master himself disturbed by these vague stirrings of a heightened social conscience. "Candidates to the Liberal party," intoned Frank McKenna, "tend to run on the left and govern in the centre, and that's a very smart thing to do."[209]

Only the issue of roads disturbed the placidity of a campaign that had otherwise "generated about as much excitement as a church quilting bee in Upper Keswick Ridge."[210] The McKenna government had constructed a toll highway between Fredericton and Moncton, and local residents were, not surprisingly, distressed by the prospect of repeated user fees. Special interest groups sprang up to protest the tolls, and the Liberal leadership campaign provided an ideal venue for them to publicize their concerns. Yet, since all three candidates, as members of the McKenna cabinet, had approved the toll highway, they could offer little more than expressions of sympathy and concern. Hoping to ratchet up the pressure on the Liberals, the president of Toll-Busters (and a former CoR candidate), Tom Taylor, threatened to enter the leadership race and to deliver his second ballot support to whichever candidate pledged to rip up the toll deal. With anti-toll sentiment highest in Camille Theriault's Moncton stronghold, it was apparent that the economic development minister had potentially the most to lose from a Taylor candidacy. Ultimately, Taylor backed down from his plan under "considerable duress" after allegedly receiving an anonymous and threatening phone call that he should only enter the race if his "business affairs were in order."[211]

Ultimately, this was a contest where organization mattered more than ideology. All three candidates had significant backing in the forty-seven-member Liberal caucus – 18 MLAs were in the Theriault camp, 9 backed Richard, 6 supported Byrne, and a further 11 were undeclared.[212] Only Theriault, however, had an organizational presence in all fifty-five Liberal riding associations. The Theriault machine's effective use of slate politics had given them a commanding delegate lead.

At the convention, opinion was divided on whether Theriault had enough support to win the contest on a single ballot. Both Byrne and Richard were convinced that a second vote would be required. For their part, the Theriault camp was supremely confident not only that they had a majority of the delegates onside but also that, even if a second ballot were required, Byrne and Richard would be unable to deliver their delegates to each other. Would Richard's Acadian supporters move en masse to a unilingual anglophone and thereby deny a fellow Acadian the premiership? Would Byrne's anglophone backers vote as a bloc for a former candidate for the Parti Acadien? Neither outcome seemed particularly plausible.

As it turned out, none of the second ballot strategies came into play. Despite giving a "phenomenal" address to the delegates ("described by many as a speech of a lifetime"), Bernard Richard came third with the rather unfortunate total of 666 votes. As the candidate's son, Matt, concluded after the totals were released: "Shit happens."[213] Despite a convention speech that "could best be described as earnest,"[214] Greg Byrne received 27 percent of the votes, a far greater total than could have reasonably been anticipated at the campaign's outset. But the day belonged to Camille Theriault, who, with 56 percent of the votes, was able to secure the prize that had eluded his father, Norbert, at a New Brunswick Liberal leadership convention twenty-seven years previously.

| Camille Theriault | 2,095 |
| Greg Byrne | 1,005 |
| Bernard Richard | 666 |

## 11 May 2002

After the brutal slate politics of their 1998 leadership contest, the New Brunswick Liberals belatedly abandoned the traditional delegated convention for 2002. In its stead would be the hybrid system successfully employed by the Ontario Liberals to elect leaders Lyn McLeod and Dalton McGuinty.[215] At delegate selection meetings in the fifty-five provincial constituencies, all New Brunswick Liberals would be eligible either to vote for their preferred leadership candidates or to indicate their uncertainty. Delegates would then be allotted to the various camps (including the undecided) on that basis. The New Brunswick Liberals were about to discover, however, that this selection method works best when there are more than two strong candidates.

From the outset, such a field seemed unlikely. Initially, the race was confined to two candidates: forty-eight-year-old farmer and businessman Jack MacDougall of Fredericton and fifty-year-old Grand Falls lawyer Paul Duffie. The two candidates had sharply different political profiles. MacDougall had no legislative experience, but as a former executive director and long-time backroom operative, he was well known in Liberal circles. His candidacy, however, was saddled with two obvious problems. First, he was essentially a unilingual Anglophone in a province that expects some fluency in both official languages from its leaders. MacDougall's linguistic shortcomings were brutally exposed in the French half of the televised all-candidates debate; according to one assessment, MacDougall's "faltering French was unintelligible."[216] Second, MacDougall had alienated many in the party when, in January 2000, he had publicly blamed Camille Theriault and his communications team for the electoral debacle of the previous year. Historically, those with ambitions to the throne have been wiser to avoid direct involvement in regicide.

By contrast, Paul Duffie, as a three-term MLA and former minister of education, had few obvious blots on his record. With most of the party brass onside, his candidacy represented an attempt to return to the glory years of Frank McKenna. At least some Liberals were concerned, however, that the party needed a new leader who could match the youthful appeal of Tory premier Bernard Lord. After a Christmas family gathering had voted 17-2 in favour of his candidacy (with his mother one of the negative votes), thirty-three-year-old Kent MLA Shawn Graham entered the race.[217] Graham had won his seat in a 1998 by-election, succeeding his father, Al, who had held the constituency for the previous thirty-one years. As one of only seven Liberals to survive the Tory rout the following year, Graham had become adept in political theatrics (including the orchestration of his own temporary banishment from the legislature). As a leadership candidate, however, Graham undertook an image makeover – shortening his hair, losing the blond highlights, wearing conservative suits – to reassure Liberal members that he had the requisite gravitas for the job.

Delegate selection began in February 2002, and the early weeks of the race were remarkably placid. Paul Duffie, for one, was pleased with the civilized tone of the contest. In past leadership races, he noted, candidates have often looked "like cry babies in the schoolyard. I can't accept that kind of approach. Our race is more mature."[218] Some commentators were clearly enthusiastic about Duffie's qualities as a "statesman":

> Looking voters straight in the eye and speaking in sincere, concerned tones, Mr. Duffie's flawless French and, later, perfect English added to his composed manner and made him stand head and shoulders above the others. During an insignificant squabble, for example, Mr. Duffie simply raised his hand, quieted them both, and took centre stage.[219]

Notwithstanding such gushing reports, at the close of the selection stage, the party announced that Graham had secured 48.9 percent of the constituency delegate total of 3,559. Duffie was at 35.6 percent, MacDougall at 8.4 percent, and a further 7.1 percent were officially undecided. Despite his impressive lead, a Graham victory was not assured. His camp not only had to find sufficient names to fill out their delegate allotment (and, at one point, they were 493 short of their quota)[220] but also had to deliver these slates to the Fredericton convention. Moreover, Jack MacDougall had already indicated that he would be supporting Duffie over Graham on the second ballot,[221] and, as the candidate of the party old guard, Duffie could have anticipated receiving the backing of the bulk of the six hundred ex officio delegates. With six weeks remaining in the race, however, Duffie shocked the party by withdrawing his candidacy and endorsing Graham. "I felt the party has basically spoken," observed Duffie, "They have identified in the early stages of this process that they like Shawn Graham."[222] That identification, continued Duffie, was going to make it almost impossible for his campaign to raise the $100,000 necessary to take the fight to the convention floor. Reaction to Duffie's announcement ranged from disappointment (as Liberal officials wondered how to salvage their suddenly "anticlimactic" convention)[223] to bewilderment ("Why a man would get out at 36 percent," commented MacDougall, "is just, after so long, is just amazing to me")[224] to glee (as "giddy" Tories salivated at the prospect of matching Bernard Lord against a Liberal leader whom they derisively dismissed as "Al's boy").[225] Ironically, Duffie did nothing to reassure those who doubted Graham's immediate readiness for the top Liberal job when, at their joint press conference, he referred to Graham as "this fine boy" and "patted him on the shoulder."[226]

With Duffie out of the race, Graham's position became unassailable. In fact, because Duffie had failed to fill 384 of his delegate allotment prior to his withdrawal, these positions were declared vacant by the party, and the number of constituency delegates was reduced to 3,175 (with Graham now at 54.9 percent, MacDougall at 9.4 percent, and the undecided ballooning to 35.7 percent of the total). Inevitably, some pressure was placed on MacDougall to withdraw in Graham's favour and save the party from lingering "over the flotsam of their torpedoed leadership campaign."[227] Yet, as an "organiser in the back corner who has always craved the limelight,"[228] it was never likely that MacDougall would voluntarily leave the race; instead, he stayed to promote the policy ideas on his innovative website (Liberalchange.com), including a pledge to reintroduce highway tolls, while providing New Brunswickers with a free pass for the station of their choice. MacDougall also chastised Graham for allegedly making $182 million worth of promises during the campaign,[229] and he took particular delight in lampooning Graham's initiative for voluntary after-school programs.[230]

Yet, with essentially no media coverage of the Liberal "race" in the five weeks preceding the convention, Shawn Graham had only to avoid some type of disaster in order to secure the leadership. "I'm being optimistic," MacDougall noted, "But I'm not naive."[231] At the convention, MacDougall's speech was adjudged to have been better than Graham's "carefully scripted, cautious address" (although, at one point, Graham inadvertently credited

THE EVOLUTION OF SHAWN GRAHAM...

MICHAEL DEADDER / MONCTON TIMES & TRANSCRIPT, 8 MAY 2002, D7

the Lord government for its work on building up provincial roads).[232] It mattered not. Even though as the self-styled "leper" of the New Brunswick Liberals, Jack MacDougall "fared far better than anyone expected,"[233] Shawn Graham cruised to victory with just under three-quarters of the ballots. At the outset of the race, the party had planned for over four thousand delegates to pack the Aitken Centre. In the end, fewer than half that total found a reason to attend the convention.

|                |       |
| -------------- | ----- |
| Shawn Graham   | 1,349 |
| Jack MacDougall | 461   |

## Prince Edward Island

### Progressive Conservatives: 1976, 1981, and 1988

#### *25 September 1976*

When the Island Tories met in the fall of 1976 to select a new leader, they had been out of office for a decade. During that period, Premier Alex Campbell's Liberal juggernaut had chewed up four Conservative leaders (two official, two interim), and his hold on provincial power seemed unshakeable. As a result, only two candidates came forward to contest the Tory leadership: sixty-two-year-old Angus MacLean, a war hero who had served as federal fisheries minister under Diefenbaker and who had been an MP for twenty-five uninterrupted years, and thirty-nine-year-old Jim Lee, former director of the provincial Tories, and one of only five Conservative MLAs after his by-election victory in Fifth Queens eighteen months previously.

The composition of the field may actually have been shaped by leadership politics at the national level. Egmont Tory MP David Macdonald had long been touted as a potential leader of the provincial party. The ascendancy of the Red Tory faction in Ottawa under new leader Joe Clark, however, led to MacDonald's elevation to the front benches in the House of Commons (and, not coincidentally, to MacLean's removal from same). With MacLean contemplating retirement in the summer of 1976, pressure began to build on him to contest the provincial leadership. "I had not considered running provincially, but now the idea had some appeal," noted MacLean in his memoirs. "On the plus side, I would be able to live at home; my concerns would be mainly my home province; and I would be associating chiefly with Islanders, people with friendly and familiar faces."[234]

Some ideological differences between Lee and MacLean became apparent during the campaign. Admittedly, at one pre-convention gathering, "neither candidate dealt with political issues" on the curious pretext that the meeting had been "designed to help PC delegates decide from a party point of view who will make the best leader."[235] Nevertheless, Lee was more prone to espouse neoconservative themes. He bemoaned, for example, the inefficiency of state planning, advocated increased protection for the rights of landowners, lamented the dangers of handouts and the welfare trap, and indicated that his preferred role for the state would be to provide "half a dozen super salesmen" for the agricultural industry.[236] By contrast, MacLean articulated a more traditional brand of conservatism. In particular, he lamented that the technocratic thrusts of Alex Campbell's Liberal administration had eroded many long-standing Island virtues:

> We've been going off on trends without looking far enough down the road as to what the end result is going to be. We tend to have been too prodigal in many directions and not sceptical enough of what has been touted as great improvements. We've fallen victim to a kind of hucksterism on a number of things ... I have a strong belief that Prince Edward Islanders have an innate sense of what is appropriate and what is right but over the past few years too many times when these fears or reservations were expressed by Islanders ... they got a snow job done on them by a lot of high-priced public relations men who were paid at tax payers' expense to leave the implication that they weren't with it, that they were old-fashioned, that they were behind the times.[237]

In matters of both style and substance, in fact, MacLean represented a throwback to traditional Island verities. MacLean chose to run a low-key campaign. His "demonstration" at the convention involved only a single piper, he bought no political advertisements, and his entire campaign budget was less than a thousand dollars. By contrast, Lee spent over five times that

amount, bought numerous ads, and distributed literature, buttons, and scarves at the convention. In fact, whereas MacLean received only two mentions in the province's major newspaper (the *Guardian*) in the twelve days leading up to the convention, Lee was able to generate newspaper coverage every day during that period.[238]

Lee's more vigorous campaign may have contributed to the relative closeness of the final result in a contest that had appeared from the outset to be something of a mismatch:

| | |
|---|---|
| Angus MacLean | 589 |
| Jim Lee | 437 |

### 7 November 1981

When Angus MacLean assumed the stewardship of the Island Tories in 1976, his stated intention was to remain as leader for only five years. The Conservatives won the 1979 provincial election, and, at mid-term, MacLean and his government remained popular with Island voters. Nevertheless, MacLean kept to his commitment. As he recalled in his memoirs: "In August 1981, I decided it was time to quit politics permanently. The five years that I had committed to the provincial party were up, and I resigned as party leader."[239] Few premiers can have taken their leave (or, at least, written about same) so matter-of-factly.

Four of MacLean's cabinet ministers entered the leadership race: forty-eight-year-old minister of education Fred Driscoll, forty-three-year-old minister of health and social services Jim Lee, thirty-three-year-old minister of energy Barry Clark, and thirty-three-year-old minister of community affairs

Pat Binns. The lengthy campaign that ensued was almost entirely devoid of controversy. All four candidates emphasized their fealty to the departing leader: "they like the way Angus MacLean does things and they perceive that Islanders agree."[240] Moreover, all four had worked amicably as cabinet colleagues since 1979. As a result, they had "nothing but respect for each other" and were, in fact, "about as friendly a group of candidates [as] you will find."[241] Finally, the four aspirants could not be distinguished by their stance on various issues; all agreed, for example, that Prince Edward Island's inordinately high energy costs were a major concern and all objected to the "bombshell dropped on the people of the Island" by Maritime Electric's application for a further rate increase.[242] Thus, Conservative delegates were left with but a single criterion upon which to make their selection: "naked leadership ability."[243]

Unfortunately, none of the candidates stood out on that measure. With the successful leadership renewal of the provincial Liberals one month previously, the Tory rank and file were casting about for someone with "the depth, the substance and background to out-manoeuvre and out-debate Joe Ghiz."[244] Yet, even if Driscoll was touted as the candidate with the "most on the ball," his "less than flamboyant style" was potentially a problem when matched against the "formidable" Joe Ghiz.[245] Jim Lee, by contrast, had long enjoyed heir apparent status after finishing a strong second to Angus MacLean in the 1976 contest. Lee was thought to be "the most well-rounded candidate,"[246] although his subservience to public opinion led some to regard Lee as "too political."[247] As well, Lee did not have a warm public persona; his marked reluctance to show either anger or surprise led one former colleague to conclude that Lee would have made "a good poker player."[248] Finally, Lee's campaign was saddled with an unofficial slogan of almost unspeakable lameness: "Shake Off the fleas, Vote for Lee."[249]

The two younger candidates had more obvious liabilities. Pat Binns had a relatively low public profile, although it was bravely advanced by supporters that Binns had "a certain kind of shyness that people find attractive."[250] His decision to contest the leadership "threw everyone for a loop," especially since he had not bothered to inform caucus members prior to the announcement.[251] As a native Westerner, Binns was tainted as a "come from away"; somewhat defensively, Binns pointed out that three previous provincial premiers had not been born and bred on the Island.[252] As for Clark, he had the unusual distinction of being the first ordained minister appointed to an Island cabinet. While Clark might eschew his ministerial collar and claim never to have been "pushy about religion,"[253] the visibility of his faith would inevitably be a liability in a province where elaborate elite accommodations have been essential to moderate religious tensions. In addition, opinions were voiced that the thirty-three-year-old Clark was "not politically

ROBERT TUCK / *EASTERN GRAPHIC*, 11 NOVEMBER 1981, 4

mature."[254] Clark's rejoinder ("I look 43 and feel that way a lot of the time")[255] could hardly have been reassuring to Tory delegates.

With each member of the field burdened with apparent liabilities, no obvious front-runner emerged in the run-up to the convention. "All four candidates are seen as solid and hard-working," concluded one observer, "and one difficulty in predicting who will win this race lies with the fact none of them are considered charismatic."[256] As it turned out, Lee had a solid, but not insurmountable, lead after the first ballot. Having delivered a "forceful speech" with "surprising flair," Clark was a clear second, with Driscoll "surprisingly" in third place.[257] Despite an apparent gentlemen's agreement prohibiting such deals, the fourth-place finisher, Binns, threw his support to Driscoll. On the second ballot, however, Driscoll's vote total actually declined, and he, too, was eliminated. Driscoll chose not to indicate any preference, although his campaign organizer visibly moved to the Clark camp. Such machinations proved unsuccessful, as Jim Lee, the only one of the four candidates without a postgraduate degree, became the master of the Island Conservatives on the final ballot.

|  | *1st ballot* | *2nd ballot* | *3rd ballot* |
|---|---|---|---|
| Jim Lee | 581 | 665 | 737 |
| Barry Clark | 348 | 463 | 577 |
| Fred Driscoll | 282 | 281 | |
| Pat Binns | 237 | | |

### 11 June 1988

From the outset, the 1988 leadership contest among Island Conservatives appeared to be a mismatch. An early entrant was Mel Gass, a forty-eight-year-old businessman and MP. Despite having won three successive federal contests in the riding of Malpeque, Gass apparently hankered for a job that promised to be more work for less money. With Gass in the race, many prominent Island Tories, including interim leader Leone Bagnall, opted out. Had Bagnall decided to enter the contest after two years experience as the first female Opposition leader in Canada, there might have been, in the words of provincial party president Eugene Rossiter, "a far different result."[258] As it stood, however, there appeared to be a distinct possibility that Gass would be acclaimed as party leader. Among the initial non-entrants had been thirty-three-year-old Summerside lawyer Andy Walker. Since entering the legislature following a 1986 by-election victory in 5th Prince, Walker's apparent leadership ambitions had frequently been the object of snide comments from the Liberal benches.[259] Nevertheless, on 3 May, Walker announced that he was not in the race owing to family commitments to his three young children. Eight days later, Walker reversed his decision and, somewhat perversely, again cited family reasons as his principal motivation:

> I have three small children whom I love very much. In two decades when they go looking for jobs, there is very little question that they will have to leave this province to work and raise their families. If present trends and attitudes in this province continue, my children will not have the opportunity to remain here.[260]

Despite Walker's insistence to the contrary, rumours began to circulate that his candidacy was that of a sacrificial lamb, that he had entered the race only to ensure that the Tories would receive some media attention in the weeks leading up to the vote. Even the candidates' unofficial slogans seemed to capture the tortoise-and-hare quality of the contest. Supporters of the underdog were urged to "Walk with Walker"; the alternative, needless to say, was to "Step on the Gas with Mel."[261]

The campaign itself was largely uneventful. The party instituted a $30,000 expenditure limit, but neither candidate came close to spending that amount.[262] Gass' campaign was predicated on his folksy appeal to ordinary Islanders. "I enjoy people," observed Gass. "I really don't consider myself a politician."[263] Walker, by contrast, emphasized that he was running "an idea campaign"; the combination of free trade and the fixed link offered Islanders an unprecedented opportunity for economic revitalization.[264] Alas, the discussion over such ideas was never joined as, running a front-runner's campaign, Gass declined Walker's repeated invitations to a leadership de-

WAYNE WRIGHT / JOURNAL-PIONEER, 13 JUNE 1988, 4

bate. On the eve of the convention, in fact, the *Guardian* editorialized that the campaign had "been about as quiet as the proverbial church mouse."[265]

Looming as a backdrop to the Conservative race was the imposing spectre of Liberal premier Joe Ghiz. Although only in office for two years, Ghiz had emerged on the national stage as a confident and articulate spokesman for Prince Edward Island's interests. While both candidates claimed Ghiz was out of touch with ordinary Islanders, they obviously had a healthy respect for his abilities. Hence, while Walker claimed to be "looking forward to going toe to toe with Joe," he also admitted that a better strategy for the Tories might be "to capitalize on the weaknesses of other cabinet ministers."[266] As for Gass, his convention speech confronted the issue of whether he had "enough pizzazz to be premier." After recounting his many alleged virtues (honesty, compassion, common sense, and the like), Gass was obliged to acknowledge: "We will leave the pizzazz to Joe."[267]

The convention was a low-key affair. Hoping to catch the attention of Islanders, the event had been scheduled for after the spring planting of crops but before the summer onslaught of tourists. Unfortunately for the Tories, the CBC cancelled its live coverage of the convention after the party balked at a proposed panel of commentators. The final result was surprisingly close. Although party president Eugene Rossiter characterized Gass' win as "a decisive victory,"[268] his final margin was a skimpy twenty-seven votes. The tortoise had almost caught the hare.

| ' Mel Gass | 599 |
| Andy Walker | 572 |

### Liberals: 1978, 1981, 1993, 1996, and 2003

#### *9 December 1978*

When Island Liberals gathered in December 1978 to select a new leader, they were also selecting a new premier. Beginning in 1966, Alex Campbell had led the Liberals to four successive majority governments. In the April 1978 election, however, the Liberal majority had been reduced to only two seats, and a chastened Premier Campbell announced his resignation in September (soon to be followed by an appointment to the provincial Supreme Court).

Many names were advanced as potential successors (including Senator Lorne Bonnell, who had lost to Campbell in 1965 in the Island Liberals' only previous leadership convention). Ultimately, only two men contested the leadership – Bennett Campbell and Gerard Mitchell – although a third, sixty-three-year-old pig farmer Anco Hamming, was ostensibly also in the race. Hamming was not a paid-up Liberal member and, in fact, had run as an independent in the spring election under the banner of "realism, responsibility, and righteousness."[269] Alas, at least the first of these qualities was absent from Hamming's leadership bid; his candidacy failed on the eve of the vote when, among the over 1,300 assembled Liberal delegates, a mover and a seconder could not be found.

Bennett Campbell and Gerard Mitchell shared many attributes. Both were thirty-four-year-old males, both had grown up in rural Prince Edward Island, and both had, at one time, taught school. Moreover, both were Roman Catholics, despite the fact that the Island had never previously been led by a Roman Catholic Liberal premier. At the levels of experience and of ideology, however, clear differences between the candidates were apparent. Bennett Campbell (no relation to the departing premier) had been first elected as an MLA in 1970 and had been in the cabinet since 1972 (serving variously as minister of education, provincial secretary, minister of finance, and interim premier). As the acting head of government, Bennett Campbell enjoyed extensive media coverage in the three months leading up to the convention and was in the enviable position (for a leadership aspirant) of being able to act decisively on his commitments. Hence, three days before the convention vote, Premier Campbell was able to announce cabinet approval of a framework to reduce building and land regulations.[270] Campbell was obviously sensitive to charges that the Liberals' cherished Development Plan

ROBERT TUCK / *EASTERN GRAPHIC*, 19 NOVEMBER 1978, 4

DUEL IN THE SNOW DEC. 9

had become overly bureaucratized. Nevertheless, as a senior cabinet minister for the previous six years, there were clear limits on how far Campbell could distance himself from the government's record. Campbell's solution was to emphasize that the government's policies were laying the foundation for future prosperity while calling for a balanced relationship between the provincial state and the private sector because "too much government involvement could be as harmful as too little."[271] According to one media pundit, "a general consensus" existed within the Liberal party that Campbell was "an able politician,"[272] and, at the convention, Campbell was to be supported by six of his nine cabinet colleagues (with the other three remaining neutral).

In contrast, Mitchell's political resumé was decidedly thinner. Mitchell had never held elected office and had, in fact, been defeated in an earlier attempt to secure a federal Liberal nomination. Mitchell did have future premier Joe Ghiz in his corner. Calling Mitchell "a man of action" who had "vigour" and "new ideas," Ghiz resigned his post as Liberal party president in order to campaign on Mitchell's behalf.[273] Otherwise, Mitchell attempted to align himself with the "dedicated and loyal Liberals" who were "crying out for a larger and more meaningful role."[274] Mitchell emphasized that he would listen to Islanders rather than bureaucrats, that he would cut government regulations "to the bone," and that he would institute travelling caucus meetings.[275] Mitchell's guise as a populist tribune seemed less credible, however, when he declined to answer questions about his backing from, and possible indebtedness to, a coterie of Charlottetown businesspeople.[276] At the convention, Mitchell gave an aggressive speech (enigmatically characterized in the media as containing "swift bursts of rapid oratorial style"),[277] but the result was a foregone conclusion.

| | |
|---|---|
| Bennett Campbell | 963 |
| Gerard Mitchell | 382 |

### 24 October 1981

In 1979, the Prince Edward Island Conservatives, under Angus MacLean, defeated the final remaining Liberal provincial government in the country. Liberal leader Bennett Campbell stayed on after the loss, but when a vacancy appeared in the spring of 1981 in the federal riding of Cardigan, he leapt into national politics, won the by-election, and was soon appointed as minister of veterans affairs. Campbell's abrupt departure propelled the Prince Edward Island Liberals into their second leadership struggle in three years. In what was reported to be a "gung ho and determined" fashion,[278] interim leader Gilbert Clements informed the provincial executive that he wished to hold the position on a more permanent basis. With ten years experience as an MLA, the fifty-two-year-old Clements was a former minister of community services, of tourism, of municipal affairs, and of environment. Admittedly, Clements had been the only Liberal minister to lose his seat in the election of 1978, but he could claim to have been "reborn from defeat" when he re-entered the provincial legislature a year later.

Facing off against Clements was Joe Ghiz, a thirty-five-year-old Charlottetown lawyer and former party president, who had never previously sought public office. Of Lebanese extraction and possessing a Harvard law degree, Ghiz was obviously an atypical Prince Edward Islander. His task, therefore, was to minimize the gulf that apparently separated him from most rank-and-file Liberal delegates. With respect to his ethnicity, Ghiz emphasized that his forbearers had emigrated to Prince Edward Island in the nineteenth century and that, in any case, Canada's success as a country was built on "people with tolerance" and "a mixture that creates a good cultural diversity and understanding."[279] As to his relatively rarefied educational background, Ghiz was at pains to emphasize that he was not "a fat cat,"[280] that he had engaged in an array of stereotypical Island activities. Hence, Ghiz bragged about picking potatoes, attending barn dances, and even, while lobster fishing, eating at sea those "small ones" that could not be legally landed.[281]

The contest soon crystallized into a clash over style rather than substance. Although both candidates were alarmed by high electricity rates and expressed concern for the disadvantaged, neither presented a detailed policy platform. Indeed, Clements emphasized that he did not "want to indicate" that he had "any magic solutions" to many Island problems,[282] while Ghiz was content to off-load his policy commitments to a future Liberal meeting convened for the purpose of drawing up a party platform. Not surprisingly, Clements stressed the advantages of having an experienced, mature leader who could relate well to ordinary Islanders, one who, moreover, already had a seat in the legislature. "I can't over emphasize the importance of having a leader who is already elected," claimed Clements, "especially since there could be several more sittings of the legislature before the next election."[283] In contrast, the Ghiz campaign talked about the importance of "fresh blood" for party renewal. Ghiz might not have a seat in the legislature but neither, it was noted, did Walter Shaw when he assumed the leadership of the Conservative party.[284] In any case, noted Ghiz, it was likely that the incoming Tory leader would soon dissolve the legislature and seek a fresh mandate from the people.[285]

Two factors, in particular, seemed to be working against Clements' candidacy. First, there was a distinct resemblance between Joe Ghiz and Alex Campbell, the one-time Liberal wonder boy who had led the party to four successive electoral victories. Both Ghiz and Campbell were thirty-six years old when they sought the leadership; both were charismatic and articulate Charlottetown lawyers. For Liberal delegates seeking to recapture the glory days of the 1960s and 1970s, the omens must have seemed clear. Second, the governing Tories were also in the throes of a leadership struggle. Gilbert Clements might have been able to compete successfully against a Conservative party led by outgoing premier Angus MacLean. But many Liberals must have worried that Clements might soon appear to be "yesterday's man" when stacked up against a more youthful and dynamic Conservative leader. Entering the convention, the leadership race was widely perceived to be very close. Both Ghiz and Clements could claim to have an impressive array of MLAs and other party notables in their camp.[286] One commentator suggested, on the eve of the convention, that it was "a real horse race, a real tight contest,"[287] while a second went so far as to predict that Ghiz would be "forced to convince delegates he is a serious alternative."[288] Such prognostications, as it turned out, were wildly off the mark. Obliged to choose between whether to "Go with Joe" or "Stay with Gilbert,"[289] Liberal delegates opted overwhelmingly for the former.

| | |
|---|---|
| Joe Ghiz | 905 |
| Gilbert Clements | 482 |

ROBERT TUCK / EASTERN GRAPHIC, 28 OCTOBER 1981, 4

### 23 January 1993

Paradoxically, it has been successful provincial political leaders who have most frequently overstayed their welcome. Those who have fared poorly in the electoral wars have confronted a cruelly unambiguous code: there is no room at the top for political losers. But there has been no corresponding rule for their victorious foes, and rare, indeed, has been the premier who has readily forsaken the office while still at the top of his or her game. Yet, Joe Ghiz was clearly one such individual. After twelve years as Liberal leader, the last seven as premier, Ghiz opted to retire even though "both he and the provincial Liberal party [were] enjoying unparalleled popularity."[290] Shortly thereafter, he was appointed as dean of the Dalhousie Law School. Just over three years later, Joe Ghiz was dead of cancer.

Given the near certainty of a Liberal victory in the impending provincial election, one might have anticipated that a bevy of aspirants would have come forward to contest the leadership. In fact, only one serious candidate emerged: Catherine Callbeck. After a single term in provincial politics (including experience in Alex Campbell's government as minister of health and social services), Callbeck had voluntarily returned to her family business in 1978. Ten years later, she re-entered politics by winning the federal constituency of Malpeque. With Ghiz's resignation, Callbeck chose, like Angus MacLean and Mel Gass, to use her position as the MP for Malpeque as a springboard for provincial party leadership. Callbeck's early declaration attracted much of the provincial caucus to her banner, and the remaining MLAs may have been "dissuaded from running by Ms. Callbeck's show of power."[291] Many Island Liberals were dismayed by the absence of a second strong candidate in the race. Yet, as one delegate from O'Leary put it: "I don't know if we could have done better. There are not too many shining lights down there [in the provincial caucus] to pick from. The members are sober, plodding, but not outstanding."[292]

Eventually, the race was somewhat enlivened by the entry of two fringe candidates: Bill Campbell and Larry Creed. A long-time social activist, Campbell's candidacy was delayed until he could secure a one-month leave from his federal civil service posting. Campbell had briefly served as Alex Campbell's executive assistant, but otherwise his political resumé was confined to having sought and lost Liberal nominations at both the federal and provincial levels. Even so, Campbell blithely concluded that, "when you add up all that experience, it comes to a lot of solid experience."[293] In "buzzword-laced" press conferences, Campbell lamented that "there's so much chaos out there" and claimed to have a "vision" for Prince Edward Island that would result in balanced budgets and full employment within a decade. Campbell also insisted that he had the backing of two Liberal MLAs, but they never came forward, and he declined to name them. "It's such an empowering experience," concluded Campbell, "going into the premier's office not owing anybody anything."[294]

If Bill Campbell's campaign had an ethereal quality, fellow outsider Larry Creed's appeal was decidedly earthier. A seasonally employed construction worker and self-styled "beans-and-baloney" candidate, Creed's campaign for a more "realistic" Liberal philosophy included selling the fleet of government cars, docking politicians' salaries, slashing expense account budgets, and appointing MLAs to government agencies and commissions.[295] Creed depicted himself as "ordinary"; thus, unlike party leaders with "professional" backgrounds, he could relate well to the concerns of most Islanders.[296] Both Campbell and Creed ran low budget campaigns. Campbell expressed surprise ("It's hard to imagine we all belong to the same family") when informed that it was inappropriate for him to crash Callbeck-sponsored delegate receptions in quest of political converts.[297] As for Creed, one report observed, apparently without irony, that his "campaign communications" would soon receive a "boost" when "a private donor provides him with a cell phone."[298]

Catherine Callbeck ran a typical front-runner's campaign. She avoided making firm commitments on most controversial policies. Frustrated by her evasiveness on the abortion question, for example, PEI Liberals for Life were ultimately compelled to endorse the candidacy of Bill Campbell.[299] Callbeck's

speeches usually emphasized her business experience and promised that "the further development of our provincial economy will be the preoccupation" of her government.[300] Callbeck may have bridled at charges that she was "vague" on most policy matters, but it was apparent that her leadership would be "a natural extension" to that of Joe Ghiz.[301]

The actual vote was without suspense. Convention organizers, presumably confident that all but a few Liberals were definitely ensconced in the Callbeck camp, made the peculiar decision to hold the all-candidates debate in cramped quarters. The media were welcome to attend, but only a few Liberal delegates were able to squeeze into the room.[302] Ultimately, Callbeck "breezed through the convention with barely a murmur of controversy or ruffled feathers"; her victory was accomplished on "one perfunctory ballot."[303] Leaving the gathering after having garnered a 5 percent vote share, Campbell remained obliviously upbeat. "Although I am not your premier," he intoned, "I still have a vision."[304]

| | |
|---|---|
| Catherine Callbeck | 1,229 |
| Larry Creed | 250 |
| Bill Campbell | 77 |

### 5 October 1996

The Liberal leadership contest of 1996 is described in Chapter 2.

### 5 April 2003

As 2003 dawned, few would have perceived the leadership of the Prince Edward Island Liberal party to be a plum position. Former leader Wayne Carew[305] had resigned shortly after the disastrous 2000 campaign, and the party's lone MLA (Ron MacKinley) had assumed the post on an interim basis. Alas, neither the party's finances nor its standing in the polls had improved under MacKinley's stewardship. Opinion soundings routinely gave the governing Conservatives a 25 percent lead,[306] and satisfaction with Premier Pat Binns remained extraordinarily high (occasionally topping the 80 percent level).[307] Party president Tim Banks was obviously alarmed by the possibility that MacKinley might seek the leadership on a more permanent basis, and the two engaged in a very public spat through the fall of 2002.[308] Yet, with the next provincial campaign not due until the spring of 2005, any other successful aspirant faced the prospect of many months of unpaid employment. In the end, MacKinley opted not to run and, instead, graciously offered his yet to be named successor a job in the party's research office at the legislature.

Who, then, did enter the contest? At previous Island conventions, experience in federal politics has been perceived as an asset – witness the triumphs of such former MPs as Angus MacLean, Mel Gass, Catherine Callbeck, and

Pat Binns. Had the Prince Edward Island Liberals held their leadership race in the spring of 2002, then Solicitor-General Lawrence MacAuley might have been a formidable candidate. Unfortunately, MacAuley's ensnarement in a patronage scandal effectively scuppered his chances. His successor in the federal cabinet, Wayne Easter, must have known that, as an ardent Chretienite, his time of influence in Ottawa was destined to be brief. Nevertheless, Easter proclaimed himself to be "very nationally minded"[309] and opted out of the race as well.

Ultimately, two candidates came forward. First to declare was Alan Buchanan, a fifty-year-old former cabinet minister, who had left politics in 1996 for an executive position with the telecommunications giant Aliant. Shortly thereafter, Robert Ghiz, a twenty-eight-year-old member of Jean Chretien's staff and, more important, son of former premier and party icon Joe Ghiz also announced his candidacy. The two men presented very different images to the voters. For obvious reasons, Buchanan emphasized the wisdom gained from over two decades of senior postings:

> My hair is pretty grey, there's no question about that and there's no denying my age. But I believe myself that I gained incredible experience in the last seven years as a member of the private sector and I stood before these people here this evening, I think, far better equipped now than I was even when I had legislative experience.[310]

In contrast, Ghiz stressed his youth and vitality. Repeatedly, Ghiz argued that it was "time for a new era in the Liberal party," that it was necessary to "start with a new group of people," and that his "passion" could "inspire a whole new generation of Liberals."[311] This difference in approach was neatly encapsulated in their respective campaign slogans: Buchanan's "Now Is the Time" contrasted sharply with Ghiz's "Building Now, for the Future."

The six-week campaign was relatively uneventful. A $30,000 spending cap was instituted by the party, and Ghiz managed to raise one-third of that amount at a farewell party organized by his friends in Ottawa.[312] Membership drives have become standard practice at universal ballot contests; in this case, both candidates claimed to have sold around two thousand new memberships.[313] Nor was much advantage gained at the three candidate debates. Both Buchanan and Ghiz pilloried the Tory administration for an impending 13 percent power hike,[314] and both seemed oddly ill-informed about the Confederation Bridge toll structure. Thus, Ghiz pledged to re-examine the rates (although these are set in Ottawa), while Buchanan claimed that the tolls had risen faster than inflation (although this is prohibited).[315] The most interesting moment of the debates probably came when Ghiz chastised the Conservatives for not restoring the 7.5 percent salary rollback imposed by the Callbeck administration on the province's civil servants.[316]

As a key member of that apparently offending Liberal administration, Buchanan was effectively skewered.

For the most part, this was a campaign about contrasting images, about youth versus experience. To his supporters, Robert Ghiz was ostensibly known as "the JFK Jr. of the Island";[317] less sympathetic observers were inclined to note that, politically, Ghiz was "still in diapers."[318] Recognizing the need to put a positive spin on his youth, Ghiz frequently quoted Jean Chretien's words of support ("Well, Robert, there is no time like the present")[319] and campaigned relentlessly ("I had to get out there. I had to prove that I'm no longer the little kid that Islanders used to see in the Christmas cards").[320] The Ghiz team even incorporated into their campaign logo a check mark with a clear resemblance to the famous Nike swoosh. Unusually, the huge multinational chose to "state emphatically that Nike does not take sides in any partisan matters and is not supporting or endorsing Mr. Ghiz or any of his opponents."[321]

In contrast, Alan Buchanan chose to emphasize the substance typically associated with age and experience. Whereas Ghiz was content to leave policy stances to be developed in some post-convention participatory exercise, Buchanan released a sixty-three-page Red Book that outlined his approach to a wide range of issues. Admittedly, some of his commitments bordered on the platitudinous ("one simple truth exists more than ever – education provides the necessary cornerstone upon which a solid society can be built and maintained").[322] Nevertheless, the booklet left the impression that Buchanan had thought long and hard about the problems confronting the Prince Edward Island government. Of course, just as Ghiz had to avoid appearing too callow, Buchanan needed to escape the charge of being "yesterday's man"; no doubt his handlers winced when Buchanan mused that the "last time" he had been "really involved" in a leadership contest had been in 1978![323]

The campaign's only controversy of note centred on Ghiz's requests to change the convention's voting rules. Rather than have balloting commence after the early-afternoon candidate speeches, Ghiz proposed that Liberals should be able to vote at any time during the day (and possibly even the preceding evening). Although Ghiz insisted that he was merely trying to make the leadership selection process as "inclusive" as possible,[324] those of a suspicious mindset wondered whether Ghiz was worried that some of his youthful recruits would be disinclined to wait out the several-hour interval between registration and voting. In any event, the Buchanan team objected strenuously to any last minute change in the rules, and the convention planning committee had little choice but to reject the proposal.[325] Even then, Ghiz pledged to pursue the matter in the long run. He was only dissuaded from launching an immediate appeal by the prospect of the organizing committee resigning en masse.[326]

Entering the convention, it was apparent that the contest was close. Approximately 4,500 Liberals registered on site to vote, but five hundred of these decamped without casting a ballot (that is, a number greater than the final margin of victory).[327] The least sinister explanation for their absence revolves around the weather. With a nasty April blizzard in the forecast ("Mother Nature must be a Tory"),[328] many Liberals may have simply opted to get home.

To the end, Robert Ghiz continued to push the theme of party renewal: members would have to make a "fundamental choice" about the future direction of the Liberal party. "Do we want to start with a clean slate and a fresh start," Ghiz asked, "or do we want to go with someone who might have a little more experience but who has been around?"[329] Most of the establishment, who presumably had also "been around," opted for one of their own and backed Buchanan (although the party's four MPs as well as party president Tim Carroll and interim leader Ron MacKinley all stayed officially neutral).[330] In contrast, Ghiz was said to be leading a "Children's Crusade,"[331] and those who shuttled between Ghiz's and Buchanan's hospitality suites could certainly detect a generational difference in support (only in the latter, for example, were there calls for the house band to play something by Neil Diamond).

Just prior to the convention, Buchanan had been named as a finalist in a competition to determine the top storyteller on Prince Edward Island.[332] Not surprisingly, he "nailed" his convention address at the Charlottetown Civic Centre.[333] As one enthusiast gushed: "Delegates and political pundits agreed that Buchanan's speech was flawless and that he had by far the strongest speech of the two candidates."[334] After his own vigorous, but relatively pedestrian, address to the convention, a worried Robert Ghiz was heard to mutter: "It's going to be tighter than I thought."[335] It was, in fact, tight. But aided by the alleged block voting of three hundred Islanders of Lebanese descent,[336] by the absence of any conspicuous political "baggage," and by a last name that was associated with "some glorious memories for many in the Liberal party,[337] Robert Ghiz won 52 percent of the vote and his party's leadership.

| | |
|---|---|
| Robert Ghiz | 2,065 |
| Alan Buchanan | 1,904 |

## New Democrats, 2002

### *13 April 2002*

With the possible exception of Quebec, no province has been more resistant to the electoral charms of the New Democratic Party than Prince Edward Island. Until the 1990s, all NDP candidates routinely lost their deposits, a circumstance that encouraged the old-line parties, in the 1950s, to raise the forfeiture fee to a then stratospheric two hundred dollars.[338] As recently as the 1982 provincial election, one riding had more spoilt ballots than votes cast for the NDP candidate.[339] This unalloyed record of electoral futility came to an abrupt end in 1996, however, when NDP leader Herb Dickieson, a well-respected doctor, won the reconstituted district of West Point-Bloomfield. Alas, many locals reportedly considered Dickieson qua physician more valuable to their well-being than Dickieson qua legislator. In 1996, Dickieson had benefited from a relatively even vote split between the two old-line parties. In 2000, Conservative premier Pat Binns targeted the riding; he made eight campaign visits to West Point-Bloomfield and announced his party's health policy from the foyer of the local hospital.[340] With the Grit vote collapsing throughout the province, Dickieson lost to the Tory candidate by twenty-two votes. Citing work and family commitments, a disappointed Dickieson soon resigned as leader.

Three relative unknowns, all, needless to say, without prior experience in elected office, sought to succeed Dickieson. The most radical candidate was Deborah Kelly-Hawkes, a forty-six-year-old counsellor from Lower Montague who had received fewer votes than had any other NDP candidate in the 2000 provincial election. On one occasion, Kelly-Hawkes had pitched a tent in front of Province House to "protest the extortion of labour"; on another, she had been arrested after allegedly keeping police officers at bay with a hammer and a pitchfork (but not a sickle). Comparing her ongoing legal troubles to those of Gandhi and Martin Luther King, Kelly-Hawkes suggested that her first-hand exposure to "the corruption of the province's legal and political systems" increased the credibility of her candidacy. A strong feminist, Kelly-Hawkes complained that women had been ruled by men "long enough" and suggested that the party elite should be gender balanced; after

WAYNE WRIGHT / JOURNAL-PIONEER, 15 APRIL 2002, 4

all, noted a *Guardian* columnist, Kelly-Hawkes was a firm believer in "male and female parody."[341]

At the other end of the NDP's ideological spectrum was thirty-eight-year-old high school teacher Gary Robichaud, a resident of North Bedeque. Self-styled as "a moderate and a fresh face," Robichaud emphasized the "relatively modest goals" of increasing party membership, revitalizing constituency associations, and preparing for the next provincial election. Robichaud's organizational focus was also apparent in his concern with retiring the party's $17,000 debt; perhaps, mused Robichaud, the NDP had erred by running candidates in all twenty-seven constituencies in the 2000 election.[342] Situated somewhere between the other two candidates was Ken Bingham, a fifty-one-year-old retired teacher from New Glasgow. Like Robichaud, Bingham stressed the need for organizational renewal and fiscal prudence. But Bingham also emphasized the need for greater social spending (in, for example, child care and home care) and decried the Island NDP's recent decision to accept some corporate donations. Robichaud, Bingham, and Kelly-Hawkes had all been unsuccessful candidates in the 2000 provincial election (receiving vote shares of 12, 10, and 2 percent in their respective ridings) and were unable to generate much enthusiasm for the race. The campaign elicited little media attention until the final few days, and the Dickieson farewell gala (at which the departing leader refused to rule out an eventual return to politics) was top-heavy with NDP notables from across the country.[343] Ultimately, Robichaud won a "landslide" victory on the first ballot and became the first Acadian to head a Prince Edward Island party since 1919. The new leader's insistence that the Island NDP was no longer a "third party" but, rather, "an equal partner in the political landscape"[344] was, however, belied by the fact that only eighty-two Islanders took part in the election.

| | |
|---|---|
| Gary Robichaud | 60 |
| Ken Bingham | 18 |
| Deborah Kelly-Hawkes | 4 |

# Notes

## Chapter 1: Choosing Leaders

1 See, for instance, Robert Krause and Lawrence Leduc, "Voting Behaviour and Electoral Strategies in the Progressive Conservative Leadership Convention of 1976," *Canadian Journal of Political Science* 12 (1979): 102 and 116, for a discussion of how leadership elections resemble general elections and the importance of examining divisions present in the wider population. See also Conrad Winn and John McMenemy, *Political Parties in Canada* (Toronto: McGraw-Hill Ryerson, 1976), 156, for an indication of how party activists are drawn disproportionately from groups more likely to support the party.

2 Anthony Sayers, "The Study of Political Leaders and Activists," in *Citizen Politics: Research and Theory in Canadian Political Behaviour*, ed. Joanna Everitt and Brenda O' Neill (Don Mills: Oxford University Press, 2002), 305.

3 Donald Smiley, "The National Party Leadership Convention in Canada: A Preliminary Analysis," *Canadian Journal of Political Science* 1 (1968): 373-97.

4 Stephen Clarkson, "The Delegate's Decision: The 1976 Leadership Convention of the Liberal Party in Ontario," paper presented to the annual meeting of the Canadian Political Science Association, Quebec City, 1976.

5 John Courtney, *The Selection of National Party Leaders in Canada* (Toronto: Macmillan, 1973), xii.

6 Roger Gibbins and Margaret Hunziker, "Issues and Leadership Conventions: The 1985 Alberta PC Leadership Convention," paper presented at the Annual Meeting of the Canadian Political Science Association, Winnipeg, 1986.

7 R. Kenneth Carty, Lynda Erickson, and Donald E. Blake, *Leaders and Parties in Canadian Politics: Experiences of the Provinces* (Toronto: Harcourt Brace Jovanovich, 1992); R.K. Carty, Donald Blake, and Lynda Erickson, *Grassroots Politicians: Party Activists in British Columbia* (Vancouver: UBC Press, 1991); David K. Stewart and Keith Archer, *Quasi-Democracy? Parties and Leadership Selection in Alberta* (Vancouver: UBC Press, 2000).

8 In the initial years, the principal investigators were Agar Adamson and Marshall Conley. Since 1991, however, the responsibility for administering these surveys has increasingly fallen on Ian Stewart. It should be noted that the 1997 survey of the New Brunswick Liberals and the 1998 survey of the New Brunswick Progressive Conservatives were joint undertakings of Ian Stewart and Bill Cross of Mount Allison University and that the 2002 surveys of the Nova Scotia NDP, the Prince Edward Island NDP, and the New Brunswick Liberals were joint undertakings of Ian Stewart and David Stewart.

9 For reasons that remain inexplicable, the Nova Scotia Liberal party's provincial executive refused to cooperate in a planned survey.

10 The advent of all-member leadership ballots in recent years has obliterated the distinction between voting delegates and the larger group of non-voting party members. Strictly speaking, therefore, the term "delegate" should not be used in the context of all-member votes.

11  J. Murray Beck, "Elections," in *The Provincial Political Systems: Comparative Essays*, ed. David J. Bellamy, Jon H. Pammett, and Donald C. Rowat (Agincourt: Methuen, 1976), 178.
12  J. Murray Beck, "Tradition and Conservatism," in *Canadian Provincial Politics*, 2nd ed., ed. Martin Robin (Scarborough: Prentice-Hall, 1978), 201.
13  Ian Stewart, *Roasting Chestnuts: The Mythology of Maritime Political Culture* (Vancouver: UBC Press, 1994), 73-88.
14  See William Cross and Ian Stewart, "Ethnicity and Accommodation in the New Brunswick Party System," *Journal of Canadian Studies* 36 (2001-2): 32-58.
15  See George Perlin, "Leadership Selection the PC and Liberal Parties: Assessing the Need for Reform," in *Party Politics in Canada*, 6th ed., ed. Hugh G. Thorburn (Scarborough: Prentice-Hall, 1991), 213-15.
16  See, for example, Stewart, *Roasting Chestnuts*, 134-54.
17  Even a partial list of the important monographs on Prairie politics would include those written by C.B. Macpherson, Seymour Lipset, W.L. Morton, David Smith, Roger Gibbins, Larry Pratt, and John Richards.
18  Again, see Stewart, *Roasting Chestnuts*.
19  At first glance, this argument may seem to be tautological; that is, it might appear that we are using leadership conventions to understand political cultures and then employing the derived apprehension of political cultures to understand leadership conventions. In fact, we are largely able to avoid this trap since we rely principally on attitudes towards public policy as our indicator of political culture – attitudes that, for the most part, cannot be directly linked to the leadership contests under scrutiny. For a fuller discussion of this problem, see Ian Stewart, "Vanishing Points: Three Paradoxes of Political Research," in *Citizen Politics*, ed. Joanna Everitt and Brenda O'Neill, 21-39 (Don Mills: Oxford University Press, 2002).

## Chapter 2: The Conventions

1   *Guardian* (Charlottetown), 4 October 1996, A3.
2   Ibid., 2 October 1996, A3.
3   Ibid., 27 September 1996, A3.
4   Ibid., 5 October 1996, A6.
5   Ibid., 26 September 1996, A3.
6   Ibid., 24 September 1996, A1.
7   Ibid., 7 October 1996, A6.
8   Ibid., 26 September 1996, A3.
9   Ibid., 19 September 1996, A2.
10  Ibid., 24 September 1996, A1.
11  Ibid., 19 September 1996, A2.
12  Ibid., 26 September 1996, A1.
13  Ibid.
14  Ibid., 28 September 1996, A1.
15  Ibid., 1 October 1996, A3.
16  *Sunday Daily News* (Halifax), 10 October 1996, 10.
17  *Guardian* (Charlottetown), 7 October 1996, A2.
18  Ibid., A3.
19  *Guardian* (Charlottetown), 8 October 1996, A2.
20  *Moncton Times and Transcript*, 18 October 1997, A3.
21  *Daily Gleaner* (Fredericton), 17 October 1997, A6.
22  Ibid., 15 October 1997, A1.
23  Ibid., 29 September 1997, A6.
24  *Moncton Times and Transcript*, 20 October 1997, D5.
25  *Daily Gleaner* (Fredericton), 22 September 1997, A1.
26  Ibid., 12 September 1997, 5.
27  *Moncton Times and Transcript*, 19 September 1997, A5.
28  Ibid., 22 September 1997, D5.
29  *Daily Gleaner* (Fredericton), 22 September 1997, A6.
30  *Moncton Times and Transcript*, 23 September 1997, A2.

31 *Daily Gleaner* (Fredericton), 9 October 1997, A4.
32 *Moncton Times and Transcript*, 18 October 1997, D15.
33 *Daily Gleaner* (Fredericton), 11 September 1997, A3.
34 Ibid., 15 September 1997, 5.
35 *Moncton Times and Transcript*, 23 September 1997, A1.
36 *Daily Gleaner* (Fredericton), 26 September 1997, A1.
37 *Moncton Times and Transcript*, 23 September 1997, A2.
38 *Daily Gleaner* (Fredericton), 16 October 1997, A2.
39 *Moncton Times and Transcript*, 20 October 1997, A2.
40 *Daily Gleaner* (Fredericton), 20 October 1997, A3.
41 *Chronicle-Herald* (Halifax), 15 July 2000, A5.
42 Ibid., 14 May 2000, A2.
43 Ibid., 20 June 2000, A1.
44 Ibid., 7 April 2000, B1.
45 *Sunday Daily News* (Halifax), 16 July 2000, 4.
46 Helen MacDonald, NDP Leadership Campaign, *Helen Today!* 15 July 2000.
47 *Chronicle-Herald* (Halifax), 23 March 2000, A7.
48 Ibid., 25 April 2000, A7.
49 Ibid., 14 May 2000, A1.
50 Ibid., 3 April 2000, A4.
51 Ibid., 16 April 2000, A4.
52 Ibid., 10 July 2000, A4.
53 Ibid., 15 July 2000, A5.
54 Ibid., 11 April 2000, A4.
55 *Sunday Daily News* (Halifax), 16 July 2000, 4.
56 Ibid.
57 *Chronicle-Herald* (Halifax), 18 July 2000, C1.
58 Ibid.
59 See David K. Stewart and R.K. Carty, "Does Changing the Party Leader Provide an Electoral Boost: A Study of Canadian Provincial Parties: 1960-1992," *Canadian Journal of Political Science* 26 (1993): 312-30.
60 In Nova Scotia after 1997, we treat both opposition parties as major parties.
61 For a discussion of this phenomenon at the national level, see Ian Stewart, "The Brass Versus the Grass: Party Insiders and Outsiders at Canadian Leadership Conventions," in *Party Democracy in Canada*, ed. George Perlin, 144-59 (Scarborough: Prentice-Hall Canada, 1988). It is important to keep in mind that, in multi-candidate races, it is possible for more than one candidate to represent continuity or change. Our focus was on the winning candidate.

## Chapter 3: From J. Buchanan to A. Buchanan

1 John Courtney, *The Selection of National Party Leaders in Canada* (Toronto: Macmillan, 1973), 119.
2 J. Lele, G. Perlin, and H. Thorburn, "Leadership Conventions in Canada: The Form and Substance of Participatory Politics," in *Social Space Canadian Perspectives*, ed. D.I. Davies and Kathleen Herman (Toronto: New Press, 1971), 205-6.
3 Alan Frizzell and Tom McPhail, "The Mass Media and Convention Voting Behaviour," *Canadian Journal of Communication* 5, 3 (1979): 20.
4 John C. Courtney and George Perlin, "The Role of Conventions in the Representation and Accommodation of Regional Cleavages," in *Party Democracy in Canada*, ed. George Perlin (Scarborough: Prentice-Hall Canada, 1988), 128.
5 Janine Brodie, "The Gender Factor and National Leadership Conventions in Canada," in Perlin, *Party Democracy in Canada*, 177-78.
6 George Perlin, Allen Sutherland, and Marc Desjardins, "The Impact of Age Cleavage on Convention Politics," in Perlin, *Party Democracy in Canada*, 192.
7 John C. Courtney, *Do Conventions Matter?* (Montreal: McGill-Queen's University Press, 1995), 336.
8 Courtney and Perlin, "Role of Conventions," 128.

9  Donald E. Blake, R.K. Carty, and Lynda Erickson, "Ratification or Repudiation: Social Credit Leadership Selection In British Columbia," *Canadian Journal of Political Science* 21 (1988): 517.

10  Agar Adamson, "The 1971 Nova Scotia Progressive Conservative Leadership Convention: How Representative?" Paper presented to the Annual Meeting of the Canadian Political Science Association, Montreal, 1972.

11  John Courtney, "Leadership Conventions and the Development of the National Political Community in Canada," in *National Politics and Community in Canada*, ed. R.K. Carty and W.P. Ward (Vancouver: UBC Press, 1986), 96.

12  Ibid., 94.

13  Courtney, *Selection of National Party Leaders*, 63; John W. Lederle, "The Liberal Convention of 1919 and the Selection of Mackenzie King," *Dalhousie Review* 27, 1 (1947): 90.

14  Heather MacIvor, "The Leadership Convention: An Institution under Stress," in *Leaders and Leadership in Canada*, ed. Maureen Mancuso, Richard G. Price, and Ronald Wagenberg (Toronto: Oxford University Press, 1994), 20.

15  The number of women who have sought the leadership is underestimated because we did not collect information on all leadership elections. Elizabeth Weir won the leadership of the New Brunswick NDP in 1988, Barbara Baird-Filliter was acclaimed as leader of the New Brunswick Conservatives in 1989, and Pat Mella was elected as leader of the PEI Conservatives in 1990 (see Linda Trimble and Jane Arscott, *Still Counting: Women in Politics across Canada* [Peterborough: Broadview Press, 2003]). The timing of their selection further demonstrates our point of the change over time.

16  Adding Mella, Baird-Filliter, and Weir to the discussion does not change the general pattern. It would shift to three of twenty-six for the Conservatives and six of eighteen for the New Democrats.

17  Sylvia Bashevkin, *Toeing the Lines: Women and Party Politics in English Canada* (Toronto: University of Toronto Press, 1991).

18  See David Stewart, "Political Realignment in Atlantic Canada," in *Regionalism and Party Politics in Canada*, ed. Lisa Young and Keith Archer, 171-87 (Toronto: Oxford University Press, 2002).

19  Agar Adamson and Ian Stewart, "Party Politics in the Mysterious East," in *Party Politics in Canada*, 5th ed., ed. Hugh Thorburn, 319-33 (Scarborough: Prentice-Hall Canada, 1985).

20  Courtney, *Do Conventions Matter?* 163.

21  Perlin, Sutherland, and Desjardins, "Impact of Age," 189.

22  For data on national parties, see Courtney, *Do Conventions Matter?* 170.

23  Excluding law, business, education, farming, and medicine.

24  We excluded the NDP from this analysis since 80 percent of their candidates came after 1987.

25  Ian Stewart, "Class Politics at Canadian Leadership Conventions," in Perlin, *Party Democracy*.

26  In this analysis, "rural" follows the Statistics Canada definition of under one thousand inhabitants; thus, while "urban" includes all communities with a population greater than one thousand, the definition of "major urban centres" varies across the three Maritime provinces. The analysis has been complicated by population shifts over the thirty-two-year-period of our study. In particular, some cities that did not previously qualify (e.g., Fredericton) now fit the criterion of a "major urban centre."

27  Of course, there are other leadership elections for which we do not have data. Long-time NDP leader Elizabeth Weir represented a Saint John riding, and a former Liberal leader, Robert Higgins, was also from that area. However, the other Liberal and Conservative leaders who contested elections were from more rural settings.

28  P.J. Fitzpatrick, "New Brunswick: The Politics of Pragmatism," in *Canadian Provincial Politics*, 2nd ed., ed. Martin Robin (Scarborough: Prentice-Hall, 1978), 121.

29  Although most of Northumberland lies to the north of the diagonal, Norm Betts' hometown of Doaktown is marginally to the south of the line.

30  Historically, NDP rules differed from those of the Liberals and the Conservatives. While the older parties required equal representation from each constituency, the New Democrats based convention representation on the size of the local party's membership. Hence, the areas where the party was strong, like Halifax, were quite likely to be "overrepresented."

31 R.K. Carty, Donald Blake, and Lynda Erickson, *Grassroots Politicians: Party Activists in British Columbia* (Vancouver: UBC Press, 1991).

32 The highest proportion of Liberals and Conservatives claiming no religion constituted 9 percent of those who voted in the 2002 Nova Scotia Liberal universal ballot. The corresponding figure for the 2002 New Brunswick Liberal convention and the 2003 PEI universal ballot was 3 percent.

33 See Rand Dyck, *Provincial Politics in Canada* (Scarborough: Prentice-Hall Canada, 1996).

34 Conrad Winn and John McMenemy, *Political Parties in Canada* (Toronto: McGraw-Hill Ryerson, 1976), 152.

35 This may be due to the popularity of former party leader Herb Dickieson, the only New Democrat ever elected to the Island legislature. Dr. Dickieson was elected from a rural constituency and may have made the party more popular in such portions of the province.

## Chapter 4: Tourists or Partisans?

1 John C. Courtney, *Do Conventions Matter?* (Montreal: McGill-Queen's University Press, 1995), 287.

2 Reg Whitaker, "Virtual Political Parties and the Decline of Democracy," *Policy Options* (June 2001): 16-22.

3 David K. Stewart, "Electing a Premier," in *Citizen Politics: Research and Theory in Canadian Political Behaviour*, ed. Joanna Everitt and Brenda O'Neill (Don Mills: Oxford University Press, 2002), 325.

4 William, Cross, "Leadership Selection in New Brunswick: Balancing Language Representation and Populist Impulses," in *Political Parties, Representation, and Electoral Democracy in Canada*, ed. William Cross, 37-54 (Don Mills: Oxford University Press, 2002).

5 Courtney, *Do Conventions Matter?* 154.

6 William Cross, *Political Parties* (Vancouver: UBC Press, 2004), 98. See also David K. Stewart and R.K. Carty, "Leadership Politics as Party Building" in Cross, *Electoral Democracy*, 67.

7 Cross, *Leadership Selection*, 43.

8 The possibility must be acknowledged that "tourists" may be less inclined than "partisans" to complete our surveys.

9 Courtney, *Do Conventions Matter?* 149.

10 Cross, *Political Parties*, 98.

11 Cross, *Leadership Selection*, 44.

12 The post-1991 period includes all of the universal ballots.

13 This universal ballot had only eighty-two voters. The mean number of voters in the four conventions was 1,545. In universal ballots the mean climbed to 4,611.

## Chapter 5: Leadership Election Support Patterns

1 R.K. Carty, "Choosing New Party Leaders: The PCs in 1983, The Liberals in 1984," in *Canada at the Polls, 1984*, ed. Howard Penniman (Washington, DC: American Enterprise Institute, 1988).

2 Robert Krause and Lawrence Leduc, "Voting Behaviour and Electoral Strategies in the Progressive Conservative Leadership Convention of 1976," *Canadian Journal of Political Science* 12 (1979): 116.

3 See David K. Stewart, "The Traditions Continue: Leadership Choices at Maritime Liberal and Conservative Party Conventions." PhD diss., University of British Columbia, 1990. Some of the analysis in this book is taken from that dissertation. See also David K. Stewart, "'Friends and Neighbours': Patterns of Delegate Support at Maritime Liberal and Conservative Conventions," in *Leaders and Parties in Canadian Politics*, ed. R.K. Carty, Lynda Erickson, and Donald E. Blake, 56-79 (Toronto: Harcourt Brace Jovanovich, 1992).

4 André Blais et al., *Anatomy of a Liberal Victory* (Peterborough: Broadview Press, 2002), 91.

5 P.J. Fitzpatrick, "New Brunswick: The Politics of Pragmatism," in *Canadian Provincial Politics*, 2nd ed., ed. Martin Robin (Scarborough: Prentice-Hall, 1978).

6 Agar Adamson and Ian Stewart, "Changing Party Politics in Atlantic Canada," in *Party Politics in Canada*, 8th ed., ed. Hugh Thorburn and Alan Whitehorn, 303-20 (Scarborough: Prentice-Hall, 2001).

7   See, for example, Vince MacLean's comments in the 1986 Nova Scotia Liberal race.
8   Robert D. Putnam, *Bowling Alone: America's Declining Social Capital* (New York: Simon and Schuster, 2000).
9   See Richard Wilbur, "New Brunswick," in *Canadian Annual Review of Politics and Public Affairs 1985*, ed. R.B. Byers, 324-31 (Toronto: University of Toronto Press, 1988).
10  *Guardian* (Charlottetown), 18 May 1988, 1.
11  *Telegraph-Journal* (Saint John), 20 January 1998, A3.
12  Ibid., 4 February 1998, A3.
13  As quoted in Chris Morris, "Interim Premier Vows to Stay the Course," *Canadian Press Newswire*, 8 October 1997.
14  *Telegraph-Journal* (Saint John), 10 April 1998, A4.
15  Ibid., 2 May 1998, A13.
16  In 2002, we were unable to identify religious differences among the candidates.
17  David Bellamy, "The Atlantic Provinces," in The Provincial Political Systems, ed. D.J. Bellamy, J.H. Pammett, and D.C. Rowatt (Toronto: Methuen, 1976), 3.
18  John Wilson, "The Canadian Political Cultures: Towards a Redefinition of the Nature of the Canadian Political System," *Canadian Journal of Political Science* 7 (1974): 438-83.
19  John A. Agnew, *Place and Politics: The Geographical Mediation of State and Society* (Winchester: Allen and Unwin, 1987), 38.
20  V.O. Key, *Southern Politics in State and Nation* (New York: Alfred A. Knopf, 1949), 110.
21  Ibid., 46.
22  Ibid., 38.
23  Alan Wilson, "Crosscurrents in Maritime Regionalism," in *Federalism in Canada and Australia*, ed. Bruce W. Hodgins, John S. Milloy, and Shawn Heard (Peterborough: Trent University, the Frost Centre for Canadian Heritage and Development Studies, 1989), 375.
24  Harry Bruce, *Down Home: Notes of a Maritime Son* (Toronto: Key Porter Books, 1988), 62.
25  G.D. Hodge and M.A. Quadeer, *Towns and Villages in Canada* (Toronto: Butterworths, 1983), 133.
26  McKenna and Buchanan were transients in the sense of living, working, and representing a riding in a part of the province where they were not born and raised.
27  Bruce, *Down Home*, 30.
28  Reginald Bibby, *Fragmented Gods: The Poverty and Potential of Religion in Canada* (Toronto: Irwin, 1987), 90.
29  Statistics Canada, *2003 General Social Survey on Social Engagement, Cycle 17: An Overview of Findings* (Ottawa: Statistics Canada, 2004).
30  Frank Jones, *Religious Commitment in Canada, 1997 and 2000* (Ottawa: Christian Commitment Research Institute, Religious Commitment Monograph 3, 2003), 107.
31  Ibid., 106.
32  George Rawlyk, *Is Jesus Your Personal Saviour?* (Montreal: McGill-Queen's University Press, 1997), 51, 105, 95, and 68.
33  Ibid., 73.
34  Warren Clark, "Patterns of Religious Attendance," *Canadian Social Trends* (Winter 2000): 27.
35  Carty, Erickson, and Blake, *Leaders and Parties*, 11.
36  Blais et al., *Anatomy of a Liberal Victory*, 190.

**Chapter 6: Town versus Country**

1   André Blais et al., *Anatomy of a Liberal Victory* (Peterborough: Broadview Press, 2002), 93.
2   Timothy Thomas, "An Emerging Party Cleavage," in *Party Politics in Canada*, 8th ed., ed. Hugh Thorburn and Alan Whitehorn (Scarborough: Prentice-Hall, 2001), 438. The Maritimes do not have edge cities in the sense that Thomas uses it, but the urban-rural distinction is clearly significant.
3   The 2001 census records the population of the Halifax urban area as 276,221 out of the total Nova Scotia population of 908,007.
4   This is the urban definition used in the Canadian census. See Ray D. Bollman and Brian Biggs, "Rural and Small Town Canada: An Overview," in *Rural and Small Town Canada*, ed.

Ray D. Bollman (Toronto: Thompson Educational Publishing, 1992), 4; and Satadal Dasgupta, *Rural Canada* (Lewiston/Queenston: Edwin Mellon Press, 1988), 3.

5  Urban growth has not always outpaced rural growth in the Maritimes. As Bollman and Biggs explain, "New Brunswick and Nova Scotia were the only two provinces where rural exceeded urban growth rates during 1981-1986." See Bollman and Biggs, "Rural and Small Town Canada," 10.

6  We used the census division to determine what counts as rural (less than one thousand) and what counts as urban (over one thousand). The home area of the candidate named was removed from the analysis. The resulting table indicates the proportion of the vote candidates received in rural and urban areas outside of their home area.

7  With regard to these elections, we did not provide separate data for candidates who received less than 5 percent of the vote.

8  The only exception was the PEI NDP in 2002.

9  Of course, we have no NDP data for New Brunswick. However, Elizabeth Weir, the leader of the New Brunswick NDP from 1988 to 2005, represented a riding in the province's largest city.

10  G.D. Hodge and M.A. Quadeer, *Towns and Villages in Canada* (Toronto: Butterworths, 1983), 20. Using a slightly different measure, Besheri and Bollman, in their analysis of 1996 census data, found that more than 60 percent of Nova Scotians lived in predominantly rural areas and that the proportions were *even higher* in New Brunswick and PEI. See Roland Beshiri and Ray D. Bollman, "Population Structure and Change in Predominantly Rural Regions," *Rural and Small Town Canada Analysis Bulletin* 2 (2): 15.

11  This is not to say that urban areas are unimportant in elections. The urban areas, particularly in Nova Scotia and New Brunswick, contain important swing areas. However, in order for these swing ridings to have an impact, a party must have won a sufficiently high number of seats in the rest of the province.

12  Hodge and Quadeer, *Towns and Villages*, 131.

13  Ibid., 135.

14  Ibid., 136.

15  Bollman and Biggs, "Rural and Small Town Canada," 39.

16  Hodge and Quadeer, *Towns and Villages*, 137.

17  Warren Clark, "Patterns of Religious Attendance," *Canadian Social Trends* (Winter 2000): 27.

18  It must be acknowledged that this difference is partially a function of the greater frequency with which urban rather than rural candidates had to compete directly with other candidates from the same locale for the support of their neighbours.

19  The place of religion in the region's politics is not explained simply by the small-town ambience. Bibby has shown that religious faith and practice is not related to community size, and others have found religion to be important in parts of the Western world that are far from rural. See Reginald W. Bibby, *Fragmented Gods: The Poverty and Potential of Religion in Canada* (Toronto: Irwin, 1987).

20  Clark, "Patterns of Religious Attendance," 25.

21  Dasgupta, *Rural Canada*, 33, noted in 1988 that the "Atlantic region experienced the lowest rate of total population growth because of outmigration of its rural population to urban centers outside the region. Its own urban centers attracted few people from the rural areas within or outside of the region."

22  Ibid., 192.

### Chapter 7: Brothers and Sisters?

1  Margaret Conrad notes the complication that, for Atlantic Canadian women, identity politics "is to a greater or lesser degree defined elsewhere and communicated through networks dominated by other regions of the country." See Margaret Conrad, "Addressing the Democratic Deficit: Women and Political Culture in Atlantic Canada," *Atlantis* 27, 2 (2003): 86.

2  Janine Brodie, "The Gender Factor and National Leadership Conventions in Canada," *Party Democracy in Canada*, ed. George Perlin (Scarborough: Prentice-Hall Canada, 1988), 186.

3  Janine Brodie, "Women and the Electoral Process in Canada," in *Women and Canadian Politics*, ed. Kathy Megyery (Toronto: Dundurn Press, 1991), 24.
4  Elisabeth Gidengil, "Economic Man – Social Woman?" *Comparative Political Studies* 28 (1995): 383-408.
5  R.K. Carty, William Cross, and Lisa Young, *Rebuilding Party Politics* (Vancouver: UBC Press, 2000).
6  Canadian 2000 Election Study, data retrieved by the authors.
7  Heather MacIvor, *Women and Politics in Canada* (Peterborough: Broadview Press, 1996), 262.
8  Brodie, "Women and the Electoral Process," 33. See also, Alfred A. Hunter and Margaret A. Denton, "Do Female Candidates 'Lose Votes'? The Experience of Female Candidates in the 1979 and 1980 Canadian General Elections," *Canadian Review of Sociology and Anthropology* 21 (1984): 394-406.
9  Richard Johnston, André Blais, Henry E. Brady, and Jean Crête, *Letting the People Decide* (Montreal: McGill-Queen's University Press, 1992), 169.
10  Penney Kome, *Women of Influence: Canadian Women and Politics* (Toronto: Doubleday Canada, 1985), 171.
11  Myra Marx Ferree, "A Woman for President? Changing Responses: 1957-1972," *Public Opinion Quarterly* 36 (1974): 393-98.
12  Lee Sigelman and Carol K. Sigelman, "Sexism, Racism, and Ageism in Voting Behaviour: An Experimental Analysis," *Social Psychology Quarterly* 45 (1982): 266.
13  Laurie E. Ekstrand and William A. Eckert, "The Impact of Candidate's Sex on Voter Choice," *Western Political Quarterly* 34 (1981): 85.
14  R.D. Hedlund, P.K. Freeman, K.E. Hamm, and R.M. Stein, "The Electability of Women Candidates: The Effects of Sex Role Stereotypes," *Journal of Politics* 41 (1979): 522.
15  John F. Zipp and Eric Plutzer, "Gender Differences in Voting for Female Candidates: Evidence from the 1982 Election," *Public Opinion Quarterly* 49 (1985): 194. See also R. Darcy and Sarah Slavin Schramm, "When Women Run against Men," *Public Opinion Quarterly* 41 (1977): 1-12.
16  Eric Plutzer and John F. Zipp, "Identity Politics, Partnership, and Voting for Women Candidates," *Public Opinion Quarterly* 60 (1996): 31. See also Elizabeth A. Cook, "Voter Responses to Women Candidates," in *The Year of the Woman: Myth and Realities*, ed. Elizabeth A. Cook, Sue Thomas, and Clyde Wilcox, 217-36 (Boulder: Westview, 1994).
17  Brenda O'Neill, "The Relevance of Leader Gender to Voting in the 1993 Canadian National Election," *International Journal of Canadian Studies* 17 (1998): 106.
18  Fred Cutler, "The Simplest Shortcut of All: Sociodemographic Characteristics and Electoral Choice," *Journal of Politics* 64 (2002): 478. See also Neil Nevitte, André Blais, Elisabeth Gidengil, and Richard Nadeau, *Unsteady State: The 1997 Canadian Federal Election* (Don Mills: Oxford, 2000), 112-15.
19  See Jon H. Pammett, "Elections," in *Canadian Politics in the 21st Century*, 5th ed., ed. Michael Whittington and Glen Williams (Scarborough: Nelson, 2000), 162.
20  *Flora: Scenes from a Leadership Convention*, National Film Board video, 1977.
21  Lisa Young, *Feminists and Party Politics* (Vancouver: UBC Press, 2000), 167.
22  David K. Stewart and Keith Archer, *Quasi-Democracy? Parties and Leadership Selection in Alberta* (Vancouver: UBC Press, 2000), 117.
23  Sylvia Bashevkin, *Toeing the Lines: Women and Party Politics in English Canada* (Toronto: University of Toronto Press, 1991), 91.
24  Ibid., 94.
25  Keith Archer and Alan Whitehorn, *Political Activists: The NDP in Convention* (Toronto: Oxford University Press, 1997), 243.
26  *Telegraph-Journal* (Saint John), 6 May 1985, 5.
27  *Guardian* (Charlottetown), 22 October 1981, 5.
28  *Moncton Times and Transcript*, 20 October 1997, D5.
29  *Guardian* (Charlottetown), 13 June 1988, 1.
30  *Chronicle-Herald* (Halifax), 1 February 1991.
31  Ibid., 27 October 1990, A3.

32 Of course, even in the absence of female candidates, one would not necessarily expect men and women to vote in an identical fashion. Thus, Janine Brodie discovered a gender gap of approximately 7 percent at both the 1983 Progressive Conservative and the 1984 Liberal national leadership conventions. See Brodie, "Gender Factor," 185.

33 *Telegraph-Journal* (Saint John), 25 February 1982, 3.

34 Ibid., 8 February 1982, 5.

35 Ibid., 27 February 1982, 5.

36 *Chronicle-Herald* (Halifax), 14 November 1980, 6.

37 Ibid., 17 November 1980, 6.

38 *Sunday Daily News* (Halifax), 31 March 1996, 3.

39 Walter D. Young, *Anatomy of a Party: The National CCF 1932-1961* (Toronto: University of Toronto Press, 1969).

40 It is unclear what one should make of Janine Brodie's claim that Brian Mulroney's receipt of the support of 7 percent more men than women was sufficient "to provide him with the margin of victory." See Brodie, "Gender Factor," 186.

## Chapter 8: Inter- and Intraparty Attitudinal Differences

1 Rand Dyck, *Provincial Politics in Canada* (Scarborough: Prentice-Hall Canada, 1986), 167.

2 Joseph Wearing, *The L-Shaped Party: The Liberal Party of Canada, 1954-1980* (Toronto: McGraw-Hill Ryerson, 1981), 89.

3 Ian Stewart, *Roasting Chestnuts: The Mythology of Maritime Political Culture* (Vancouver: UBC Press, 1994), 88.

4 Fred Fletcher, "The Mass Media and the Selection of National Party Leaders: Some Explorations," in *Party Democracy in Canada*, ed. George Perlin (Scarborough: Prentice-Hall Canada, 1988), 118.

5 See Robert Krause and Lawrence Leduc, "Voting Behaviour and Electoral Strategies in the Progressive Conservative Leadership Convention of 1976," *Canadian Journal of Political Science* 12 (1979): 96-136; and Richard Johnston, "The Final Choice: Its Social, Organizational, and Ideological Bases," in Perlin, *Party Democracy*, 203-42.

6 David Stewart, "Friends and Neighbours: Patterns of Delegate Support at Maritime Liberal and Conservative Conventions," in *Leaders and Parties in Canadian Politics,* ed. R. Kenneth Carty, Lynda Erickson, and Donald E. Blake (Toronto: Harcourt Brace Jovanovich, 1992), 78.

7 Data on each of the attitudinal variables discussed in this section can be found in Table 8.2.

8 It is important to keep in mind that the question does not ask whether patronage is good!

9 Donald Smiley, "The National Party Leadership Convention in Canada: A Preliminary Analysis," *Canadian Journal of Political Science* 1 (1968): 378, 386, 396.

10 George Perlin, *The Tory Syndrome* (Montreal: McGill-Queen's University Press, 1980), 174.

11 Roger Gibbins and Margaret Hunziker, "Issues and Leadership Conventions: The 1985 Alberta PC Leadership Convention," paper presented at the Annual Meeting of the Canadian Political Science Association, Winnipeg, 1986.

12 Krause and Leduc, "Voting Behaviour," 120.

13 Ibid., 127.

14 Richard Johnston, "The Final Choice: Its Social, Organizational, and Ideological Bases," in Perlin, *Party Democracy*, 219.

15 Ibid., 214-17.

16 R.K. Carty, Donald Blake, and Lynda Erickson, *Grassroots Politicians: Party Activists in British Columbia* (Vancouver: UBC Press, 1991).

17 David K. Stewart and Keith Archer, *Quasi-Democracy: Parties and Leadership Selection in Alberta* (Vancouver: UBC Press, 2000).

18 Agar Adamson, "The 1971 Nova Scotia Progressive Conservative Leadership Convention: How Representative?" Paper presented to the Annual Meeting of the Canadian Political Science Association, Montreal, 1972.

19 See Chapter 2 for a fuller discussion of this convention.

20 The protection of agricultural land was also significantly associated with voting but not in any structured pattern.

21  Leaving linguistic questions aside.
22  NS PC 1971, NS PC 1991, NS Liberal 1992, NS NDP 1980, NS NDP 1996, NB Liberal 2002, PEI NDP 2002.
23  NS NDP 1980, NS NDP 1996, PEI NDP 2002.
24  NS NDP 2000, NB Liberal 1998, PEI Liberal 2003.

**Chapter 9: Rebels without a Cause?**

1  For a discussion of this phenomenon, see John Courtney, *The Selection of National Party Leaders in Canada* (Toronto: Macmillan, 1973), 185-90.
2  Patrick Martin, Allan Gregg, and George Perlin, *Contenders: The Tory Quest for Power* (Scarborough: Prentice-Hall Canada, 1983), 156.
3  Courtney, *Selection*, 89.
4  For several reasons, we have decided not to include Deborah Kelly-Hawkes in our discussion of fringe candidates. First, we received only one completed questionnaire from a Kelly-Hawkes supporter. Second, the PEI NDP is itself a fringe entity, and distinguishing between serious and fringe candidates for the party leadership is conceptually confused. Third, many of the factors that inform the subsequent analysis (such as the nature of media coverage, pre-convention polls, patronage motivations, unoccupied hospitality suites, and, ultimately, public humiliation) have no relevance to a leadership race for the PEI New Democratic Party. One could, in fact, advance a persuasive argument that it is the winner of such a contest rather than any fringe candidate who, in the long run, suffers far greater public embarrassment.
5  Unfortunately, the small numbers involved make it impossible to pick out specific provincial, temporal, institutional, or partisan patterns.
6  Frederick J. Fletcher and Robert J. Drummond, "The Mass Media and the Selection of National Party Leaders: Some Explorations," in *Party Democracy in Canada*, ed. George Perlin (Scarborough: Prentice-Hall Canada, 1988), 99.
7  *Chronicle-Herald* (Halifax), 6 November 1980, 5.
8  Ibid., 13 November 1980, 7
9  Ibid., 17 November 1980, 1.
10  *Mail-Star* (Halifax), 10 December 1990, A2.
11  *Cape Breton Post* (Sydney), 6 June 1992.
12  *Mail-Star* (Halifax), 8 June 1992.
13  *Guardian* (Charlottetown), 7 January 1993, 1.
14  Ibid., 18 January 1993, 8.
15  *Chronicle-Herald* (Halifax), 28 October 1995, A2.
16  *Guardian* (Charlottetown), 19 September 1996, A1.
17  Ibid., 4 October 1996, A3.
18  *Chronicle-Herald* (Halifax), 7 April 2000.
19  Fletcher and Drummond, "Mass Media," 98-100.
20  George Perlin, for example, similarly divided delegate motivations into policy, patronage, and affective. See George Perlin, *The Tory Syndrome* (Montreal: McGill-Queen's University Press, 1980), 151-72.
21  Proportional representation electoral systems are designed to be sensitive to minority viewpoints. Accordingly, it is difficult to identify any party operating in such a system as completely lacking in electoral credibility. For an analysis that ignores this understanding, see Herbert P. Kitschelt, "Left-Libertarian Parties: Explaining Innovation in Competitive Party Systems," *World Politics* 40 (1986-88): 193-234.
22  For a recent attempt to modify Duverger's law, see Jae-On Kim and Mahn-Geum Ohn, "A Theory of Minor Party Persistence: Election Rules, Social Cleavage, and the Number of Political Parties," *Social Forces* 70 (1992): 574-99.
23  Examples of this type of party would include Screaming Lord Sutch's Monster Raving Loony Party of Great Britain and the Rhinoceros Party of Canada. The latter promised to build a giant glue factory in Winnipeg to help keep the country together.
24  J. David Gillespie, *Politics at the Periphery: Third Parties in Two-Party America* (Columbia: University of South Carolina Press, 1993), 10. Cited in John C. Berg, "Prospects for More

Parties in the United States," paper presented at a conference entitled Party Politics in the Year 2000, Manchester, England, January 1995, 4.

25 One analysis of National Front supporters in Great Britain was obliged to aggregate twenty-two separate studies of voting intentions to generate a reliable sample size. See Martin Harrop, Judith England, and Christopher T. Husbands, "The Bases of National Front Support," *Political Studies* 28 (1980): 271-83.

26 Robert Krause and Lawrence Leduc, "Voting Behaviour and Electoral Strategies in the Progressive Conservative Leadership Convention of 1976," *Canadian Journal of Political Science* 12 (1979): 103-5.

27 Cited in Lawrence Leduc, Jr., "Party Decision-Making: Some Empirical Observations on the Leadership Selection Process," *Canadian Journal of Political Science* 4 (1971): 99.

28 While a scrutiny of other leadership data sets is beyond the scope of this analysis, it is noteworthy that, at the 1993 national PC leadership convention, the camps of fringe candidates Patrick Boyer and Garth Turner were disproportionately populated with late-comers. While only 15 percent of the delegates who supported the main contenders, Kim Campbell and Jean Charest, on the first ballot reached their decision at the convention, the proportion for Boyer and Turner was 31 percent. Turner, in particular, seems to have profited from this phenomenon. Fully 47 percent of his support came from delegates who were swayed by his speech to the convention. The corresponding figures for Campbell and Charest were only 10 percent and 16 percent, respectively. When there are two or more fringe candidates in the race, it may well be that one of them attracts the lion's share of the late converts.

29 Losing candidates are rarely happy with the mid-campaign release of polls as is clear in the appendix of this book. See, for example, the reactions of Ken MacInnis and Ray Frenette (in 1985).

## Chapter 10: Going My Way?

1 The variant of the universal ballot employed by the New Brunswick Liberals in 2002, under which elected voters are explicitly tied to a particular candidate on the first ballot, represents an exception to this generalization.

2 Mark Graesser, "Leadership Crises in an Opposition Party: The Liberal Party of Newfoundland," in *Leaders and Parties in Canadian Politics: Experiences of the Provinces*, ed. R.K. Carty, L. Erickson, and D.E. Blake (Toronto: Harcourt Brace Jovanovich, 1992), 38.

3 The Telegram News Staff, *Balloons and Ballots* (Toronto: The Telegram, 1967, 122).

4 Peter C. Newman, *The Distemper of Our Times* (Toronto: McClelland and Stewart, 1968), 188.

5 Jonathon Manthorpe, *The Power and the Tories* (Toronto: Macmillan, 1974), 62-63. In 1968, Mitchell Sharp withdrew in favour of Pierre Trudeau immediately prior to the federal Liberal leadership convention. Sharp recounted: "I met with my principal workers this morning at breakfast, and without exception, they will follow my lead and support Mr. Trudeau." See Martin Sullivan, *Mandate '68* (Toronto: Doubleday Canada, 1968), 330.

6 This listing includes only those conventions for which we have survey data. It should also be noted that the 1967 Conservative list of candidates excludes both John MacLean and Mary Walker Sawka since none of their supporters appeared in the data.

7 John C. Courtney, *Do Conventions Matter?* (Montreal: McGill-Queen's University Press, 1995), 226.

8 Ibid., 229.

9 Donald E. Blake, R.K. Carty, and Lynda Erickson, "Ratification or Repudiation: Social Credit Leadership Selection In British Columbia," *Canadian Journal of Political Science* 21 (1988): 530.

10 Robert Krause and Lawrence Leduc, "Voting Behaviour and Electoral Strategies in the Progressive Conservative Leadership Convention of 1976," *Canadian Journal of Political Science* 12 (1979): 114.

11 George Perlin, *The Tory Syndrome* (Montreal: McGill-Queen's University Press, 1980), 2-7.

12 Norman Snider, *The Changing of the Guard* (Toronto: Lester and Orpen Dennys, 1985), 34.

13 *Chronicle Herald* (Halifax), 19 March 1979, A1.

14 Jean Chrétien, *Straight from the Heart* (Toronto: McClelland and Stewart, 1985), 202.
15 A.K. McDougall, *John P. Robarts: His Life and Government* (Toronto: University of Toronto Press, 1986), 71.
16 Terry Morley, "Leadership Change in the CCF/NDP," in Carty, Erickson, and Blake, *Leaders and Parties*, 120.
17 Audrey McLaughlin, *A Woman's Place* (Toronto: Macfarlane, Walter and Ross, 1992), 72.
18 Jack Horner, *My Own Brand* (Edmonton: Hurtig, 1980), 162.
19 Sullivan, *Mandate '68*, 330.
20 Ron Graham, *One-Eyed Kings: Promise and Illusion in Canadian Politics* (Toronto: Totem Books, 1986), 178.
21 Patrick Martin, Allan Gregg, and George Perlin, *Contenders: The Tory Quest for Power* (Scarborough: Prentice-Hall Canada, 1983), 166.
22 Martin Goldfarb and Thomas Axworthy, *Marching to a Different Drummer* (Toronto: Stoddart, 1988), 40.
23 Martin, Gregg, and Perlin, *Contenders*, 167.
24 L. Ian MacDonald, *Mulroney: The Making of the Prime Minister* (Toronto: McClelland and Stewart, 1984), 204.
25 *Chronicle Herald* (Halifax), 9 June 1980, 12.
26 Fraser Mooney, telephone interview with Ian Stewart, 19 June 2002.

## Chapter 11: Prince Edward Island and the Garden Myth

1 *Donald MacKinnon v. Government of Prince Edward Island and the City of Charlottetown,* [1993] 1 P.E.I.R. 216 (P.E.I.S.C.T.D.) at 256.
2 David Milne, "Politics in a Beleaguered Garden," in *The Garden Transformed: Prince Edward Island, 1944-1980*, ed. Verner Smitheram, David Milne, and Satadal Dasgupta, 38-72 (Charlottetown: Ragweed Press, 1982), 40.
3 John McClellan, "Changing Patterns of Land Use," in Smitheram, Milne, and Dasgupta, *Garden Transformed*, 102.
4 Department of the Provincial Treasury, *Province of Prince Edward Island: 29th Annual Statistical Review, 2002* (Charlottetown: Department of the Provincial Treasury, 2003), 54.
5 Ibid., 4; Maurice Beaudin, ed., *The Economic Region of Prince Edward Island* (Charlottetown: Canadian Institute for Research on Regional Development, 1998), 31; William Janssen, "Agriculture in Transition," in Smitheram, Milne, and Dasgupta, *Garden Transformed*, 115.
6 J.M. Bumsted, "The Only Island There Is: The Writing of Prince Edward Island History," in Smitheram, Milne, and Dasgupta, *Garden Transformed*, 14.
7 William Janssen, "Agriculture in Transition," in Smitheram, Milne, and Dasgupta, *Garden Transformed*, 116.
8 Ibid., 124.
9 Angus J. MacLean, *Making It Home: Memoirs of J. Angus MacLean* (Charlottetown: Ragweed Press, 1998), 274.
10 *MacKinnon v. P.E.I.* at 248.
11 *MacKinnon v. P.E.I.* at 247.
12 David A. Milne, "Prince Edward Island: Politics in a Beleaguered Garden," in *The Provincial State in Canada*, 2nd ed., ed. Keith Brownsey and Michael Howlett (Peterborough: Broadview, 2001), 113.
13 Lester B. Sellick, *My Island Home* (Windsor: Lancelot Press, 1973), 97.
14 Maurice Beaudin, ed., *The Economic Region of Prince Edward Island* (Moncton: Canadian Institute for Research on Regional Development, 1998), 134.
15 PEI Department of Tourism, http://www.gov.pe.ca/tourism/index.php3.
16 McClellan, "Changing Patterns," 106.
17 Judith Adler, "Tourism and Pastoral: A Decade of Debate," in Smitheram, Milne, and Dasgupta, *Garden Transformed*, 131.
18 Betty Howatt, "Friends of the Island," in *Crossing That Bridge: A Critical Look at the P.E.I. Fixed Link*, ed. Lorraine Begley (Charlottetown: Ragweed, 1988), 172.
19 Kevin J. Arsenault, "Recalling the Unanswered Question," in Begley, *Crossing That Bridge*, 120.

20 Adler, "Tourism and Pastoral," 142.
21 Ibid., 138.
22 Janssen, "Agriculture in Transition," 127.
23 Rand Dyck, *Provincial Politics in Canada* (Scarborough: Prentice-Hall Canada, 1996), 92.
24 Sellick, *My Island Home*, 85.
25 Adler, "Tourism and Pastoral," 142.
26 Milne, "Prince Edward Island," 112.
27 For a discussion of the transformation of the legislative elite in Prince Edward Island, see John Crossley, "Who Governs in Prince Edward Island? A Profile of Members of the Legislative Assembly, 1965-1996," paper presented to the annual meeting of the Canadian Political Science Association, St. Catharines, ON, 1996.
28 Lorraine Begley, "Introduction," in Begley, *Crossing That Bridge*, 2.
29 Milne, "Politics," 41.

## Chapter 12: New Brunswick

1 Statistics Canada, http://www.12.statcan.ca/english/census01.
2 For a discussion of the return to major party status for the New Brunswick Conservatives, see Jacques Poitras, *The Right Fight: Bernard Lord and the Conservative Dilemma* (Fredericton: Goose Lane, 2004).
3 For a full discussion of this phenomenon, see William Cross and Ian Stewart, "Ethnicity and Accommodation in the New Brunswick Party System," *Journal of Canadian Studies* 36 (2001-2): 32-58.
4 P.J. Fitzpatrick, "New Brunswick: The Politics of Pragmatism," in *Canadian Provincial Politics,* 2nd ed., ed. Martin Robin (Scarborough: Prentice-Hall, 1978), 124.
5 For a spirited chronology of the French-English flash points in New Brunswick, see Philip Lee, *Frank: The Life and Politics of Frank McKenna* (Fredericton: Goose Lane, 2001), 40-46.
6 Arthur T. Doyle, *Front Benches and Back Room* (Toronto: Green Tree, 1976), 133.
7 Richard Wilbur, *The Rise of French New Brunswick* (Halifax: Formac, 1989), 125-27.
8 John Edward Belliveau, *Little Louis and the Giant K.C.* (Hantsport: Lancelot Press, 1980), 40.
9 Robert Garland and Gregory Machum, *Promises, Promises: An Almanac of New Brunswick Elections, 1870-1980* (Saint John: University of New Brunswick Press, 1979), 193).
10 Richard Starr, *Richard Hatfield: The 17-Year Saga* (Halifax: Formac, 1987), 61.
11 Fitzpatrick, "New Brunswick," 126.
12 Michael Cormier and Achille Michaud, *Richard Hatfield: Power and Disobedience* (Fredericton: Goose Lane, 1992), 205.
13 Starr, *17-Year Saga*, 169.
14 Ibid., 194.
15 Herman Bakvis and Laura G. Macpherson, "Quebec Block Voting and the Canadian Electoral System," *Canadian Journal of Political Science* 28 (1995): 658-92.
16 Rand Dyck, *Provincial Politics in Canada* (Scarborough: Prentice-Hall Canada, 1996), 174.
17 Garland and Machum, *Promises, Promises*, 167.
18 Cormier and Michaud, *Power and Disobedience*, 218.
19 Fitzpatrick, "New Brunswick," 126.
20 Cormier and Michaud, *Power and Disobedience*, 100-1.
21 Peter H. Russell, *Constitutional Odyssey: Can Canadians Be a Sovereign People?* (Toronto: University of Toronto Press, 1992), 141.
22 McKenna's national persona as a stalwart defender of linguistic minorities did not always jibe with his government's actions at home. In 1989, for example, the Acadian Society of New Brunswick released a "scathing denunciation" of McKenna, when his government tried to uphold the constitutionality of unilingual traffic tickets. See *Toronto Star,* 7 December 1989, A13.
23 Andrew Cohen, *A Deal Undone: The Making and Breaking of the Meech Lake Accord* (Vancouver: Douglas and McIntyre, 1990), 237.
24 See Michael Behiels, "The Dilemma of the Linguistic Minorities: Introduction," in *The Meech Lake Primer*, ed. M. Behiels, 212-15 (Ottawa: University of Ottawa Press, 1989).

25  David Pye, "Interest Group Articulation in Public Policy Formation: A Study of New Brunswick's Meech Lake Hearings, January-February, 1989," MA thesis, University of New Brunswick, 1990, 112-22.
26  Cormier and Michaud, *Power and Disobedience*, 134.
27  Ibid., 138.
28  Richard Johnston, André Blais, Elisabeth Gidengil, and Neil Nevitte, *The Challenge of Direct Democracy: The 1992 Canadian Referendum* (Montreal: McGill-Queen's University Press, 1996), 178-81.
29  Cormier and Michaud, *Power and Disobedience*, 148.
30  William Cross, "Leadership Selection in New Brunswick: Balancing Language Representation and Populist Impulses," in *Political Parties, Representation, and Electoral Democracy in Canada*, ed. W. Cross (Don Mills: Oxford University Press, 2002), 50.
31  Cormier and Michaud, *Power and Disobedience*, 154.

### Chapter 13: Nova Scotia

1  Andrew Robb, "Third Party Experiences on the Island," in *The Garden Transformed: Prince Edward Island, 1944-1980*, ed. Verner Smitheram, David Milne, and Satadal Dasgupta (Charlottetown: Ragweed Press, 1982), 94.
2  David Lewis, *The Good Fight: Political Memoirs, 1909-58* (Toronto: Macmillan, 1981), 153.
3  Ron Crawley, "Class Conflict and the Establishment of the Sydney Steel Industry, 1898-1904," in *The Island: New Perspectives on Cape Breton's History*, ed. Kenneth Donovan, 148-50 (Fredericton: Acadiensis Press, 1990).
4  David Frank, "The Cape Breton Coal Industry, and the Rise and Fall of the British Empire Steel Corporation," in *Cape Breton Historical Essays*, ed. Don MacGillivray and Brian Tennyson, 110-13 (Sydney: College of Cape Breton Press, 1980).
5  David Frank, "Tradition and Culture in Cape Breton Mining Communities in the Early Twentieth Century," in *Cape Breton at 200*, ed. Kenneth Donovan (Sydney: University College of Cape Breton Press, 1985), 203.
6  David Frank, "Working-Class Politics: The Election of J.B. McLachlan, 1916-1935," in Donovan, *The Island*, 189.
7  *Halifax Herald* (Halifax), 28 October 1941, A1.
8  Ibid., 24 October 1945, 2.
9  Ian McKay, "The Maritime CCF: Reflections on a Tradition," in *Toward a New Maritimes: A Selection from Ten Years of New Maritimes*, ed. Ian McKay and Scott Milson (Charlottetown: Ragweed Press, 1992), 72.
10  Ibid., 77.
11  William John White, "Left-Wing Politics and Community: A Study of Glace Bay, 1930-1945," MA thesis, Dalhousie University, 1978.
12  J. Murray Beck, *Politics of Nova Scotia*, vol. 2 (Tantallon: Four East Publications, 1988), 196.
13  Lewis, *Good Fight*, 160.
14  Ibid., 245-47.
15  Terrence D. MacLean, "The Co-operative Commonwealth Federation in Nova Scotia, 1937-56," in *More Essays in Cape Breton History*, ed. R.J. Morgan (Windsor: Lancelot Press, 1977), 29. For a dissenting view on this matter, see McKay, "Maritime CCF," 77-79.
16  J. Murray Beck, *Politics of Nova Scotia*, vol. 1, *Nicholson-Fielding, 1712-1896* (Tantallon: Four East Publications, 1985), 219.
17  Brian Cuthbertson, *Johnny Bluenose at the Polls* (Halifax: Formac, 1994), 277.
18  MacLean, "Co-operative Commonwealth Federation," 34.
19  Gerry Harrop, *Clarie: Clarence Gillis, MP, 1940-1957* (Hantsport: Lancelot Press, 1987), 32, 41, 67, 35.
20  McKay, "Maritime CCF," 83.
21  J.H. Aitchison, "The Provincial Election," unpublished paper, 1967, 2.
22  Ian McKay claims that, in the 1970s, "the Cape Breton seats were never won by the party. They were won by a skilled and inventive machine which had less and less to do with even mildly left-wing principles." See Ian McKay, "Left, Right and Centre: Three NDPs in the Maritimes," *New Maritimes*, July-August 1984, 10.

23 *Chronicle-Herald* (Halifax), 29 March 1974, 2.

24 Ibid., 23 March 1974, 4.

25 Ibid., 3 April 1974, 4.

26 Ibid., 28 March 1974, 4.

27 Ibid., 27 March 1974, 4.

28 Paul MacEwan, *The Akerman Years* (Antigonish: Formac, 1980), 65.

29 Peter S. MacIntosh, "The Politics of Discord: Turmoil in the Nova Scotia New Democratic Party, 1967-80," MA thesis, Dalhousie University, 1982, 45-48.

30 MacEwan, *Akerman Years*, xiv.

31 See MacIntosh, "Politics of Discord," 26-44.

32 Ibid., 57, 83-84.

33 MacEwan, *Akerman Years*, 33.

34 Ibid., xiv.

35 MacIntosh, "Politics of Discord," 41-42.

36 Ibid., 100.

37 *Chronicle-Herald* (Halifax), 13 November 1980, 7.

38 Agar Adamson, "Does MacEwan's Real Ale Give the NDP Heartburn?" paper presented at APPSA (Atlantic Provinces Political Science Association), Wolfville, 1985, 10.

39 *Halifax Herald* (Halifax), 9 October 1981.

40 Parker Barss Donham, "What Next, Alexa?" *Atlantic Insight*, December 1981, 22.

41 Harry Bruce, "The Fiery Baptism of Alexa," *Atlantic Insight*, November 1982, 23.

42 Glenn Wannamaker, "Launching A Separatist Ship," *Atlantic Insight*, November 1982, 15.

43 *Chronicle-Herald* (Halifax), 7 November 1984, 5.

44 Ibid., 1.

45 For an insightful analysis of the CBLP, see Patrick Jamieson, "The Only Honest Politician: Paul MacEwan and the Strange World of Fourth Party Politics in Cape Breton," *New Maritimes*, October 1986, 3-9.

46 Ian Stewart, *Roasting Chestnuts: The Mythology of Maritime Political Culture* (Vancouver: UBC Press, 1994), 62-63.

47 See David Stewart, "Political Realignment in Atlantic Canada," in *Regionalism and Party Politics in Canada*, ed. Lisa Young and Keith Archer, 171-87 (Toronto: Oxford University Press, 2002).

48 *Chronicle-Herald* (Halifax), 27 February 1998.

49 Ibid., 14 February 1998.

50 Ibid., 14 March 1998.

51 See, for example, Robert Michels, *Political Parties: A Sociological Study of the Oligarchical Tendencies of Modern Democracy* (New York: The Free Press, 1962).

52 Robert C. Tucker, *The Marxian Revolutionary Idea* (New York: Norton, 1960).

53 *Guardian* (Charlottetown), 21 July 2003, A5.

54 *Chronicle-Herald* (Halifax), 4 July 2003, B1.

55 Ibid.

56 John DeMont, "One Last Whistle," *MacLean's*, 6 August 2004, 16.

57 http://www.tv.doc.ca/newinreview/oct98/environ/legacy.htm.

**Chapter 14: The End of the Affair?**

1 The initial movement to conventions from caucus as a means of selecting leaders complicated the relationship between leaders and caucus by effectively removing from caucus the ability to remove the party leader. The universal ballot further complicates this relationship. However, the democratic implications of "dumping" a leader who was endorsed by a wider public in an election are also controversial and illustrate the complexity of the relationship between parties, leaders, and the broader electorate.

2 See, for example, George Perlin, "Leadership Selection the PC and Liberal Parties: Assessing the Need for Reform," in *Party Politics in Canada*, 6th ed., ed. Hugh G. Thorburn, 202-20 (Scarborough: Prentice-Hall, 1991).

3 Peter Woolstencroft, "Tories Kick Machine to Bits: Leadership Selection and the Ontario Progressive Conservative Party," in *Leaders and Parties in Canadian Politics: Experiences of the*

*Provinces*, ed. R. Kenneth Carty, Lynda Erickson, and Donald E. Blake (Toronto: Harcourt Brace Jovanovich, 1992), 225.

4　Heather MacIvor, "The Leadership Convention: An Institution under Stress," in *Leaders and Leadership in Canada*, ed. Maureen Mancuso, Richard Price, and Ronald Wagenberg (Don Mills: Oxford University Press, 1994), 23-24.

5　David K. Stewart and Keith Archer, *Quasi-Democracy: Parties and Leadership Selection in Alberta* (Vancouver: UBC Press, 2000) 67-94.

6　Leonard Preyra, "From Conventions to Closed Primaries?" in *Party Politics in Canada*, 8th ed., ed. Hugh G. Thorburn and Alan Whitehorn (Toronto: Pearson Education, 2001), 455.

7　Patrick Malcolmson, "Two Cheers for the Leadership Convention," *Policy Options*, December 1992, 23-25.

8　John C. Courtney, *Do Conventions Matter?* (Montreal: McGill-Queen's University Press, 1995), 293.

9　Somewhat unexpectedly, the Nova Scotia Conservatives opted to return to the delegated convention to select its party leader in February 2006. The Nova Scotia Liberals followed suit.

10　*Daily Gleaner* (Fredericton), 24 October 1997, A3.

11　*Telegraph-Journal* (Saint John), 27 October 1997, A3.

12　Ken Carty, "Transforming the Politics of Party Leadership," paper presented at the annual meeting of the Atlantic Provinces Political Studies Association, Halifax, 1994.

13　Interview, 18 February 1999, in Bradford R. Hatch, "The Coronation of a Prince? An Examination of the 1998 New Brunswick Liberal Leadership Convention," Honours thesis, Acadia University, 1999, 87.

14　*Telegraph-Journal* (Saint John), 21 October 1997, A13.

15　Ibid., 9 October 1977, A7.

16　Ibid., 27 October 1997, A11.

17　Ibid., 26 January 1998, A2.

18　Hatch, "Coronation," 87.

19　Ibid., 65.

20　*Telegraph-Journal* (Saint John), 28 March 1998, E3.

21　Hatch, "Coronation," 79.

22　*Telegraph-Journal* (Saint John), 1 April 1998, A8.

23　Ibid., 14 April 1998, A3.

24　*Globe and Mail*, 4 May 1998, A3.

25　*Telegraph-Journal* (Saint John), 4 May 1998, 4.

26　Ibid., 6 March 1998, A1.

27　Ibid., 8 April 1998, A3.

28　*Daily Gleaner* (Fredericton), 18 March 1998, A7.

29　Daniel Latouche, "Universal Democracy and Effective Leadership: Lessons from the Parti Québécois Experience," in Carty, Erickson, and Blake, *Leaders and Parties*, 183-88.

30　Alan Cairns, "Political Science, Ethnicity, and the Canadian Constitution," in *Federalism and Political Community*, ed. David P. Shugarman and Reg Whitaker (Peterborough: Broadview Ross, 1989), 115.

### Chapter 15: Conclusion

1　See, for example, Ian Stewart, *Roasting Chestnuts: The Mythology of Maritime Political Culture* (Vancouver: UBC Press, 1994).

2　See, for example, Ian Stewart, "More Than Just a Line on the Map: The Political Culture of the Nova Scotia-New Brunswick Boundary," *Publius* 20 (1990): 99-111.

3　These figures are taken from Statistics Canada's 1985 and 2003 General Social Surveys.

4　John Crossley, "Picture This: Women Politicians Hold Key Posts in Prince Edward Island," in *In the Presence of Women*, ed. Jane Arscott and Linda Trimble (Toronto: Harcourt Brace, 1997), 280.

5　The 1997 Canadian Election Study.

6　The 2000 Canadian Election Study.

7　Stephen Clarkson, "The Delegate's Decision: The 1976 Leadership Convention of the Liberal Party in Ontario," paper presented to the annual meeting of the Canadian Political Science Association, Quebec City, 1976, 1.

8 Harold D. Clarke, Jane Jenson, Lawrence LeDuc, and Jon H. Pammett, "Absent Mandate: Canadian Electoral Politics in an Era of Restructuring," in *Party Politics in Canada,* 8th ed., ed. Hugh G. Thorburn and Alan Whitehorn (Toronto: Prentice-Hall, 2001).
9 Bonding social capital is defined by Putnam in terms of "in-group loyalty." See Robert D. Putnam, *Bowling Alone: America's Declining Social Capital* (New York: Simon and Schuster, 2000), 23.

**Appendix: Leadership Election Profiles**
1 *Chronicle-Herald* (Halifax), 5 February 1971, 4.
2 Peter Kavanagh and John Buchanan, *The Art of Political Survival* (Halifax: Formac Publishing, 1988), 50.
3 *Chronicle-Herald* (Halifax), 6 March 1971, 1. On the eve of the convention, Chambers' editorial cartoon showed a "dark horse" rapidly gaining on the three nervous leadership aspirants.
4 *Chronicle-Herald* (Halifax), 12 February 1971, 21.
5 Ibid., 15 February 1971, 17.
6 Ibid., 3 March 1971, 1.
7 Ibid., 20 February 1971, 2.
8 Ibid., 22 February 1971, 3.
9 Ibid., 3 March 1971, 1.
10 Ibid., 7 February 1991, A2.
11 Jeffrey Simpson was to single Cameron out as a paragon of political virtue in his *Spoils of Power* (Toronto: HarperCollins, 1988), 167-71.
12 *Globe and Mail*, 8 November 1990, A3.
13 Donald Cameron, interview with Ian Stewart, Halifax, 8 June 1992.
14 Even Cameron's supporters avoided his hospitality rooms at the convention, preferring to freeload in the suites of his major competitors.
15 *Chronicle-Herald* (Halifax), 14 January 1991, C2.
16 *Kentville Advertiser* (New Minas), 25 December 1990, 1A.
17 *Casket,* 16 January 1991, B6.
18 *Cape Breton Post* (Sydney), 1 February 1991, 1.
19 See the *Chronicle-Herald* (Halifax), 13 December 1990, A1; and the *Daily News* (Halifax), 14 December 1990, 4.
20 *Pictou Advocate,* 9 January 1991, 7.
21 *Chronicle-Herald* (Halifax), 24 January 1991.
22 The *Bulletin* (Bridgewater), 24 October 1990.
23 *Cape Breton Post* (Sydney), 3 January 1991, 1.
24 *Sunday Daily News* (Halifax), 18 November 1990, 11.
25 *Daily News* (Halifax), 15 November 1990, 4.
26 Ibid., 29 January 1991, 4.
27 *Chronicle-Herald* (Halifax), 17 January 1991.
28 *Mail-Star* (Halifax), 2 February 1991, B1.
29 *Globe and Mail*, 16 November 1991, A5.
30 Kavanagh and Buchanan, *Art of Political Survival*, 66.
31 *Globe and Mail*, 8 February 1990, A2.
32 *Daily News* (Halifax), 28 September 1990, 4.
33 Thornhill was actually charged twelve days after the convention, but by the end of the year the Crown had dropped all charges.
34 *Daily News* (Halifax), 15 November 1990, 4.
35 See, for example, *Chronicle-Herald*, 10 December 1990, A1.
36 *Chronicle-Herald* (Halifax), 17 January 1991.
37 Ibid., 9 February 1991, A2.
38 Ibid., 6 October 1995, C1.
39 Ian Stewart, "Despoiling the Public Sector? The Case of Nova Scotia," in *Corruption, Character, and Conduct: Essays on Canadian Government Ethics,* ed. John W. Langford and Allan Tupper, 90-112 (Don Mills: Oxford University Press, 1994).
40 *Chronicle-Herald* (Halifax), 24 August 1995, A4.
41 Ibid., 28 October 1995, A2.

42  Ibid., 30 October 1995, B1.
43  Ibid., 24 October 1995, A2.
44  Ibid., 28 October 1995, A2.
45  Ibid., 30 October 1995, A1.
46  Ibid., 13 October 1995, A4.
47  Progressive Conservative Party of Nova Scotia, *Grassroots Connection*, October 1995, 5.
48  *Chronicle-Herald* (Halifax), 26 October 1995, A1.
49  Ibid., 27 October 1995, D1.
50  Ibid., 30 October 1995, A1.
51  Ibid., B1.
52  Ibid.
53  *Chronicle-Herald* (Halifax), 5 May 1980, 21.
54  Ibid., 9 June 1980, 13.
55  Ibid., 12.
56  *Chronicle-Herald* (Halifax), 5 May 1980, 21.
57  Ibid.
58  See, for example, the full-page article in the *Chronicle-Herald* (Halifax), 31 May 1980, 7.
59  *Chronicle-Herald* (Halifax), 28 May 1980, 15.
60  Ibid., 9 June 1980, 12.
61  Ibid.
62  Ibid., 13.
63  Ibid., 1, 12.
64  Ibid., 1.
65  Ibid., 25 February 1986, 6.
66  Ibid., 22 February 1996, 1.
67  Ibid., 13 February 1986, 8.
68  Ibid., 22 February 1986, 1.
69  Ibid., 6 February 1986, 3.
70  Ibid., 22 February 1986, 8.
71  Ibid.
72  Ibid., 24 February 1986, 16.
73  Ibid., 18 February 1986, 23.
74  Ibid., 8.
75  Ibid., 12 February 1986, 3.
76  Ibid., 22 February 1986, 8.
77  Ibid., 24 February 1986, 16.
78  Some of this discussion of the Nova Scotia Liberals' 1992 convention appeared previously in Ian Stewart, *Roasting Chestnuts: The Mythology of Maritime Political Culture* (Vancouver: UBC Press, 1994), 80-82, 136-53.
79  *Chronicle-Herald* (Halifax), 27 May 1992, A2.
80  Ibid., 24 April 1992, A1.
81  A memo describing a senior editor at the *Cape Breton Post* as "a large fat man with a bad heart, a bit of a hare lip and an incurable penchant to drape himself in red suspenders" was inadvertently sent to several media outlets (*Mail-Star* [Halifax], 30 April 1992, A1).
82  *Cape Breton Post* (Sydney), 6 June 1992, 1.
83  Ibid., 1 May 1992, 1.
84  *Chronicle-Herald* (Halifax), 30 May 1992, B1.
85  Ibid., 29 May 1992, A2.
86  *Daily News* (Halifax), 10 April 1992, 3.
87  Ibid., 30 May 1992, B1.
88  *Cape Breton Post* (Sydney), 9 April 1992, 11.
89  *Daily News* (Halifax), 9 April 1992, 8.
90  *Cape Breton Post* (Sydney), 1 June 1992, 6.
91  *Chronicle-Herald* (Halifax), 30 March 1992, A1.
92  *Daily News* (Halifax), 16 May 1992, 10.
93  Ibid.

94 *Cape Breton Post* (Sydney), 6 June 1992, 1.

95 *Daily News* (Halifax), 9 June 1992, 3.

96 *Mail-Star* (Halifax), 13 June 1992, A1.

97 An intriguing postscript to the convention raised legitimate concerns about the security of tele-democracy. While insisting that the party had instituted safeguards to prevent large-scale vote buying, President Young acknowledged that the Liberals had "opened the system in a trusting sort of way" (*Cape Breton Post* [Sydney], 30 April 1992, 10). Alas, this trust may have been misplaced. There are unsubstantiated claims that one Liberal, Sydney Mines lawyer Nash Brogan, "bought" a personal identification number for himself and for 231 friends (who turned the PINs over to him). Since it was possible for an individual to vote as many times as he or she had PINs, Brogan (or anyone else for that matter) could have wielded tremendous influence for an initial outlay of only $5,800. Given the amounts of money typically associated with serious campaigns for party leadership, this does not seem to be a particularly large sum. Brogan has alleged that he cast the 232 votes for MacInnis on the first ballot and for Savage on the second. If this is true, he determined the outcome of the election. It is parenthetically worth noting that unsubstantiated allegations of vote-buying circulated well before the convention (see *Chronicle-Herald* [Halifax], 30 May 1992, A9).

98 See Peter Clancy, Jim Bickerton, Rod Haddow, and Ian Stewart, *The Savage Years: The Perils of Reinventing Government in Nova Scotia* (Halifax: Formac, 2000).

99 *Chronicle-Herald* (Halifax), 28 February 2002, B1.

100 Ibid., 23 February 2002, A5.

101 Ibid., 19 March 2002, A1.

102 Ibid., 13 February 2002, A3.

103 Ibid., 14 February 2002, A5.

104 Ibid., 10 January 2002, A3.

105 Ibid., 22 March 2002, A1.

106 Ibid., 20 February 2002, A5.

107 Ibid., 16 January 2002, A4.

108 Ibid., 12 March 2002, A6.

109 Ibid., 16 March 2002, A1.

110 Ibid., 13 March 2002, A5.

111 Ibid., 29 March 2002, A1.

112 Ibid., 12 April 2002, B1.

113 Ibid., 27 February 2002, B1.

114 Ibid., 15 February 2002, A5.

115 Ibid., 25 February 2002, A4.

116 Ibid., 20 February 2002, A5.

117 Ibid., 27 February 2002, B1.

118 Ibid., 28 February 2002, B1.

119 Ibid., 14 March 2002, B1.

120 Ibid., 12 April 2002, A3.

121 *Sunday Daily News* (Halifax), 14 April 2002, 5.

122 *Chronicle-Herald* (Halifax), 12 April 2002, B1.

123 Ibid., 15 April 2002, A1.

124 Ibid., 9 November 1980, 2.

125 Ibid., 13 November 1980, 2.

126 Ibid., 7.

127 Ibid., 17 November 1980, 5.

128 Ibid., 13 November 1980, 7.

129 Ibid., 9 November 1980, 2.

130 Ibid., 17 November 1980, 2.

131 Ibid., 13 November 1980, 7.

132 Ibid., 14 November 1980, 1.

133 Ibid., 13 November 1980, 7.

134 Ibid., 15 November 1980, 1.

135 Ibid., 17 November 1980, 5.

136   Ibid., 30 March 1996, A4.
137   Yvonne Atwell, "Commentary," *Atlantis* 27, 2 (2003): 110.
138   Walter D. Young, *Anatomy of a Party: The National CCF 1932-1961* (Toronto: University of Toronto Press, 1969).
139   *Daily News* (Halifax), 10 February 1996, 5.
140   *Chronicle-Herald* (Halifax), 1 April 1996, A2.
141   Yvonne Atwell did, in fact, secure the Preston riding for the NDP in the 1998 provincial election.
142   *Sunday Daily News* (Halifax), 31 March 1996, 5.
143   *Chronicle-Herald* (Halifax), 1 April 1996, A3.
144   *Sunday Daily News* (Halifax), 31 March 1996, 5.
145   *Chronicle-Herald* (Halifax), 2 April 1996, 31.
146   Ibid., 2 May 2002, D1.
147   Ibid., 6 March 2002, A1.
148   Ibid., 9 March 2002, C3.
149   Ibid., 10 April 2002, A5.
150   Ibid., 12 April 2002, A4.
151   Ibid., 30 May 2002, C1.
152   Ibid., 2 May 2002, D1.
153   Ibid., 30 May 2002, A4.
154   Ibid., 5 March 2002, A3.
155   Ibid., 16 April 2002, A6.
156   Ibid., 30 May 2002, C1.
157   See, for example, *Telegraph-Journal* (Saint John), 20 February 1982, 3.
158   Ibid., 1 February 1982, 3.
159   Ibid., 15 February 1982, 3.
160   Ibid., 1 February 1982, 3.
161   Ibid., 18 February 1982, 3.
162   Ibid., 4 February 1982, 3.
163   Ibid., 11 February 1982, 3.
164   Ibid., 27 February 1982, 5.
165   Ibid., 15 February 1982, 3.
166   Ibid., 1 February 1982, 3.
167   Ibid., 26 February 1982, 5.
168   Ibid., 27 February 1982, 5.
169   Ibid., 1.
170   Ibid., 10 February 1982, 3.
171   Ibid., 8 February 1982, 5.
172   Ibid., 15 February 1982, 3.
173   Ibid., 27 February 1982, 5.
174   See William Cross and Ian Stewart, "Ethnicity and Accommodation in the New Brunswick Party System," *Journal of Canadian Studies* 36 (2001-2): 32-58.
175   *Telegraph-Journal* (Saint John), 8 April 1985, 8.
176   Ibid., 19 April 1985, 4.
177   Ibid.
178   Ibid.
179   Ibid., 6 May 1985, 2.
180   Ibid., 19 April 1985, 4.
181   Ibid., 22 April 1985, 7.
182   Ibid., 3 May 1985, 2.
183   Ibid., 22 April 1995, 7.
184   Ibid., 23 April 1995, 5.
185   Ibid., 24 April 1985, 1.
186   Ibid., 4 May 1985, 1.
187   Ibid., 6 May 1985, 1.
188   Ibid., 25 April 1985, 4.

189 Ibid., 29 April 1985, 3.
190 Ibid., 27 April 1985, 8.
191 Ibid., 29 April 1985, 3.
192 Ibid., 19 April 1985, 4.
193 Ibid., 24 April 1985, 4.
194 Ibid., 6 May 1985, 4.
195 Ibid.
196 Ibid., 3 May 1985, 5.
197 Ibid., 4 May 1985, 4.
198 Ibid., 5.
199 Ibid., 6 May 1985, 2.
200 Ibid., 14 January 1998, A4.
201 Ibid., 27 January 1998, A1.
202 Ibid., 31 January 1998, E2.
203 Ibid., 20 January 1998, A3.
204 Ibid., 2 February 1998, A3.
205 Ibid., 4 February 1998, A3.
206 *Globe and Mail*, 27 April 1998, A19.
207 *Telegraph-Journal* (Saint John), 7 April 1998, A3.
208 Ibid., 3 April 1998, A5.
209 Ibid., 8 April 1998, D6.
210 *Globe and Mail*, 27 April 1998, A19.
211 *Daily Gleaner* (Fredericton), 15 April 1998, A1.
212 *Telegraph-Journal* (Saint John), 26 January 1998, A2.
213 *Daily Gleaner* (Fredericton), 4 May 1998, A3.
214 http://www.dailygleaner.com/050598/PROVINCE/116350.htm.
215 The federal Liberals also used this method to elect Paul Martin in 2003.
216 *Telegraph-Journal* (Saint John), 11 March 2002, A1.
217 Ibid., 11 May 2002, A8
218 *Moncton Times and Transcript*, 11 March 2002, A7.
219 *Telegraph-Journal* (Saint John), 11 March 2002, A5.
220 Ibid., 29 March 2002, A1.
221 *Moncton Times and Transcript*, 28 March 2002, A2.
222 *Telegraph-Journal* (Saint John), 29 March 2002, A4.
223 Ibid., A2.
224 Ibid., 28 March 2002, A10.
225 Ibid., A2.
226 Ibid., 30 March 3 2002, A2.
227 Ibid., 3 April 2002, A2.
228 Ibid.
229 *Moncton Times and Transcript*, 18 March 2002, A7.
230 *Telegraph-Journal* (Saint John), 4 April 2002, A2.
231 *Moncton Times and Transcript*, 30 April 2002, A5.
232 *Telegraph-Journal* (Saint John), 13 May 2002, A8.
233 *Moncton Times and Transcript*, 13 May 2002, A5.
234 Angus J. MacLean, *Making It Home: Memoirs of J. Angus MacLean* (Charlottetown: Ragweed Press, 1998), 221.
235 *Guardian* (Charlottetown), 18 September 1976, 1.
236 Ibid., 14 September 1976, 3; see also 22 September 1976, 5.
237 Ibid., 16 September 1976, 5.
238 The information in this paragraph is from Arthur Brendan Curley, "An Analysis of the 1976 Progressive Conservative and 1978 Liberal Leadership Conventions in Prince Edward Island," honours thesis, Acadia University, 1979, 36-38.
239 MacLean, *Making It Home*, 248.
240 *Guardian* (Charlottetown), 7 November 1981, 3.
241 Ibid., 7 November 1981, 3.

242  Ibid., 29 October 1981, 2.
243  Ibid., 31 October 1981, 1.
244  Ibid.
245  Ibid., 7 November 1981, 1.
246  Ibid.
247  Ibid., 31 October 1981, 1.
248  Ibid., 10 October 1981, 3.
249  Ibid., 7 November 1981, 1.
250  Ibid., 31 October 1981, 1.
251  Ibid., 7 November 1981, 1.
252  Ibid., 5 October 1981, 3.
253  Ibid., 22 October 1981, 3.
254  Ibid., 31 October 1981, 1.
255  Ibid.
256  Ibid., 7 November 1981, 1.
257  Ibid., 9 November 1981, 1.
258  Ibid., 11 June 1988, 3.
259  Ibid., 12 May 1988, 2.
260  Ibid.
261  Ibid., 13 June 1988, 1.
262  Ibid., 11 June 1980, 1.
263  Ibid., 3 June 1980, 3.
264  Ibid., 12 May 1988, 2.
265  Ibid., 8 June 1988, 4.
266  Ibid., 3.
267  Ibid., 13 June 1988, 1.
268  Ibid., 3.
269  Ibid., 24 November 1978, 3.
270  Ibid., 6 December 1978, 1.
271  Ibid., 22 November 1978, 1.
272  Ibid., 9 December 1978, 1.
273  Ibid., 2 December 1978, 5.
274  Ibid., 29 November 1978, 3.
275  Ibid., 22 November 1978, 3.
276  Ibid., 29 November 1978, 3.
277  Ibid., 11 December 1978, 1.
278  Ibid., 24 October 1981, 3.
279  Ibid., 3 October 1981, 3.
280  Ibid., 22 October 1981, 5.
281  Ibid., 3 October 1981, 3.
282  Ibid., 21 October 1981, 3.
283  Ibid.
284  Ibid., 24 October 1981, 3.
285  Ibid., 3 October 1981, 3.
286  Ibid., 6 October 1981, 3; 1 October 1981, 3; 17 October 1981, 3.
287  Ibid., 24 October 1981, 1.
288  Ibid., 23 October 1981, 1.
289  Ibid., 24 October 1981, 3.
290  Ibid., 23 January 1993, 1.
291  Ibid., 22 January 1993, 12.
292  Ibid., 20 January 1993, 4.
293  Ibid., 16 January 1993, 7.
294  Ibid., 7 January 1993, 1.
295  Ibid., 14 January 1993, 3.
296  Ibid., 22 January 1993, 12.
297  Ibid., 14 January 1993, 3.

298  Ibid.
299  Ibid., 18 January 1993, 3.
300  Ibid., 13 January 1993, 4.
301  Ibid., 12 January 1993, 3.
302  Ibid., 23 January 1993, 3.
303  Ibid., 25 January 1993, 1.
304  Ibid.
305  Carew had been acclaimed party leader subsequent to Milligan's resignation after the 1996 defeat.
306  *Guardian* (Charlottetown), 20 January 2003, A2; 6 March 2003, A2.
307  Ibid., 20 December 2002, A1.
308  See, for example, *Guardian* (Charlottetown), 19 October 2002, A3.
309  Ibid., 23 January 2003, A3.
310  Ibid., 20 February 2003, A2.
311  Ibid., 18 February 2003, A1; 21 February 2003, A1.
312  Ibid., 27 February 2003, A3.
313  Ibid., 6 March 2003, A1.
314  Ibid., 27 March 2003, A4.
315  Ibid., 14 March 2003, A2.
316  Ibid., 14 March 2003, A1.
317  Ibid.
318  Ibid., 11 January 2003, A3.
319  Ibid., 21 February 2003, A2.
320  Ibid., 31 March 2003, A3.
321  Ibid., 21 March 2003, A3.
322  Alan Buchanan, *Now Is the Time, Charlottetown,* 2003, 15.
323  *Guardian* (Charlottetown), 15 February 2003, A2.
324  Ibid., 21 March 2003, A5.
325  Ibid., 22 March 2003, A2.
326  Ibid., 31 March 2003, A3.
327  Ibid., 8 April 2003, A4.
328  Ibid., 4 April 2003, A1.
329  Ibid.
330  Ibid., 12 April 2003, A6.
331  Ibid.
332  Ibid., 1 April 2003, A3.
333  Ibid., 12 April 2003, A6.
334  Ibid., 4 April 2003, A1.
335  Ibid., 7 April 2003, A1.
336  Ibid., 12 April 2003, A6.
337  Ibid., 7 April, A6.
338  Andrew Robb, "Third Party Experiences on the Island," in *The Garden Transformed: Prince Edward Island, 1944-1980,* ed. Verner Smitheram, David Milne, and Satadal Dasgupta (Charlottetown: Ragweed Press, 1982), 92.
339  Agar Adamson, "The 1982 Prince Edward Island General Election: An Innocent's Comment," paper prepared for the Canadian Political Science Association annual meeting, Vancouver, 1983, 4.
340  *Guardian* (Charlottetown), 12 April 2002, A3.
341  The material in this paragraph came from the *Guardian* (Charlottetown), 13 April 2002, A5.
342  *Guardian* (Charlottetown), 12 April 2002, A3.
343  Ibid., 13 April 2002, A1.
344  Ibid., 15 April 2002, A2.

# Bibliography

Adamson, Agar. "Does MacEwan's Reality Give the NDP Heartburn?" Paper prepared for the 1985 APPSA annual meeting, Wolfville.

–. "The 1971 Nova Scotia Progressive Conservative Leadership Convention: How Representative?" Paper prepared for the 1972 CPSA annual meeting, Montreal.

–. "The 1982 Prince Edward Island General Election: An Innocent's Comment." Paper prepared for the 1983 CPSA annual meeting, Vancouver.

Adamson, Agar, and Ian Stewart. "Changing Party Politics in Atlantic Canada." In *Party Politics in Canada*, 8th ed., ed. Hugh Thorburn and Alan Whitehorn, 302-20. Scarborough: Prentice-Hall, 2001.

–. "Party Politics in the Mysterious East." In *Party Politics in Canada*, 5th ed., ed. Hugh Thorburn, 318-30. Scarborough: Prentice-Hall Canada, 1985.

Adler, Judith. "Tourism and Pastoral: A Decade of Debate." In *The Garden Transformed: Prince Edward Island, 1944-1980*, ed. Verner Smitheram, David Milne, and Satadal Dasgupta, 131-54. Charlottetown: Ragweed Press, 1982.

Agnew, John A. *Place and Politics: The Geographic Mediation of State and Society*. Winchester: Allen and Unwin, 1987.

Aitchison, J.H. "The Provincial Election." Unpublished paper, 1967.

Archer, Keith, and Alan Whitehorn. *Political Activists: The NDP in Convention*. Toronto: Oxford University Press, 1997.

Arscott, Jane, and Linda Trimble. *In the Presence of Women: Representation in Canadian Governments*. Toronto: Harcourt Brace, 1997.

Arsenault, Kevin J. "Recalling the Unanswered Question." In *Crossing the Bridge: A Critical Look at the P.E.I. Fixed Link*, ed. Lorraine Begley, 112-22. Charlottetown: Ragweed, 1988.

Atwell, Yvonne. "Commentary." *Atlantis: A Women's Studies Journal* 27, 2 (2003): 19-112.

Bakvis, Herman, and Laura G. Macpherson. "Quebec Block Voting and the Canadian Electoral System." *Canadian Journal of Political Science* 28 (1995): 658-92.

Bashevkin, Sylvia. *Toeing the Lines: Women and Party Politics in English Canada*. Toronto: University of Toronto Press, 1991.

Beaudin, Maurice, ed. *The Economic Region of Prince Edward Island*. Moncton: The Canadian Institute for Research on Regional Development. 1998.

Beck, J. Murray. "Elections." In *The Provincial Political Systems: Comparative Essays*, ed. David J. Bellamy, Jon H. Pammett, and Donald C. Rowat, 176-96. Agincourt: Methuen, 1976.

–. "Nova Scotia: Tradition and Conservatism." In *Canadian Political Politics*, 2nd ed., ed. Martin Robin, 171-204. Scarborough: Prentice-Hall, 1978.

–. *Politics of Nova Scotia*. Vol. 1: *Nicholson-Fielding, 1710-1896*. Tantallon: Four East Publications, 1985.

–. *Politics of Nova Scotia*. Vol. 2: *1896-1988*. Tantallon: Four East Publications, 1988.

Begley, Lorraine. "Introduction." In *Crossing the Bridge: A Critical Look at the P.E.I. Fixed Link*, ed. Lorraine Begley, 2-5. Charlottetown: Ragweed, 1988.

Behiels, Michael. "The Dilemma of the Linguistic Minorities: Introduction." In *The Meech Lake Primer*, ed. Michael Behiels, 210-17. Ottawa: University of Ottawa Press, 1989.

Bellamy, David. "The Atlantic Provinces." In *The Provincial Political Systems*, ed. David J. Bellamy, Jon H. Pammett, and Donald C. Rowatt, 3-19. Agincourt: Methuen, 1976.

Belliveau, John Edward. *Little Louis and the Giant K.C.* Hantsport: Lancelot Press, 1980.

Besheri, Roland, and Ray D. Bollman. "Population Structure and Change in Predominantly Rural Regions." In *Rural and Small Town Canada Analysis Bulletin* 2 (2): 1-15. Ottawa: Statistics Canada, January 2001.

Bibby, Reginald W. *Fragmented Gods: The Poverty and Potential of Religion in Canada*. Toronto: Irwin, 1987.

Blais, André, Elisabeth Gidengil, Richard Nadeau, and Neil Nevitte. *Anatomy of a Liberal Victory: Making Sense of the Vote in the 2000 Canadian Election*. Peterborough: Broadview Press 2002.

Blake, Donald E., R.K. Carty, and Lynda Erickson. "Ratification or Repudiation: Social Credit Leadership Selection in British Columbia." *Canadian Journal of Political Science* 21 (1988): 512-38.

Bollman, Ray D., and Brian Biggs. "Rural and Small Town Canada: An Overview." In *Rural and Small Town Canada*, ed. Ray D. Bollman, 1-44. Toronto: Thompson Educational Publishing, 1992.

Brodie, Janine. "The Gender Factor and National Leadership Conventions in Canada." In *Party Democracy in Canada: The Politics of National Party Conventions*, ed. George Perlin, 172-87. Scarborough: Prentice-Hall, 1988.

–. "Women and the Electoral Process in Canada." In *Women and Canadian Politics*, ed. Kathy Megyery, 3-59. Toronto: Dundurn Press, 1991.

Bruce, Harry. *Down Home: Notes of a Maritime Son*. Toronto: Key Porter Books, 1988.

–. "The Fiery Baptism of Alexa." *Atlantic Insight*, November 1982, 22-27.

Buchanan, Alan. "Now Is the Time," campaign materials, 2003.

Bumsted, J.M. "The Only Island There Is: The Writing of Prince Edward Island History." In *The Garden Transformed: Prince Edward Island, 1944-1980*, ed. Verner Smitheram, David Milne, and Satadal Dasgupta, 10-38. Charlottetown: Ragweed Press 1982.

Cairns, Alan. "Political Science, Ethnicity, and the Canadian Constitution." In *Federalism and Political Community*, ed. David P. Shugarman and Reg Whitaker, 112-40. Peterborough: Broadview Press, 1989.

Carty, Ken. "Transforming the Politics of Party Leadership." Paper prepared for the 1994 APPSA annual meeting, Halifax.

Carty, R.K. "Choosing New Party Leaders: The PCs in 1983, the Liberals in 1984." In *Canada at the Polls, 1984*, ed. Howard Prenniman, 54-78. Washington: American Enterprise Institute, 1988.

Carty, R.K., Donald Blake, and Lynda Erickson. *Grassroots Politicians: Party Activists in British Columbia*. Vancouver: UBC Press, 1991.

Carty, R.K., William Cross, and Lisa Young. *Rebuilding Canadian Party Politics*. Vancouver: UBC Press, 2000.

Carty, R. Kenneth, Lynda Erickson, and Donald E. Blake. *Leaders and Parties in Canadian Politics: Experiences of the Provinces*. Toronto: Harcourt Brace Jovanovich, 1992.

Chrétien, Jean. *Straight from the Heart*. Toronto: McClelland and Stewart, 1985.

Clancy, Peter, Jim Bickerton, Rod Haddow, and Ian Stewart. *The Savage Years: The Perils of Reinventing Government in Nova Scotia*. Halifax: Formac, 2000.

Clark, Warren. "Patterns of Religious Attendance." *Canadian Social Trends* (Winter 2000): 23-27.

Clarkson, Stephen. "The Delegate's Decision: The 1976 Leadership Convention of the Liberal Party in Ontario." Paper prepared for the 1976 CPSA annual meeting, Quebec City.

Cohen, Andrew. *A Deal Undone: The Making and Breaking of the Meech Lake Accord*. Vancouver: Douglas and McIntyre, 1990.

Conrad, Margaret. "Addressing the Democratic Deficit: Women and Political Culture in Atlantic Canada." *Atlantis: A Women's Studies Journal* 27, 2 (2003): 82-89.

Cook, Elizabeth A. "Voter Responses to Women Candidates." In *The Year of the Woman: Myth and Realities*, ed. Elizabeth A. Cook, Sue Thomas, and Clyde Wilcox, 217-36. Boulder: Westview, 1994.

Cormier, Michael, and Achille Michaud. *Richard Hatfield: Power and Disobedience*. Fredericton: Goose Lane, 1992.

Courtney, John. "Leadership Conventions and the Development of the National Political Community in Canada." In *National Politics and Community in Canada*, ed. R.K. Carty and W.P. Ward, 93-111. Vancouver: UBC Press, 1986.

–. *The Selection of National Party Leaders in Canada*. Toronto: Macmillan, 1973.

Courtney, John C. *Do Conventions Matter? Choosing National Party Leaders in Canada*. Montreal: McGill-Queen's University Press, 1995.

Courtney, John C., and George Perlin. "The Role of Conventions in the Representation and Accommodation of Regional Cleavages." In *Party Democracy in Canada*, ed. George Perlin, 123-44. Scarborough: Prentice-Hall Canada, 1988.

Crawley, Ron. "Class Conflict and the Establishment of the Sydney Steel Industry, 1898-1904." In *The Island*, ed. Kenneth Donovan, 144-64. Fredericton: Acadiensis Press, 1990.

Cross, William. "Leadership Selection in New Brunswick: Balancing Language Representation and Populist Impulses." In *Political Parties, Representation, and Electoral Democracy in Canada*, ed. William Cross, 36-54. Don Mills: Oxford University Press, 2002.

–. *Political Parties*. Vancouver: UBC Press, 2004.

Cross, William, and Ian Stewart. "Ethnicity and Accommodation in the New Brunswick Party System." *Journal of Canadian Studies* 36 (2001-2): 32-58.

Crossley, John. "Who Governs in Prince Edward Island? A Profile of Members of the Legislative Assembly, 1965-1996." Paper presented to the annual meeting of the Canadian Political Science Association, 1996.

Curley, Arthur Brendan. "An Analysis of the 1976 Progressive Conservative and 1978 Liberal Leadership Conventions in Prince Edward Island." Honours thesis, Acadia University, 1979.

Cuthbertson, Brian. *Johnny Bluenose at the Polls*. Halifax: Formac, 1994.

Cutler, Fred. "The Simplest Shortcut of All: Sociodemographic Characteristics and Electoral Choice." *Journal of Politics* 64 (2002): 465-90.

Darcy, R., and Sarah Slavin Schramm. "When Women Run against Men." *Public Opinion Quarterly* 41 (1977): 1-12.

Dasgupta, Satadal. *Rural Canada: Structure and Change*. Lewiston/Queenston: The Edwin Mellon Press, 1988.

DeMont, John. "One Last Whistle." *MacLean's*, 6 August 2001, 16.

Department of the Provincial Treasury. *Province of Prince Edward Island: 29th Annual Statistical Review, 2002*. Charlottetown: Department of the Provincial Treasury, 2003.

Donald MacKinnon v. Government of Prince Edward Island and the City of Charlottetown, [1993] 1 P.E.I.R. 216 (P.E.I.S.C.T.D.).

Donham, Parker Barss. "What Next, Alexa?" *Atlantic Insight*, December 1981, 22.

Doyle, Arthur T. *Front Benches and Back Rooms: A Story of Corruption, Muckraking, Partisanship and Political Intrigue in New Brunswick*. Toronto: Green Tree, 1976.

Dyck, Rand. *Provincial Politics in Canada*, 3rd ed. Scarborough: Prentice-Hall, 1996.

Ekstrand, Laurie E., and William A. Eckert. "The Impact of Candidate's Sex on Voter Choice." *Western Political Quarterly* 34 (1981): 77-87.

Ferree, Myra Marx. "A Woman for President? Changing Responses: 1957-1972." *Public Opinion Quarterly* 36 (1974): 390-99.

Fitzpatrick, P.J. "New Brunswick: The Politics of Pragmatism." In *Canadian Provincial Politics*, ed. Martin Robin, 120-37. Scarborough: Prentice-Hall, 1978.

Fletcher, Frederick J., and Robert J. Drummond. "The Mass Media and the Selection of National Party Leaders: Some Explorations." In *Party Democracy in Canada: The Policies of National Party Conventions*, 96-122. Scarborough: Prentice-Hall Canada, 1988.

*Flora: Scenes from a Leadership Convention*. National Film Board video, 1977.

Frank, David. "The Cape Breton Coal Industry, and the Rise and Fall of the British Empire Steel Corporation." In *Cape Breton Historical Essays*, ed. Don MacGillivray and Brian Tennyson, 19-132. Sydney: College of Cape Breton Press, 1980.

–. "Tradition and Culture in Cape Breton Mining Communities in the Early Twentieth Century." In *Cape Breton at 200*, ed. Kenneth Donovan, 203-18. Sydney: University College of Cape Breton Press, 1985.

–. "Working-Class Politics: The Election of J.B. McLachlan, 1914-1935." In *Cape Breton at 200*, ed. Kenneth Donovan, 186-219. Sydney: University College of Cape Breton Press, 1985.

Frizzell, Alan, and Tom McPhail. "The Mass Media and Convention Voting Behaviour." *Canadian Journal of Communication* 5 (1979): 17-26.

Garland, Robert, and Gregory Machum. *Promises, Promises: An Almanac of New Brunswick Elections, 1870-1980*. Saint John: University of New Brunswick, 1979.

Gibbins, Roger, and Margaret Hunziker. "Issues and Leadership Conventions: The 1985 Alberta PC Leadership Convention." Paper prepared for the 1986 CPSA annual meeting, Winnipeg.

Gidengil, Elisabeth. "Economic Man – Social Woman?" *Comparative Political Studies* 28 (1995): 383-408.

Gillespie, J. David. *Politics at the Periphery: Third Parties in Two-Party America*. Columbia: University of South Carolina Press, 1993.

Goldfarb, Martin, and Thomas Axworthy. *Marching to a Different Drummer: An Essay on the Liberals and Conservatives in Convention*. Toronto: Stoddart, 1988.

Graesser, Mark. "Leadership Crises in an Opposition Party: The Liberal Party of Newfoundland." In *Leaders and Parties in Canadian Politics: Experiences of the Provinces*, ed. R. Kenneth Carty, Lynda Erikson, and Donald E. Blake, 32-52. Toronto: Harcourt Brace Jovanovich, 1992.

Graham, Ron. *One-Eyed Kings. One-Eyed Kings: Promise and Illusion in Canadian Politics*. Toronto: Totem Books, 1986.

Harrop, Gerry. *Clarie: Clarence Gillis, MP, 1940-1957*. Hantsport: Lancelot Press, 1987.

Harrop, Martin, Judith England, and Christopher T. Husbands. "The Bases of National Front Support." *Political Studies* 28 (1980): 271-83.

Hatch, Bradford R. "The Coronation of a Prince? An Examination of the 1998 New Brunswick Liberal Leadership Convention." Honours thesis, Acadia University, 1999.

Hedlund, R.D., P.K. Freeman, K.E. Hamm, and R.M. Stein. "The Electability of Women Candidates: The Effects of Sex Role Stereotypes." *Journal of Politics* 41 (1979): 512-24.

Helen MacDonald (NDP leadership campaign). *Helen Today*. 15 July, 2000.

Hodge, G.D., and M.A. Quadeer. *Towns and Villages in Canada*. Toronto: Butterworths, 1983.

Horner, Jack. *My Own Brand*. Edmonton: Hurtig, 1980.

Howatt, Betty. "Friends of the Island." In *Crossing the Bridge: A Critical Look at the P.E.I. Fixed Link*, ed. Lorraine Begley, 172-74. Charlottetown: Ragweed, 1988.

Hunter, Alfred A., and Margaret A. Denton. "Do Female Candidates 'Lose Votes'? The Experience of Female Candidates in the 1979 and 1980 Canadian General Elections." *Canadian Review of Sociology and Anthropology* 21 (1984): 394-406.

Jamieson, Patrick. "The Only Honest Politician: Paul MacEwan and the Strange World of Fourth Party Politics in Cape Breton." *New Maritimes*, October 1986, 3-9.

Janssen, William. "Agriculture in Transition." In *The Garden Transformed: Prince Edward Island, 1944-1980*, ed. Verner Smitheram, David Milne, and Satadal Dasgupta, 113-29. Charlottetown: Ragweed Press, 1982.

Johnston, Richard. "The Final Choice: Its Social, Organizational and Ideological Bases." In *Party Democracy in Canada*, ed. George Perlin, 203-42. Scarborough: Prentice-Hall, 1988.

Johnston, Richard, André Blais, Elisabeth Gidengil, and Neil Nevitte. *The Challenges of Direct Democracy: The 1992 Canadian Referendum*. Montreal: McGill-Queen's University Press, 1996.

Johnston, Richard, André Blais, Henry E. Brady, and Jean Crete. *Letting the People Decide: The Dynamics of a Canadian Election*. Montreal: McGill-Queen's University Press, 1992.

Jones, Frank. "Religious Commitment in Canada, 1997 and 2000." Religious Commitment Monograph 3, Christian Commitment Research Institute, Ottawa, February 2003.

Kavanagh, Peter. *John Buchanan: The Art of Political Survival*. Halifax: Formac Publishing, 1988.

Key, V.O. *Southern Politics in State and Nation.* New York: Alfred A. Knopf, 1949.

Kim, Jae-On, and Mahn-Geum Ohn. "A Theory of Minor Party Persistence: Election Rules, Social Cleavage, and the Number of Political Parties." *Social Forces* 70 (1992): 574-99.

Kitschelt, Herbert P. "Left Libertarian Parties: Explaining Innovation in Competitive Party Systems." *World Politics* 40 (1986-88): 193-234.

Kome, Penney. *Women and Influence: Canadian Women and Politics.* Toronto: Doubleday Canada, 1985.

Krause, Robert, and Leduc Jr., Lawrence. "Voting Behaviour and Electoral Strategies in the Progressive Conservative Leadership Convention of 1976." *Canadian Journal of Political Science* 4 (1979): 96-136.

Latouche, Daniel. "Universal Democracy and Effective Leadership: Lessons from the Parti Québécois Experience." In *Leaders and Parties in Canadian Politics: Experiences of the Provinces,* ed. R. Kenneth Carty, Lynda Erickson, and Donald E. Blake, 173-202. Toronto: Harcourt Brace Jovanovich, 1992.

Lederle, John W. "The Liberal Convention of 1919 and the Selection of Mackenzie King." *Dalhousie Review* 27, 1 (1947): 84-92.

Leduc Jr., Lawrence. "Party Decision-Making: Some Empirical Observations on the Leadership Selection Process." *Canadian Journal of Political Science* 4 (1971): 96-118.

Lee, Phillip. *Frank: The Life and Politics of Frank McKenna.* Fredericton: Goose Lane, 2001.

Lele, J., G. Perlin, and H. Thorburn. "Leadership Conventions in Canada: The Form and Substance of Participatory Politics." In *Social Space, Canadian Perspectives,* ed. D.I. Davies and Kathleen Herman, 204-11. Toronto: New Press, 1971.

Lewis, David. *The Good Fight: Political Memoirs, 1909-1958.* Toronto: Macmillan, 1981.

MacDonald, L. Ian. *Mulroney: The Making of the Prime Minister.* Toronto: McClelland and Stewart, 1984.

MacEwan, Paul. *The Akerman Years: Jeremy Akerman and the Nova Scotia NDP, 1965-1980.* Antigonish: Formac, 1980.

MacIntosh, Peter S. *The Politics of Discord: Turmoil in the Nova Scotia New Democratic Party, 1967-80.* MA thesis, Dalhousie University, 1982.

MacIvor, Heather. "The Leadership Convention: An Institution under Stress." In *Leaders and Leadership in Canada,* ed. Maureen Mancuso, Richard G. Price, and Ronald Wagenberg, 12-27. Don Mills: Oxford University Press, 1994.

–. *Women and Politics in Canada.* Peterborough: Broadview Press, 1996.

MacLean, Angus J. *Making It Home: Memoirs of J. Angus MacLean.* Charlottetown: Ragweed Press, 1998.

MacLean, Terrence D. "The Co-operative Commonwealth Federation in Nova Scotia, 1937-56." In *More Essays in Cape Breton History,* ed. R.J. Morgan, 21-41. Windsor: Lancelot Press, 1977.

Malcolmson, Patrick. "Two Cheers for the Leadership Convention." *Policy Options* 13, 10 (1992): 23-25.

Manthorpe, Jonathon. *The Power and the Tories: Ontario Politics, 1943 to the Present.* Toronto: Macmillan, 1974.

Martin, Patrick, Allan Gregg, and George Perlin. *Contenders: The Tory Quest for Power.* Scarborough: Prentice-Hall Canada, 1983.

McClellan, John. "Changing Patterns of Land Use." In *The Garden Transformed: Prince Edward Island, 1944-1980,* ed. Verner Smitheram, David Milne, and Satadal Dasgupta, 101-14. Charlottetown: Ragweed Press, 1982.

McDougall, A.K. *John P. Robarts: His Life and Government.* Toronto: University of Toronto Press, 1986.

Mckay, Ian. "Left, Right and Centre-Three NDPs in the Maritimes." *New Maritimes,* 1984, 8-10.

–. "The Maritime CCF: Reflections on a Tradition." In *Toward a New Maritimes,* ed. Ian McKay and Scott Milson, 66-83. Charlottetown: Ragweed Press, 1992.

McLaughlin, Audrey. *A Woman's Place: My Life and Politics.* Toronto: Macfarlane, Walter and Ross, 1992.

Michels, Robert. *Political Parties: A Sociological Study of the Oligarchical Tendencies of Modern Democracy.* New York: The Free Press, 1962.

Milne, David. "Politics in a Beleaguered Garden." In *The Garden Transformed: Prince Edward Island, 1944-1980,* ed. Verner Smitheram, David Milne, and Satadal Dasgupta, 38-72. Charlottetown: Ragweed Press, 1982.

–. "Prince Edward Island: Politics in a Beleaguered Garden." In *The Provincial State in Canada,* 2nd ed., ed. Keith Brownsey and Michael Howlett, 110-38. Peterborough: Broadview, 2001.

Morley, Terry. "Leadership Change in the CCF/NDP." In *Leaders and Parties in Canadian Politics: Experiences of the Provinces,* ed. R. Kenneth Carty, Lynda Erickson, and Donald E. Blake, 120-46. Toronto: Harcourt Brace Jovanovich, 1992.

Nevitte, Neil, André Blais, Elisabeth Gidengíl, and Richard Nadeau. *Unsteady State: The 1997 Canadian Federal Election.* Don Mills: Oxford, 2000.

Newman, Peter C. *The Distemper of Our Times: Canadian Politics in Transition, 1963-68.* Toronto: McClelland and Stewart, 1968.

O'Neill, Brenda. "The Relevance of Leader Gender to Voting in the 1993 Canadian National Election." *International Journal of Canadian Studies* 17 (1998): 104-30.

Pammett, Jon H. "Elections." In *Canadian Politics in the 21st Century,* 5th ed., ed. Michael Whittington and Glen Williams, 158-72. Scarborough: Nelson, 2000.

Perlin, George. "Leadership Selection in the PC and Liberal Parties: Assessing the Need for Reform." In *Party Politics in Canada,* 6th ed., ed. Hugh G. Thorburn, 202-20. Scarborough: Prentice-Hall 1991.

–. *The Tory Syndrome: The Tory Syndrome: Leadership Politics in the Progressive Conservative Party.* Montreal: McGill-Queen's University Press, 1980.

Perlin, George, Allen Sutherland, and Marc Desjardins. "The Impact of Age Cleavage on Convention Politics." In *Party Democracy in Canada,* ed. George Perlin, 187-201. Scarborough: Prentice-Hall Canada, 1988.

Plutzer, Eric, and John F. Zipp. "Identity Politics, Partnership, and Voting for Women Candidates." *Public Opinion Quarterly* 60 (1996): 30-57.

Poitras, Jacques. *The Right Fight: Bernard Lord and the Conservative Dilemma.* Fredericton: Goose Lane, 2004.

Preyra, Leonard. "From Conventions to Closed Primaries?" In *Party Politics in Canada,* 8th ed., ed. Hugh G. Thorburn and Alan Whitehorn, 443-59. Toronto: Pearson Education, 2001.

Progressive Conservative Party of Nova Scotia. *Grassroots Connection.* October 1995.

Putnam, Robert. *Bowling Alone: America's Declining Social Capital.* New York: Simon and Schuster, 2002.

Pye, David. "Interest Group Articulation in Public Policy Formation: A Study of New Brunswick's Meech Lake Hearings, January-February, 1989." MA thesis, University of New Brunswick, 1990.

Rawlyk, George. *Is Jesus Your Personal Saviour?* Montreal: McGill-Queen's University Press, 1997.

Robb, Andrew. "Third Party Experiences on the Island." In *The Garden Transformed: Prince Edward Island, 1944-1980,* ed. Verner Smitheram, David Milne, and Satadal Dasgupta, 73-100. Charlottetown: Ragweed Press, 1980.

Russell, Peter H. *Constitutional Odyssey: Can Canadians Be a Sovereign People?* Toronto: University of Toronto Press, 1992.

Sayers, Anthony. "The Study of Political Leaders and Activists." In *Citizen Politics: Research and Theory in Canadian Political Behaviour,* ed. Joanna Everitt and Brenda O'Neill, 301-20. Don Mills: Oxford University Press, 2002.

Schellenberg, Grant. *2003 General Social Survey on Social Engagement, Cycle 17: An Overview of Findings.* Ottawa: Statistics Canada, Ministry of Industry, July 2004.

Sellick, Lester B. *My Island Home.* Windsor: Lancelot Press, 1973.

Siaroff, Allan. Paper prepared for the 2004 APPSA annual meeting, Moncton, New Brunswick.

Sigelman, Lee, and Carol K. Sigelman. "Sexism, Racism, and Ageism in Voting Behaviour: An Experimental Analysis." *Social Psychology Quarterly* 45 (1982): 263-67.

Simpson, Jeffrey. *Spoils of Power: The Politics of Patronage*. Toronto: HarperCollins, 1988.

Smiley, Donald. "The National Party Leadership Convention: A Preliminary Analysis." *Canadian Journal of Political Science* 1 (1968): 373-97.

Snider, Norman. *The Changing of the Guard: How the Liberals Fell From Grace and the Tories Rose to Power*. Toronto: Lester and Orpen Dennys, 1985.

Starr, Richard. *Richard Hatfield: The 17-Year Saga*. Halifax: Formac, 1987.

Stewart, David. "Political Realignment in Atlantic Canada." In *Regionalism and Party Politics in Canada*, ed. Lisa Young and Keith Archer, 171-87. Toronto: Oxford University Press, 2002.

Stewart, David K. "Electing a Premier." In *Citizen Politics*, ed. Joanna Everitt and Brenda O'Neill, 321-37. Don Mills: Oxford University Press, 2002.

–. "Friends and Neighbours: Patterns of Delegate Support at Maritime Liberal and Conservative Conventions." In *Leaders and Parties in Canadian Politics*, ed. R. Kenneth Carty, Lynda Erickson, and Donald E. Blake, 55-79. Toronto: Harcourt Brace Jovanovich, 1992.

–. "The Traditions Continue: Leadership Choices at Maritime Liberal and Conservative Party Conventions." PhD diss., University Of British Columbia, 1990.

Stewart, David K., and Keith Archer. *Quasi-Democracy? Parties and Leadership Selection in Alberta*. Vancouver: UBC Press, 2000.

Stewart, David K., and R.K. Carty. "Does Changing the Party Leader Provide an Electoral Boost: A Study of Canadian Provincial Parties: 1960-1992." *Canadian Journal of Political Science* 26 (1993): 312-30.

–. "Leadership Politics as Party Building." In *Political Parties, Representation, and Electoral Democracy in Canada*, ed. William Cross, 54-67. Don Mills: Oxford University Press, 2002.

Stewart, Ian. "The Brass versus the Grass: Party Insiders and Outsiders at Canadian Leadership Conventions." In *Party Democracy in Canada*, ed. George Perlin, 144-59. Scarborough: Prentice-Hall Canada, 1988.

–. "Class Politics at Canadian Leadership Conventions." In *Party Democracy in Canada*, ed. George Perlin, 160-71. Scarborough: Prentice-Hall Canada, 1988.

–. "Despoiling the Public Sector? The Case of Nova Scotia." In *Corruption, Character, and Conduct*, ed. John W. Langford and Allan Tupper, 90-112. Don Mills: Oxford University Press, 1994.

–. *Roasting Chestnuts: The Mythology of Maritime Political Culture*. Vancouver: UBC Press, 1994.

–. "Vanishing Points: Three Paradoxes of Political Culture Research." In *Citizen Politics: Research and Theory in Canadian Political Behaviour*, ed. Joanna Everitt and Brenda O'Neill, 21-39. Don Mills: Oxford University Press, 2002.

Sullivan, Martin. *Mandate '68: The Year of Pierre Elliott Trudeau*. Toronto: Doubleday Canada, 1968.

*Telegram* News Staff. *Balloons and Ballots: The Inside Story of Robert Stanfield's Victory*. Toronto: The *Telegram*, 1967.

Thomas, Timothy. "An Emerging Party Cleavage." In *Party Politics in Canada*, ed. Hugh Thorburn and Alan Whitehorn, 431-42. Scarborough: Prentice-Hall, 2001.

Tucker, Robert C. *The Marxian Revolutionary Idea*. New York: Norton, 1960.

Wannamaker, Glenn. "Launching a Separatist Ship," *Atlantic Insight*, November 1982, 12-15.

Wearing, Joseph. *The L-Shaped Party: The Liberal Party of Canada, 1954-1980*. Toronto: McGraw-Hill Ryerson, 1981.

Whitaker, Reg. "Virtual Political Parties and the Decline of Democracy." *Policy Options* (June 2001): 16-22.

White, William John. *Left-Wing Politics and Community: A Study of Glace Bay, 1930-1945*. MA thesis, Dalhousie University, 1978.

Wilbur, Richard. "New Brunswick." In *Canadian Annual Review of Politics and Public Affairs 1985*, ed. R.B. Byers, 323-31. Toronto: University of Toronto Press, 1988.

–. *The Rise of French New Brunswick*. Halifax: Formac, 1989.

Wilson, Alan. "Crosscurrents in Maritime Regionalism." In *Federalism in Canada and Australia: Historical Perspectives, 1920-88*, ed. Bruce W. Hodgins, John S. Milloy, and Shawn Heard Heick, 367-80. Trent University: The Frost Centre For Canadian Heritage and Development Studies, 1989.

Wilson, John. "The Canadian Political Cultures: Towards a Redefinition of the Nature of The Canadian Political System." *Canadian Journal of Political Science* 7 (1974): 437-83.

Winn, Conrad, and John McMenemy. *Political Parties in Canada.* Toronto: McGraw-Hill Ryerson, 1976.

Woolstencroft, Peter. "Tories Kick Machine to Bits: Leadership Selection and the Ontario Progressive Conservative Party." In *Leaders and Parties in Canadian Politics: Experiences of the Provinces,* ed. R. Kenneth Carty, Lynda Erickson, and Donald E. Blake, 203-25. Toronto: Harcourt Brace Jovanovich, 1992.

Young, Lisa. *Feminists and Party Politics.* Vancouver: UBC Press, 2000.

Young, Walter D. *Anatomy of a Party: The National CCF, 1932-1961.* Toronto: University of Toronto Press, 1969.

Zipp, John F., and Eric Plutzer. "Gender Differences in Voting for Female Candidates: Evidence from the 1982 Election." *Public Opinion Quarterly* 49 (1985): 178-97.

# Index

unions: attitudes by party, 100, 101-2,
103, 105, 113; movement, ranking of
importance to party philosophy, 105-8
United Mineworkers of America, 173, 175
universal ballot: associated with increase
in over-60 delegates, 33, 47; attractive to
previous supporters of another party, 52;
compared with traditional conventions,
48; concern about less committed
delegates, 48; Conservatives (NS), 1995
convention, 210-11, 212; delegates,
length of party membership, 54; effect
of endorsement on vote transfer, 141-42;
effect on conventions over time, 59-60;
first use by Parti Quebecois, 8-9; and
gender shift of delegates, 31-32; growth
of support for, in Maritime provinces,
188-92, 203; introduced by Parti
Quebecois in 1985, 8-9, 187; New
Democrats (NS), 2002 convention, 232;
no impact on voters persuading others,
58; no perceived difference in ideological attitudes than regular conventions,
113; not associated with large percentage of "tourist" votes, 49, 51; percentage
of delegates making choice early, 55, 58;
pre-convention strategies, of candidates,
192-96; views of academic researchers,
187-88, 196-97

Valcourt, Bernard, 4, 19
Vautour, Angela, 172
Veniot, P.J., 156
Volpe, Jeannot, 20
vote-buying allegations: Conservatives
(NB) 1997 convention, 21; Liberal (NS)
2002 convention, 222

vote transfers: effect of endorsement,
by first-choice candidates, 131-42;
motivations for, 137-40; research on,
130; by women candidates, 95
voters. *See* delegates
voting methods: hybrid system, 242;
multi-site universal ballot (Conservatives (NB), 1997), 19-21; preferential
ballot system, 142; single site all-
member vote (Liberals (PEI), 1996),
16-18; traditional delegate system,
22-24, 26, 187; universal ballot, 26, 187,
188-96. *See also* tele-voting; universal
ballot; vote transfers

Walker, Andy, 54, 69, 250-52
Wappel, Tom, 115
Wark, Larry, 230
Weir, Elizabeth, 172, 190
Wells, Clyde, 164
Westray mine disaster, 219
White, Jim, 69, 81, 199, 211-13
Winters, Robert, 132, 138
women: acceptance as leaders, in
Maritime provinces, 201; Canadian
female candidates, 87; Maritime
candidates, 30, 46, 204; percentage
of delegates, 28, 31-32; tendency to
support women candidates, 88-89,
92-97
Woolstencroft, Peter, 188

Young, Doug, 26, 40, 91, 166, 168, 198,
233-35
Young, John, 219, 220
youth (under 30) delegates, 28, 32-33, 46

Printed and bound in Canada by Friesens

Set in Stone by Artegraphica Design Co. Ltd.

Copy editor: Joanne Richardson

Proofreader: Megan Brand

Indexer: Annette Lorek